SAKE & SATORI

JOSEPH CAMPBELL

SAKE & SATORI

ASIAN JOURNALS — JAPAN

EDITED AND WITH A FOREWORD BY DAVID KUDLER

JOSEPH CAMPBELL FOUNDATION

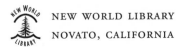

NEW WORLD LIBRARY
NOVATO, CALIFORNIA

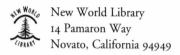 New World Library
14 Pamaron Way
Novato, California 94949

Cover design by Mary Ann Casler
Text design and typography by Tona Pearce Myers
Illustrations by Carol Pentleton

Library of Congress Cataloging-in-Publication Data
Campbell, Joseph, 1904–1987
  Sake and satori : Asian journals, Japan / by Joseph Campbell.
    p.   cm.
Includes glossary and index.
  ISBN 1-57731-236-8 (alk. paper)
  1. Japan—Civilization—1945– 2. Japan—Religious life and customs.
3. Japan—Description and travel. 4. Campbell, Joseph, 1904—Journeys—Japan.
I. Title. II. Kudler, David.
  DS822.5 .C367 2002
  952.04—dc21   2002007500

First printing, November 2002
ISBN 1-57731-236-8
Printed in Canada on acid-free, partially recycled paper
Distributed to the trade by Publishers Group West

10 9 8 7 6 5 4 3 2 1

CONTENTS

———◦◦◦◦———

ABOUT THE COLLECTED WORKS OF JOSEPH CAMPBELL

At his death in 1987, Joseph Campbell left a significant body of published work that explored his lifelong passion, the complex of universal myths and symbols that he called "Mankind's one great story." He also left, however, a large volume of unreleased work: uncollected articles, notes, letters, and diaries, as well as audio- and videotape recorded lectures.

The Joseph Campbell Foundation was founded in 1991 to preserve, protect, and perpetuate Campbell's work. The Foundation has undertaken to archive his papers and recordings in digital format, and to publish previously unavailable material and out-of-print works as *The Collected Works of Joseph Campbell.*

THE COLLECTED WORKS OF JOSEPH CAMPBELL
Robert Walter, Executive Editor
David Kudler, Managing Editor

EDITOR'S FOREWORD

When Joseph Campbell arrived in Colombo, Ceylon, on March 4, 1955, he was in a foul mood. He had come to India some six months before, funded by grants from the Bollingen Foundation, and driven by his own deep desire to see the country that had dominated his professional life and his dreams for so many years.

Since a chance meeting with Jiddu Krishnamurti on a transatlantic steamship in 1924, Campbell had been fascinated with the religions and philosophies of Asia, and particularly India. When his mentor, renowned Indologist Heinrich Zimmer, had died in 1943, leaving behind a huge volume of notes for uncompleted scholarly texts, Campbell had agreed with Zimmer's widow Christiane to fashion these notes into a collection of posthumous works. He had spent the next twelve years devoting most of his professional energy into these books. Indeed, he had traveled to India with the proofs for the last volume, *The Art of Indian Asia*, in his suitcase.

Campbell had arrived in India expecting to find the breath of *brahman*—the World Soul of the Hindu religion—that inspired the classical Indian art and literature that he and Zimmer had studied. What he had found instead was a society obsessed with *bakhti*, the rituals of devotion, and centered around what Campbell came to call "the Baksheesh Complex":

what he felt was a national expectation of getting something for nothing. In his journals, he said:

> The squalor of India is not a result of Indian poverty alone, but also of an indifference to dirt, the inefficiency of city officials, and an intentional spectacle of poverty presented by professional beggars: moreover, the assault that the visitor endures from the beggars gives him an exaggerated view of the seedier aspects of the Indian scene. This whole matter of Indian poverty and squalor may be summed up as a function of the Baksheesh Complex, which has two major forms of manifestation: that of the beggar, that of the retired pensioner. The formula for both is *Something for Nothing*.
>
> India's pretext of spiritual superiority is another consequence of the Baksheesh Complex and does not accord with the actualities of the modern international scene. India is in fact receiving all of her progressive ideals (spiritual principles) as well as machines (technological principles) from the West.[1]

Campbell had faced beggars and hucksters, pimps and fakirs, and like many Westerners before and since it had put him in a state of moral shock. He had had many wonderful, enriching experiences as well, but by the time he had finished up his tour, he was sick at heart.

The Indian government itself had dealt the final insult. As Campbell had applied for an exit visa, he had discovered that he would have to pay income tax on all the money that he had brought into the country. In Campbell's eye, this was nothing but the last, egregious, institutional form of baksheesh. As he wrote to the Indian Minister of Finance:

> I arrived in New Delhi, August 30, 1954; lectured, gratis, at a number of Indian colleges and institutions; spent as much as I could afford on Indian textiles; gave as generously as I could to your temples and beggars; overlooked the anti-American propaganda in the newspapers; learned to admire and love the Indian people, as I had long admired and loved their culture—and when it came time for me to buy my ticket to depart (that is to say, today), my way was blocked by your income tax officials, to whom I am compelled to pay 519 rupees—not on any moneys earned in India (for I have not received one rupee here) but out of the funds that I brought into India and spent here. After this final experience of the baksheesh motif—played *fortissimo*, now, by the government itself—I am afraid that I am going to find it harder than it used to be, to speak and write about the Indian character with the respect it deserves.[2]

Campbell's thoughts and feelings about the contradictions of Indian philosophy and society dominate the journals from which this volume and *Baksheesh & Brahman* are drawn as he moves from a Hindu to a Buddhist world. He was ready for a different experience than the dirt and squalor that had overwhelmed him in India, and he found it in Ceylon, Southeast

Asia, and especially Japan. Reading his daily musings, one sees a sensualist delight in the pleasures of these newfound lands. He experienced anew the joy of discovery, not only in the Buddhist temples and Shintō shrines, but also in the bath- and teahouses.

Now, by his own testimony, Campbell was a very happily married man.[3] He wrote his wife, choreographer Jean Erdman, regularly, and looked forward to his final month in Asia, when she would join him on a teaching junket. Yet he indulged in the fleshpots of Tokyo with a man-of-the-world (and almost entirely voyeuristic) verve.

From the sybaritic glee that Campbell took in immersing himself in Japanese nightclubs, baths, and theaters, he soon moved to the scholar's joy of immersing himself in this new country's language and religion. As his stay lengthened—and especially once the first copy of *The Art of Indian Asia* arrived—Campbell's physical, spiritual, and intellectual reaction to his stay in India mellowed, and he gained new perspectives on India, Japan, and his own psyche, as well as on geopolitics, a subject he had previously avoided considering.

Campbell's timing in traveling to East Asia was politically fortuitous. Nineteen fifty-five was a relative slack-water period in the Cold War: two years after the cessation of hostilities in Korea, one after the French departure from Indochina. America's post–World War II occupation of Japan was officially over (though an enormous U.S. military presence remained in the country, much to Campbell's repeatedly voiced dismay) and its involvement in Vietnam had not yet begun. Joseph McCarthy's hearings in the U.S. Senate, seeking to unearth Communists among the employees of the Department of State and the army (whom Campbell refers to somewhat sneeringly as "our Fifth Amendment boys"[4]), had ended. Yet the politics of East and West, Capitalist and Communist were very much in the air, and Campbell, a lifelong nonpartisan, found himself increasingly drawn to defend his native land.

The difficulty for Campbell was that he found the Americans working and traveling in Asia to be, for the most part, woefully uninformed, misinformed, and unconcerned about the cultures of the nations they were visiting. A classic example occurred during a dusty tour-bus ride back from the spectacular ruins of Angkor Wat. As he was to recount many times in later years, he overheard an American tourist moan to his wife, "I'd give everything I have to have had three Coca-Colas instead of all those temples."[5]

As he considered this dilemma—his love of America and what it stood for on the one hand, and the poor showing that its representatives made abroad—several initiatives shaped themselves in his mind that were to inform the rest of his career. The first was his course of lectures on world culture and religion for the Foreign Service Institute, the training program of the U.S. State Department, that he undertook soon after his return to the United States and continued well into the 1970s.

The second was the germ of the idea that was to become the series of books known as *The Masks of God*—four comprehensive volumes on comparative religion and myth aimed not only at his fellow academics but also at the broader American populace.[6] These books would engage most of his writing energy from his return home until the last volume, *Creative Mythology,* was issued in 1968.

The third initiative that he undertook after his travels in Asia was his series of popular lectures. From his homecoming until his death in 1987, Campbell embarked on an ongoing succession of lectures at colleges and churches, public venues (such as New York's Cooper Union) and private conferences, on radio and television,[7] seeking to educate the public about world myth and religion.

Indeed, it is in these journals that Campbell finally identifies his field of study: "Resolution: *Comparative mythology . . .* is indeed my field."[8] Amazing as it may seem to us, Campbell had always avoided defining precisely what it was that he was studying and teaching. He had studied English, biology, and medieval literature as a young man; he was on the Sarah Lawrence College English faculty. It was only now, at the age of fifty, that Campbell—the obdurate generalist—felt ready to name his specialty.

It is in these journals too that Campbell begins to realize and take into account some of his own preconceptions. In the notes that provide the first manifesto for what is to become *The Masks of God,* Campbell wrote, "As a contemporary Occidental faced with Occidental and contemporary psychological problems, I am to admit and even celebrate (in Spengler's manner) the relativity of my historical view to my own neurosis (Rorschach formula)."[9] It is in this self-aware mode that Campbell embarked on the new phase of a career that was to reshape his ideas on comparative mythology, and ours.

NOTES ON THE TEXT

The journal entries were not made daily, although Campbell organized them so. Often they were composed at the end of a trip, and sometimes he would spend an entire day catching up on the previous week. He wrote some of it, at least, with an eye to eventual publication, although certainly not in the form presented here. The book is therefore at some points closely written, at others wide-ranging and informal. There is much philosophical meat in these pages, and each reader will chew and digest it according to his or her own constitution. The extensive endnotes should help; they offer pointers also to Campbell's later work, where ideas that appear here briefly bear full fruit.

The text has been edited to preserve the flow and interest of Campbell's narrative. Cut from the text are tentative itineraries, times of missed appointments, names of people met in passing and never seen again, long quotes from contemporary newspapers, and other details. Also removed are several political meditations that are later repeated in more cogent forms. Punctuation has been altered where necessary for ease of reading, and the occasionally awkward sentence has been recast. Many of Campbell's frequent lists are now run on in narrative text. Nowhere has the meaning been altered.

Campbell was inconsistent in the way in which he presented Japanese and other Asian names in these journals. We have chosen to present East Asian names in the conventional Western manner, with the family name after the personal name. The only exceptions are names such as Chiang Kai-shek and Ho Chi Minh and other historic figures that are best known to Western readers in their traditional order.

Campbell himself footnoted his work. These parenthetical notes, quotations, and citations can be found at the bottom of the page within the text proper. Endnotes, on the other hand, were added by the editors and their contributors, and mark historical, linguistic, and bibliographic references.

Sanskrit and Japanese words have been transliterated with full diacritical marks.

Campbell from time to time included rough drawings to illustrate his text. These have been redrawn and placed without captions in the text where they occurred. The photographs included were all taken with Campbell's camera, either by his own hand or by a traveling companion. The maps were commissioned by the editors to help the reader follow the geography of Campbell's travels.

CHAPTER I

THE BUDDHA LAND

CEYLON,[1] THAILAND, AND CAMBODIA

Friday, March 4, 1955   *Colombo*

Up at 6:00. Morning tea and newspaper.

A few retrospective thoughts about India:

1. The Indians are great talkers. The man who will talk to you like a saint, however, about God, Soul, the Gītā, and Illumination, may well have betrayed a great many of his friends, and when you meet these friends you will certainly hear about it.
2. The Indians are great talkers. In New York I heard all the talk about the Unity of Religions. In India I found more disunity (Communalism principle) than anywhere in the modern West.
3. The Indians are great talkers. They talk of "Thou art That," and they treat human beings worse than they treat animals.
4. I cannot believe that the Brahmans in the past were less arrogant and cruel than the worst of them today. We have the evidence of the Buddhists, for example, in the fifth century B.C., and we have also the evidence of the Laws of Manu and the Institutes of Viṣṇu.
5. Swami Nikhilananda has frequently said that the altruistic principle is an insecure base for ethics, while the metaphysical is a secure one. Actually, however, the altruistic ethic of the West has yielded a society in which mutual regard is more evident than it is in India.

6. The great lesson of India is that men and women can survive under conditions that one would think impossible—and not only survive, but be charming.

7. The Indians are charming. Poverty: Charm: Eloquence: Inconsistency: Inefficiency.

After breakfast, I wrote up my diary for yesterday on a veranda overlooking the sea, then went to town to try to get organized—and the following plan developed:

I shall leave tomorrow morning by taxi for a three-day tour of the chief sites of Ceylon. I shall return Tuesday to Colombo and leave Wednesday morning for Bangkok, Siam.[2] I found that I could move into the Grand Oriental Hotel this afternoon and return to it Tuesday. Then I took a cab out to visit the museum, but found it "closed on Fridays," and to meet Dr. Paranavitana, the Commissioner of Archaeology,[3] but found him "out of station, until Tuesday." So I returned to the Galle Face Hotel for lunch, and after lunch taxied to the Grand Oriental.

Wrote a letter to Jean and after tea took a cab to the zoo, to watch an amusing elephant dance. A handsome zoo, designed, I learned from my cab driver, by a German—Hagenbeck, no doubt.[4]

At dinner, listening to a rather poor orchestra, I thought: the pleasure that the Occidental finds in the Orient is that of being an Occidental in the Orient: the tension between the two worlds is experienced (one way or another) and this is what yields the pleasure.

I went for a brief walk around the block after supper and retired early. Colombo's rickshaw boys, by the way, don't seem to have the imagination of those of Calcutta: all they can think of to offer are "Movies?" "Cold beer?"

Saturday, March 5   *Anuradhapura*

Departing from the hotel in a small taxi at 8:15, I was driven north, through Negombo and Chilaw, to Puttalam, where I arrived at 11:20 for lunch at the Rest House.

Miles and miles of coconut lands, all the way. One field of tobacco. Also, bananas, jackfruit, etc. The people, definitely, look better off than the Indian. One notes also, no turbans, few head loads, and less head wagging. The bullock carts have characteristic wattle tops.

The whole region is surprisingly Catholic: churches everywhere. One Hindu temple with a large running horse in the place of Nandi.

The people have a slightly Indonesian look. Two of the men whom I talked with in Colombo were from Indonesia. Remember the great sea trade from Sumatra too, in the ninth century. Buddhism also linked with Indonesia. From here, perhaps the influence upon Malabar and Cochin.

After a pleasant lunch in the pleasant rest house, my drive cut northeast to Anuradhapura, where I arrived about 2:00. Drive through wild forestland; good road. Huge anthills with cobra holes all along the way.

Installed in the cute little Grand Hotel, I went to see the monuments: Issurumuniyagala (my God, what they have done to this!), Sacred Bo-Tree and Brazen Palace, Ruvanweliseya Dagaba (huge: and again, what they have done to the precious images!), Thuparama Dagaba—ruins, ruins everywhere. One gets very strongly the impression of a once tremendous and magnificent center. Nice driving along well-kept roads and through country with lovely trees, grazing cattle, quiet people. Buddha images. Abhyagiri and Jetavanaramaya Dagabas. More ruins—and a lovely, huge lake, from which one sees the tremendous domes of the Ruvanweliseya and Abhyagiri—the first, restored, the second in ruins. The other *stūpas*[5] are considerably smaller.

I concluded my tour with a visit to the museum, where I found a number of fine things, and a few of particular interest:

1. Two "*garbha* stones" with twenty-five square holes, within each of which a little bronze image or symbol was contained. In the center of one, a Bodhisattva on a lotus. A number of swastikas.
2. A Vajrasattva image from the seventh century. (Definite Mahāyāna in both of these!)
3. Chinese pottery from the eighth to tenth centuries. (The China trade.)

After my trip (Hot!) I had tea on the veranda of the hotel and began a letter to Vann, summarizing my India experiences. Then people began to arrive: a German foursome: some scattered English: an American couple (seventy-ish) from New York (Mr. & Mrs. Harry Englander), who commenced conversation and with whom I had dinner. Going to Tokyo (shall meet them there). Just came from two years in Pakistan (engineering). Spoke favorably of the Pakistanis, but I could not gain much of an impression of what is going on there. When all had cleared away, I had a glass of lukewarm beer and went to bed.

Sunday, March 6   *Mihintale—Polonnaruva*

Off at 8:10 for Mihintale, about six miles from Anuradhapura. A lovely hill, with a great series of steps up to various *stūpas* and promontories: a hot but beautiful climb. Magnificent prospect of the land, with the great *stūpas* of Anuradhapura visible in the distance.

Then a drive to Polonnaruva. Lunch and rest at the pretty rest house, which is on an artificial lake. From 2:00 to 4:00, a view of the monuments: Old Parakrama Bahu I⁶ with the "Library Dagaba" nearby; next, a great compound of ruins, including the Vata-da-ge, Thuparama, Stone Book, and Satmahal ("Seven-Storied") Prasada; further, Gal Vihara and nearby the vast area including the Ruvanweliseya, Buddha Sima Prasada, and Jetavanaramaya.

I got back to the rest house about 4:00, pretty hot & tired: tea; naps; letters—and a long evening chat with Melford, a young Englishman in the colonial service, who was three years in the Gold Coast, and is now going to England on leave after three years in Malaya. Lots of interesting news:

1. The coast of Ceylon, from Colombo to Puttalam (with all its coconut groves, thatch cottages, etc.) greatly resembles the African Gold Coast⁷— only does not seem to be so prosperous. The Gold Coast, apparently, is one of the most flourishing of the Colonies. There is a law against land being owned by non-natives, and this has prevented the development of a planter situation like that of East Africa. The natives, furthermore, are coming steadily into their own as modern citizens. They are excellent doctors and surgeons (development of the witch doctor principle); not so hot, however, as engineers.

2. Three eras of history are represented simultaneously in the native population of West Africa (this goes also, I should say, for India).
   a. Among the peasants—an archaic/medieval,

b. among the politicians and pedagogs—the nineteenth century; and

c. among the doctors, engineers, etc.—the twentieth century.

3. In Malaya—the Communist movement is represented, about 90 percent, by the Chinese; as follows:

   a. a basic core of Communist guerrillas, who were formerly equipped and encouraged by Great Britain

   b. a reinforcement in arms through the Japanese, who left equipment behind, for the annoyance of the British

   c. young Chinese "idealists" (Padover's term), trained in and graduated from the Chinese schools in Malaya

   d. the Chinese "rich men" of the various districts who bribe the Malayan district officers; the "rich men" themselves being threatened by the Chinese Communists, who, one way or another (families, properties, etc., in China), have them under their power

4. Victory over the Communists is being attained and may yet be won:

   a. through starvation (air-poisoning of their jungle crops; strict control of all sales of preserved foods: puncturing all tins as soon as sold, etc.),

   b. through jungle forts (paratroops into treetops, ropes to ground: clearing of forest for helicopter landings; construction of jungle forts).

5. The cost of the war is 1,000,000 Malayan dollars per day (over US $500,000). Drain on Malayan economy—but that's the idea.

6. Among the troops now being used against the Communists are Fijians (great rugby team), Gurkas, Aborigines (five kinds), and Malayan. Few Chinese enlist.

7. The Great Dilemma of democratic politics in the Orient is this: that the native regimes, which have to be supported, are inevitably corrupt (Rhee,[8] Chiang,[9] etc.). If one insists on reform, one is immediately accused of meddling in internal affairs. Meanwhile, one is preaching and teaching the very principles that condemn the crowd that one is supporting.

8. The British policy has been to induct the native peoples into the democratic system as steadily as possible, and to retire when there is no use holding on (the French, on the other hand, don't know when they're through). Example: registering voters and instruction in voting ("I always feel that I am driving the first nail into my own coffin when I do this.")

Monday, March 7   *Polonnaruva—Sigiriya—Kandy*

Off, at about 8:00, from the Polonnaruva Rest House for a visit to Sigiriya. Stiff climb. Encountered my Englishman about halfway up, at the level of the frescoes. He was troubled a bit by vertigo, but pushed on; we went through the lion's feet and scaled to the top. Amazing view. Amazing brickwork structures. Must have been a fantastic affair. Then down we went again. A company of priests at the bottom offered us coconut milk, after which we drove to the rest house for a cup of tea.

Procession in Kandy

Next, to Kandy: a very pretty little city around a charming lake (made me think, a little, of Lucerne). On the way: rubber plantations, tea, coffee, cocoa, coconut, pepper. Visited the Temple of the Tooth, the beautiful botanical gardens, and the new, handsome, still-growing university.[10]

At about 5:00, my friend and I fell into an amusing adventure. We drove in his car to see the temple elephants bathing, but were told that they had already bathed and were now in a procession of some kind. We drove to find the procession, and presently, lo! an elephant ahead. Traffic jam. We got out of the car and walking fast with our cameras, caught up to the elephant—more ahead; and both before and behind the great last elephant Kandyian dancers and drums. Behind the whole procession, a slowly walking Buddhist monk, shading his head with a palm, and walking on a long white cloth (in two pieces: picked up from behind and placed before him). We were tall and conspicuous, and were cordially invited into the enclosure into which the dancers, monk, and reliquary from atop the last elephant were gathered. "One hour of dancing," we were told. But instead, it was one hour of speeches—and we were trapped—sitting in places of honor. The elephants went back along the road; the dancers too—and there we were.

"We have fallen into a deep trap," I said.

"We can't go now," said my friend.

But toward the close of the third speech, I said, "When this one ends, let's get up and go."

We did so, and nobody seemed to mind. The most helpful of our hosts came up and talked with us. The speeches, which had been in Singhalese, had been made by police officers and lawyers, and were on the subject of the evil of crime. We had been lured into an anti-crime meeting by a troupe of elephants.

Meanwhile, of course, our driver had lost us. We started walking back to town, and then hopped a bus.

After I had bathed and rested, I came down for dinner, to find my friend (Melford) having a drink with a late-middle-aged English couple, Major & Mrs. Blake, from South America, who had just spent six weeks as guests of the state in Siam. Very nice words about Siam. I should visit, not only Bangkok and Chiang Mai, but also Korat—the Major's verdict: practically no Communism in Siam. Government corrupt? Yes! But the people are well-off and happy. A threat: the Thai of the north (South China) now do so want to join their southern brothers, who left them eight hundred years ago!!

I found Mrs. Blake very edgy and un-nice about Americans ("your people," she called them, when addressing me), and the major very strongly against the U.N. and open diplomacy. Otherwise an apparently civilized and pleasant couple.

Tuesday, March 8   *Kandy—Colombo*

Good-bye to my friend Melford after breakfast, and a fine drive, then, back to Colombo. Pause, on the way, at a tea factory, where I became acquainted with the secrets and the grades:

1. BOP (the best)
2. BOPF (Fannings)
3. BP
4. OP (Orange Pekoe)
5. Pekoe
6. Dust 2
7. Dust 1 (the finest grain)

Arrived at the Grand Oriental Hotel at noon, to find everything in good order: ticket ready for Bangkok, room reserved here and in Bangkok, and a letter from Jean—also, one from Arthur Gregor, and a wild affair from Ed Solomon (Sarah Lawrence),[11] who expects to arrive in India in March or April and wants quick information.

After lunch I went to the Colombo museum (excellent bronzes) and chatted with Dr. Paranavitana (Archaeological Commissioner for Ceylon) and Dr. Devendra, who is to be the editor of a Buddhist encyclopedia.[12]

They told me that Sigiriya was an imitation of Kubera's Kailasa, and that the frescoes of the *apsarases* probably ran all around the sides. On top was a garden, not a castle. The approach wound up the sides somewhat like a ziggurat.[13]

In the car, on the way back to Colombo, I meditated a bit about India and Ceylon, Hinduism and Buddhism, Religion and the modern world. One does not find in Ceylon the utterly abject castoffs that abound all over India. The wealth seems not to be so unevenly distributed. Is this the result of the Buddhist, non-caste ideology? If so—the caste system can be regarded as greatly responsible for the peculiarly Indian spectacle of squalor. The Buddhist shrines are conspicuously cleaner and more neatly kept than the Hindu. Their art is more cleanly brash. I am amazed at the strength of the Buddhist tone in the newspapers. The fundamental anti-Westernism seems to be comparable to that of India: a pride in the old-fashioned virtues: vegetarianism, nondrinking, etc. The monks seem to me to be little different from the Hindu—except that we don't seem to have any wild *sadhus* here. A more clarified, less archaic atmosphere.

One religion or another—I think—they're all out of date, and in their variety are the various hues of a sunset—Catholic *bhakti,* Hindu *bhakti,* Buddhist *bhakti:* Buddha's tooth, Christ's Cross, Śiva's *lingam.* As Jason said, the other day: "In the Madura temple, watching all those people, finally something cracked in me and I couldn't take it any longer: I sat down and laughed. People, I thought, will worship anything—absolutely anything—and so what?"[14]

Wednesday, March 9   *Bangkok*

A radical change of world. Up at 4:00 A.M. to catch 5:00 o'clock bus to the airport: bus late: 5:30. Standing in the somnolent lobby of the Grand Oriental Hotel, waiting. The other person leaving from the hotel was a dapper young Japanese.

Lots to do at the airport about passports, customs, and papers—then into a vast new KLM Super Constellation. Very few passengers and a dismal Dutch hostess. Only five passengers in tourist class. Breakfast rather dull. Lots of camera work by the young Japanese boys and Germans in the cabin: shooting (and I with them) the disappearance of Ceylon—and later, the arrival of Malaya: first a lovely scattering of islands; then the jungle land of the peninsula; then fields—threaded with rivers that looked, at first, like roads: houses lining the riverbanks: boats on the rivers, seen from above.

We landed at the great airport in Bangkok about 1:00 P.M. Indian time: 2:30 P.M. Bangkok time—I realized that I am now exactly halfway round the world: 2:00 P.M. here is 2:00 A.M. in New York. And lo! we have come, indeed, into the American sphere: on the airfield, American army planes; in the airport—a flock of American tourists: we are served, immediately, Pepsi-Cola. It is very hot.

A very long bus ride to the hotel; bus filled with an American tour—widows and old gentlemen from the rural parts mostly (Bennington, Vt., was on one bag): a noisy man singing "East Side, West Side" and taking up more room than he should. "Look at them horns!" anent the water buffalo. I noted *wooden houses instead of clay*: Chinese-style hats, water jars on carrying sticks, etc. Chinese-style people and clothes. And a new sensation: most of the people are vertical instead of horizontal, and although poor, do not have the look of utter squalor.

Discharged at the Metropole Hotel—which is a bit out from the center—I found myself in the sort of place that one might find, say, in a new Nevada hotel run by Chinese. The price of the room shocked me: 250 ticals air-conditioned (= $12.50) without meals (contrast the normal Indian twenty-five rupees [= $5.00] *with* meals). Not air-conditioned I would pay 130 ticals (= $6.50): that I took; but I determined to look for something cheaper elsewhere. Then I took a shower (no hot water), changed into lighter clothes, and walked along the new-looking street toward the town. Found the Trocadero Hotel and made reservations for next week. Found the World Travel Service, and made reservations for two hours tomorrow. Found the telegraph office and wired Jean for $750. Came home for dinner and after dark went for a little stroll.

My first impression: a large Chinatown. After India, it has an air of fun-in-life and prosperity. People are cleanly and neatly dressed. Lots of new buildings going up everywhere. Men and women; boys and girls in the cafés, however, mostly men. The Orient, all right; but people don't seem to be having as much trouble as the Indians with inherited habits. A relief to see people without their religion painted all over their faces. Even the Buddhist monks in their bright yellow robes (clean, for a change) seemed comparatively simple.

Furthermore, there is the electrical air here of a town on the threshold of a considerable future. Last week the great SEATO[15] meeting took place in Bangkok, and it became the capital of the alliance. In the vast new Postal and Telegraph building, there is a special window for SEATO wires.

Thursday, March 10

Up for a seven o'clock start on a launch trip, up the river and through some of the canals and smaller streams. A wonderful world of people in boats— boat restaurants, boat markets, boat transports of every kind; also, wooden homes, shops, and workshops, warehouses, etc., all along both banks, thickly packed. The navigating of the boats through the teeming, narrow channels was something marvelous: motorboats with lighters and loaded skiffs in tow. One had the sense of a happy, well-fed people, an abundance of fruits and rice (barges down to the gunwales, loaded with rice, coming down the river by the dozen). Something very different from India—even though this trip reminded me at many points of the backwaters around Cochin.

We made two stops on the launch trip. The first was at a great shed, sheltering about ten of the longest canoe-barges I have ever seen: one was over one hundred fifty feet long; the others only a little shorter. These were the royal barges and war canoes—golden prowed with dragon and Garuda figureheads, the latter having a hole, for the firing of a canon, between the spread legs of the birds. Date of the barges, said to be eighteenth century or so, made of teak. Our second stop was at the tall Dawn Temple. We climbed to about halfway up the central tower, and the Hindi woman in the party wrote "Zahria Pakistan 1955" on the inside of the top parapet.

After lunch, I went on another tour—to the royal palace and the adjacent temples: golden, pagoda, temple of the Emerald Buddha. Fabulous colors—and I ran out of color film, of course. One charming episode: an American gentleman of about seventy, from California, was standing beside me and I pointed out a frieze of Thai *apsarases,*[16] up near the ceiling. "Angels," I said. "You know," he said, with a kind look in his eyes, "there are pictures of Greek angels, Indian angels, American angels, Buddhist angels—and they're all different. I wonder which is right!"

Wired Jean twice today for money; once for my pocket, once for my fares ($750 + $600). After dinner at the Metropole Hotel, I went to my room, and wrote a set of letters to India—including Sri Krishna Menon.

Friday, March 11

No particular plan for the day. Had expected a morning tour but it didn't come through. Strolled about town, purchasing razor blades, films, etc., visiting the Chartered Bank of India, to see if my money had arrived; and then bumped into the gentleman who had asked about the angels—Mr. Farrell, of California. Joined him and his wife for a visit to the National Museum (great room of bronzes) and a large standing Buddha. By the time we were finished it was lunchtime, and when I returned to the Metropole I found that the World Travel Service had phoned. I got in touch with them immediately after lunch and was told that there would be room for me on a one day excursion that they were running to Angkor tomorrow. Did I want to go? I did. Quick changes of plan. Trip to the bank, and my first money had arrived.

After settling my travel and money affairs, I went into the Trocadero bar for a bit of air-conditioning and a cup of tea, and had been there about half an hour, when a rather fierce-looking guy came walking in and went walking around the room like a lion in a cage—sort of angry, and as though he had just been pulled out of a drunk or a beating of some kind.

He looked dimly familiar. Too loudly, he ordered ham and eggs, and, continuing his ravaged walk, suddenly stopped before me.

"Say!" he said, "Aren't you Campbell?"

"Hello there, Don," I said, gradually remembering. It was (my God!) Don Bigelow, whom Jean and I had met in Baroda—Fulbright representative of America to India.[17]

He sat down at my table, and in his hoarse voice—which he always seems to be trying to test for a better sound—began rehearsing his rough experiences: a bad BOAC[18] landing in Calcutta; a late flight; the horrible BOAC; the horrible Hindus, with whom he had lived a year: he had told them off when he was about to leave: they had asked him what he thought of India and he let them have it: a graceless, selfish, dreary people.

I too felt that there was something definitely wrong about the Hindus. One enters the country and is shocked by the squalor, the callousness of the rich, and all those other things enumerated in my early notes. Gradually, then, one gets used to the negative aspects and the positive begin to emerge. These, too, I have noted. One even begins to accept the low Indian standard as a kind of norm. But then one leaves, and even in Ceylon it is evident that life can easily be better. Here in Thailand, one is actually amazed at how bright it can be; whereas for all the American tourists here in Thailand, this place seems below par. Now that I can look back upon India, I think that what finally got me down the most was the arrogant assumption of spiritual superiority by a people in whose lives and society one can see the evidence only of a conspicuously materialistic self-interest, with a heavy sauce of *bhakti,* which is what the Hindus seem to mean by spirituality. Bigelow agreed that the spiritual arrogance was the worst of it. In Rangoon he had bumped into Santha Rama Rau and Faubian Bowers,[19] and Santha, after hearing all his complaints, had said, with perfect confidence, that, yes, but India was, after all, *the* great civilization.

It appeared that Bigelow was going to be on the trip tomorrow to Angkor. It appeared, also, that there were going to be a number of American tourists in the party. It appeared, finally, that he had met somewhere, somehow, a dismal couple who might be typical of what was coming and was going to have a drink with them at 7:00 P.M. Would I like to come? I said I would come at seven-thirty. Their name was Wallace and they were in the Trocadero Annex. The husband was about seventy and the much younger wife, somewhat desperate, was already throwing herself at Bigelow.

I returned to my own hotel, just down the street, for a bit of a nap and preparatory packing for tomorrow, then brought my smaller bag to the Trocadero, to be kept for me until my return from Angkor, and went over to the Wallace apartment in the Annex. The door was opened by a large, smiling, broad-faced, sandy blond woman of about forty-five, in a dressing gown and with her grease on her face. "My friend, Don Bigelow, told me to come," I said. "He isn't here yet," she said, still smiling, "but come in, come in. Pour yourself a drink and I'll finish dressing." I said I thought it would be better if I went over to get Don and returned in about half an hour. She consented, and I went downstairs; but instead of going to see Don immediately, I went for a brief walk, and returned to learn that Don had already gone up to the Wallace apartment. When I got there, he was sitting with a drink in his hand, while Margaret (Mrs. W.) went on with her dressing. I poured my drink and sat down. Then Mr. Wallace's quavery voice called from the bathroom for his trousers and a rather large-bellied pair was handed to him by his wife. She managed then to step into her dress and get it up over her while adroitly discarding her dressing gown and Don then opined that he had better go and change his garments too. We had decided to go to the Oasis, around the corner. (A place recommended to me by the two women I met in Darjeeling, and of which Mrs. W. had also heard a good report.) Mr. Wallace appeared: a mild, large, rather plump, oldish man; he greeted me perfunctorily (and why not?) poured himself a drink and sat down. Don went out to change and Mrs. W. went into the bathroom to finish her pruning. I was left with the old man.

"Well, of course," he said, "I'm not a professor, so I don't really understand these things; but it seems to me you can't give freedom to people until they're ready for it. Now you take the case of so-and-so, this friend of mine: he tells me that in such-and-such a place they built fine homes for the people, and what did they do? They used the bathrooms for wood and coal bins. Now, I don't know logic, of course, but it seems to me reasonable to think that people shouldn't be given things, or have things thrust upon them, till they're educated to use them." Etc. etc. One always gets it immediately from the man of money. This one has a large flat in San Francisco, a hotel room, for the moment, in Hong Kong, where he and his wife are keeping their spare luggage; this room at the Trocadero (air-conditioned), which he will keep while going to Angkor—and no idea, particularly, of why he is making the trip.

When Don returned, we finished off the drinks and walked around to the Oasis: a nightclub with a Thai band playing good Hawai'ian, American, and South American music. Two girl singers; one smoky, the other cuddly. Nice crowd—mostly Thai—and a very good dinner for about two dollars. First Mr. Wallace had to dance with his wife, so that she would be available to Don and myself. First I, then Don, then I again danced with her. "Sometimes," she said, "I feel so lonesome.... That's why I have to keep doing things."—Well, that was it all right: about the most dismal marriage picture I have seen. Married for money and the old man didn't die.

Saturday, March 12   *Cambodia*

Up at 4:00 to catch a bus at 4:45; but the bus did not arrive until 5:30. In it were an oldish man and a youngish wife: not the couple of last night, but another. This bus was an auxiliary affair: the real bus had gone on, full up, to the airport. And when we arrived, sure enough, there was a whole company of wealthy old gentlemen, petulant as babies, and forceful, variously younger wives—two, at least, with voices like men. I thought of Jung's *enantiodromia* formula:[20] here, however, it seemed to be represented with unusual force. Is this the soul of the U.S.A. that I behold?

The plane got off in due time, and I sat in the back seat with Bigelow: across from us a young anthropologist from Oregon, here on a Fulbright, to study and teach something about the teaching and study of native languages. When we got to Cambodia it appeared that neither of these Fulbright boys could speak French—or, probably, any language but English; and I could not but remember the first question that the Fulbright authorities at Columbia put to me: What about my languages? (German, French, Sanskrit, a bit of Hindi; also, Spanish and a bit of Italian, Russian, Latin and Greek.) I don't quite get it!

At the Siem Reap airport there was an extremely superior young Frenchman with a black beard, who certainly despised the arriving Americans, and though I despised his superiority, I could not but admit that he had some reason on his side. We were certainly a pitiful spectacle. It took a while to deal with the customs, and in the meantime another plane arrived on the small airfield—with a small party of French.

We were taken to the large, French-style hotel, in a bus that stalled on the way (fan-belt trouble), but finally arrived and then began, almost immediately, our tour of the sites.

First: Angkor Wat. Don and I got out ahead of the crowd; looked carefully at the mural reliefs, clockwise, to halfway round; then entered the courts and climbed the towers. Next finished the murals, clockwise, and met the crowd at the gate. Lots of color photos.

Bus back to the hotel for lunch. Off again at 3:00.

A quick drive through one of the Angkor Thom gates (to be visited tomorrow) and an arrival at Preah Khan. A wonderful adventure. I was so excited that I opened my camera before reeling back the film, and so, spoiled all of the shots of the morning. Five of us: Don Stern, the anthropologist, a young English historian from Singapore, and a young Swiss named Henri, sort of got detached from the party in the labyrinths of Preah Khan, and found, when we reached the bus, that the whole party had been sitting for fifteen or twenty minutes waiting—the atmosphere was not very good!

Our next stop was Neak Pean, which proved to be one of the prettiest symbolic compositions I've ever seen. Two serpents, tails enlaced, enfold a lotus structure, their heads, however, leaving an opening at the side opposite to their tails. Avalokiteśvara, as the Horse Cloud (Balaha), is shown carrying a great number of human souls to this entrance. They cling to his sides and hang from his tail. Within the main sanctuary of the lotus isle is a Mucalinda Buddha.[20a] The four sides of the sanctuary show the images of gods.

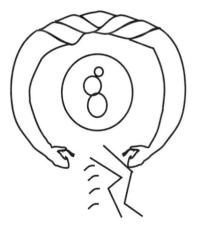

The bus guide rushed us along and we dashed next to a couple of other sanctuaries, at one of which, in my rush, I sprained my right ankle—not badly, but enough to make the ankle swell and hurt. We got back to the hotel in time for a bath and pleasant dinner, before going to bed.

I felt pretty distinctly, however, that I did not want very much to be

Mucalinda-Buddha sanctuary at Neak Pean

with the main crowd again tomorrow. Two of the prize remarks:

1. We drove quickly past a ruin and the Oregon anthropologist cried, "Hey, aren't we going to look at that?" One of the men of the party leaned forward and said, "Say, you sound as though you *wanted* to see those things!" "Well," was the quiet answer, "that's what I came here to do!"

2. At the conclusion of the day, the oldest gentleman in the party said to his wife: "I'd give everything I have to have had three Coca-Colas instead of all those temples."

Sunday, March 13   *Angkor Thom*

Ankle not too bad. Aroused by the bugle practice of some kind of Boy Scout or army unit in the neighboring fields. After breakfast I managed to get the manager of the hotel to let five of us have a jeep for a quick dash out to Banteay Srei (thirty-five kilometers over a rugged road) and then a look at Angkor Thom.

The drive out was one-and-a-half hours, through roads lined by the most primitive villages I've ever seen: palm-thatch houses up on stilts; very simple people. The boys lined the roads, holding out flowers. We found a couple of small parties at Banteay Srei before us; had a fine visit to the pretty temple; then drove back to the elephant and Garuda terrace and the great heads of the Bayon. While in the latter place, it came time for me to change films again, and I found that in my hysterical moment yesterday, I had failed to put my new film in correctly, so that it had not moved beyond picture number one. No color shots, consequently, of Angkor!

After lunch, the plane home to Bangkok: arrival at about 6:00. I find that my bag has not been delivered to the Trocadero Hotel, where I am to stay. Hunt. Discovery at the Oriental. Quick change. And off to a performance of Siamese dance—actually a kind of Chinese-American, Siamese opera–musical comedy. Story: Swan maiden (Kinnara). The final dance, where the prince had to recognize his bride among her six sisters in the palace of the Kinnara king, was charming. The rest was rather dull.

I got back to the hotel too late for anything to eat; so, had three bottles of beer in the air-conditioned bar and went to bed.

Monday, March 14   *Bangkok*

Woke up feeling like hell: bad case of the runs. Went to a clinic near the hotel to see about my ankle. Nice experience of the role of the doctor in Thailand. Wired Jean about money again and picked up my travel vouchers and tickets for my trip to Chiang Mai: otherwise, a day, largely, of sitting around and recovering. Had various chats in the hotel with various members of the Angkor party, and at 5:00 P.M. set off for the station.

What a contrast with India! Clean station, clean, decently dressed people, quietness and orderliness. Had plenty of help from boys and porters who showed me to my compartment—or rather, upper berth, American style. Presently the occupant of the lower arrived: Mrs. Quentin Roosevelt— widow of the young man whom I met, with his father, Theodore Jr., at the Wallaces' in Mount Kisco, some years ago.[21] Once every three years she leaves her three little girls with their grandparents and comes to the Far East for a three-month holiday and painting spree. Across the aisle from us was a young Thai couple with a lot of luggage, on their way north. They were cute and kind, and helped us considerably with the porters and waiters.

The train, narrow guage, made in Japan, American style, was rather amusing, particularly when, at retiring time, it became apparent that there were to be no curtains to screen off the berths. Mrs. R. and I had dinner together—brought to us from the dining car; and presently, all were tucked away.

Tuesday, March 15 *Chiang Mai*

All day in the train, till 5:30 P.M. An excellent way to see the length of Thailand. Rice fields; then hilly country and second-growth forest; when low mountains began to appear, I recalled what Jean had said about this part of the world; namely, that the landscapes looked like Chinese paintings. Indeed it does.

At one junction our train was divided in two and two, sturdy, wood-burning engines pulled us through the mountains, the rest of the way; at one point, however, our little affair could hardly get its load around a bend. We stopped and then inched along, with a man out in front of the engine dusting something onto the rails to help the traction.

After our Thailand couple got off, we located a Rev. Dr. H. Gaylord Knox, of the American Presbyterian Mission, who was on his way to Chiang Mai for some kind of mission conference. He was very nice and told us a number of helpful things about the objects that we were seeing on the stations and in the hills.

The general picture on the station platforms was considerably different from that of India: fewer people, less commotion, less noise, better clothing.

The tendency is to carry things, not on the head, but on bamboo sticks, over the shoulder; however, some of the platform vendors carried their trays on their heads—with stacks of fried chicken parts, fruits of various kinds, bowls of soup, rice dinners, etc. Dr. Knox introduced us to a lovely thing called something like *yum-yum:* steamed rice packed into a joint of bamboo and baked: one strips the bamboo away, and there is a lovely, sealed packet of tasty rice.

He told us also, that if we had taken this train ride one month from today, we would be arriving drenched with water: people greet each other with splashes of water at that time (April 15, 16, 17), to bring the rains that will nourish the crops of May.

He showed us, also, the large leaves used here for roofing: they do not burn.

At the Chiang Mai station, Dr. Knox was met by two young missionaries, who packed us into their jeep truck and let us down at the distinctly odorous Chainarong Hotel. Our rooms were up on the second (i.e., top) floor hall, at the back; Mrs. R.'s no. 2; mine no. 8. I took a shower (no hot water, however, in Thailand) and a nap—feeling rather fatigued from my upset entrails and sprained ankle. When I went downstairs at about 7:30, the proprietress at the desk told me that Mrs. R. had already gone to the Chinese restaurant near the movie theater just down the street. I joined her there for a fairly good Chinese dinner, after which we took a walk around the block, looking at the closing shops. Carved wooden elephants, etc., silver bowls beaten out of Indian rupees—and black false teeth, for the betelnut chewers.

Wednesday, March 16

At 1:30 A.M. there was a powerful rap at my door: sounded like the police. "What's the matter?" I yelled; and, getting up out of a sound sleep, opened the door. There stood an American youth of moderate stature with an almost empty bottle of whiskey in his hand. "Excuse me," he said quite clearly, "but would you like to have a drink?" "For God's sake!" I said, and I slammed the door. Immediately, the knock was repeated. I opened. "Are you the rugged type?" said the youth. "No," I answered; "but I'm damned tired. I've been traveling for weeks and I want to sleep." Whereupon, the face of a young Thailander appeared beside my challenger. "Please excuse," he said. "I'm sorry. Please excuse." The two retired and I shut the door.

Precisely one hour later there was another rap at my door. "Say, what the hell *is* this?" I shouted, and I got up and opened. This time three Thai officers of some kind, in dark blue uniforms, with red bands about their caps, were in the hall, and a man who looked like one of the hotel clerks said, when he saw me, "Please excuse; so sorry." "For God's sake!" I said; and I shut the door.

One half hour later, there was the sound of a buzzer and a red light went on across the hall from me (could be seen over the top of my front wall). I heard the voice of the youth who had rapped at my door saying, "You've got a fire here. Put it out." There was a considerable noise in the hall and I got up to see what was going on. The officers in blue were in the hall; so were a number of the servants of the hotel. The young man's bed had caught fire. They were rapping at a door down the hall, across from Mrs. R.'s, out of which there presently came the proprietress in a dressing gown. I shut my door and went back to bed. When all had become quiet again, the American voice began to say loudly, "Well! Have you got another room. I want another room." A second American voice then came along the hall, with a gentle laugh. "Well, how are you feeling?" "Why, this is the kind of place," said the first voice, "that catches fire!"

I went off to sleep, in spite of the roosters that now were crowing as though a new eon were dawning, and in the morning went downstairs to learn who my countrymen were. They were, respectively, Major House and Major Britain of the U.S. Air Force.

After breakfast at the Chinese restaurant, Mrs. R. and I went in a rickshaw to the U.S. consul's compound and chatted a while with his wife, who offered to drive us tomorrow to the Leprosy Colony, directed by Dr. Buker (whose name had been given to me by the Dr. Cockran whom I met in the Air Ceylon bus going to Colombo). I returned, then, to my room to write in my diary and to nap (not feeling too well yet—and rather tired after a succession of troubled nights), while Mrs. R. went forth to meet a young Thailand lady to whom she had an introduction.

At lunchtime Mrs. R. returned to the hotel with her prey—a nice young woman, trimly dressed, Western style—and we all had lunch at the Chinese place. Her name was something like Mrs. Suchat. She let us have one of her cars for the afternoon and we were driven by her chauffeur up a lovely mountain that rises from the plain to a considerable height (reminded us both of the Colorado situation). I keep recalling what Jean said about the Chinese-painting look of the mountains in these parts. It is quite true. The curious mist that lies over all distances and the sudden type of the hills, with a peculiar vegetation composed largely of bamboo, bananas, teak, and various plants entirely unknown to the West, make for a quite distinctive impression. We stopped at the foot of a long dragon staircase that led up to a nice Buddhist temple, now being painted up freshly. A magnificent view. Mrs. R. finally settled to paint a picture of the landscape, and I wandered around with my camera, having a peaceful and pleasant time. A curious detail was a pair of white, guardian Ganeśas with four arms and very short trunks at the main entrance to the main enclosure. Lots of gold—umbrellas—a gold *stūpa*—mural of the Buddha life in a sort of Siamese-Italian-primitive style. Two nice old monks, who came down for a while to watch Mrs. R. paint. Thunder was rolling over the hills and presently drops began to fall. We returned to the car and to the hotel. Once again the Chinese restaurant and a brief walk before retiring: this time, for a sound night's sleep.

Thursday, March 17

After breakfast—again at the Chinese restaurant, which is the only safe place in town for the alien stomach—I drove with the Mrs. U.S. consul and two other ladies to the Leper Colony while Mrs. R. went in Mrs. Suchat's car to some temple that she wanted to paint. The visit to the colony was extraordinarily interesting—particularly after what I had seen of India's lepers. It is an institution dating from 1908, underwritten by the American Leprosy Mission, with about five hundred inpatients and two thousand who are being treated in various nearby towns. The idea is to give the lepers a sense of responsibility and ability to work. Some are carving little wooden elephants and carts; some are working on new buildings or in the fields. There are a number of dormitories, but most live in cottages for two, with the names of the donors painted over the doors. The men live in one area and the women in another. There are also a few families of lepers. We visited the hospital, church, and a great part of the grounds. The lepers are not even urged to become Christians and the colony does not itself provide a pastor:

but many of the lepers have become Christians and these take care of the church affairs themselves. The principal medical treatment, apparently, is by way of D.D.S. tablets, which gradually alleviate the symptoms and sort of stabilize and immunize the patient's condition. When they are ready to return to normal life they are released—but some do not want to leave.

This mission (Presbyterian sponsored, in the main) and that of the nuns on St. Thomas Mount in Madras have pretty well cured me of my anti-missionary bias—particularly since I now don't think it matters very much whether people practice one form of religion or another. Something certainly has to be said to the credit of the social orientation of the Christian tradition, which has sent these missionaries out into very difficult and dangerous areas to spread the benefits of Western science, as well as the Gospel. And I think it can be said that these benefits (those of science, that is to say) cannot be shrugged away.

Thailand is giving me a rather good picture of an Oriental nation taking on the Western benefits without too much agony of spirit—largely because these people are not troubled, as the Indians are, by a profound inferiority complex. They do not have to compensate for every benefit received by pretending to some nonexistent spiritual advantage.

After returning from the colony I took a stroll through the Chiang Mai market—which is one of the model markets of the world: the meat section is screened, to keep the flies out, and the rest is pretty and orderly, with nice-looking vendors sitting at their stands, under red parasols. The only time I heard that "Good day, sir. Please come in, just to look!" was, of course, from an Indian merchant with his textile stall. And the only beggars were three lepers sitting quietly at one of the entrances. ("Why these?" I thought, "with the colony less than twenty minutes away!")

I sent my bag to the Thai Airways office and went to the Chinese restaurant for lunch. Mrs. R. arrived just before I left and we promised to get in touch with each other in New York. Then I caught the bus—and the plane back to Bangkok.

The plane was full of military men (Thai and American) and a missionary party, which included one pleasant lady, who, when we landed, introduced me to her husband and family and drove me to my hotel.

I took a shower, ate dinner in the air-conditioned bar, went for a brief after-dinner stroll, and retired at 9:00.

Friday, March 18   *Bangkok*

I have decided not to do any more traveling in Thailand. Have a rather nice little room at 55 ticals ($2.75), and believe that I might be able to finish up a few chores here before setting off for Japan. Spent the morning writing up my diary and now, at exactly noon, am exactly here.

After lunch I started reading V. E. Sarachchandra's *The Sinhalese Folk Play*,[22] which I have to review for Salmony[23]—one of my two remaining chores (the second, a preface for Eranos volume II,[24] I hope to finish in Hong Kong, so that I may enter Japan soul free). Also, I procured my Japanese and Hong Kong visas for the coming trip. I have decided to add a two-day stay in Formosa, if I can get the visa tomorrow.

For dinner I went around to the Oasis and listened to the lively band—the two girl singers are something that one would simply not find in India: here, however, they are quite in the groove. When I came home I wrote a couple of letters and at eleven retired.

Saturday, March 19

Went, after breakfast, in a bicycle-rickshaw to the Chinese legation (Nationalist Chinese) for my visa to Formosa, and spent the rest of the day reading Sarachchandra on the folk plays of Ceylon. A very nice little book. Had lunch at the hotel and for dinner went around to Chez Eve—which is not as pleasant as the Oasis: a good piano, but the rest of the band is not so hot. Wrote some more letters and retired about ten.

Sunday, March 20

A really quiet day. Finished the *Folk Play* book, wrote my review, and mailed it off to Jean to be typed.

At lunch today, in the hotel dining room, who should walk up to speak to me but Johnny Girshory—now grey-haired and a bit on the old side. She is playing companion to some wealthy lady on the world tour of the *Coronia*. The hotel is now full of those people: wealthy and old. I had coffee at her table, and after lunch she went off to paint some river scene. I returned to my work and finished the day. For dinner I went back to the Oasis. To bed about ten.

Monday, March 21

A day of considerable importance, because at 5:00 P.M. I finished my Editor's Foreword to the next Eranos volume (*The Mysteries*). I worked on the piece all day. Had lunch in an American-style lunch counter that I discovered last night next to the Oasis. When I had finished the Foreword I went out to a bookstore and bought myself McGovern's *Conversational Japanese*. After my shower and before dinnertime, I studied the first chapters, and began to feel like a new man. The point is that I am now free of all commitments—first time since the Zimmer papers fell upon me thirteen years ago.[25]

Tuesday, March 22

A day of letter writing and of concluding all my travel arrangements. All meals in the hotel. Tomorrow morning I'm off for Rangoon.

And though I haven't *done* very much these past few days, in the way of seeing the sights in this nice little city, I've recovered my equilibrium and feel that the days were very well spent. Also, something of the rhythm and feeling of the life in Bangkok has soaked into me: and I can say that I like it.

The other day, as I was out walking, I passed three large Indian women, dressed in their saris and with the jewels in their noses and ears. They looked quaint—as do also the Sikhs on their motorcycles who occasionally appear in these streets. But one of the women then squatted on the curb—and I suddenly realized what a difference the prospect of an Indian and a Thailand city. Here most of the people, most of the time, are vertical and moving. I suddenly saw the streets of Calcutta and Bombay, with the people picking the lice from each other's hair, and I wondered—I wonder—whether India will ever catch up.

As for Thailand—my impression is good. It is said that the government is corrupt; but when I broached this theme to Dr. Knox, who has lived here some forty years, he did not agree. He told me, moreover, of an interesting law; namely, that if a man does not inhabit or work the land for which he has paid, he may lose it. All land belongs, legally, to the crown; and to hold a claim to it, one has to work it. The majority of the farmers in Thailand, therefore, own their land.

The literacy rate is something like 70 percent. The country is under-, not overpopulated—and food is abundant.

My impression of the press is that its international position is anti-Communist and pro-American: not at all in the between position of India.

Burma,[26] Hong Kong, and Formosa[27]

Wednesday, March 23   *Rangoon*

A considerable change of scene. Up at five. Bus to the airport. A handsome four-motor Thai Airways plane—with only three Sikh families heading home and an Englishman named Smithson, who drove me to the hotel in his station wagon.

In Bangkok they gave me a Burmese visa for three days. Actually I shall be here a little less than three full days—10:30 A.M., March 23, to 5:00 A.M. March 26; but since four dates are involved this is counted four days; hence my visa is valid only till March 25. A normal sort of Oriental situation. I have, therefore, to go to the Immigration Office for a one-day extension. I went to the Immigration Office and climbed upstairs through a fantastic crowd (Indians, mostly, but also a great many other nationalities) to the desk of the head man: a mild little, greatly wall-eyed person, who gave me a long blank to fill out, and then sent me off to get a 1.50-rupee stamp— in another building. I went to the Court Building—and again ran into an interesting crowd—this time mostly Burmese. They are a cute lot, I must say. (But we'll come to that later.) I found the tables in a long corridor where the stamps are sold and was told to come back tomorrow: stamps are "out of stock." (This means, of course, that no legal business can be effectively initiated in Rangoon, the capital of Burma, till tomorrow.) They told me to try at another place, opposite the Hong Kong Bank: I did so, but the story was the same. So I went back to the Immigration Office and my wall-eyed friend said that he would start my passport on its way, so that it would be ready in time: I could affix the stamp tomorrow.

I went next to the Strand Hotel (which is close to all of these offices) and was sitting, sort of getting my bearings, when my friend Mr. Smithson came in. We had a couple of beers together, after which he went in to get lunch and I decided that this was the kind of hotel that would have a good barber shop—so I got a haircut (first since Bombay: distinctly needed). I went next to write a couple of letters, and then, it being about 3:30 P.M., took a taxi and asked to be shown the town.

What interested me most were the long and busy dock front on the Irrawaddy River, the flower and fruit market, the immense number of movie houses, with movies from all over Europe, America, and Asia, the Shive Dagon Pagoda area, and the very colorful, somewhat chic, little people. As Smithson remarked on the drive in this morning, in Rangoon one sees women—in contrast, for example, to Calcutta—and they give a lot of color to the city. They dress very trimly here, in tight white bodices and with varicolored sarongs, tight about the hips (the men wear the same sarong). Also, they pay attention to their hair and have a number of cute ideas about hairdos (not just the pigtail of India). And finally, a number of them wear a sort of light-yellow, musklike pancake powder all over the front of the face—which adds another color and is amusing. In the sun they carry pretty, colorful parasols.

In fact, I would say that Rangoon is one of the most interesting cities, visually, that I have seen. The population is greatly mixed: Burmese, Chinese, and Indian. Hordes of the dock coolies are Indian; the hotel servants at the Strand are Indian; the people lying down in the streets are Indian; and the beggars are Indian: Also, the shopkeepers who call after you are Indian. I've come to the conclusion that for Indians begging is neither a necessity nor a habit, but a trait of character. The baksheesh formula remains the key to the whole national structure. It is the key even to the international "neutralist" position, which has the function of inviting competing handouts from both sides. It is not "balance of power" politics, as it was in England's great day, but "balance of baksheesh." In fact *bhakti* might be said to be a technique for getting baksheesh from God. (The way of the kitten; the way of the baby monkey.[28]) And while we're on the Indian theme: Smithson told me a good one about the Taj Mahal Hotel. When the architect who had designed the building saw the finished structure, he shot himself. They had built it with the front to the back.[29]

But to return to Rangoon and Burma. The main product of the south is rice, of the dry country peanuts, beans, pulses, and in the north there are mineral deposits—but nobody can work them because of the bandits. There is a good deal of graft in the business operations. The newspapers are carrying a case right now of graft in the government buying of rice.

The airfield, one immediately notes, is not very good. That in Bangkok is much better. Smithson tells me that, actually, the new Bangkok airport has drawn a good deal of the international traffic away from Rangoon. Apparently Burma and Thailand form the Continental Divide here: Burma is sticking to the Indian Orient. Neutralist, Oriental costumes. It is more picturesque, consequently—or rather, no! It is picturesque in another way—rather, it's picturesque in a more archaic way than Thailand. The two are the great rice producers also. And their people, racially, are Tai Shan.

Well, anyhow, after my drive around the city, I had tea at the Strand and then walked slowly back to the Railway Hotel. I lay down for a rest, studied my *Conversational Japanese,* had dinner, tried to wash in a sort of modified Woodstock way from a washbowl, and went to bed.

Thursday, March 24

Up at seven—and the little fat housekeeper woman invited me down the whole length of the hall to have a bath. After breakfast I sat in the lobby and read the newspaper.

Forgot, yesterday, to note that the Russians have just awarded a "Stalin Peace Prize" (created in parody of the Nobel Prize) to a little eighty-year-old Burmese writer, Thakin Kodaw Hmaing,[30] who will build a Palace of Peace and Culture with the fund that he will establish with the prize money. In his speech of acceptance the old man followed the Moscow-Nehru line in abusing the atom bomb and SEATO. Definitely, we are again in the neutralist zone; not Communist perhaps, but no less anti-American than the Communists.

At about ten I went to the stamp desks again and was told to return at noon; so I went for a nice long picture-taking walk to a small golden pagoda and along the docks. Passed, also, a community of refugee thatch huts—which fascinated me (refugees, this time, from the troubles in the north). I returned to the stamp desk at noon and was told to return at two.

Went back to my hotel for lunch and a brief rest; then returned to the stamp desk. "Another ten minutes," said the man with a smile.

It appeared that although the 1.50-rupee stamps had not come in yet, 2-rupee stamps were now available. I bought one and went to the Immigration Office. My wall-eyed man passed on my stamp to a wall-eyed boy who had an extra thumb and who sat at a desk beside a third wall-eyed man. It took a long while to get around to my passport, and when we got to it, I was told that two photos were needed. Fortunately I had some back at the hotel. Returned by rickshaw, fetched the photos, paid 10 rupees, and took my passport with the one-day extension, which it took me one day to get, to the Foreigners Registration office, where I was told that I now had to fill out a certain "D-Form" for my departure permit. I should come back tomorrow at eleven for this permit.

I went next for an interesting walk along another stretch of docks and photographed a couple of cute boat families; then returned to the Strand for tea, and went back to my own hotel for a rest and dinner. After dinner I took still another long walk through the very lively markets and streets. Rangoon certainly is an amusing place, with its cute little sidewalk restaurants filled with nice little people. In a way, the streets tonight, with all their restaurants and life, reminded me of the boulevards of Paris. And in a way, also, I think that all this is more like what I expected of India than what I found there. The main difference? A kind of chic! Which comes, perhaps, of letting the women loose.

Friday, March 25

A surprise to me is the number of Christian churches and schools (Catholic and Baptist, mostly) and Mohammedan mosques in Rangoon. One sees the Buddhist monks everywhere—as in Ceylon and Thailand—and the most prominent religious structures are the Buddhist pagodas; apparently, however, the number of Christians and Mohammedans in the city is considerable.

Today I walked from the hotel to the Dagon Pagoda, and encountered on the way a lively procession, with a tiny boy dancer in the lead, accompanied by a band of musettes and bamboo clappers. A long file of young women carrying trays of flowers on their heads came next; after which there were a couple of women dancers with their band. And finally, four boys riding ponies came along, beneath gold umbrellas. I took a lot of photos and followed the procession up to the temple. At one point they were passed by another procession coming back from the temple, and the fun was immense. When they reached the temple they simply made a U-turn and started back.

I went on into the Dagon Pagoda, where I spent about an hour and a half with a guide, and when I came out, I walked back, past the hotel, to the main section of the city, where I retrieved my passport from the Foreign Registration office, made arrangements for my air passage tomorrow to

Hong Kong and had lunch at the Strand Hotel. Then I walked back to the Railway Hotel and lay down (damn tired) for a rest.

At about 2:30 I got up and started out on another long walk; to Royal Lake—where I sat for a while under a tree among a bunch of Hindu youngsters who were swimming and generally horsing around, and then, by a long roundabout route, back to the Strand Hotel.

My final impression of Rangoon, gathered largely on this walk, is that it is the dirtiest city I've visited (Calcutta included); garbage literally dumped in the gutter to stink, in many places; dirt everywhere, for the streets, I believe, are never cleaned; many utterly squalid neighborhoods, of thatch (which frequently catch fire), or of filthy tenement alleys with open-drain gutters over which the front-room floorings may extend. The people, however, have more personal style than the Indians. Also, we have no cows in the streets, very few bullock carts—and, somehow, there is an air of people being better off than in Calcutta: very few beggars, cripples, or destitutes—and when there *are* beggars, they are usually Indians.

After my walk, I had tea at the Strand, then returned by rickshaw (tricycle with sidecar) to the Railway Hotel, to pack, shave, have dinner, and go early to bed.

Saturday, March 26 (fifty-first birthday)   *Hong Kong*

Up at 2:30 A.M. to catch a 3:00 A.M. airlines bus, which arrived at 4:30! Meanwhile, conversed with a nice Japanese man, Mr. Nagai, of Tokyo, and an Indian from East Africa, who were also waiting for the bus. The plane didn't take off till about 6:30. Pause in Bangkok: then, a wonderful flight to Hong Kong.

Passed over Indochina, going out to sea at a point south of Hanoi: mountains and wilderness, very few villages, no towns. I thought: "So Indochina goes Communist. What does it mean? What does it matter?"[31]

We approached Hong Kong above a thick flooring of cloud, came down through the clouds, and broke into view of the beautiful island cluster, the water being dotted with junks. Customs. Bus to the Peninsula Hotel. Arrival. Hong Kong time 5:30 P.M.

I felt ridiculous in my tropical white ducks and light shirt: Hong Kong is a large and well-dressed, temperate-zone city, and the weather is fairly cool.

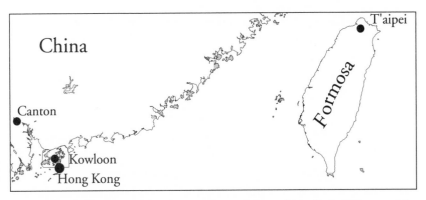

From the Peninsula Hotel, I took a rickshaw (cute little Chinese rickshaw man, loaded me and my luggage aboard and trotted away) to the Miramar Hotel, where I had reserved a room, but where no room had been reserved. They sent me on to the Shamrock Hotel, just a bit further down Nathan Ave. Nice, clean, new Chinese-run hotel. The room boy said that he would get me anything I wanted. "If a girl is required the hotel will supply one. Girls brought in from outside sometimes cause trouble." He also said that the hotel had a tailor and immediately produced one, who tried to sell me before I had even found my bearings. I told him: "Tomorrow"; and went upstairs to have a nice Chinese dinner, after which I went for a stroll along Nathan Ave. The rickshaw boys are almost as great a nuisance as they were in Calcutta. Wire to Jean, and to bed.

Sunday, March 27

Up at about eight. Breakfast upstairs: beautiful views from the top-floor restaurant. Good breakfast, too: first real orange juice since I left America.

After breakfast, I walked the length of Nathan Ave., to the Peninsula Hotel, where I booked myself for a tour of Hong Kong (discovering, to my surprise, that I am now not in Hong Kong but in Kowloon, on the mainland). Amusingly, and fortunately, my companion on this tour was a chap named Campbell—Daniel Campbell from South Carolina, an electronics engineer with Philco; has been nine years in Tokyo. A nice guy with glorious cameras. We had a wonderful day, being driven out to Aberdeen (for lunch in the floating restaurants) and back. Incredible views. Return to Kowloon about 4:30 for tea.

I think that something like this must have been what I was expecting in India. A great and vivid city—in population smaller than either Calcutta or Bombay, but in urbanity so far beyond them that it seems a much larger, stronger, more serious city than either—and the people are lively, healthy looking, busy, clean, shod, dressed, and intelligent. The hotel services are by servants with an idea of what they are doing. The shops are attractive and sophisticated. The women are elegant (the great sensation is the split skirt) and the men manly. I must say, the more I see of the rest of the Orient, the more it seems to me that there is something really wrong with India—and that the cause of her misery is not England (Hong Kong is a colony) but herself.

Campbell and I had a good talk at tea, and there were certain things he said about Japan that are valid also for India—probably for the whole Orient:

1. Americans are admired for their ingenuity—which is regarded, however, as an inferior talent. It is thought that if the Japanese were as fortunately situated as the Americans, they would be able to do much better than the Americans in the fields in which Americans excel.
2. The gadgets—not the fundamental, life-transforming factors—of the machine age are what are liked, bought, and imitated. A Japanese in a $2,000 house will have a $1,000 radio and television set, but no refrigerator. Japan has cameras but no refrigerators.
3. The front part of the home of a successful Japanese businessman will be in the Western style, and the number of the Western rooms, there for the entertainment of his Western friends and associates, will be the measure of his prestige. But his living quarters will be Japanese and without furniture; and when he returns in the evening, he puts off his Western garb and dons Japanese. The comparable situation in America would be, to have a log cabin as a residence, in which one would wear Daniel Boone's leather leggings and raccoon-skin cap.[*]

---

[*] The fact is, however, that many Americans do have this arrangement, for their weekends and holidays, in the form of a "little place" in the woods. Our National Parks are fairylands of pioneering make-believe. The problem is that of keeping in touch simultaneously with two worlds: that of the practical, rational, modern present and that of the past, from which one's systems of ethics, ideals, feeling-values, etc., were inherited. For the Westerner the dichotomy is not as great as for the Oriental, because (a) the Occidental past is generically related to the world's modern present, and (b) the stress on the reduction of the individual to the patterns of the collective archetypes has never been as strong in the West as it is in the Orient. The problem of the Westerner who wishes to hold to the two worlds of his present and his inherited past is therefore not as great as that confronted by the Oriental.

4. The appearance of law and order that one may observe in the legal codes, etc., of Japan, Campbell said, is deceptive. Actually, if you are hit by a car in the street and bring suit, you may find yourself thrown in jail for obstructing the passage of some personage who has known how and whom to bribe. The whole operation of the law is governed by the pulling of wires behind the scenes—in the grand old Oriental style. In contrast, in a colony like Hong Kong, where the final word is that of the British, we have clean streets, well-built houses, solid roads, and effective law.

After tea I returned to my hotel for a bath, a nap, and dinner, then went for an evening stroll (harried by the rickshaw boys) and went early to bed.

Monday, March 28

Up at 8:30—just in time to catch the last drop of water for my shave. (Hong Kong is suffering from an acute water shortage. Water is available only from 6:30 to 8:30 A.M., and from 6:00 to 8:00 P.M.) At 10:15 I turned up at the Peninsula Hotel for my tour—again with Campbell—of the so-called "New Territories"—inland to within a couple of miles of the Red China border. There is a railroad line (Kowloon-Canton) that carries passengers right through.

I was impressed by the fine schools that are being built in the back-country, the general state of well-being of the whole countryside: the excellent roads (certainly by far the best that I have seen in the Orient), the number of new cars (learner drivers are everywhere), the multitude of British military establishments (lots of jeeps and trucks on the roads)—and, in general, the impression of a colony optimistic about its future. A great many new and excellent factories (largely textile) are to be seen.

We had lunch at a charming Riviera-like inn by a lovely cove, and returned to the Peninsula Hotel about 4:30. Tea with Campbell, and a good-bye till Tokyo.

I arranged, next, for a night tour this evening in the company of Mr. and Mrs. Gutherie (the couple who were in the airlines truck with me on the day of the Angkor Wat adventure) and their guide, then returned to my hotel for a bit of rest.

At 7:00 P.M., off with the party to Hong Kong: (a) a touch of Chinese opera; (b) dinner at that floating restaurant in Aberdeen; (c) a night drive up over the road of views; (d) a finale in a night shot full of Chinese gentlemen and their Chinese dancing partners. Our guide got us one of his former girls, born in Saigon, sold there to a Chinese woman who brought her to Hong Kong to be a source of income, and now, at twenty-three, still at it: demure, cuddly, delicate, and ladylike; Mrs. Guthrie renamed her Tina (the girl was called simply Cissy). At about 12:50 we dashed for the last ferry—and I got to bed at 2:00 A.M.

Tuesday, March 29

Up at 8:15; breakfast in the hotel. Then, the ferry to Hong Kong, where I spent the day strolling about the wonderful streets, enjoying the sense of being in a full-fledged city again, and trying to make up my mind to buy something. Finally bought a couple of shirts at Mackintosh's. Had lunch in the Parisian Cafe (first full-fledged restaurant I have been in since leaving New York). And finally, at 2:00, rather tired, went to a movie that Campbell highly recommended: Hitchcock's *Rear Window*. The movie theater might have been in New York.

I took the ferry home at about five. Bathed and rested; then went out for dinner at a "Russian" restaurant, which was actually Chinese with a number of Russian dishes. A brief walk and to bed.

Wednesday, March 30

In the Monday morning paper there was an article by Carl T. Rowan (lecturer and observer for the U.S. State Department)[32] on the "Deep, Dangerous Chasm" that he found between India and the U.S.A. A number of points echo my own observations.

1. "I was asked about everything from sex and sin to segregation, the implication being that I should be against all three." (Better, it seems to me: divorce, drinking, and segregation.)
2. "Indians are for peace because they are spiritual and Americans for war because they are materialistic."
3. "I was not long in India before I realized that I was dealing with a national Jekyll-Hyde complex. First, I saw the friendly warmth, the generous hospitality of Indian people. This struck me more than anything except the panorama of poverty during my first few days here. But when I went out to lecture or took part in political discussions, the other side of India would emerge. The man who had poured lavish

hospitality on me as an individual would become my passionate foe as an American."

Some of the Indian explanations of their "neutralist" position that he quotes are also worth remembering.

1. "All Asia wants economic progress. It is almost as if India were racing with China to show that she can produce more relief for the miserable through Democracy than the Reds can through totalitarianism. If India fails, the Communists conquer all Asia.... In the showdown, India stands for democracy."

2. "India must have peace. We must have some years of peace at any price.... We've got problems to solve—problems we can solve only if we have peace."

3. "We are jammed up against China and Tibet. Russia is only a Blitzkrieg away through Afghanistan and the Khyber Pass. If we seem less dedicated to freedom, more soft-spoken toward our neighbors, remember that the threat of annihilation is much closer to us."

Got up this morning at 8:15, had breakfast upstairs, and strolled to the Peninsula Hotel; made a date with the Gutheries for cocktails this afternoon, and returned to my room to bring my diary up to date. Went out for lunch in what turned out to be a second-rate restaurant, and again returned to my room to write—diary and letters. Out, then, for the cocktail date and back to the hotel for a nap. Out for a fine steak dinner at the "Russian" restaurant of last night. Home to pack, and early to bed. *Finis* Hong Kong.

Some Hong Kong titbits:

1. Slit skirts are of three degrees: (a) to the knee, (b) to mid-thigh, (c) a bit higher. When the object sits down the slit is drawn up, and when she crosses her legs, the tableau is magic.

2. Driving in the Hong Kong streets is rendered dangerous by the idea held by some Chinese that if they can manage just to miss being hit, the scare will drive away the bad spirits!

3. The women carry their babies on their backs, like papooses, in cute little slings.

4. Wooden-soled slippers on the pavement make a sort of xylophone sound; particularly charming if the shoes are small. And since no two shoes make quite the same sound, there is a delightful little music in the streets.

Thursday, March 31   *T'aipei*

Up at 6:30 and to the Peninsula Hotel for breakfast and to catch the Thai Airways bus. Opened conversation with a chap who had been on the last air trip I took; he turned out to be Martin Wilbur of Columbia—and we knew each other from New York and Sarah Lawrence.[33]

Interesting chat in the plane, comparing notes on India—though, like a good professor, he managed not to be the one who did most of the talking. His impression of Nehru's capitulation to the Chinese was not so strong as mine, and he seems to have let Indian hospitality blind him somewhat to the strength of the anti-American feeling.

We reached T'aipei about 1:30. From the plane one could see miles and miles of well-tended, well-cultivated fields. "Much better agriculture," said Wilbur, "than the Indian. The Indians are not good farmers." When the plane approached the airport the hostess made us all pull our blinds: war zone: not to peek! We all peeked—and saw nothing, of course, but more hills and fields.

Wilbur went to the YMCA and I to the Grand Hotel, which is a bit too far out of town. The hotel is jammed with army officers and newspaper people: all Americans. I took a little taxi drive after lunch, to view the town: the President Building, museum, movie district, university, and then Green Lake—a charming little spot some fifteen minutes out of town. When the drive was finished, I took a walk in the neighborhood of the hotel and returned for tea (no one else but me), a shower, and a spell of writing.

The scenery of Formosa is romantic in a way that would have appealed, I believe, to Rousseau. The clouds today are low on the heavily-wooded hills, and the rice fields stretch to the edges of the hills: pleasantly winding streams are numerous, with people quietly boating: an air of eighteenth-century repose in the country lies over the land, even though twentieth-century factory smoke pours up from the stacks, which are numerous. The city is by no means as potent as Hong Kong, but it is a large and strongly built industrial city, somewhat dull because of the unimaginative brick and concrete architecture, but nevertheless an impressive little city. And everywhere, in the city and in the fields, are the Free China soldiers—military jeeps and trucks fill the roads. Definitely there is an army here.

I'm rather pleased and amused by the picture of this hotel. It is situated well outside of the city proper and in a large estate of its own—somewhat as the Hotel Cecil in relationship to New Delhi. But the social tone is American, not British. And I must say, it is a very good tone. A lot of high army brass, apparently, has settled its families here: they are nice-looking, well-behaved people, with well-behaved youngsters. The dining room this evening had something of the atmosphere of a ship's dining salon: there was to be a bingo game at nine, and some of the tables were talking about it. At several of the tables were Chinese people—and at one, a cute American family with two charming young Chinese friends. My roommate (the hotel is jammed) is an eighth-grader, whose father has just been sent out here for a two-year stint. The atmosphere is that of a community that does not expect to be dislodged by the Communists very soon—or even to be troubled by their bombs. There is a great deal of road building in progress on the island and the hotel is building an annex bigger than itself.

After dinner I took a brief stroll down the hill, and went early to bed.

Friday, April 1

After breakfast, took a long walk into town, to try to find Miss Dorothy Whipple at the U.S.I.S. office,[34] whose name had been given to me by Martin Wilbur. I was given a couple of wrong-road directions, and so presently took a bicycle rickshaw and at 11:45 entered the correct office. Miss Whipple arranged for me to meet a Dr. Jao, who would guide me on a visit to the university at 3:00 P.M., and invited me, meanwhile, to accompany herself and another lady on a picnic, up on a lovely hill called Yang Ming Shan (Grassy Peak). Dr. Jao was cordial and very helpful, told me all about the college situation, showed me the excellent university museum (ethnology: the aborigines of Taiwan are extremely interesting), and finally introduced me to the president of the university, with whom I had a fine talk. From the university, we went to the Teachers College and viewed a quite good exhibition of the student paintings—Eastern and Western style, in watercolors and oils, the watercolors (as in India) being generally better than the oils.

After a shower and nap, I went to a cocktail party at a Mr. and Mrs. Cockran's, where I met a lot of the government people. Pleasant crowd. Was invited for dinner tomorrow night with a Mr. George Gurow, and Miss Whipple promised to try to arrange for something for me to do tomorrow.

Invited Miss Whipple to dinner with me at the hotel and we found there some of the people from the cocktail party. Joined them for dinner and after dinner went for drinks to their home. To bed about midnight.

The Formosan picture, as far as I can see:

The fifty years of Japanese rule were fortunate for the island:[35] good plants, factories, and buildings constructed; good roads and railways; good agricultural practices established; excellent university founded, etc. However, the native Taiwanese were at a disadvantage in their participation in the educational system and government. This situation has been corrected under the present regime.

The population is about 80 percent (or more) literate. The island is well-off as far as food and shelter is concerned. The villages are of brick and stone: the people are clean and decently dressed: beggars hardly exist.

The population consists of about eight million Taiwanese and two million mainlanders—recent arrivals, of the Kuomintang group,[36] who are the leaders in the government. The KMT are strongly anti-Communist, and believe that though they cannot reconquer the mainland, they can support, by their threat and presence, subversive movements, which are said to be increasing on the mainland. The idea of sealing off the battle and settling for an independent or U.N.-protected Formosa does not appeal to these people. In contrast, therefore, to the other "Overseas Chinese" in the Far East, those of Formosa are definitely anti-Communist and do not constitute a subversive factor.

As for the eight million Taiwanese, it is said that they too are fundamentally anti-Communist.

(In the midst of this situation, Nehru's speech yesterday denouncing the American support of the Formosans as an aggressive support of colonialism sounds ridiculous. The man, on all his cruising around Asia, should have allowed a few days for a visit to this sanctuary!)

It seemed to me, as I conversed with Jao and the president of the university, that efforts should be made to bring American students to Taiwan and Taiwanese to the U.S.A. Exchange arrangements, however, would not be practical, since the lectures here are delivered in Chinese.

Apparently, the U.S. government has caught on to the idea of giving grants to bring Chinese students from Malaya, etc., to Taiwan for a bit of democratic instead of Communistic Chinese education.

Saturday, April 2

At 8:15 A.M. I was called to the phone and heard Wilbur's voice instead of Miss Whipple's. He had left a note for me yesterday, which I had not received (while I was at the phone it was handed to me), inviting me to go with him on a trip to a mountain spot (Wu-lai), where I met a lot of the government people; a pleasant crowd. I was told we might have an opportunity to see some aboriginal dances. If I was going, I should be at the railroad station in time to catch an 8:50 A.M. bus. I made a wrong decision; that is to say, I decided, on the spur of the moment, to go with Wilbur and leave a message for Miss Whipple. Quick dressing, no breakfast, taxi—and I just made it.

We drove in a bus, up a lovely valley, with mist on the hilltops that gradually descended and turned into a light rain. Romantic, Chinese-landscape scenery. At one point, the whole crowd had to get out of the bus and walk across a swinging bridge, over which the bus then followed. At another point, we had to have our passports checked (I had forgotten mine, but got through just the same).

And finally, at the end of the line, we got out for a little walk further along—through a mountain village, along a mountain trail, amidst beautiful scenery, to a point across the chasm from a lovely waterfall. In the village there was an old woman with a vividly tattooed face—once the sign of the married woman, but during the Japanese occupation forbidden. Only the old women (with very few young exceptions) now have this mark.

Tatooed woman

Downhill from the walk along which we went we heard a steady drum beat: ♫ ♩ / ♫ ♩ / ♫ ♩ / ♫ ♩ /. The "aboriginal dance," no doubt. We would go down there on the return. A little girl overtook us as we walked, and when we arrived at the little restaurant across from the waterfall, opened her package of souvenirs of Wu-lai for us while we sipped tea. (Compare what India would have offered!) It was raining pretty steadily by now. We started back and descended to the sound of the drum. A nice little high-school girl came up with an umbrella, to cover my head, and conducted us to a little theater shelter, full of youngsters, and with a few KMT soldiers. Three girls were singing to a tom-tom, which one of them beat; and our little hostess joined the three. After a lot more singing the little girls then presented their "aboriginal dances." It was a cute affair. The dances were largely arm and hand dances with gay steps that brought the dancers around the floor in the way of Russian girl dancers. I was reminded most strongly of the Indian and Hawai'ian arm dances—a couple of hip sways occurred. The girls were distinctly Mongolian, though, not Chinese.

After this little party, we returned to the village for a decent Chinese lunch, with a drink called "Old Whisky" that had very little kick. The bus finally brought us back to town and we said good-bye to our Chinese companion, a Professor Chen.

From the YMCA, where Wilbur is staying, I phoned Miss Whipple and Mr. Gurow; then I took a bus back to my hotel, bathed, rested, and at 7:30 drove to Mr. Gurow's for a delightful and very tasty dinner. Nice crowd, good talk until about 2:00 A.M.

I found that my own tendency, in talking about India, was to lay considerable stress on the anti-Americanism that I found there. I am really wondering why we are continuing to send money to those people.

A Mr. Wang, who was at the party, brought out something of what might be called the basic Oriental view of the danger of American aid: we should not try to spread "the American way of life": the Orient should be aided to develop in its own style.

Discussing China and Japan, he said that Japan has taken over Western patterns wholesale but superficially: the Oriental style remains beside them, dissociated. The Chinese, on the other hand, have taken over fewer elements (more selectively) but have assimilated them more deeply.

He pointed out, also, that Orientals regard it as degrading when their women marry Westerners.

CHAPTER 11

THE REALM OF THE SENSES

TOKYO, JAPAN

Sunday, April 3 *Tokyo*

A day of rain. After breakfast, read the paper and packed. When it came
to paying my bill it appeared that the office, in a mix-up, had given it to
another occupant of the room who left on an early train, thus overcharg-
ing him 110 Taiwan dollars. They asked me if I could send him U.S. $5 to
his U.S. home, and they would give me the 110 Taiwan dollars. But then I
learned that I am unable to convert my Taiwan cash into any other money
on God's earth. This dished the deal—and I was left, besides, with a 175
Taiwan dollar surplus.

The airlines car didn't call for me till 12:45. Wilbur was aboard.
Approaching the airport, we saw a large military event leaving it: U.S.
Secretary of the Army Robert Stevens had just arrived in a large
Constellation, and every military man in the neighborhood above the rank
of captain had been on the receiving line. There was a lot of confusion at
the airport, but we finally got aboard—and had a fine flight to Tokyo,
arriving about 8:30 P.M. Airlines bus to the (very expensive) Nikkatsu
Hotel.

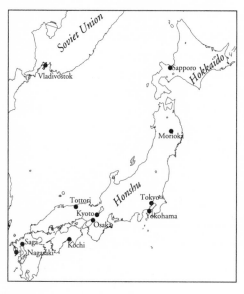

But, hurray for Tokyo and the Japanese. This tops Hong Kong and scores supreme for the cities of Asia visited so far. As I hoped: both are here—the past and the present; and in good form.

My hotel is an absolutely modern, absolutely clean, perfectly efficient, fine affair, with intelligent, trim hall boys and good service. The hot water is hot; the fixtures work; the room is attractive; *and*—the Japanese touch: when I entered I found the matchbox placed in a studied and pretty way against the ashtray, the desk blotter aptly placed on the desk, and the bureau drawers drawn partly out, in an ordered way.

Having settled, I went out to look for a bite to eat, moved toward the brightly lighted area leftward of the hotel, entered a little street hung with lanterns, passed a number of Chinese restaurants in search of something Japanese, and saw a sign advertising a Japanese striptease with the scholium "On Limits," i.e. OK for U.S. GIs—so in I went. A cozy nightclub atmosphere; crowds on the stairs: up I went to a little den with a mediocre band, a bit of dance space, a bit of bar with about five stools, and lots of tables for two all around the walls. Young boys with Japanese girls and lots of excess girls filled the room: young waiters and pretty waitresses (the latter in a Japanese-servant rig that was definitely cute). The hostesses all were in modest evening gowns. Obviously, there would be no food, so I ordered a whisky and soda, thinking to stay for a minute and leave, when the drink was down, to go and eat. However, a little thing came and sat beside me. "May I join you?" "Fine," I said; "so what'll you have?" A whisky and soda. Presently a tall seminude appeared in a spotlight and stalked around luxuriously to music, took off her bra, and began sitting alluringly close to a guy's arms. Then her act was over, she withdrew, and the band resumed its squawking for the dance floor. Well, it was nice to see a girl after all these weeks, but otherwise, things were very dull. My little hostess, Chiku, aged twenty-four, giggled a good deal and insisted that my arm should be around her, then asked to be kissed and finally wanted to dance. Not at all, it seemed to me, in what I had heard was the Japanese tradition: absolutely without style. I decided to wait for another nude and then go; which I did.

But the remarkable thing about this little GI joint was the age of the patrons: boys, I should say, just out of high school. One had passed out at the bar and the girls were mothering him. Nobody was over college age. And the girls, of course, were taking a lot of their money simply by ordering drinks very fast. The drinks, I can testify, were mostly ice, and the waiters usually managed to take them away before they were finished.

Chiku was very eager that I should return; for I had given her a good tip. She accompanied me downstairs, gave me the card of the house, made me give her a kiss and returned to her work. Hours: 1:00 P.M. to 1:00 A.M; my departure was at 11:00 P.M.

Monday, April 4

I went to bed last night without dinner—and woke up about four, cold and hungry. The weather had changed and was really chill. After a 9:15 breakfast in the hotel coffee shop, in the arcade basement, I found that there was a sharp wind blowing: the sort of wind that rips down the Riverside Drive side streets.[37] I had no topcoat, but decided to brave it and hunt for the American Express office. The town is full of vivid, lively people, a wonderful cocktail of East and West: women in kimonos, wearing wooden clogs, but mostly people completely at home in Western dress. One curious phenomenon: because of the soot in the air from charcoal burners, quite a few people wear a wad of cheesecloth over their mouths and nostrils—like Jains.[38]

The people at the American Express were not very good at giving me advice on how to see the town, and there was only one letter for me—from Mother. I went for a long walk around the Ginza district, then phoned my friend Campbell from Hong Kong and things began:

Lunch with Danny Campbell at the old Union Club (now Peers Club)—a club for U.S. Army personnel, with a nice-looking crowd. Met a pleasant chap named Stan Spivak who lunched with us. Danny had to go back to his office at about one, but we arranged to meet for a steam bath and steak dinner at six.

After lunch I went for another long walk and ended up at a really first-rate revue, at the Nichigeki Music Hall on the fourth floor of the Nichigeki Theater. Lots of gorgeous girls, good bands, elegant style: the girls not *quite* as naked as in Paris but a lot more active; no filth, it seemed to me—though I might have a different opinion if I had understood the comedians. One charming number toward the end brought a modern Japanese gentleman with glasses and a briefcase into collision with a sort of Kabuki-style, folk religious procession: I don't know what the point was, but it looked good. The American-style jazz and acrobatic dancing was better than good, and there were a couple of good French Apache numbers.[39] The title of the show: "The Seven Keys to Love (Not Reported by Dr. Kinsey)."

Well—it was a great pleasure to run into something like this after India. Of course, India's present ideas about "purity" and "spirituality" close them off from this sort of thing: they have no feeling for it whatsoever. As a result—their prostitutes are the filthiest whores in the world. So it goes! The rejected factor manifests itself in an inferior mode, whereas when accepted it adds a tone and sophistication to the whole picture of life.[40]

After the show, I was joined by Danny, and we proceeded to the Tokyo Onsen near Ginza: a charming affair; the N.Y.A.C. steam rooms and rubbing rooms, from now on, are to be a rank disappointment. Here a little thing in bra (Peter Pan, I think) and shorts goes to work on you for an hour. Mine's name was Otako, and she gave me the best massage of my life. Being steamed and bathed by her, also, was a pleasantly comforting and relaxing affair. Part of the delight (perhaps the greatest part of it) is the sense of being waited on completely: one is returned to the state of infancy for a gentle hour. Price ¥1,000, about $13. Definitely something that should become a sort of regular event.

Danny left the bath a little earlier than I did, to fetch a young woman who was coming up from Yokosuka navy base to have dinner with him, and I met them at 7:15 at Suehiro's (about a block from Tokyo Onsen) for one of the best steaks I've eaten in my life. "They massage the cows," said Danny, and I think he's right.[41] The girl, Dorothy Riggs, is quite handsome and, apparently, quite gone on my handsome bachelor friend. And the restaurant is one of the best in the world. One has to make *no* concessions to enjoy it, as one has to, even in the best restaurants in India: service, food, decor—excellent.

After dinner we drove around a bit and then went to one of Tokyo's unnumbered pinball (pachinko) emporiums. It is said that Japan's chief industries are the three Ps—Paper, Pachinko, Prostitution. After pachinko, we went to the nightclub Latin Quarter, which has an elegant band (Philippino, with an exceptionally good featured drummer) and a floor show mainly of male singers. Miss Riggs had to leave during the floor show, to catch her train back to Yokosuka. I remained and when Danny returned we proceeded to another night spot (11:00 P.M.), the Ginbasha, on Ryokan Avenue. Here we sat at a little table with a couple of hostesses, danced and watched the floor show, till closing time at about 1:30 A.M. The contrast with my club of last evening was immense. The girls—"Janie" and "Katie"—were perfectly poised little ladies: charming, decorous, handsome; without the least touch of the aggressive, but easily responsive to the patterns of conduct of their clients. Most of the people in the large nightclub were Occidentals— officers and government people. The floor show was good: a couple of remarkable contortionist dancers with a deadpan composure (identical twins, I should say) and a girl who danced with a pigeon. All very decent.

We left our ladies and took a brief drive, to view the night situation at 2:00 A.M. Those nightclub hostesses (like our own) whose customers did not come through with a bid for the night (at ¥7,000 = $20), change into street clothes and head for Fourth Street and Y Avenue, and neighbor-hood—where the price is down to about ¥2,000. The total take, Danny thinks, of a good Tokyo prostitute is about $400 to $500 a month. At the nightclubs we paid ¥2,000 each for the company of our little friends, and they also received a percentage on the drinks.

Tuesday, April 5

Today I went around to the Yashima Hotel, at Ginza Street and W Avenue, and arranged to move in the day after tomorrow. The Nikkatsu is much too expensive: ¥3,000 per day for room and bath. At the Yashima I shall have a room (no bath) and breakfast for ¥1,500 per day—and a good excuse (no bath) for going frequently to Tokyo Onsen. I went also to the Imperial Hotel[42] (*very, very* touristy) and arranged to go on a bus tour of Tokyo this afternoon—following which I would go to another "bath" that Danny had recommended, over in the Sumida section of town.

I lunched in the Imperial Coffee Shop and toured in the bus from 1:15 to 5:30 P.M. An excellent tour of a really wonderful city. Then I got into a taxi to go to my "bath"—and ran into one of the most awkward events of the year.

My taxi driver had a hard time locating the place, so I arrived at about 6:20. We turned into a pretty little garden area, with a cluster of Japanese wooden cottages and a row of parked American cars. Three Japanese ladies (middle-aged) in kimonos greeted my arrival with polite bows. What was it, exactly, that I would like?

"Well," I said, "I had caught a bad cold (and I certainly had: the chill of yesterday morning had been pretty bad) and should like a hot bath; steam..."

They looked at each other. "Steam?"

"Well," I said, "a good hot bath and a rest, with plenty of time to cool off."

"Fine," they said. "Will you stay all night?"

"No," I said, "just a couple of hours."

"Three hours?"

"OK," I said, "Three hours."

I was conducted through a little garden, into one of the pretty cottages, doffed my shoes, and went upstairs to a Japanese room with a low table in the center, a smaller table beside it, and a bowl of hot coals beside that. My hostess bade me sit on a little seat that faced the smaller table and place my feet under the table, under its heavy covers. It was warm as toast in there—the rest of the room was chill. My legs were resting on some kind of brazier, which contained hot coals. Tea was brought to me, and a servant began busying herself about the room and in the room adjoining. "*Gāru-san*[43] come soon," she said as she left; and she shut the door.

It dawned on me, as I peacefully sipped my cup of tea, that I had made a little mistake, and was not quite in a hot bath establishment. I was alone for about half an hour: then the panel before me slid open and *gāru-san* was there, right side to me and her head at a cordial tilt. She was in a pretty kimono, and her hair had been frizzled with the permanent waves that are fashionable now in Japan. I rose to greet her and observed a light eczema of some kind on her right cheek, which she had covered with powder.

"What is your name?" she said.

"What is yours?" I asked, and she told me (but I have forgotten).

"Mine," I said, "is Joe."

She bade me sit down again at the little table and she sat beside me, at my right hand. Then she asked me quietly what I wanted, and I told her: "A good hot bath." She nodded.

"And a massage," I added.

"A massage!?" she said, and her brow furrowed.

"Well," I said, "whatever you do here."

At this moment the panel slid open again and one of the older women knelt beside me. "Everything all right?" she said.

"Oh yes indeed," I said politely.

"And three hours?" she said.

"Three hours will be fine," I answered.

"That will be ¥4,200," she said (about $12!). The most expensive bath of my life! But I was in it—so I put the yen on the table. Everybody smiled and bowed; the lady left, and my girl and I were alone, now, for three hours.

We talked a little about Tokyo and Japan. Her English was a little hard to understand, so, to say a little took quite a while.

When a little time had elapsed, she said, "You like bath now?"

"Yes," I said, "now will be fine."

"Now?" she said.

"Yes now," I said.

She had a very serious look. She seemed to think and decide. She looked at me. "All right," she said. She got up.

"Get up," she said. I got up. "Put on kimono." She pointed to a heavy, man's kimono on a shelf. While I got out of my clothes and into the kimono, she removed her obi and top kimono. Then she helped me tie my sash and we started downstairs—narrow stairs, out into the yard, which was a pretty garden. I followed her in the moonlight to another cottage and she led me to a small, neat, Japanese room with a tiny, rectangular bath, full of hot water, flush with the floor.

"Get in!" she said. I removed my kimono and got in. She removed hers and got in too. Well—so this was different. The tub was very small indeed and the water very hot. She made it too hot and we had to get out. Then we got back in again and sat in steaming water, to our necks.

Physically, the position was extremely intimate; but there was nothing very intimate about the mood; and so we sat there, quietly splashing the water over each other's shoulders, to keep warm. "Enough?" she said, after about ten minutes. "Enough," I said. "Sit down," she said, and she pointed to a little wooden stool. I sat down and she knelt beside me and gave me a good soaping. Then she began pouring hot water over me with a little wooden bucket. When she had finished she gave me another bucketful of water for a bit of private washing then turned around to wash herself. When we had finished, she dried me, helped me back into my kimono, and conducted me again through the garden and back into the little room. It was now quite clear to me what sort of place I was in.

"What time is it now?" she said. We had used up an hour. Two hours to go.

She sat across from me—our feet and legs under the warm table, not touching. I think that by now it was as clear to her as it was to me that I had not come to get what most people came for. She looked very thoughtful for a moment, as she considered the two hours ahead. "I don't *have* to stay two hours," I said, "if you find this thing too difficult." "No," she said. "It is OK."

Then, after a brief pause, she managed to initiate the conversation. Was I married? Yes. "Papa-san?" No. We talked of Jean and the dance; marriage and children; and why she herself hadn't married. This broke the ice, and there was a lot beneath.

She was twenty-two years old; her father was "an old man" of fifty-two (when I told her that I was fifty-one, she had a hard time believing). She had to help earn money. She had a married sister with a couple of children (husband a typist) and a younger brother at school. She had been in this geisha establishment one year.

She didn't know how many girls they had in the establishment; there were two completely distinct sections, one for Japanese, one for foreigners—she was in the foreign branch: she didn't like Turks, Scandinavians, and elephants (I couldn't make out how the elephants got in here!). She liked Americans when they were gentlemen: sometimes the young ones were rough.

"My poor broken body," she said, several times. I asked for the technical details of how she protected herself from disease—and she said she went to the doctor for injections when she felt something itching: she could usually tell the next day. She didn't know how to tell if the man she was with was sick, and if he didn't use a rubber she might be infected. But she protected herself against children. "Blue eyes and red hair not so good," she said. She told me of one girl who had had ten abortions; another, eight. "Very bad, very bad," she said. And we both sat still, a while, thinking how bad. "This is very hard work," she had said several times.

"Now," I said, "I have just paid four thousand two hundred yen for three hours with you: how much of that goes to you?"

"I'm ashamed to tell you," she said. "I won't tell you."

I waited a little.

"Do the men who visit you," I said, "ever leave you money?"

"I never asked you for any money," she said.

"I know," I said; "you didn't ask me. But suppose I left something: would that be unusual?"

She changed the subject. "When people phone me at my house, I send them here. I work only here."

The talk began to lag a bit after an hour and so I thought we should have a change of scene. "Would it be possible to lie down somewhere?" I said.

She tilted her head and looked as she had looked when standing at the door. "You want to go to bed with me?" She then looked as she had looked before we started for the bath. "In there," she said. I pushed open a sliding wall and there was a vast pile of mats made up nicely as a large bed for two. She followed, after a few moments, and we got in, fully wrapped in kimonos. To let me take her sashes off, she had to sit up; then she lay down again and I could stroke her nice smooth skin.

"You Japanese women," I said, "have the smoothest skin in the world." She smiled a little. I stroked some more and she lay there, absolutely inertly.

"When people make love to you," I said, "do you ever have any feeling?"

"Feeling?" she said. "I never feel them." She had misunderstood.

"No," I said, "I mean inside: do you feel any emotion?"

She sort of laughed and shrugged it off.

After a little pause she said, "I think you are happily married."

"Yes," I said, "I think I am." So we talked some more about Jean: then about herself and of how she should get married and get out of this work. She shook her head and looked grimly desperate.

There were some sounds outside of people on the stairs. "The girl next door," she said. "She is sick. She was getting a permanent wave and something happened. Something has happened to all her hair." We listened a little, and then there was a call on the stairs.

"They want to know," she said, "if you want a taxi." Our three hours were up, and we were both, I think, very much relieved. I dressed and gave her a decent tip.

"They gave you a hard job," I said, "and you did it nicely." We bowed.

"Come on, Joe," she said, and she led me downstairs. In the garden stood a tall American gentleman, chatting easily with about six of the women of the establishment—one in full geisha regalia. My poor sparrow and I went to my waiting cab. I kissed her cheek and neck. "Good night," I said, "you were very sweet." And my driver drove me back to the Nikkatsu Hotel. 10:15 P.M. No dinner. No hunger, either. I piled into bed.

Wednesday, April 6

Booked myself this morning for the night tour of Tokyo, then went to the American Express, where I found a couple of nice letters from Jean and one from Helen McMaster; after which I went for a lovely long walk, cherry-blossom viewing, around the Imperial Palace Garden. It was a beautiful day, and there were lots of other people cherry-blossom viewing too.

Returning to the hotel at about 12:45, I found a note from my friend Danny Campbell, inviting me to lunch at noon. I phoned the Union Club but missed him.

I had a bit of lunch in the Nikkatsu Coffee Shop, then started walking to where I thought the American Embassy would be, to get my passport extended for another two years, and to try to find Jean's friend, Bryan Battey. On the way, whom do I bump into but Danny Campbell! Brief chat, and a tentative date for tomorrow noon. He is departing Saturday for the U.S.A. He directed me to the embassy, where I arranged my passport extension and met Battey. Battey drove me to the American Cultural Center, where Jean danced in January, and showed me a fine report that he had written about Jean's event for the Washington U.S.I.S. office. I left him at about 4:00 P.M., and strolled back to my hotel.

The night tour of Tokyo was great. A circuit, first, of the brightly lighted areas: the Japanese have a fabulous talent for the handling of lighted signs. An hour, next, at the Kabuki Theater, where we saw a whole Kabuki play. And finally, supper and fun for forty at a geisha house, the restaurant Mita: an excellent supplement to my experience of last evening; for this time I could see something of the proper mood and functioning of one of these establishments, and it was simply delightful.

Low table around three sides of a pleasant room; with additional area at the other end, where two samisen players[44] and two little geisha girls performed. First, two comparatively formal dances. Next, a little game (scissors-paper-stone), audience being introduced to rules of the game. Next, "How to Play Baseball"—a cute dance game to samisen music with baseball movements (pitching, batting, catching, running, "outa, safe,") and finally the scissors-paper-stone element, to see who wins—the loser sits down and someone else comes up. The girls called up the man from the visiting group—and managed, finally, to break the ice of the party completely. Finale: "Auld Lang Syne" for the whole crowd. And then the same girls—who had seemed so alien at the start— were driven to their homes in our bus, in full regalia—a wonderful idea of the mood and skills of the geisha house! They took what came and gave it a great time.

Thursday, April 7

Spent the morning dealing with money affairs, at Pan American Airways and American Express, after moving to the Yashima Hotel: nice little room, without bath: a good excuse for more baths at Tokyo Onsen. After lunch, went to the Nichigeki Theater to see a sort of Paramount Theater show. Well done, in its kind, with a rapid-fire sequence of colorful scenes: house full of kids and families: completely *à l'américain*. Trip, next, to Tokyo Onsen and then to Suehiro's for a grandiose steak dinner. Spent the evening walking in the enchantingly lighted little streets of my new neighborhood. Sent a birthday telegram to Charlie.[45]

Friday, April 8

Spent a good part of the day trying to make contact with Danny, who was likewise trying to catch me. We kept missing. At 11:00 A.M. went to the

Shimbashi Enbujo (Theater) to see the first half of the spring program of the Azuma Odori—"the celebrated geisha of Shimbashi"...the group, part of which came to New York last year. A perfectly beautiful event—went on until about 2:15. Got in touch with Battey during the afternoon and he invited me to a "modern" dance recital this evening at 6:00 P.M.—Bac Ishu's Oriental Ballet, "Human Buddha"—presented in a huge auditorium (filled), with full symphony orchestra and immense cast. Not so good: more like third-rate Balanchine[46] than like modern dance. Driven to my hotel by the Batteys: had a snack in one of these cute coffee shops that are so abundant in Tokyo, and went early to bed—today is the Buddha's birthday.

Saturday, April 9

A day somewhat cloudy, but the cherry blossoms are at their best, so I went for a huge walk: to Ueno Park, through the wonderful museum, and then to Asakusa, where I walked around admiring the wonderful little streets and great crowds and then began visiting theaters—all that weren't movies turned out to be a sort of cross between burlesque and "little theater": at least one of the short plays (three or four acts) was darned good—and it was followed immediately by a kimono striptease that was simply wonderful. One little joint, the Asakusa Strip Tease, put on a series of jobs to a jammed house that were certainly the best of the kind that I've ever seen. Finally was caught by Danny; had a drink with him and Dorothy Riggs in the Yashima bar. He leaves tonight.

Dinner with the Batteys—who very very much want Jean to be here next August and January.

Sunday, April 10

Practically all day at the Kabuki Theater—11:00 A.M. until 4:15 P.M. Never got so much theater for my money in my life. Simply great. Invited Dorothy Riggs to come with me, to take her mind off Danny's departure.

After the show, said bye-bye to Dorothy, went to Tokyo Onsen, had a grand steak dinner again at Suehiro's, took the subway up to Asakusa and strolled around again in the extraordinarily prettily lighted streets. When it started to rain I went into another theater—same sort of thing as yesterday. Left at nine and went home—again in the subway—and to bed.

Monday, April 11

A lovely sunny day—so I went again to Ueno Park, to see and photograph the blossoms. They have begun to lose their petals. The park was still full of cherry-blossom viewers. Came back to the hotel about 1:30 and took a bath and nap, to freshen up for another session of Kabuki. 4:30 to 10:15 P.M., Kabuki! (Kabuki isn't merely theater: it's a form of life!) Home, and after a hot chocolate in the little coffee shop across the street, to bed.

Tuesday, April 12

A long letter to Jean—my first since arriving in Tokyo; then, to the Maruzen bookshop, to get started on my Japanese career of study: grammars, readers, and a bit of philosophy. A wonderful bookshop, full of Japanese, English, French, and German books—and not a single Bollingen volume.47 Not a single Bollingen volume in Hong Kong either. Great job of selling the Orient!

Today, at last (first moment since my arrival in dizzying Tokyo), I feel that I can begin to settle into something like a sober stride. I think I'll spend this week and next in Tokyo, with a weekend at Kamakura, etc., to see how that might be as a place for Jean and me to stay if she decides to accept Battey's bid for her to teach here in August. Then I'd like to visit Nikko and after that transfer my center to Kyoto.

This afternoon at 2:30 I went to the Azuma Odori Theater again for part two of the program—2:30 to 5:30 P.M. Then to Suehiro's sukiyaki restaurant for a delightful dinner, served by three charming little Japanese ladies. The more I see of these wonderful women, the more apt the saying seems: for the perfect home, one should have an American house, a Chinese cook, and a Japanese wife. The husband, in such circumstances, I guess, can be anything at all.

Wednesday, April 13

Morning, by train to nearby Samezu, to get my driver's license: am to return tomorrow at two. Got back to my hotel by eleven and studied Japanese till 4:30. Next, to my Tokyo Onsen, then to Asakusa to see the big U.S.A.-type revue at the large theater. Next, a bit of burlesque across the street, and home at ten.

Thursday, April 14

To the Kanze Kaikan, Noh theater, to buy a ticket for this afternoon; then to Samezu again, to pick up my license. Noh plays from 5:00 to 10:00 P.M., then home to bed.

Friday, April 15

Studied Japanese practically all day, with a trip at noon to the American Express and at five to Tokyo Onsen. After a fine steak dinner at Suehiro's, a long stroll through the Ginza area trying to read the signs in katakana[48] (which I now have learned), and home to a bit of letter writing and bed.

I am beginning to have some ideas about Japan, India, and the modern world; but shall wait a bit before trying to put them down.

Saturday, April 16

A nice, old-fashioned, rainy day. Good day for thoughts, and a study of Japanese.

I have now seen Noh, Kabuki, Azuma's geisha troupe, two American moviehouse–style revues, one hot revue, two burlesque performances, three striptease shows, and one GI night spot; have visited two stylish nightclubs, Suehiro's elegant Japanese-style and Western-style restaurants, one geisha house, a number of little coffee shops, and my Tokyo Onsen. Have also walked through numerous miles of Tokyo's streets and parks; have dwelt in two hotels—an expensive and a moderate priced—and have visited a number of shops. Some general impressions have begun to become fixed in my mind.

1. In contrast to India: the literacy rate is over 90 percent (highest in the world), in contrast to India's 5 percent to 20 percent (perhaps the lowest): one immediately obvious correlate—a dramatically higher general intelligence. Jobs are done efficiently, intelligently, and well. But a multitude of other contrasts are evident also, and the literacy rate no doubt contributes greatly to these. As follows:

2. Whereas in India one feels that a situation of cultural catastrophe exists— the ancient civilization gone and the new not yet generally effective, with a group of bewildered amateurs now searching romantically into their own past for India and into the West for the means of social health, stalled midway between—in contrast to this, in Japan both East and West are vividly and wonderfully present, in every phase of life. That is to say, in India the

West-East tension is inadequately objectified, and so exists excessively as a spiritual or psychological tension of ideas, feelings, premonitions, and resistances, while in Japan the two worlds are brought into an actual concrete interplay, and the result is a life-enhancing integration-in-process. What I shall find when I get into the country, of course, I don't yet know. But in the city (and India has no city, in the sense that Tokyo is a city), what I find is a vivid cocktail of East and West—with its own martini flavor, which is neither gin nor vermouth: and as a martini matures and gets better in the icebox, with the passage of time, so too will this.

3. Whereas in India there is a pathological necessity to criticize and abuse the West as "materialistic," while vaunting the native "spirituality," there seems to be very little (if any) of this in Japan. India's reactionary, fundamentalist, ignorant and consequently stupid pride is perhaps her chief impediment. The machine, modern morality, and even modern dress represent a challenge to the good old "four square" gospel of the Vedas— which, of course, they do. Unable to resolve the tension of these pairs of opposites, India is at present in a condition, not merely of physical, but also of psychological, paralysis. Japan, on the other hand, jumped at the modern *means* of life with a ready will. The result is a condition of progressive spirituality that is immensely impressive.

4. This leads me to begin to believe that Japan has understood better than modern India the final import of the Indian doctrine of non-duality. The Indian psyche is locked in duality: East vs. West, Spiritual vs. Material, Hindu vs. Moslem, caste vs. outcaste, new vs. old. The Japanese, on the other hand, understand how to *rock with the waves*. The relative world is relative and the transcendent, transcendent. There is no point or position, idea or feeling in the relative world that has an absolute value; and yet *all* things are Buddha things.

5. A query, then, with respect to the contrast of Hinduism and Buddhism:
   a. It is with the Upaniṣads that India first breaks into the non-priestly sphere of a generally accessible transcendent realization: the chief teachers were not brahmins but laymen.
   b. With the Buddha (a *Nepalese;* a *kṣatriya*) this realization is freshly taught, in a definitely anti-brahminical style and with a primarily psychological inflection.
   c. Mahāyāna Buddhism, and then Zen, carried this teaching forward to its ultimate implications.
   d. With Śaṅkara's Vedanta, India lapsed into a fundamentally negative position—not greatly different, finally, from that of Jainism, which is fundamentally dualistic.
   e. India's dualism, pride of race, archaic style, etc., are perhaps as intrinsic to Hinduism as their Jewish counterparts are to Judaism. Japan's readiness for new forms is perhaps a function of her Zen.

6. In the Japanese theater I have found an excellent projection of the modern Japanese syndrome:

   a. In the Noh, Kabuki, and geisha traditions the ancient pattern is maintained. New works, however, are being produced in these forms: it is
possible, therefore, for the Japanese to experience the new world—or
rather the continuation of their ancient world into the new—in a style
appropriate to their historical past.

   b. In the vast movie-theater-style revues there is an enthusiastic imitation
of the American-Western style—but with an inevitable Japanese feeling
for theater, decor, humor, etc. that is conditioned by the Kabuki. This
reaches right down into the burlesque. One can feel distinctly the force
of the native Kabuki in practically every scene. Furthermore, in every
one of these shows there is at least one act or scene presenting traditional
Japanese materials on the stage and in the style of the modern revue.

   c. In the striptease stunts there is another very amusing sign of the dual
world. The Japanese physique is distinguished by relatively short thighs:
to match the long-legged ideal of the American striptease, therefore, the
girls wear very high heels—and the effect is generally quite definitely
OK. The Japanese woman has in reserve, however, the possibility of the
low-slung effect also: and this is occasionally rendered, *by the same girls,*
in the absolutely inimitable kimono striptease—where a whole new set
of values and effects becomes suddenly evident.

7. The contrast of the Japanese theater—strong, healthy, and professional in
style—with the Indian (which can hardly be said to exist) suggests an
interesting series of thoughts.

   a. India today is a nation of amateurs in *every* field—amateurs and half-
baked fakers. As in all amateur events, there is a compensatory over-
estimation of the value of the deed evident in all Indian spiritual, political, scientific, and aesthetic performances.

   b. There is a dissociation between the Indian folk arts (Kathakali, etc.) and
modern Indian experience. This is due largely to the failure of the
Indians to support their own arts. The arts, supported and flourishing,
assist in the process of spiritual integration. Religion, on the other hand
(which is India's "strength"), resists the new and tends to impede integration.

   c. The arts of the theater are associated everywhere, one way or another,
with prostitution. In Japan this association is overt in the tradition of
the geisha ("art person"). Prostitution is a recognized profession here,
and so exists in a highly inflected, civilized, and differentiated set of
manifestations. One can find what one wants or requires, on every
level—and this has contributed to the grace and decorum of life. It represents and facilitates a life-furthering momentum. In India, on the
other hand, where the inevitable association of the arts with prostitution led, during the nineteenth century (if not earlier), to a genteel sup-
pression and rejection of the arts, not only prostitution, but civilization
itself, has declined. Aesthetic taste is abominable. The whorehouse

quarters are unspeakable. The arts are dead. And "*all life is sorrowful.*" I am sure that in the days when Indian culture may be said to have flourished (up to, say, A.D. 1200) the situation was comparable to that of present-day Japan.

And this leads me to a couple of new formulae:

8. Where the *gei-sha* ("art person") principle is repressed, civilization declines. Its fosterage leads to cultural adulthood (India today being my example of an infantile culture).

9. Where the *gei-sha* ("art person") principle is repressed, religion declines—into vulgar image worship or psalm singing.

10. The *gei-sha* ("art person") principle is at the root of the glory of Japan; its motto: "What is it you want or require? Can do! I can supply your demand in a humble, willing, likeable way."

At 12:00 noon I set off for another session of Noh, and this one beat the world's record for duration: 12:30 to 6:50 P.M.! Three plays were presented and one comic interlude. I bought a copy of P. G. O'Neill's *A Guide to No* at the theater and caught up a bit on my lesson; I find that I have seen the following:

April 14th: *Arashiyama*, by Zempō (O'Neill, p. 5), and *Fuji's Drum*, by Zeami (p. 32). April 16th: *Chikubu Shima*, by Zenchiku (p. 13); *Genji Kuyō*, by Zeami (p. 40); and *Kurama Tengu*, by Miyamasu (p. 90).

Chikubu Shima was particularly interesting to me, since it presented in essence the whole adventure of the Hero. The boat to the temple-island was marvelously rendered by means of a simple frame placed on the ground, within which the three characters settled for the voyage, hero and goddess-guide sitting; old man-dragon deity standing in the stern with a punting pole.

It is interesting to compare Noh with Kabuki. Many elements are shared: the combination of music, dance, and drama—Noh emphasizing music, however, and Kabuki drama and dance. Kabuki's dance opens out into great action at times: Noh's remains dense and intense. Noh's music is carried largely by three drums and flute with chorus; Kabuki stresses the samisen. Both theaters have approaches to the stage: Noh's however is along the back wall and Kabuki's is through the house. Noh uses no scenery or sets; Kabuki stresses surprising stage effects: Kabuki even uses trapdoors.

The modern Japanese revue, by the way, takes over the trapdoor effects: also the runway! And Kabuki takes over the house cries of the popular burlesque.

Rode home in a trolley and went then to Ten-ichi for some tempura, then to Mon (across from my hotel) for ice cream and coffee. Home at 8:45, for a bit of Japanese before bed.

CHAPTER III

FROM SAKE TO SATORI

TOKYO AND KYOTO

Sunday, April 17   *Environs of Tokyo*

9:45 A.M. train from Tokyo Station for Yokosuka, where Dorothy Riggs met me with her car and drove me for a little tour of Yokosuka, Hayama, Zushi, and Kamakura. The day was wet and windy, but this did not destroy the scenery (reminded me a little of the Monterey Peninsula) nor did it prevent literally thousands of Japanese tourists from visiting Kamakura by bus. Saw the great Buddha figure of Kamakura;[49] visited the Tsurugaoka Hachimangū Shrine, saw the crowds going out to Enoshima, had a late lunch at a little Japanese restaurant in Yokosuka called Mikado, and took the 3:50 train back home. Evening studying Japanese. Concluded that Kamakura was *not* the place for Jean and me to set up house this August: too many people, and the swimming (in spite of the beauty of the shoreline) a bit foul.

Monday, April 18   *Tokyo*

Studied Japanese until noon, then out for a haircut and lunch at the Imperial. Back home for more Japanese, and at 4:00 P.M. started off to have dinner with Mr. and Mrs. Wilbur, out in a little residential section of Tokyo which it took more than an hour to reach. Cute spot though, very Japanese. And as I came along the street I heard music, and there were five people in Kabuki costumes doing a little dance in procession. Mrs. Wilbur later told me that this was one of the stunts put on for advertising by the local real estate people who are trying to advertise and build up their neighborhood.

At dinner was a young Nisei[50] from California named Laverne Senyo Sasaki, who is studying to be a Buddhist preacher at the University of Tokyo. There were also two ladies, one American, one Japanese, with ideas about things that didn't quite come out—largely because my own somewhat passionate judgments of India and enthusiastic remarks about Tokyo gave an emphatic slant to the conversation: indeed, *too* emphatic. I have got to reform. Wilbur said—half-jokingly but wisely—that I was obviously suffering from shock.

I believe I am, and I believe the shock can be analyzed and dissolved as follows:

I. The sixfold shock:
  1. India's anti-Americanism, fellow-traveler style
  2. The depth and extent of India's poverty
  3. India's squalid *bhakti*
  4. The pattern of India's male-female coexistence
  5. The conceit and complacency of India's "spiritual" position
  6. The depth, extent, and importance of the Western influence in India

II. The sixfold reaction, conditioned by:
  1. My strong anti-Communist sentiments
  2. A belief that such poverty must be somebody's fault—and in this case not England's
  3. An ever-present contrast, in my experience, with the monuments and philosphies of India's past
  4. My own displeasure on finding myself in a world without women
  5. A recognition of the flimsiness of my own earlier celebration of the Indian superiority: a disillusionment about Coomaraswamy (the incongruity now makes me feel that I want to laugh every time I see an Indian)
  6. The obvious importance of this influence gives force to my whole reactions to the Indian anti-Westernism

III. The means of cancelling the shock:
  A. Change the order of the items:
    4. The pattern of India's male-female coexistence
    3. India's squalid *bhakti* (infantilism)

> 2. The depth and extent of India's poverty
> 6. The depth, extent, and importance of the Western influence in India
> 5. The complacent conceit of India's "spirituality"
> 1. India's anti-Americanism
>
> B. Interpret the headings analytically.
>> a. Headings 4, 3, 2, and 6 anthropologically and historically
>> b. Heading 5 psychologically
>> c. Heading 1 in terms of a sociological analysis, giving due recognition to the negatives on the American side

And now let me take a vow not to let myself discuss India again in terms of my personal reactions, emotions, and experiences.[51]

The force of my feelings this evening was partly caused by the contrast with India that I have felt in Japan, for instance:

> 4. The comparative ease with which Japan seems to be making the changeover to a modern, personalized male-female relationship
> 3. The beauty of Japan's shrines and temples and the ubiquitous evidence here of taste
> 2. The lack of any display of poverty: no sense here of people being interested primarily in baksheesh
> 6. A willing grasp of the Western machine as a means for heightening life
> 5. An attempt to adjust, psychologically, to the new age
> 1. An anti-Americanism based, not on a haughty reaction to American aid, but on
>> a. The bombings
>> b. An army of occupation
>> c. An American-forced constitution
>> d. The pressures of American politics and economics

Came home from the party with Sasaki, who offered to give me the introductions I shall need for Kyoto. I already have the feeling here that I had in India of my voyage developing of itself.

Tuesday, April 19

Off to the Meijika Theater for an 11:00 A.M. to 4:20 P.M. performance of Kabuki. This time, there was no English program available, so I haven't any idea of what I saw. The first was a short two-scene piece about a child abducted by a bird who seems to turn up in scene two as an abbot visited by his bereaved and now delighted mother. The second took up the rest of the five hours: a work in many scenes, wherein a samurai slays an unpleasant woman and drops her into a well, and a woman slays a man who then gets up and lives for a moment, only to die downstairs. I could not follow this piece at all. But the fascination of the optical and musical effects was as great as ever. Kabuki seems to me to have achieved what Wagner tried to achieve—a perfect synthesis of music and theater—plus the dance.

Home for a bit of Japanese—then went downstairs to wait for a date that I thought I had made for tonight with the Batteys. Fell into conversation with a Nisei from Vancouver over here on business. Batteys didn't turn up (date is actually for tomorrow). Went across the street to Mon for a hotdog and cocoa with my new friend from Canada, returned for a half hour chat in his room, and then went to bed. During the chat I again found myself talking the wrong way about India.

Wednesday, April 20

In the morning paper, Einstein's formula for success: $A = XYZ$. A is success in life, X is work, Y is play, and Z is keeping your mouth shut. If it weren't for the fact that I seem to have a much lower resistance to silence than most people I might be able to add Z to my mixture. Meditation for the acquisition of Z:

   a. OK, nobody's talking; so what! and
   b. Formulate a question

I also find in the morning paper that what I saw yesterday were four plays, not two; as follows: *Rōbensugi no Yurai, Shinpan Utazaimon, Banchō Sarayashiki,* and *Yodogoi Shusse no Takinobori.*

Spent the greater part of the day at my Japanese; can now read both katakana and hiragana[52] scripts: am beginning, also, to catch words in people's conversations. In the mail today, I received a great load of mail forwarded from Ceylon: all of Jean's early letters, a very nice surprise.

I invited the Batteys out to dinner and discussed Jean's summer possibilities. Important: U.S.I.S. does not pick up people from scratch and set them up to a tour. Rather, it comes in with a lift for people already assured of a money-making run in the area to be visited. "They are too deeply committed to the principle of individual enterprise to do anything else." This, of course, is why the American cultural propaganda is a failure: those who have hit the bandwagon are not precisely the ones to give foreigners the idea that America is a civilized nation.

After dinner at Suehiro's, we went to a cute little coffee bar with classical music on its phonograph in the Ginza neighborhood. Home at about 11:00 P.M.

Thursday, April 21

Morning at my Japanese. Noontime went to a doctor to see about the ankle that I sprained at Angkor: it is still swollen and today developed a new set of pains. He gave me an Ace bandage and some advice. Nice guy: he thinks it will still take quite a while for this to go down, with me walking so much.

At 5:00 P.M. I went to the Noh theater again and saw *Hagoromo*, by Zeami—the play about the swan-maid–angel. I had been hoping to see this, and was delighted by the performance.

Had a snack at Mon, across the street, and retired to write letters and study. To bed about 11:00 P.M.

Friday, April 22

Morning on Japanese. Noon to American Express to find letter from Jean accepting the idea of teaching here in August. Spent the early afternoon writing letters and from 4:30 to 10:00 P.M. attended the second part of the Meijika Kabuki. What seemed to me to be two very long works in numerous acts, and a fabulous dance-play at the conclusion. The last features two men (a samurai and a clown), a woman (chiefly partner of the samurai), and eight acrobatic, tumbler-dancers (bearing cherry-blossom branches; companions of the clown). The dance lasted about an hour.

This Kabuki group seems to go in for long pieces of a slowly moving sort, emphasizing dialogue. The pictorial aspect of the production is so good, however, that I felt no sense of tedium, even though I had no idea of what was going on. The music, also, is remarkable: largely one samisen and one singer—but with occasional flute and additional voices.

This, I think, concludes my present dose of Kabuki and Noh. I am setting my sails, now, for Kyoto: expect to leave Monday or Tuesday.

Saturday, April 23

Morning studying Japanese and catching up a bit on mail. Toward noon, a long walk to American Express through the Ginza area. Lunch—ham sandwich and coffee have become my standard Tokyo lunch: price, about sixty cents at a coffeehouse with lots of dim-light atmosphere and a good orchestra playing pleasant music.

At 1:00 P.M. the Batteys picked me up in their car and we went for a drive into the suburbs of Tokyo. Lovely countryside, and happy motoring until son David, asleep in the backseat, woke up and became the normal American child. We met another American family in the U.S. service at a finicula stop and not only the children but also the parents made a great noise and show of themselves over the heads of a large number of peacefully watching Japanese families—what the hell is it about the American family?

After the finicula ride, we drove some more and at about 7:00 P.M. stopped at a sweet little Japanese inn in Ome for dinner. But David ran loose and wild to such an extent that we were very politely asked to leave before dinner was served. Mortified departure. Dinner, finally, at the Batteys', and to bed about eleven.

New news for Jean. The Batteys think she should give a recital in Tokyo as well as teach.

Sunday, April 24

Morning, to Tsukiji Honganji Temple, to attend a Sunday morning service, held in English and Japanese, under the auspices of the International Buddhist Association. The temple architecture is based on the Occidental plan of a Protestant church: the architectural elements are from Indian Buddhist sanctuaries (largely Sāñcī and Ajaṇṭā); the shoes are not removed when one enters; there are chairs in which to sit; and both upstairs and in the basement there are offices. The temple grounds are large, enclosed by a modified imitation of the Sāñcī railings. Youngsters are playing baseball in the yard. Just outside one of the gates is a man selling goldfish, which little children carry away in cute, transparent plastic bags. There is a mild smell of fish in the air from the fish market just across the corner.

The temple interior is large and a bit chill and gloomy: the congregation for this service was small—about twenty-five people. The service began with a layman introducing the Reverend So-and-so, who, then facing the altar, read a prayer in English which we all followed in our prayer books—faith and trust in the Buddha, *dharma,* and *sangha,* etc. Hymns then were sung, in English and in Japanese. A sermon in Japanese was delivered by another Reverend So-and-so; one in English (on "sincerity") by my young friend, the Reverend Sasaki of Sacramento; and the service concluded with more hymns. Following the service, one was permitted to make one's "incense offering" by dropping money into a box and a pinch of incense into an incense urn.

Sasaki introduced me as a professor of comparative religion to the other two reverend gentlemen, and one of them immediately asked me whether I had any faith of my own. I replied that since I found that all the great religions were saying essentially the same thing in various ways, I was unable and unwilling to commit myself to any one, but tried to teach and understand the ultimate tenor of their various yet homologous symbolic languages. The gentleman said that he thought everyone should be committed to a single religion, and that for him Buddhism was the only one. He felt that a person with such a religion could teach comparatively better than a nonreligious scholar. I replied that I thought that such a person would inevitably favor his own religion; indeed, I declared, I have seen and heard plenty of such people from various faiths. Their position is always: "You worship God your way and I His way."

We parted cordially, and I returned to the hotel, after another stroll in the Ginza area and lunch in that dim coffeehouse.

The Tsukiji Honganji Temple is the headquarters of the Shinshū sect in Tokyo: the great center is in Kyoto. Founded in 1630, the temple has been destroyed many times by fire. The present structure dates from 1935. The image on the main altar is of Amida Buddha; and it was to Amida that the prayers of the service were addressed.[*][53]

Sasaki's sermon and the whole setup suggest to me a few problems that I should like to clarify:

What is the relation of this modern, Occidental-style temple and service to the big temple in Honolulu? What is the relation of the International Buddhist Association to the sectarian situation? What is the relation of the Shinshū sect to the other orthodox Buddhist sects in Japan, and why has it furnished the platform for the I.B.A.?[54] When Sasaki and

---

[*] See *An Official Guide to Japan with Preparatory Explanations on Japanese Customs, Language, History, Religion, Literature, Etc.* (Tokyo: Japanese Government Railways, 1933), p. 291.

his friends speak of and pray to Amida Buddha, do they think of him as a historical character, or as purely a *Dhyāna* Buddha?[55] If as a *Dhyāna* Buddha, what do they think of the Amida legend? (Purely symbolic? or meant to be believed literally by the simpler faithful?) Sasaki spoke of the need for the individual to grasp and integrate the grace or spirit of Amida. This seems to me to contradict the fundamental Amida formula; namely, that to pronounce the name is sufficient. What is the position of the I.B.A. on such a point, and what that of the traditional sectarians?

It is possible that all of these questions are conceived from a standpoint quite alien to the thinking of a Japanese Buddhist. During the course of my conversation after the service, I had occasion to refer to the Catholic dogma of the Assumption of the Virgin as both scientifically and meta-physically untenable. (Heaven is not a *place:* a physical body has to be in a *place:* it extends in space and endures in time—no space—no body.)[56] I was told that such an image has to be taken symbolically. I replied that the Roman Catholic Church insists on the Assumption as a literal fact.

"You mean, if one were there one could have seen it?"

"Definitely. It is claimed that people were there and that people liter-ally did see the Virgin ascend. Moreover, the body of Jesus also ascended." (And, I might have added, we are all to ascend at the moment of the Resurrection of the Dead.)

"We Buddhists," I was then told, "treat such things as symbols. The Buddha, for instance, is said to have been born from his mother's side. We don't ask ourselves whether that was a literal fact."

"Well," I said, "in the West we tend to give such themes a concrete reading—and religion then comes under the criticism of science. Young people become confused, and reasonably abandon their faith."

I spent the afternoon on my Japanese and at six went to Tokyo Onsen for my final Turkish bath and massage—Otako-san singing little geisha songs while she worked, and a new song called "Samisen Boogie-Woogie." A fine steak dinner at Suehiro's after the bath, and then a long stroll home.

Monday, April 25

Anniversary (eighth month) of my departure from New York. Shall leave for Kyoto tomorrow. Bought my third-class ticket yesterday for the 9:00 A.M. express.

Today I finally got up my nerve and purchased two new lenses for my camera (a wide-angle and a telephoto), as well as a leather bag in which to carry my photographic affairs and a universal viewfinder. I then went around the city viewing buildings and finally went to a little studio where I could try all this out in a strictly measured area. They supplied a nude model, whom I viewed happily through 135 mm, 50 mm, and 35 mm lenses—finding, however, to my distress, that the difference between the 50 and 35 was not great enough to warrant the money I had spent on the latter. I hurried back to the store (for it was now 5:00 P.M.) and swapped my wide-angle for an extra-wide-angle lens of 28 mm. This cost another four thousand yen but made me happy.

For dinner, I went tonight to Irene's Hungaria, a very nice little cellar restaurant, full of Americans. Returned home to pack and retired at peace with the world.

Tuesday, April 26   *Kyoto*

Nine A.M. to 4:20 P.M. Third-class: a perfectly beautiful train ride. There is no comparison possible with the trains of India! Clean crowd, very orderly and considerate, with neat packages, all nicely dressed and un-smelly, with cute little packets of things to eat. The train was swept of its clutter of tangerine skins and discarded wrappings six times during the trip.

The countryside is incredible: the farms are like gardens, perfectly kept and groomed—full of people working. The mountains and sea everywhere. Vast, busy, modern cities and charming hamlets.

Kyoto, a city of over a million, was more like Tokyo than I had expected: great and busy modern streets and buildings, but proportionately many more of the quaint little streets and temple compounds than Tokyo. As soon as I was settled in my room in the Kyoto Hotel (a small room and bath for more than I wanted to pay), I went out for a stroll, hunting for some of the restaurants that the Batteys had named for me. Had dinner at one that I found myself: the Alaska, on the top floor of a seven- or eight-storey building, with all glass walls and a fine view of the valley in which Kyoto nestles. Then strolled, enchanted again, through the multitudes of charmingly lighted little streets—all swarming with droves of schoolchildren, who are brought here in great busloads to see the ancient capital and the religious center of their country. They flood the little streets, doll shops, pachinko games, movie theaters, coffee shops, and Japanese-style inns.

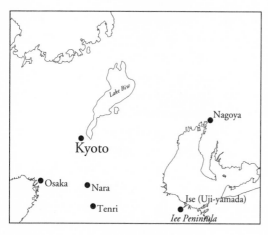

Wednesday, April 27

Up at 5:00 A.M., and write three letters before breakfast: one to Mr. Phillip Karl Eidmann,[57] in the Honganji Temple compound (Feuerring's[58] suggestion), one to Mrs. Ruth Sasaki (Alan Watts's former mother-in-law),[59] and one to Miss Ellen D. Psaty (Salmony's former student).[60] After breakfast I asked to be moved to a cheaper room, and went off for a morning's walk. Strolled from the hotel to the Sanjō-Shijō area, then across the river and up to the Yasaka Shrine, then back to Kawaramachi Street. Streetcar to the railroad station area and into the Japan Tourist Office, where I got some advice on where to study Japanese: I have a date this afternoon, 5:00 P.M., for an interview at the Japanese Language School at Nakadachiuri. Took a streetcar up to the school corner, to locate the place, then returned to the hotel for a spaghetti lunch in the grill. I moved into the new room.

After lunch, a sightseeing bus: Higashi Honganji Temple, a magnificent wooden structure, with a wonderful atmosphere, the "junior headquarters" of the Shinshū sect, the same as that of the temple I visited in Tokyo. The sect was founded by Shinran (i.e. Kenshin Daishi), A.D. 1173–1262, as a reform movement. It rejects celibacy of priesthood, vegetarianism and ascetic practices, and claims salvation by faith in Amida (*Namu Amida Butsu*[61]). It suffered many persecutions, including an eleven-year siege in the sixteenth century in Osaka.* Unlike the Tokyo temple, here the style is completely Japanese: beautiful wooden columns, mat flooring, a great sense of quiet space. It is one of the finest temple structures in Japan.

Next we visited the Imperial Palace; then paused at some shops, and

---

* *Guide to Japan,* p. 695.

finally visited the Heian Shrine and gardens. I took as many photographs as possible (black-and-white) with my new lenses.

After the tour, went to the language school and arranged to begin tomorrow: three hours a day, in a class with one other pupil, who is two weeks ahead of me. Bought the books (Naganuma's Japanese course) and went home to study. Dinner in the hotel dining room—rather dreary.

Thursday, April 28

Up at 5:30, to continue studying my new books, trying to run through as far as to lesson thirteen. Not too hard; but many new words and constructions. Eight o'clock breakfast, 8:35 streetcar; school 9:00 to 12:00—full of priests and nuns. Good teaching. I think it's going to work. Tomorrow is a holiday (the emperor's birthday),[62] and I shall be able to have a makeup session in the morning.

From one to six, I witnessed an extraordinarily interesting dramatic pantomime at the Mibu-dera Temple, the so-called Mibu-Kyōgen, which dates back to 1299. (My guide says: "It is performed from April 21 for ten days and is entirely in pantomime. There are more than thirty characters, and an orchestra of flutes, gongs, and drums. The dresses worn by the actors date in some cases from the Genroku Era (1688–1703). There are also a number of old masks in the temple.")

The temple is of the Ritsu sect, and was founded in A.D. 991. The chief image enshrined is one of Jizō-bosatsu (who appears in and is celebrated in the pantomimes), which is attributed to Jōchō, a celebrated sculptor of the eleventh century.[63]

The pantomimes are presented on a high balcony built on the south side of one of the temple structures (the Great Prayer Hall, Daibutsu-den), which faces a large pavilion where the crowd sits—a great company of little families—lots of kids—and again the miracle of five hours of excellent behavior.

A young Japanese law student named Hisashi Mita came and sat beside me and helped me to know what was going on. Six little plays were shown. (Apparently there is a repertoire of about twenty-three pieces.)

    1. *Hōroku Wari.* A tale of two quarreling merchants. One, a drum seller, goes to sleep, and the second, a seller of plates, steals his drum. The judge reprimands the plate seller and the drum seller destroys his shop.

2. Tale of a priest with a wife and child. The townspeople suspect something and insist on entering to see the image.[64] The wife, wearing a mask (on top of her mask) poses as Kannon carrying a child.[65] The people depart, but return, and the priest this time, in his confusion, has put the mask on his wife upside down. The wife is driven from town and the priest, with his baby on his back, is led in ignominy through the streets with a red rope tied around his waist and passed between his legs from behind.

3. Five robbers divest voyagers of their kimonos, but presently enter an inn where a celebrated samurai does them all to death.

4. An assassin (Yogitsu?) attempts the life of the shōgun but is defeated.

5. *The Hungry Souls' Wrestling Match with the Ogres.* Three poor "hungry souls," shivering with fear, are enabled by the grace of the Bodhisattva Kṣitigarbha (Jizō-bosatsu—principal figure of the Mibu-dera Temple) to become strong enough to overcome a horde of ogres.

6. *Benkei's Ship.* Benkei is carrying Yoshitsune and Yoshitsune's wife in a vessel. A storm demon seeks to sink the craft, but Benkei rattles his beads and, after a fierce contest, the demon is overcome.

The musical accompaniment of these pantomines remained the same throughout the afternoon: a basic rhythm marked by a gong, the secondary beats, variously, by a drum struck with two sticks, and a flute playing - - - | - - | - - - | - - | etc. all afternoon.

The characters were all masked and moved in a manner suggesting Noh, but not so slowly. No singing, and no words, however.

The balcony stage was of almost exactly the same structure as the Noh stage at the Kanze Kaikan in Tokyo. Indeed, I had the feeling, distinctly, that I was witnessing a sort of proto-Noh. I also had the feeling that I was witnessing something not very different from the religious pantomimes and morality plays of the European Middle Ages. These plays are said to have originated (circa A.D. 1170–1250) during the Kamakura period "to give the illiterated [*sic*] masses the teaching of Buddhism."[66] Noh originated about a century later: Kan'ami, circa 1333–84, and Zeami, 1363–1443.

After the performance, I had coffee with Hisashi (nicknamed Shō), and made a date with him to visit Nara on Sunday. Then to the hotel for a pleasant tempura dinner in their tempura restaurant, and an evening of work on my Japanese.

Friday, April 29

The emperor's birthday. Japanese flags all over the place. Morning from 9:00 to 11:00 at my Japanese school. After lunch, two geisha shows: the first, that of the Gion geishas at the Gion Kaburenjō Theater and the second, that of the Pontochō geishas at the Pontochō Kaburenjō Theater—the latter was the better and rather charming, though not so good as the Shimbashi geishas were, in the Azuma Odori in Tokyo. These spring geisha festivals are given every year, as advertisements of the geisha houses in the various geisha areas represented. In the programs are photos of the girls arranged according to house. Both of the little plays seen today were based on Lady Murasaki's *Tale of Genji*. The Pontochō piece, about a fox-woman and her human husband, was quite delightful. All the machinery of the Kabuki stage was used with wonderful effect.

I went to the second show with Ellen Psaty and two of her friends (one American, one Japanese) and after the performance we went (minus the Japanese lady) to Kyoto's Suehiro restaurant for a six-hundred-yen steak dinner—simply great. I told them all about my India adventures with Salmony, and left them with the promise of further events together in the future.

Before the first of the two geisha shows, I attended their "Tea Ceremonial," which was a sort of farce. A large roomful of people served a little cake and bowl of "whipped" tea, while two little geisha students sat on a high platform illustrating the act of whipping the tea. We were rushed through in lively style so that the next horde could be admitted.

Saturday, April 30

Morning and early afternoon bringing my diary up to date. It is now 3:15 P.M. Next, a letter to Jean; and the rest of the day will be spent I believe, on my Japanese.

Dinner at Prunier's: not so good: like a Midwestern restaurant and bar, with television set going full blast—in spite of a very elegant entrance and reception.

Sunday, May 1   *Nara*

A fabulous and memorable day: one of the richest of my year in the Orient. My little friend of last Thursday, Hisashi Mita, arrived at 8:10 A.M., to pick me up. There was a slight drizzle, but we set off, just the same. A fast train to Nara brought us there by 9:35, and our walk began. The weather gradually cleared.

The first phenomenon of the day was Nara's May Day parade: not very different in appearance from what I had seen before in New York—except, of course, a good deal smaller. "We have these in America too," I said. "But here," said Hisashi, "I think it is a little different. There is an anti-American side to it." "There's an anti-American side to May Day parades in America too," I said.

We talked a bit about these things during the course of the day. Among the questions that came up were:

1. American mistreatment of the negro (same theme as in India)
2. Capitalism vs. the worker (I pointed out—as I had in India—that our bricklayers get $28 per day or more: here—as in India—it is about $1.00, and $1.00 is high.)

Hisashi told me also that the students discuss in English the problem of Science vs. Religion (taking over, I suggested, a Western problem, which does not properly concern the Orient, since God is not the final term of Oriental religious thinking).

Our first stop was at the Sarusawa Pond, across which the Kōfukuji's Five-Storied Pagoda could be seen, reflected in the water. Hisashi pointed out the tree associated with the death of some legendary court lady of the past. We next walked pleasantly through the Deer Park to the Shintō Kasuga Shrine, where there was a ceremony of some kind in progress. This shrine was first constructed in A.D. 768 and has since been reconstructed many times—formerly every twenty years. All along the ways to it, and all around it, are stone lanterns, with the names of their donors inscribed on them—also, a few new lanterns of wood, with the names of department stores inscribed!* I stood a while and watched the very formal ceremonial: seven priests and two musicians—their elegant black lacquer shoes on the ground at the side of the temple area. And in another area, a sort of

---

* *Guide to Japan,* pp. 724–5.

veranda, were three women, sitting in absolute silence. Prayers were recited; staffs bearing paper slips (like leaves) were placed, regularly spaced, before the altar, various priests did various things, and the whole suggested in its decorum what I have seen of Noh.

Our third visit was to the Shin'yakushiji Temple (A.D. 747), which contains a large, wooden, seated image, surrounded by eleven (formerly twelve) "kings," and an eleven-faced Kannon.[*] And our fourth visit was to the great Tōdaiji Temple, which contains the vast Daibutsu, an image of Vairocana (Birushana-butsu), who is regarded by the Kegon sect as the spiritual body of Śākyamuni).[67] The image weighs 452 tons, is 53 feet 6 inches high, sits in the preaching *mudrā* (*seppō-in*),[68] with the right hand in the fear-not posture (*semui-in*) and the left in that granting boons (*yogan-in*). The image was commenced in 743 and finished in 749. It is flanked by gold-covered images

Daibutsu, the Mahāvairocana Buddha, at the Tōdaiji Temple, Nara

of Kannon (Nyoirin Kannon = Cintāmaṇi Avalokiteśvara),[69] on the right, and Kokūzō (Ākāśagharba),[70] on the left.[**] A number of little families were sending their children through the "lucky hole" in one of the pillars of the temple, and there was a great deal of picture taking going on.

The whole temple area was decorated with banners for the Ten Thousand Lights Festival, which is to take place tonight and the two nights following. This ceremony is celebrated at this temple only once in a hundred years—and it is a wonderful chance that today is the day. The time is to be from 7:00 to 9:30 P.M.

---

[*] *Guide to Japan*, p. 733.
[**] *Guide to Japan*, pp. 727–30.

Our fifth visit (last of the morning) was to the Kaidan-in. This is a large room filled with the platform of a single shrine. One can mount the platform and walk around it. The Four Kings are at the four corners, and within the central pagoda sit two small Buddha figures, that to the observer's left in the meditation posture, and the other in the posture of teaching: they are said to be Śākyamuni and Tahō Nyorai, though which is which, and who the latter is, I do not know.[*]

We stopped for lunch in a little outdoor restaurant, where we had tea, something called *oyako-donburi* (a bowl of rice mixed with chicken, boiled onion, and egg), and a bit of *takuan* (salt-marinated turnip slices). Then our sightseeing was resumed.

The temple bell at the Tōdaiji Temple, Nara

Our sixth visit of the day (first of the afternoon) was to the belfry, wherein there hangs one of the largest bronze bells in Japan (cast A.D. 752, broken 989, recast ca. 1239).[†] Visit seven was to the Sangatsu-dō, which

---

[*] *Guide to Japan,* p. 730.
[†] *Guide to Japan,* p. 731.

contains a great Kannon[*] and fourteen other statues, and visit eight was to the Nigatsu-dō.[†]

Visit nine was one of the great events of the day, namely, to the Shōsōin Treasure House—which is within a large, walled area, opened to the Japanese only once a year, but to foreign visitors by special permission. Hisashi managed to induce the very gentlemanly custodian to let us in. The area contained, as its main glory, the great and curious treasure house itself—a structure like a very large and handsome log cabin, raised on mighty stilts—of Japanese cypress and dating from the eighth century. Within this are kept many works of art and craft from the Tempyō period (A.D. 710–94), which the custodian showed me in photographs (eighteen volumes), when we had returned to the gate building. Also in this area is a smaller building in the same log-cabin style, but square, containing a complete set of the Buddhist scriptures, another large building enclosed in concrete and resembling in proportions the main treasury, and a small but beautiful wooden sanctuary. We spent about an hour and a half looking at pictures of the treasures after we had viewed the buildings: largely textiles of unique designs.

We had walked, I should say, somewhere between ten and fifteen miles and were beginning to be tired. We went to the elegant Nara Hotel for dinner, and then returned by cab to the Tōdaiji Temple for the great Ten Thousand Lights Festival (Mantō-e).[71]

The image and temple interior were extremely impressive in the dim light, illuminated by a multitude of flickering wicks placed all around the great platform. There took place a preliminary ceremony of worship, conducted by some fourteen or fifteen priests, who ascended the platform and chanted from some *sūtra*. Great offering stacks of rice cakes and oranges were very neatly arranged before the prodigious image. There were not many people present and I had a good position from which to view this event. The great Buddha could easily be experienced as the partially realized presentiment of supreme consciousness looming through the darkness beyond the comparatively bright foreground of the ceremony and the chant. The character and function of ritualistic worship as an assistance and guide to meditation was evident in an exceptionally strong way in this rite.

---

[*] *Guide to Japan,* p. 732.
[†] *Guide to Japan,* p. 731.

The vast enclosure between the temple and the great gate was illuminated by six braziers placed around the dance platform that had been built in front of the large, ancient, bronze lantern just in front of the temple entrance. Two great bronze drums, six feet in diameter, were at either side of the platform, and stage left was a pavilion in which the musicians sat: stage right was another pavilion that remained empty. The music: about five flutes, two small drums, two or three *shō*,[72] and two or three very short, reedy musettes. The costumes of the dancers and of the men who beat the big bronze drums were those of Japanese warriors of the period antedating that of the samurai.[73]

The night performance commenced at 7:00 P.M. with the sound of a deep bell, from somewhere in the distance. Then, to the music of one flute and the great drum, stage left, a single, male dancer appeared with a spear. Very slowly he ascended to the platform, and executed a stately dance. Next, to the same music, but the drum stage right, another man executed the same dance. Next to the music of flutes, *shō*, bells, and the drum stage left, four men danced. Then again, but to the drum stage right, a dance of four. The fifth dance (drum stage left) was performed by a single dancer wearing a golden animal mask and the same warrior costume. It was a long dance, one of its passages being performed in silence. Two flutes and two small drums were played. And the last dance, to the same sort of music, was performed by two dancers wearing black human masks. The evening concluded with an orchestral selection accompanied by the two great drums.

The dances consisted largely of stately turning strides, from straight to bent knees, silent stamps, great slow arm swings, knee bends with occasional spring jumps (vertical) and once or twice, genuflections to the floor.

At 9:30, we caught a cab to the station. Got to bed at about eleven.

Monday, May 2   *Kyoto*

A rather quiet day, after the great Nara visit of May 1. Actually, I should have gone back to Nara for the second night of the three-night festival, but I felt that I had to work hard on my Japanese, to pick up on my class; furthermore, the weather was a bit overcast and dull. Morning, nine to twelve, at the Japanese school. Lunch in a little cake shop, and all afternoon and evening on my Japanese. Dinner in Prunier's Pontochō Grill: not as bad as the other Prunier restaurant, but too expensive.

CHAPTER IV

AN AMERICAN BUDDHIST IN KYOTO

Tuesday, May 3

Father Moss, my schoolmate, was to be absent today, so it was arranged that I should take my classes in the afternoon, with a young American housewife who is at lesson six. I spent the morning studying, and at one went to the school.

"Is your husband in the government service?" I asked.

"No," said the young woman, "he is with the University Field Service."*

I confessed that I knew nothing of the group, and it was explained that it was a new organization that had fourteen or fifteen men in the field making surveys and sending in reports—in Japan, India, etc.

"Your husband, then, speaks Japanese?" I said.

"Well . . . ," she parried, "a little."

So here it is again!74

At 3:00 P.M. a new phase of my visit to Japan commenced, when I went to the Nishi Honganji Temple compound to pay a visit to a young man of about thirty-three whose name had been suggested to me by Jacob Feuerring

---

* Or something like that.

in New York. I entered the compound by the Ōmiya Gate, turned to the left, and came to the back entrance of a small Japanese house. Two Japanese bowed to greet me when I said "Eidmann-san?" and I doffed my shoes to enter. I was conducted through the house and shown into a pleasant room opening onto a lovely garden where there sat on the floor, with his legs out flat beneath a low Japanese table, a paralyzed young man, who greeted me easily and bade me sit down on the cushion at his right. Then commenced a highly interesting, but rather demanding, monologue that lasted until about 7:30 P.M. It was punctuated by the visit of a tall young man, named Fillmore, who is in the army (but wearing civilian clothes) and hopes to remain in Japan to enter Tokyo University. He was just back from Tokyo, where he had been attending to the problem of his papers.

"Did anything happen May Day?" Eidmann asked.

Fillmore smiled. "No," he said. "But they expected something to happen. They were convinced that there was going to be some kind of Communist disturbance and had machine guns planted all around the camp. The colonel, on the emperor's birthday, said, 'No Communists? What are all those flags with the red ball?' They were the Japanese flags hung out for the holiday."

At about six a nice Japanese dinner was served by Eidmann's housekeeper and shared by a young Japanese who had been introduced to me as Eidmann's secretary and is a Shinshū priest. There is also a Korean houseboy, likewise a student of Shinshū.

Shortly after dinner the secretary and Eidmann staged an absolutely formal tea ceremony for my benefit, and I heard a great deal about the mysteries of tea. Whipped tea had been served to me also at the time of my arrival.

The first major event, after my arrival and the preliminaries of becoming acquainted, was a tour of the large temple compound, with Eidmann in his wheelchair being pushed by the secretary, and me walking alongside.

I learned that the Nishi Honganji Temple is one of the most important and influential Buddhist institutions in Japan.[*][†]

---

* See *Guide to Japan*, pp. 146–47.

† Briefly summarizing the historical situation:

    A.D. 552—Buddhism enters Japan, when the King of Kudara (Paekche), in Korea, presents *sūtras* and images of Buddha to the Imperial Court of Japan. These are followed by priests and nuns, temple architects and image carvers.

Eidmann told me during the course of our tour of the temple compound that the Honganji Temple (which is the great center of the Shinshū)

A.D. 592–628—Prince Shōtoku makes Buddhism the religion of the Court, issues a code, and organizes the national administration on the basis of Buddhist teachings, builds temples and monasteries, charity hospitals, orphanages, and homes of refuge for the widowed and the aged.

A.D. 645–794—Nara period: development of "the Six Sects of the Southern Capital (Nara): Sanron, Jōjitsu, and Kusha, now extinct; and Ritsu, Hossō, and Kegon.

Many commentaries on the *sūtras* were composed. The main character of the religion is still that of the Chinese *Mahāyāna* (Daijō Bukkyō), the basic principle being faith in the Three Treasures (*ratnatraya*, i.e. the oneness of the Perfect Person (Buddha), the Truth (*Dharma*), and the Community (*Saṅgha*). This principle was demonstrated artistically in ceremonies and supported by a system of philosophy.

A.D. 794–1185—Heian period: a strong national bent is given to the imported religion, chiefly by the application of the doctrine of Honjisuijaku, according to which the Shintō deities are regarded as various manifestations of Buddhas and Bodhisattvas. The two great teachers were:

Saichō (Dengyō Daishi, 767–822), founder of Tendai; and Kūkai (Kōbō Daishi, 774–835), founder of Shingon.

The two great centers from which these doctrines then emanated were, for Tendai, Mt. Hiei, northeast of Kyoto, and for Shingon, Mt. Kōya, south of Nara.

Tendai is described as being based on "pantheistic realism," and Shingon as presenting "an esoteric philosophy" with "a complex symbolism."

A.D. 1185–1392—Kamakura period: four new sects arise for the purification of Buddhism, which has become "secularized and corrupt":

Zen, founded by Eisai (1141–1215) and Dōgen (1200–53)

Jōdo, founded by Hōnen (1133–1212)

Shinshū, founded by Shinran (1173–1262)

Hokke, founded by Nichiren (1222–82)

Jōdo and Shinshū are essentially one in doctrine, both teaching that the only way to salvation lies in absolute trust in the all-saving power of Amitābha Buddha, a doctrine which is generally styled "salvation through the absolute faith in another's power" (*tariki-hongan*). The two sects, however, have some important differences. While the Jōdo sect lays emphasis on repetition of the formula *Namu Amida-butsu*, or "Glory to Amida Buddha…" the Shinshū sect regards faith in Amida Buddha as the all sufficient and only essential thing, the repetition of the formula being considered merely an expression of a thankful heart. Another important difference is that the Shinshū sect discards the principle of celibacy of the clergy, together with all ascetic practices. Further more, the Shinshū sect is more logical in its observances. Its adherents believe in Amida Buddha alone, and although they worship before the founder's image as the revealer of the Amida doctrine, the sect has discarded all other images.

has never capitulated to the efforts of the Court to reduce Buddhism to a nationalistic, patriotic, political tool. When, during the last war, the government issued a statement that those who died in the service of their country would become, if they were Shintōists, Shintō gods, and, if Buddhists, Buddhas, the Honganji was the only Buddhist group that had the courage to publish a counterstatement to the effect that dying for Japan had nothing to do with Buddhahood: those spiritually ready to become Buddhas would become so; others, however, might go to hell. The Honganji, indeed, has always been regarded with suspicion by the government.[*]

According to Eidmann, between Nishi Honganji and Higashi Honganji there is no rivalry or contention. They are two institutions representing the same principles and sect.

During the course of our tour of the Nishi Honganji Temple I was shown two Noh theaters and a beautiful garden.

About Noh: it appears that the origins of Noh are closely associated with the Honganji (there is another Noh theater, I read, in the Higashi Honganji Temple).[†] In one of the two Noh theaters in the Nishi Honganji there is an annual performance in which representatives of all the schools of Noh participate. (The event this year will be on May 21. Eidmann will get me a ticket.) The other Noh theater in this temple is the oldest Noh theater in Japan. Only members of the temple family, royal family, etc.,

---

[*] As we read: "The new sect passed through many vicissitudes and under persecution was compelled to shift its headquarters many times. At Ishiyama, Osaka, its temple became a powerful stronghold, which successfully resisted a siege by Oda Nobunaga (1534–82), lasting for eleven years. But it was again compelled to seek a resting-place in Kii Province, and still another in Osaka. Ten years later, it became permanently settled, by favor of Toyotomi Hideyoshi, at the present site in Kyoto. In 1602 Tokugawa Ieyasu, fearing the growing power of the sect, sought to weaken it by giving a former abbot permission to found another branch of the sect. This younger branch is known as the Higashi Honganji Temple from the location of its chief temple.

"In 1617 the buildings of the Nishi Honganji were destroyed by fire, but they were soon restored, a building being added by transference from the site of Hideyoshi's famous Juraku Museum. This new building is called Hiunkaku, and is now protected as a 'National Treasure.' Again in 1636 another building was added.

"It may be noted that the Nishi Honganji Temple has 9,837 local temples, and more than six million adherents" (*Guide to Japan*, p. 695).

[†] *Guide to Japan*, p. 694.

can attend the performances here presented. Seeing these outdoor Noh theaters let me know the reason for the form of the modern Noh stage.[75]

Outdoor Noh

About gardens: the plans of the garden architect cannot be realized in one generation. They are consulted for decades; the branches of the trees are bent and trained to follow the designated forms. Every stone is considered. The temple garden that I saw was somewhat marred by the removal of one background building at the time of the war and collapse of two trees at the time of a big wind some two or three years later. But new trees have been planted and in another few decades the garden will be back in trim.

The buildings that we visited included many wonders. The two main temple halls were much like the main hall of the Higashi Honganji that I had seen on the sightseeing tour. There were also a number of court rooms of the shōgun, etc., with a "Nightingale Floor"[76] and squeaking door approaches to protect the shōgun against a sneak attack. The rooms had screenlike paintings on gold backgrounds: one charming room of sparrows, another of waves. On the outer doors were great tigers (from stuffed models) and an eagle—quite majestic. The visit, with Eidmann in his wheelchair telling the stories, gave me a strong sense of the period—and of the crucial importance of this temple in the history of Japan.

Eidmann talked of the influence of Buddhism, and particularly of the Honganji Temple, in America. It is estimated that there are about 450,000 Buddhists in the United States. There are Honganji temples in a number of American cities (including New York), and it is planned ultimately to have missions in every state. The Nisei form a kind of core, but they are by no means an overwhelming majority.

Eidmann's presence in the Honganji compound (invited by the abbot) is connected, I suspect, with the interest in America. He has just gained an M.A. from Kyoto University with a translation of some Shinshū text and is very busy on translations, articles, hymns, etc. He plans to proceed, however, after another four or five years in Japan, to Siam, then Burma, and finally India, to study the history and present state of Buddhism in the Orient.

The tea ceremonial was an extraordinarily interesting little affair, conducted with perfect and absolute decorum by Eidmann's secretary in full regalia, according to the rules of the Yabu-no-uchi school. (The other two chief schools today are the Ura-senke and the Omote-senke.) The manner of movement and posture of the tea master were very much like those of the Noh—indeed, this whole thing is closing into one great picture. Eidmann told me what I was to do when my time came to do things, and the tea master performed without a hitch, as though his guest were the mikado.

I asked Eidmann about the relationship of tea to Zen, and he was inclined to think that tea, originally, was independent of Zen, but that Zen took it over and read into it a sense that had not been there before. The prodigious decorum of tea is perhaps to be attributed as much to the aristocratic decorum of the classes that fostered it as to the spirit of ritual. Today, tea is a kind of social hobby—excellent for social climbing and with all kinds of fancy phases. One can tell immediately in what tea school a person has been trained: every detail of posture and gesture is regulated, with the very slightest differences as hallmarks. And all the implements used are variously shaped (very slightly differing) according to the school.[*]

---

[*] The history of tea in Japan is given as follows in the *Guide to Japan*, pp. 236–40:

A.D. 645–794—Nara Period. The drinking of tea was already known in Japan during the reign of the Emperor Shōmu (A.D. 729), who was said to have invited one hundred Buddhist monks to the Imperial Palace to have tea. The leaves were probably imported into Japan by the ambassadors to the Tang Court and prepared in the way then in fashion.

A.D. 794–1185—Heian Period. In 805 a priest named Saichō brought back some seeds from China, where he had stayed for studies for some years, and planted them on Mt. Hiei, near Kyoto. Many tea gardens are mentioned in literature in the succeeding centuries, as well as the delight of the aristocracy and priesthood in the beverage.

A.D. 1185–1392—Kamakura Period.

Eidmann showed me his certificate of admission to, and certificate of graduation from the tea school. He told me also that in Japan a young lady, before she can hope to get married, must have at least two of the four following certificates: tea, flower arrangement, music, sewing—or, occasionally, she can substitute for one, calligraphy.

Discussing the contemporary scene, Eidmann said, "I hate to see the United States tying its defense to Japan. It seems to me, if we want to blow up the Communist world, the best thing we could do would be to give them the J-Bomb."[77] The problem: Japanese politics is run, not by or for principles and ideals, but in terms of loyalties and obligations. One votes for and supports those to whom one thinks one is obligated. When such a focal figure dies or disappears from the political scene, people turn to their

---

A.D. 1392–1573—Muromachi Period. The tea plant, a native of southern China, was known from very early times to Chinese medicine, and was highly prized for possessing the virtues of relieving fatigue, delighting the soul, strengthening the will, and repairing the eyesight. Taoists considered it an important ingredient of the elixir of immortality and Buddhists used it extensively to prevent drowsiness during their long hours of meditation. *Among the Buddhists, the southern Zen sect, which incorporated so many of the Taoist doctrines in their belief, formulated an elaborate ritual of tea.* The monks gathered before the image of Bodhidharma and drank tea out of a single bowl with the profound formality of a holy sacrament. *It was this Zen ritual which finally developed into the ceremonial tea of Japan in the 15th century.* By the 15th century, under the patronage of Yoshimasa of the Ashikaga Shōgunate, the tea ceremony had been fully constituted and made into an independent and secular performance. Tea became a means by which purity and refinement could be worshipped.

The Tea House (*suki-ya*) to accomodate not more than five persons, consists of: a service room (*mizu-ya*), where the tea utensils are washed and arranged before being brought in; a waiting room (*yoritsuki*), in which the guests wait until they receive the summons to enter the tea-room; a garden path (*roji*), which connects the yoritsuki with the tea-room; and the tea-room proper (*cha-shitsu*), which is generally nine feet square, with a special entrance for the host and another for the guests, the latter (*nijiriguchi*) being so small that they have to creep in. The room takes four and a half mats (*tatami*), the half mat filling the space in the center of the room, and at one corner of this half mat a square hearth is fitted into the floor, so as to form a brazier, on which is placed an iron kettle. By the hearth sits the host.

The utensils consist of the tea-bowl (*cha-wan*), tea-caddy (*cha-ire*), bamboo tea-whisk (*cha-sen*), bamboo spoon (*cha-shaku*), etc. The full ceremony takes about two hours. (For procedure, see *Guide*, pp. 238–40.)

next loyalty or obligation. Also, when the U.S. forced universal suffrage on Japan it opened the political machine to a multitude without any specific loyalties or obligations vis-à-vis the figures running for election. The behavior of this mass at election time is a large X quantity, subject to the most whimsical motivation. There is little chance that a pattern of consistent loyalty to any ideal or system of political ideals could be made to steady them effectively. Americans, thinking of Japanese politics in such terms as we can properly apply to our own, are completely out of touch with the hidden facts of the situation. Indeed, the Japanese themselves sometimes think that their loyalty is to the ideals of which they speak and write.

Wednesday, May 4

Studied Japanese in the morning. Class in the afternoon, one to three; then back to the hotel, to write letters and diary.

At 6:30 Ellen Psaty arrived, in a chipper mood, and we went to an elegant Japanese restaurant, named Tsuruya, for dinner. Our room opened onto a lovely garden, there was a bright three-quarter moon, and in a large banquet room at an angle to ours we could see a company of gents with the geisha girls entertaining: first, the samisen and dances; then, by magic, the whole company of gents being lured into letting down on their dignity and dancing too. There was one moment when the whole room was filled with gracefully capering Japanese gentlemen and appreciatively helpful geishas.

Ellen said: only the geishas can make them relax. They never let go at any other time. (The tension of the Japanese formality accounts, I believe, for the tendency of Japanese to weep when emotionally stirred. They weep, apparently, very easily. It requires also, I think, that there should be this ancient art of the geishas, to afford the safety valve—since the relationship to the wife is largely formal and definitely part of the public pattern.)

Ellen spoke of her researches into the life of a certain Japanese artist whose children, legitimate and illegitimate, are still alive. The principle that she had found operating here, as in everything else in Japan, is that of the *hidden motivator*. In Japanese business, in Japanese politics, in Japanese life, there is always the official front and front personage. The heads of

Japanese firms are chosen for their family connections, names, etc., and they know precisely what their role is and do not try (as do Americans elected or appointed for such reasons) to become the actual instead of apparent directors. The actual director (the politician behind the man behind the shōgun) is always deep out of sight, and must be diligently searched for to be found.

Thursday, May 5

Our seventeenth wedding anniversary. Telegram to Jean in the morning. Also, in Japan, Children's Day and a national holiday.

At 9:15 A.M. went to Eidmann's, and at 11:30 P.M., returned home: meanwhile, fourteen hours of almost continuous talk from my young master—and a long walk, with several interesting stops. We set off after an elegant Japanese lunch and went by taxi to the area of the Chion-in Temple—a prodigious institution of the Jōdo sect. This sect has six branches, and the Chion-in is the head temple of the most flourishing.[*] This temple is one of the largest in Japan and covers an area of about thirty acres. Some of the buildings date back to A.D. 1633–39.[†] We strolled past the great *sammon* (two-storied gate), paused before a stone covering a spot where a meteor fell, and paused for a delicious drink of *amazake*[78] at a little garden, and went on for a visit to a convent of Jōdo nuns, where Eidmann is to lecture in a couple of days.

The younger nuns, with their heads completely shaved and uncovered, and wearing a boyish looking type of service jumper, looked to me at first like boys: but Eidmann assured me that they were older than they seemed to be. This convent is a school, where they come to study. They may leave the order at any time they please, but seldom do; and there are about thirty at a time in this convent. In all, apparently, there are about a thousand Jōdo nuns—devoted primarily to the recitation of the *Namu Amida-butsu*. We were greeted by two older nuns—cute little darlings in sturdy black kimonos, with grey, and then white, under-kimonos (visible at the neck), who talked attentively and with typical Japanese politeness with Eidmann

---

[*] *Guide to Japan*, p. 148.
[†] *Guide to Japan*, p. 700.

and had their young nuns serve us whipped tea and cakes. When we departed they accompanied us to the road and bowed us away.

Our path took us, next, down the hill and across the river to the Pontochō, where there was a great jam of people, just getting out of the Odori. Eidmann explained the geisha institution. The Japanese never entertain in their homes. (In contrast to India.) Instead, the head of the family has a geisha house where he regularly entertains. One is introduced to such a house by a friend; one is billed by the month; and the function of the house is to take care of one's catering problems. The geishas of Kyoto are today the most honored in Japan. There are three geisha sections: Gion, Pontochō, and Shimabara.

We paused, to look at the river and take a brief rest, then went to a shop specializing in tea paraphernalia, where Eidmann made a few purchases and I was shown the different forms of the utensils of the three chief schools. We stopped for "*sofuto aisukureemu*" (soft ice cream) at a crowded restaurant where Eidmann's secretary joined us and the young man who had been pushing the wheelchair took his leave; and then we resumed our walk.

Visits to a couple of bookstores revealed the fact that a number of new Russian volumes, in Russian, as well as Russian magazines, are on display, whereas the English books for sale (except in the department store Maruzen) are largely secondhand. Problem: why the dearth of books in English? Expense? Can't be it; because in India there were lots of paperbacks, while here I haven't seen any. Eidmann tells me that Maruzen has an import monopoly of some kind. Apparently, our booksellers just haven't made a good connection here.

The remainder of the walk consisted largely of visits to little shops, with a pause at a Chinese restaurant for dinner; then a walk through the Shimabara geisha section (less high-class than the others: the geishas were actually sitting outside of their houses, at the doors), and back to the Nishi Honganji. They got me an excellent masseur to massage my right ankle and leg, which are still sore from the Angkor sprain and get a bit tied up from the pressure of the Ace bandage during a long walk (today, about six hours, not counting pauses). I returned to my hotel about 11:15 P.M.

Among the matters discussed during the day were the following:

The development of a Honganji literature and service in English.

According to Eidmann, the service now in use—which is what I experienced in Tokyo—was developed by a man named Ford who is now living in Honolulu. (Must try to meet him on my way home.) He was an Anglican clergyman before becoming a Buddhist, and modeled the service that he developed on the Anglican pattern. Eidmann is himself at work, now, trying to improve the situation—culling appropriate Buddhist hymns from the old collections, finding appropriate tunes, etc. The problem of the Honganji sponsorship of publications in English is also a serious one—which he is helping the abbot (who is a member of the great Ohtani family and a cousin of the emperor) to solve.

The Shinshū attitude toward monasticism was explained by Eidmann as a consequence of the conviction that the valid succession had been broken and that there could be no true *arhats*[79] in Japan. Under such circumstances the monastic life could not conduce to its proper end. At this point I was moved to open my eyes and exclaim, "My God!" but I refrained. Implied here is a belief in the spiritual effect of an apostolic succession; a belief that in modern Japan Buddhism cannot conduce to its proper end; and that monasticism is the supreme form of life. I must ask about this some more. At this point, it seems to me, a great chasm begins to yawn between what I should have thought was the true sense of the doctrine and the ecclesiastic interpretation of the problem of enlightenment.

Eidmann declares that *arhats* do exist in Burma; that they have been identified by examination and that monasticism is therefore validated in Burma. In Thailand too there are probably *arhats*. In Ceylon there are none.

The Hīnayāna in Burma was a twelfth- or thirteenth-century reaction against the excesses of the Tantric Mahāyāna of the centuries immediately preceding. In Ceylon, all the Mahāyāna texts were burned.

The relationship of Zen to Buddhism is not completely clear. There is a possibility that Bodhidharma was not a Buddhist at all, but a Vedantist (Bodhidharma's date, which I think was A.D. 527, is earlier, however, than the date of Śaṅkara, I believe; for was not the latter circa A.D. 800?).[80] Furthermore, the chief development of Zen was Chinese: all of the sages whom Suzuki cites were Chinese.[81] Zen, as described by Suzuki at least, is hardly Japanese. Its closest affinities would seem to be Taoism. (Indeed Lao-tzu's *Tao-te Ching* is a fundamental text for the understanding of all so-called Buddhist philosophy in Japan.[82])

The fundamental principle of Zen would seem to be: "Do what you have to do, perfectly, and without reservations."

Paradoxically, however, there are Zen monasteries and Zen monastic disciplines. Moreover, Zen lore and life is full of what would seem to us to be superstitious practices: amulets, etc. Zen pays respect to all the Buddhas and Bodhisattvas.

Zen's relationship to tea has been noted above.[83] The relationship to painting is similar: a lay tradition is taken over and reinterpreted, and the tradition then again becomes a lay tradition serving nonreligious ends.

[T]he Zen or Contemplative sect... "seeks salvation by meditating and divine emptiness." Its doctrines may be summed up in the following injunction: "Look carefully within and there you will find the Buddha!" This sect found adherents among the powerful leaders and samurai of the Shōgun's government at Kamakura, owing to the fact that in Zen each believer must work out his own salvation by austere discipline, bodily and mental, and thus develop the measure of will-power and self-control needed by a true samurai. We see a marked development of this in Bushidō,[84] which was greatly influenced by Zen principles.*

Some rather shocking information came out about the anti-Buddhist, pro-Christian activity and propaganda of the Occupation:

Temple landholdings were confiscated, as a part of the general land reform. All of the temples except the Honganji are dependent on land rents; as a consequence, many are now in very critical financial straits. This accounts somewhat for the conspicuous decline of the other sects and prosperity of the Shinshū since the war.

It was required of every religious institution that, like the Christian churches, it should have a congregation to become legally recognized as a corporate body; and without this recognition there could be no tax exemption. Many Buddhist temples, on the other hand, do not have and never were supposed to have, congregations in the Protestant Christian sense.

MacArthur patronized a vast distribution of Bibles (one finds them, indeed, in many Japanese hotel rooms), contributing a letter over his own signature that only the Christian can be truly democratic.

---

* *Guide to Japan*, p. 146.

One can readily understand from this latter point why there is, and must inevitably be, a very strong anti-American, and even pro-Communist tendency among Buddhists. One-third of the Ceylonese clergy is Marxist, and the Southeast Asians are tending to favor Russia against the West, not so much because Russia is anti-Democratic as because Russia is anti-Christian.

One should perhaps note in this connection that the leaders whom we are supporting in the Orient are predominantly Christian: e.g. Chiang Kai-shek in China, Romulo in the Philippines, and Diem in French Indochina. What Rhee is, I don't know; but I shouldn't be surprised...[85]

Eidmann feels that the Buddhists of Asia (Ceylon, Burma, Thailand, for example) will never accept India as the leader of Asia. Here Nehru & Co. are doomed to disappointment. He feels also, however, that there is such a strong anti-Western tide that Japan, which is regarded as the most Westernized of the Asian powers, will not be accepted as the leader either. This would seem to leave China in a pretty good spot.

An interesting surprise turned up when I asked Eidmann why he was so greatly interested in Brazil and Portuguese. He replied that of the five chief Portuguese writers of the past century, two were Buddhists and wrote from Japan, namely, Antero de Quental (a poet) and Wenceslau de Morais (1854–1929, a writer of prose). He also pointed out to me that a work written in Portuguese on the subject of Indian medicine was one of the important contributions to the progress of European medicine in the sixteenth century, namely *Coloquios dos simples e drogas he cousas medicinais da India* (Goa, 1563).

We talked a bit of the Fulbright and Foundation situation and it was his opinion (as it was also Ellen Psaty's) that these grantees have cut a rather poor figure in Japan (as I should say they have in India too.) They don't seem to know anything about the material or culture and certainly nothing about the language. "The Ford people seem to be a cut above the Fulbright," was his opinion.

Finally, a motif that I forgot to record for yesterday's talk with Ellen: "The Japanese male and the American female," she said, "are the spoiled children of the world—and spoiled children aren't nice."

Friday, May 6

Awakened at 4:30 A.M. by a knock at my door—and an anniversary telegram from Jean (time problem: Japan, New York!) Back to sleep and up at 7:00 A.M. Spent the morning writing up my diary and at 12:30 went to Eidmann's again, this time to see an annual Shintō procession, which stops for breath at the Nishi Honganji gate. The procession is the passage of the fox-god Inari from his city residence to his country residence.*

---

* [See *Guide,* pp. 142–45.]

The chief shrines are in Uji and Yamada—about three hours ride from Kyoto: to be visited at some later date.

Shintō in its early stages taught the innate goodness of the human heart. *Follow the genuine impulses of your heart,* was the essence of its ethical teaching. Its pantheon of "eight million gods," with the Sun Goddess, Amaterasu-Ōmikami (Great-Heaven-Shining-Goddess) at its head (she is enshrined in the Naikū, or Inner Shrine, of the Daijingū Shrines at Uji-Yamada), embraces many nature gods and goddesses of the sea, rivers, winds, fire and mountains and many deified persons.

Under the influence of Confucianism, which came to Japan along with Buddhism in the middle of the 6th century (which marked the end of the Archaic period, and the opening of the Asuka Period: A.D. 552–645), the conception of *loyalty or filial piety* was introduced to the Japanese ethical code.

And *Buddhism* had an overwhelming influence upon Shintō after its introduction—culminating in the creation of the *Double Aspect Shintō* (*Ryōbu*). The theory is that the Buddhist pantheon in general represents the indestructible parts of the gods, while the deities in the Shintō pantheon are their partial appearances or incarnations. The real entity, or prime noumenon, is called the *Honji,* the original, and the manifestation, the *Suijaku.* In this combination every god (*Kami*) is regarded as a manifestation of a certain Buddhist deity. This state of things lasted for well nigh a thousand years.

Muromachi Period (1392–1573), Momoyama Period (1573–1615):

In the fifteenth century further progress was made in the systematization of Shintō theology. The name of Ichijō Kanera (1402–81) is prominent in this connection. Shintō, according to Kanera, teaches the existence of many deities, but metaphysically speaking they are one, because each deity is but a manifestation of the universal soul in a particular aspect of its activity and all the gods are one in spirit and entity, especially in the virtue of veracity.

Edo Period (1615–1868):

In the course of the eighteenth century Shintō entered a new path and prepared for another revival. All the earlier Shintō theorists had depended much upon either Buddhism or Confucianism in interpreting Shintō ideas; now the time became ripe for *purging the alien elements to a certain degree and restoring early Shintō by means of historical scholarship.* This was made possible by the *philological studies of the ancient records compiled in the eighth century.* The greatest of the philologists and the pioneer of "Pure Shintō" was

Appropriately, during the course of the Shintō procession that I went to the Honganji gate to see, a limousine with bride and groom, as well as parents, pulled to a stop, to wait for the street to clear. A number of little women with children on their backs spotted the bride within (a very serious little thing, dressed as a geisha) and came over to peer.

The procession was rather amusing. In the vanguard were two white and green trees carried on litters by many men: these represented the Sacred Tree of the Amaterasu myth: There followed various sorts of men in costume and finally three large, cloth-enclosed tabernacles on immense beams, carried by a great lot of rather hilarious fellows. Many had a bit more sake in them than they could handle, and I noticed as I went back by streetcar to my hotel that the path of the god was pretty well strewn with unconscious devotees.

Motoori Norinaga (1730–1801). His contention was that Shintō, when purged of all foreign accretions and influences, represented the pure, and therefore the best, inheritance of humanity from the divine ages.

Another aspect of the revival of Shintō was *the appearance of popular teachers in the first half of the nineteenth century*. Their followers today make up the so-called Shintō sects. There are two forms of Shintō:

1) *Jinsha Shintō* (Shrine Shintō), also known (up to 1945) as "National Shintō Faith," "State Shintō," and "Official Cult." The *jinsha* (shrines) belonging to this form of Shintō were maintained at the expense of the central or prefectural governments, city, town or village authorities. With the promulgation of the Religion Corporation Ordinance of December 1945, however, official support of these shrines was abolished, and all the *jinsha* are now maintained chiefly by their respective believers. As of December 1949 there were 87,802 *jinsha* belonging to this National form of Shintō.

2) Sectarian or Denominated Shintō, consisting of about 160 sects. Some of the oldest of these are Fusō-Kyō, Izumo Taisha-Kyō, Konkō-Kyō, Kurozumi-Kyō, Misogi-Kyō, Mitake-Kyō, Shintō Tai-Kyō, Shinri-Kyō, Shinshū-Kyō, Shintō Jikkō-Kyō, Shintō Shūsei-Kyō, Taisei-Kyō, and Tenri-Kyō. [I must hunt for some explanation of these.]

Worship in Shintō consists of obeisances, offerings, and prayers. Obeisance takes the form of a humble bow which lasts for a minute or two. The *offerings* presented before the altar are primarily food and drink. Formerly cloth was offered, but eventually *a symbolic offering known as gohei* or *nusa* came into use, consisting of strips of paper which represent lengths of cloth. These symbolic offerings are attached to a wand or twig of the evergreen *sakaki* tree and placed before the altar. [This is what I saw at the Shintō shrine in Nara.] The presentation of offerings regularly follows the formal *norito prayers,* which

When I arrived at Eidmann's I found a Japanese gentleman present, who was introduced to me as Professor Kasugai.[86] Eidmann made an appointment for me for tomorrow, to be shown through the great Chion-in Temple (which we merely skirted yesterday) by Professor Kasugai. The conversation, first with Kasugai and then with Eidmann alone (for Kasugai left us after we had seen the Shintō procession), made, among others, the following points:

The Buddhist iconography of India is extremely uncertain. It is even possible that there is not a single image that can be identified with absolute certainty. The Hindus, who know very little about the subject, and the Europeans, who know little more, have been very glib with their identifications; but when one compares the Japanese Buddhist iconography with that of Ajaṇṭā, etc., the sense of certainty fades. For example, at Ajaṇṭā one sees continually three figures: a Buddha seated in the center with deer below his pedestal, and with a Bodhisattva at either hand, one with a Buddha figure as his crest jewel and the other with a *stūpa*. These have been

---

appeal to the deity by virtue of vivid expression of address. *Great stress is laid on the formality of the prayers rather than their contents.* To make them impressive the words were originally the most solemn that Japanese possessed. *Norito* prayers are uttered not only in front of the shrine altar, but also within a sacred precinct, on a river bank, or in the home.

Purification is essential before worship, and is achieved by three principal methods: exorcism (*harai*), cleaning (*misogi*), and abstention (*imi*). Exorcism is performed by presenting offerings, after which the priest waves over the person to be purified the above mentioned *gohei* or *nusa* wand and pronounces a formula of purification. [This too I saw in Nara: the priest appeared for a moment before the meditating young women and waved his *gohei*.] The misogi is a cleansing rite for the removal of accidental defilement acquired by contact with unclean things, such as might be caused by death or disease. It is effected by ablutions, usually by the mere sprinkling of water and salt. Near the oratory of the shrine on the left side of the pathway, there usually stands a font at which the worshipers wash their hands before worship. *Imi,* or abstention, is a method of acquiring a positive purity by avoidance of the source of pollution. It was the duty rather of priests than of laymen to practice the necessary austerities, which consist chiefly in the observance of certain prohibitions.

Formerly Shintō priests scarcely ever performed the funeral service, the dead being given over to the care of Buddhism, but now Shintō funeral services have become quite common. On the other hand marriages until recent years were never celebrated with religious rites, whether Buddhist or Shintō. Now it is fashionable to have the wedding ceremony performed at a Shintō shrine.

identified as Gautama in the Deer Park preaching the first sermon, Avalokiteśvara, and Maitreya[87]—but such a trio does not constitute an accepted trinity. When Avalokiteśvara appears at the side of a Buddha, the Bodhisattva at the other side is Amitābha (Kannon and Amida in Japan). The whole subject has to be reviewed very carefully from this, the Japanese, end—with the Chinese caves as intermediate monuments. Nara, Honan, and Ajaṇṭā-Elūrā are about contemporary.

Rev. Phillip Eidmann and Prof. Shin'ya Kasugai

I was surprised and unsettled by this discussion, but not convinced. When asked what the symbol of Gautama flanked by the two Bodhisattvas, Maitreya and Avalokiteśvara, might symbolize, I suggested that the two great Bodhisattvas of the later Mahāyāna might be there to symbolize the content or import of the doctrine—as a kind of apologia for the Mahāyāna addition of such figures to the Theravāda teaching. My two friends were surprised and could not deny the possibility, but suggested that such an interpretation was probably too Western. The Mahāyāna, they thought, did not feel the need to justify itself. I brought up the justification implicit in the legend of Nāgārjuna and the Nāgas—but this only led us, by a little jump, to questioning how much we knew about Nāgārjuna, of whose actual writings absolutely nothing remains.[88]

I asked what the attitude of Buddhist sectarians was to the Buddhas and Bodhisattvas not included in their sectarian cult. Shinshū, for example, pays worship only to Amida. The answers were a bit confused and indecisive. It seems the problem is not much considered. In one sect, I was told (but I've forgotten which) the devotee selects his personal Bodhisattva by tossing a pellet onto a sheet of Bodhisattva names.

A couple of interesting items came out about Tibet and Japan. Apparently in the Noh dramas there occur a few words that could not be understood until they were recognized, rather recently, as Tibetan. Apparently, also, the *vajra*[89] is used in the Shingon school rites. Tantra is hush-hush in Japan. Apparently it was here, but no one will talk of it.

The Nishi Honganji is strongly unfriendly to Shintō. However, until this year, the men in the fox-god Inari's procession were allowed to slake their thirst at the Honganji gate; that, in fact, is why they stop here. This year some of the patrons of the temple pointed out the inconsistency in this custom, and, for the first time, the water was refused. Eidmann expected a bit of trouble of some kind, but nothing happened.

After the procession and before my departure Eidmann showed me something about the Japanese technique of handling Chinese in their writing—numbering the signs in a Japanese order but writing them on the page in a Chinese sequence; also, using a Chinese ideograph sequence as a single noun (somewhat in the way of a Sanskrit agglutinated term).[90]

When I got back to the hotel I found a couple of letters from Jean and another anniversary telegram, forwarded from Tokyo. Among other nice things, she tells me that *The Art of Indian Asia* has finally arrived.[91] Nice anniversary event.[92]

I went to Suehiro's for dinner and spent the evening at my diary.

Saturday, May 7

At 10:30 A.M. Professor Kasugai arrived, to take me on a wonderful visit to the Chion-in Temple.

The atmosphere in the cloister area (a handsome wooden cloister: the first in wood that I have ever seen) was closer to what I remember from the monk world of India than anything I have yet found in Japan (the nuns reminded me, rather, of New York). Kasugai and I were in that part of the temple compound at 11:15, when a group of young monks were standing in two rows, chanting *Namu Amida-butsu,* while waiting for the abbot to appear in his red robe. The abbot appeared, preceded by an older monk and followed by another who was in a robe of blue, and the younger group then followed the abbot past us to the main temple, where we later found them in a service of noonday worship which was attended by a small lay company as well. Such services take place in the morning and evening also. But I must say, as the young monks passed me one by one, they did not seem to me to be the smartest looking young men that I've seen in Japan.

The buildings of this great temple are magnificent: the *sammon* (two-storied gate), the *hondō* (main hall), the assembly hall ("hall of one thousand mats"), and the inner apartments. Kasugai and I had lunch in a lovely room of the latter area, sitting on the mat floor, Japanese style (it took me five minutes to get the blood back into my legs) with a handsome picture of Amida (Central Asian manner) hanging on the wall. We then visited the belfry (the bell was cast in 1638, the largest of its kind in Japan: 17.9 feet high, 8.9 feet in diameter, 9.5 inches thick, 74 shot tons). We ascended also to the gardens and ridges higher up, where there were graveyards and other buildings.

Everywhere I turned, everywhere we went, there were beautiful gardens—and part of the charm were the anecdotes about this stone and that, this and that lantern, that Kasugai was able to recount as we walked around. Comparable anecdotes go along with the bowls of the tea ceremony, and, no doubt, with many more of the cherished objects in Japan.

During the course of our visit to the Chion-in grounds, we came to a little Shintō shrine on the Chion-in estate. "It is bad that we have this here," said Kasugai. It is a cute little shrine, with two white fox figures sitting with lifted tails at either side of the central object on the little altar. When we turned away, there approached and passed us, on their way to the shrine, two women, apparently from the Gion geisha quarter (which is not far away). "You see," said Kasugai, "that is the type that comes here to worship the White-Tailed Fox-God."[93]

After having conducted me through the Chion-in Temple estate, Kasugai brought me to his home for a look at his library. I met his little girl and boy, and his pleasant little wife, who served us tea and cakes while we talked about books.

Kasugai has a theory that the first form of Buddhism to enter China was the Hīnayāna (Sarvastivādin, Vinaya, and Agama Śastra) via the Northern Caravan trail through the Gobi area; that the Mahāyāna (Śunyatavādin) then came through the southern route; and that a third period (Gandhavyuha and Saddharma Pundarīka) is represented by the works in Chinese Turkestan patronized by the medieval traders.

We looked at some pictures of the carvings in the Chinese cave temples at Longmen, Honan, which date from the fifth to seventh centuries A.D., and discussed a little the fact that Ajaṇṭā, Honan, and Nara are about contemporary.[94] The close connections suggest that medieval Buddhism should be studied from the standpoint of the Japanese sects, some of which continue the medieval traditions without change.

We looked at some handsome pictures of the now-destroyed (in 1949) Hōryūji frescoes. Here Amida is a prominent figure, flanked on his proper right by Mahāsthamaprapta (as Padmāpami, with a jewel as the crest jewel of his tiara: Mahāsthamaprapta is Seishi in Japan, and personified religious energy[95]) and on his proper left by Avalokiteśvara (holding a sort of boat hook in his hand, with an image of the Buddha as the crest jewel of his tiara; his Japanese name is Kannon, who personifies the quality of mercy: Kuan-yin is patroness of seamen and merchants in China: Kannon (compassion) is in all things—an Indian motif). These frescoes are dated A.D. 708, and they include a glorious, seated figure of the Bodhisattva Suryaprabha, with a lovely red lotus in his left hand. Compare all this with the Indian tendency (which I am afraid I followed too easily in *The Art of Indian Asia*) to find Avalokiteśvara wherever the lotus is held in the hand.[96]

Kasugai led me next (about 3:00 P.M.) to the Seiren-in Temple (Blue Lotus Temple), where there is a charming garden of the hill garden type. This temple is of the Tendai sect, I believe (founded by Dengyō Daishi, ca. A.D. 800), and on one of the altars we found a *vajra* and *vajra* bell,[97] which Kasugai said were characteristic of the Shingon sect (Kōbō Daishi, also ca. A.D. 800).[98]

My final event with Kasugai was a visit to the Heian Shrine and garden; after which we parted with great bows.

I spent all evening writing up my diary.

CHAPTER V

UNIMPEDED

KYOTO AND NARA

Sunday, May 8 *Kyoto*

A remarkable and very fruitful day. Went around to Eidmann's at 10:00
A.M., to meet and talk with Professor Takamine,[99] the leading Kegon
scholar of Japan, and left at about 9:00 P.M. Takamine left at about 1:00
P.M., but Kasugai arrived just then and remained through tea. Then
Eidmann coaxed me to stay through dinner, and finally brought in a
masseur to massage my ankle again. The conversation ran largely along the
themes of Buddhist philosophy.

Discussing Eidmann's translation of and commentary on *The Tractate
of the Golden Lion,* I opened the affair by asking the meaning of the following sentence:

"In the Perfected Mahāyāna (i.e. Kegon), everything, every speck of dust
even, can be seen as conditioned arising. Thus even in a hair there are innumerable golden lions." I asked how the second sentence followed from the first.

We were sitting on the floor, around the low table that covers
Eidmann's legs, Takamine in the place of honor, with his back to the kakemono[100] and facing Eidmann, I at Eidmann's right, and the secretary at

Eidmann's left. The secretary and I had our pens and notepaper ready for news. Takamine spoke in Japanese, the secretary—under correction from Eidmann—translated, and I put my next question.

The first question was answered with the help of an apt diagram that Eidmann gave in his paper, where he distinguished between the *ri-ji-muge* doctrine and the *ji-ji-muge* doctrine:

Ri-ji-muge distinguished from *ji-ji-muge*

Ri stands for Reason, Principle, Noumenon, or Absolute.
Ji stands for the particular, phenomena, the objects of the universe.
Muge means unimpeded, undivided.

Ri-ji-muge means that the Noumenon and Phenomenon, the realm of the Absolute and that of Life and Death are identical: undivided, unimpeded. In this school, however, one *thing* equals another only indirectly, i.e., only because the two things are both identical with the one transcending *ri* and not because of their own essence. The Kegon school declares that this doctrine is not that of the true immanence of the Universal Buddha.

Ji-ji-muge means, literally, "Phenomenon-Phenomenon-Undivided," or more freely, the direct identity in essence of all phenomena.

While *ri-ji-muge* causes us to seek for the Buddha in the mind, the *ji-ji-muge* concept causes us to look for the Universal Buddha in the body. Following out the former idea, the flesh is regarded as a shackle imprisoning the enquiring spirit, so that by retiring from the world one should reduce it to proper submission and thereby obtain enlightenment. With the *ji-ji-muge* school, however, illumination can be found only through perfecting the flesh by bringing out its latent potentialities, and thereby uncovering the Buddha hidden in the human heart.

I summed up the dichotomy by saying that *ri-ji-muge* is the *Way of Sitting* and *ji-ji-muge* the *Way of Moving in the World,* and both Eidmann and Takamine accepted this as OK. The two views arise from, and rationalize, these two attitudes, which might be termed the alternate bridges to a transcendent realization where the distinctions implied in the metaphysical argument disappear.[101] (Compare the reply of Ānanda Mayī to my query about renunciation and affirmation.)[102]

Takamine made the point, however, that simply moving in the world is not enough—moving in the world mechanically; for in that case one is aware only of the *ji* and *ji* as separate from each other. *In order to experience the* ji-ji-muge *two things are necessary:*

a. Compassion (*karuṇā: jihi*)
b. The Vow (of Bodhisattvahood, *praṇidhana: gan*); here we have, apparently, the main formula of Kegon

Haru, Eidmann's secretary, summed up the stages of the shift of perspective from the mechanical to the enlightened view, as follows: "Seeing a thing, one realizes, first, that 'no thing exists'; that is the negative side: simultaneously, however, the postive side must be realized, namely, that 'that is *tathatā*.'"

In sum, to use the Indian terms: we have here the way of *neti neti* and that of *iti iti*.[103] The particular point about Kegon is that it follows the way of *iti iti* with Compassion (*karuṇā: jihi*) and the Vow (*praṇidhana: gan*) as its "effective means."

According to Takamine, in Kegon, religious practice cannot be separated from life: all work and viewing is practice. In the Kegon communities there are annual short retreats; but these are not very different in purpose from the retreats for laymen in the Catholic Church. They are not the means through which enlightenment is attained. They are, rather, interludes of thought and quiet consideration.

It is to be noted that this idea of the normal life task and path as "practice" is precisely what, in Zen (as presented by Suzuki), has seemed to me to be the most important thing about Zen. We shall come to the problem of Zen in a moment.

According to Eidmann, Kegon is the fundamental doctrine of *all* truly Japanese Buddhism. All of the specifically Japanese sects may be characterized as manifestations or aspects of Kegon. Also, Japanese art developed largely out of Kegon. Jishū (the Kegon position) is the most influential, furthermore, in Japan today.

Zen, according to Takamine and Eidmann, originally had no Kegon. Its basic text was the Diamond *Sūtra* (indeed, there is a discussion as to which *sūtra* Bodhidharma handed to his disciples, the Diamond or the Lankavatāra). The doctrine of the Sixth Patriarch (Hui-neng: Enō) is based on *śunyatā*.[104]

Hui-neng's disciple's disciple's disciple (Ch'eng-ti: Chōkan) took in Kegon; from there on . . . but see Suzuki's article on Kegon and Zen in his series of *Essays in Zen*.[105] (The legend now appears that Bodhidharma's *sūtra* was really the Kegon *sūtra*.)

Among the ideas taken over by Zen from Kegon is that of all work and viewing as practice.

Japanese Zen has two main streams. Sōtō Zen follows the way of *ri-ji-muge*, meditation and monastic practice; Rinzai Zen follows the Kegon way of *ji-ji-muge*. Suzuki presents, principally, his interpretation of the Rinzai.

On either path (Sōto or Rinzai) Zen stresses practice—not philosophy. While practicing, one attains satori[106]—and here philosophy is again superfluous. From the standpoint of Zen, therefore, the distinction made philosophically between *ri-ji-muge* and *ji-ji-muge* is a quibble. On the other hand, from the standpoint of Kegon it would appear that in the Sōtō the way is that of *ri-ji-muge* while in the Rinzai it is *ji-ji-muge*.

Takamine left at about this point, and presently Eidmann and I were discussing the doctrine of the multiple bodies of the Buddha.* During this phase of the day, Kasugai dropped in (all dressed up in striped trousers— looking very neat and alert; for he had just come from a ceremony confirming the status of a new Zen master), and the conversation continued. The following are the main points:

The doctrine of the Three Bodies, which has been so greatly emphasized by scholars in the West, belongs to the *Prajñāpāramitā* teachings: it evaporates (Kasugai's word) after the period of the *Prajñāpāramitā Hṛdāya Sūtra*.[107]

The *Prajñāpāramitā* teaching played no role in the philosophical

---

* See the article "Busshin," on the bodies of the Buddha, in *Hōbōgirin*—an encyclopedia of Buddhism published by the French Institute in Tokyo: only three volumes have appeared: it is written in French, but the headings are in Japanese.

thinking of Japan, except in Hossō.[108] Dengyō knew the *Prajñāpāramitā Hṛdāya Sūtra,* and wrote commentaries, but his followers of the Tendai sect used only the commentaries.

Zen is the closest of the truly Japanese sects to the three-body view of the *Prajñāpāramitā.* Shinshū (like Tibetan Buddhism) gives the Buddha seven bodies, classifying them as four with three subheadings. Tendai uses a four-body system, but in such a way that it resembles the Tibetan system of seven bodies. Nichiren is a two-body system. This is not the same, however, as that of the *Uttaratantraśastra.*[109] Shinran's two-body system is different from that of Nichiren: different also from his own four-body system. Still another two-body system is that of the Mahāsāṅghika.[110] In the *Sarvāstivādinśastra (Daibibasharon)*[111] a one-body system is offered. Systems have been built from one body (*ichi-shin*) to ten (*ji-shin*).[112]

It is a Western tendency to try to find connections and homologies between such things as these various theories of the bodies of the Buddha. In the Orient, on the other hand, such theorizing is eschewed. Best: *don't try to connect.* Nevertheless, an aid to the understanding of the Kegon conception of the infinite will be found in a study of the nineteenth-century work of Cantor on *The Infinite in Mathematics* (ca. 1880).[113] Kegon's infinite is comparable.

The Buddhism of the Yazunembutsu-shū is Kegon without the Pure Land *sūtras.* Its chief theme is "the interpenetrating name of the Buddha."

In Shinshū (Honganji) *ri* is *tariki* ("the other power") and *ji* is the individual. The two are united in "*the moment of the awakening of faith* (i.e. of realization)"; this realization being that of:

ichi soku issai	one is the same thing as everything
issai soku ichi	everything is the same thing as one

Shinshū is not *bhakti.* "The rituals of Shinshū have no meaning or aim; and that is their meaning."

Anecdote: A Christian lady saw a Buddhist praying. "What are you praying for?" "Nothing." "Whom are you praying to?" "No one." The lady moved away. The Buddhist got up and said to her: "And, Madam, there is no one praying." Compare the anecdote of Śaṅkara up a tree.[114]

Yet it can be said that Shinshū has an aim—a psychological aim. According to the *Dai-kyō (Sukhāvatī-vyuha)* the dual aim is: *anshin* (peace of mind), and *san shin ichi shin* (the realization that the three [essentials] are one); these three are: earnest thought, faith serene, and desire for *nirvāṇa*. Another and somewhat different statement of the aims will be found in the *Kan-gyō* (*Amitabha-jñāna Sūtra*), but at the time of our discussion this formula could not be recalled.

The distinguishing characteristic of the attitude of one who has attained the Awakening of Faith and lives in it is: *gratefulness to the world—to the tea, the teacup, the table, everything—which has made and makes existence and enlightenment possible.* This idea of religion as gratefulness has permeated Japan.

There do exist in the Shinshū community true *myōkōnin:* those who have attained the awakening of faith and live in it.

In Zen there are today but five recognized masters—including the one recognized in the ceremony that Kasugai had just attended. One is of the Sōtō sect; the others are Rinzai. Two are about fifty-two years old (including the one celebrated today); the others range around eighty.

The attitude of the Jōdo sect approaches that of *bhakti* (in contrast to Shinshū). There are ceremonies of a sort that resemble certain "sealing ceremonies" of the Mormons, which confirm or dedicate the individual. (I did not understand this phase of the discussion at all.) Kasugai (a member of the Jōdo sect) could not say that there were any members of the community now "living in the Buddha knowledge." "The members of the sect do not live in the Buddha knowledge; but they die in it." (I *think* I caught this correctly.)

The monks of the Jōdo sect (but not the nuns) are, for the most part, married. What the sense is of a married monk is a bit obscure: so much so, indeed, that there is no word in Japanese that can be applied to the wife of a monk. This circumstance is the result of history: Japanese laws vs. monasticism. And effort is about to be made, however, to repair the situation: young men are to be sent to Thailand, to follow the path of the true *bhikkhus*.

The difference between the Hīnayāna and the Mahāyāna was formulated by Eidmann as follows:

The aim of the Hīnayāna is to achieve egolessness through realizing that the self is egoless: the self is the Buddha; whereas, the aim of the Mahāyāna is to achieve egolessness through realizing that the universe is egoless: the Universe is the Buddha: and I am egoless by participation. The Hīnayāna can be said, therefore, to be psychological and the Mahāyāna metaphysical in stress; yet the end (egolessness) is the same.

Shinshū returns in aim to the psychological position, while preserving the vocabulary of metaphysics. See the point above about the psychological aim of Shinshū.[115] Zen remains metaphysical.

Problem of the antiquity of the Bodhisattva doctrine. The Buddha taught the prior existence of Buddhas; in one place seven, in another twenty-five, in another, many. Problem: whence did he derive this idea? Compare the *tirthankaras* of the Jains. What was the relationship of Buddha's belief about himself to the doctrines of his Jain rival Mahāvīra? Can we say, that, like reincarnation, we have here a basic Indian archetype which the teachers automatically accept and then rerender according to their diverse modes of realization?

Big jump: it is Kasugai's view that gold was not known in India before the time of Aśoka. Problem: the gold amulet of Lauriya-Nandangarh.

Another jump: the publicized Rangoon congress of Buddhists actually is two congresses:

    a. A completely unimportant meeting of the World Fellowship of Buddhists, which meets regularly, every two years—with such vague aims and effects as their name would suggest; and

    b. A three-year conference, now in progress, concerned with reediting the scriptures—and this one is very important.[116]

Finally we jumped to an example of Zen in the Noh drama: Beatrice Lane Suzuki, *Noh Gaku* (Wisdom of the East Series), last play, *Yuki* ("The Snow").[117]

Monday, May 9

Up at six to prepare my Japanese language lesson for today, and language class from nine to twelve. All afternoon bringing this, now very complicated, diary up to date.

I have a couple of points to make now of my own.[118]

The May 2 edition of *Time* reports on page thirty-six the inaugural lecture of Professor C. S. Lewis[119] as Professor of Medieval and Renaissance English Literature at Cambridge University, from which I lift the following:

"...whereas all history was for our ancestors divided into two periods, the pre-Christian and the Christian...for us it falls into three...the pre-Christian, the Christian, and what may reasonably be called the post-Christian....It appears to me that the second change is even more radical than the first. Christians and Pagans had much more in common with each other than either has with a post-Christian. The gap between those who worship and those who do not..." In politics, art, and religion, the old frames have been shattered.

But the biggest change of all is that born of machines. "How has it come about, that we use the highly emotive word 'stagnation,' with all its malodorous and malarial overtones, for what other ages would have called 'permanence'?...I submit that what has imposed this climate of opinion so firmly on the human mind is *a new archetypal image* [italics mine]. It is the image of old machines being superseded by new and better ones....Our assumption is *that everything is provisional and soon to be superseded* [italics again mine], *that the attainment of goods we have never yet had, rather than the defense and conservation of those we have already, is the cardinal business of life,* would most shock and bewilder [our ancestors]....I conclude that it really is the greatest change in the history of Western Man...."

This, precisely, is one of the ideas that has been most forcefully represented to me by the experiences of my voyage of this year.

The fundamental idea of Buddhism, namely, "All is without a self," would seem to me to go along very well with the idea of the discarded machines (though not, indeed, with that of striving for goods we have never yet had). There is, in fact, a good deal about both Buddhism and Hinduism that can easily appear to a Westerner (and certainly did to me, in the sweet long ago) as though it were exactly what he needed. However, the attitude of worship or piety in the Orient is totally different from anything that the post-Christian can properly use. Moreover, the Oriental doctrines are all mixed up with such problems as that represented by the Buddhist examination and confirmation of *arhats* and the Hindu proclivity to *samādhi*. It now seems to me best to leave these doctrines exactly where they are—namely, in the Orient—and to initiate the next Western step from a completely Western position. Comparisons being odious, as I have noted above,[120] let's not even use the Oriental words. Clues may be taken from the East (or from anywhere), but let's not then try to read our own reactions back into the Oriental context.

All of this implies great warnings and danger signals for me in the work ahead on my *Basic Mythologies of Mankind*.[121]

1. Beginning from the beginning, I am to follow motifs objectively and historically. Also, I am to record interpretations objectively and historically, on the basis of contemporary texts.

2. As a contemporary Occidental faced with Occidental and contemporary psychological problems, I am to admit and even celebrate (in Spengler's manner) the relativity of my historical view to my own neurosis (Rorschach formula).

3. The historical milestone represented is that of the recognition of the actual unity of human culture (the diffusion and parallelism of myths) together with the relativity of the *mores* of any given region to geographical and historical circumstance (Bastian, Sumner, Childe). The time has come for a global, rather than provincial, history of the images of thought.

4. The moral object of the book is to find for Western Man (specifically, the post-Christian Occidental) suggestions for the furtherance of his psychological opus through a transformation of unconscious into conscious symbols, a confrontation of these with the consciously accepted terms of the present period, and a dialogue of mutual criticism. This, however, is to be the minor aim, subordinated strictly to 3.

5. Make no great cross-cultural leaps, and even within a given culture, do not try to harmonize what the philosophers of that culture itself have not harmonized. Stick to the historical perspective and all will emerge of itself.

As for the problems of the young Orientals of today—Asia for the Asians: let them work them out for themselves. They will solve their problems, I think, by imitating in their own several ways our problems, and so in serving ourselves we shall serve the world.

I am finding, by the way, that my present residence and work in Japan is, somehow, helping me to assimilate the shock of India. A couple of interesting contrasts are to be noted:

1. In India, 80 percent illiterate, and the literate classes largely Anglicised, the Orient survived primarily on the folk level, in folk terms, and in a squalid condition.

2. In Japan, 90 percent literate, and this literate class fundamentally Oriental still—in spite of the miraculous grasp of the machine—one experiences the Orient in a more elegant style, in quite good form, and with its spirit still noble.

3. In India it was possible, because of the general knowledge of English, to

penetrate quickly into the Indian sphere—leaving Occidentals behind. But the penetration was into rotten wood, as it were; and it was not easy to find where the wood was still sound. In Japan, on the other hand, where very few speak English, and those few not well, one does not come quickly *into* the Japanese sphere; yet one comes immediately *against* it, and one can feel the wood. Fortunately, with Eidmann to help, I am finding some cracks that are letting me way in (the nuns, Kasugai's home, Takamine's conversation). But I can actually feel Japan as the living Orient every time I step into the street; and the Noh and Kabuki experiences were already at least as impressive as anything encountered during my first several months in India—indeed, up to the time of Ahmedabad (save for the four days in Orissa).

But halt! It is now 10:30 P.M., and I have still to prepare for tomorrow's class.

Tuesday, May 10

Up at 6:00 A.M. to resume preparations for the class. Japanese from nine to noon, then a visit to the Daimaru Department Store, to recover my light meter which I left there last week for repair; then lunch in a nearby restaurant, and back to my room, to study Japanese. At 5:00 P.M. I went to the Nishi Honganji compound for a "Mongolian" dinner (a sort of sukiyaki) and chat with Eidmann. Our range of subjects, as usual, was wide.

Gate 1

The lanterns in Japanese gardens: are they originally Japanese, or were they brought from the mainland? Such lanterns are not Chinese (and yet it seems to me that I saw two in porcelain at the Chion-in Temple). Those found in Korea may well have been brought from Japan, but in Manchuria one lone stone lantern has been found, which is a kind of enigma. Also, the torii before the Shintō shrines are probably not derived

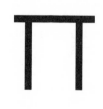

Gate 2

from the Buddhist Sāñcī-type of gate, but an independent invention. The gate before the Chinese Buddhist temples, on the other hand, with straight uprights, is probably from India.

The cultural activities of the U.N. and UNESCO in the Orient are strongly slanted toward a propagandizing, and even enforcement, of Occidental moral values; e.g. the propaganda against polygamy. In the face of this pressure the Pakistani and Indonesian premiers are to be commended for having dared to take second wives.

There is a very strong run of Communism in the universities of Japan. This was greatly furthered by the Occupation, which expelled up to one-third of the members of the faculties as Fascists (the work of our lovely Fifth Amendment boys,[122] no doubt, whose great cause, when they themselves are called to the bench, is Academic Freedom). One university in Kyoto is completely and openly Communist today, namely Ritsumei University. The Christian Dōshisha University is very strongly Communist and is prominent in all Communist-style student agitations. There the students even participated in the election of the president of the university (a length to which our Harold's enthusiasm for student participation in the business of the college perhaps would not extend).[123] The Japanese do not have a tradition of open argument and debate, but the Communist groups are trained and geared for precisely that, and so, always win out in direct confrontations. The Japanese are using more devious methods, therefore, to combat them, and are gradually regaining ground. For example: a Communist-run committee called for an all-college meeting to be held at 1:00 P.M. The professors, to allow plenty of time for the meeting, called off all classes for that day after 9:00 A.M. Result: practically no one on hand for the meeting.

My own guess, from what Eidmann told me, is that the Communists in the universities of Japan are about where they were in those of the U.S.A. during the late thirties and early forties—perhaps even a bit ahead of that point.

America's handling of the hundreds of students now coming from Asia is, on the whole, very bad. There is no professional direction given to their studies: practically none of their advisors knows anything about the cultures from which they come; people who *do* know such things (and there *are* such people in our country: they could be found if an honest effort were made to discover them) are never consulted. Why is it that a large percentage of the intellectual leaders of the Communist movement in the Oriental countries were trained in American colleges. And why is it that those trained in Russia do not have comparable reactions against their teacher but become, in the main, ardent Communists?

We had a couple of pretty little cakes that looked like tiny money bags, made by a man who is the sole possessor of the secret formula, which has been handed down from father to eldest son. These cakes are made particularly for the Cake God, the God of Cakes, who has been brought from India. Nuns cover their eyes when they approach his shrine. He holds his consort on his lap, and he has an elephant's head—undoubtedly Ganeśa;[124] perhaps in a Tantric form. I'd like to know a bit more.

Resuming our discussion of Shinshū Buddhism, I learned:

1. That the Shinshū term for the gratitude to the world and everything in it that is coextensive with the Awakening of Faith is *hōnō kansha.*
2. That Shinshū does not regard Amida as a concrete, anthropomorphic person, or his realm as an actual place: Amida and his Realm are described as an "apparitional body and realm, which appear as a result of practice." (This is in contrast to the belief represented in the *Amirabha-jñāna Sūtra,* where it is said that one, by practice, develops an eye that really sees an actual Buddha and Buddha Realm. *I* wonder, however, whether the language of the *sūtra* may not be metaphorical, after all. In any case, Eidmann assures me that in Shinshū there is no question at all of anthropomorphic, concretistic superstition.)
3. The *practice* recommended by Shinshū is primarily that of listening to sermons and talks. The Shinshū clergy are the best lecturers in Japan. Small teaching groups are favored. One is to listen to sermons—not seeking for enlightenment, but just sitting and listening. Listening and practicing the attitude of Gratitude (*hōnō kansha*) are the Shinshū Way.
4. We can know nothing, absolutely nothing; all that can be said is but a *stepping-stone* (not a direct path, but a stepping-stone). The closest we can come to the absolute is the name and title *Namu Amida-butsu,* which arises with the instant of faith.
5. In Shinshū homes there are no images; only words—tablets usually written by the patriarch, who writes some one or two hundred every morning. The statues of Amida in the temples are an innovation of about three hundred years ago.
6. One who has attained the Awakening of Faith and lives in it is known as a *myōkōnin.*

The U.S.I.S. could do a good work by sending books to the universities of Japan—not the government universities (these already have an excessive grip on the educational situation), nor the Christian universities (for these are already pretty well taken care of), but the numerous private universities throughout the country, whose libraries are in a pitiful state. Any book would certainly be read a hundredfold.

In selecting students from Japan to educate, why choose those who will never have any influence? In Japan, family position is decisive. It is known now (with perhaps a 10 percent margin of error) who will be influential twenty years from now. The others, inevitably, will return to disappear. The democratic approach is fine, but the realistic is effective.

When I arrived Eidmann was tutoring the little son of the patriarch of the Honganji, who will himself be the patriarch—and consequently, one of the most influential men in Japan—in a few decades. I dare say Eidmann's effect will be greater than that of many of the millions now being poured into Fulbright, Ford, and Rockefeller aids—and he is working without any U.S. aid at all. Compare the situation in Ahmedabad, where the Sarabhais (like the Honganji patriarch here) are the ones who are doing the best work in bringing the most appropriate people from America to India—at least in the cultural sphere.

Wednesday, May 11

Up at 6:00 A.M. again for my Japanese. Class from 9:00 to 12:00.

The hotel is full, today, of musicians—members of the company of the NBC Symphony that is now touring Japan, to vast acclaim. I was sitting in the lounge, reading *Time* for this week, when Eidmann's friend Fillmore appeared. He was waiting for a member of the symphony orchestra. We sat and talked, and presently the member appeared: behold, George Graber, Jean's fat drummer. Greetings—and could we have dinner together tonight? Why, sure! Had I heard the symphony? I did not say that I had not come to Japan to listen to a New York orchestra, but simply: "No, I'm sorry, I missed it!"

All afternoon on my Japanese.

Graber phoned at seven, and we went, together with a young army chap named Smith, to Suehiro's, for a nice steak dinner. Home by 9:30 to catch up on the mail, and at midnight to bed.

Thursday, May 12

Due to a mix-up at the phone desk, Graber, in room 611, got my 6:00 A.M. call and I, in room 711, his 7:15 call. Breakfast with Graber and off to school. He and all the rest of the symphony are enormously impressed by Japan and the Japanese audiences and hope to return. "Apparently the audiences for American art are all outside of the United States," said he.

In class I feel that I've begun to leave my classmate a bit in the rear.

When I returned to the hotel I found a wire from Dorothy Riggs,[125] to say that she would be arriving this evening for a three-day visit to Kyoto. It's a bit wet, however: not the best weather for visits to Kyoto and Nara. I spent the afternoon on Japanese and mail. At last, I'm catching up.

I find in a little article written by Eidmann, the following classification of the Buddhist schools:

Hīnayāna
1. Permanent *ātman* schools (*Vātsiputriyas*)
2. "Things but no *ātman*" (*Qavastivādins*)
3. "Void of *ātman* and past and present *dharmas*" (*Mahāsāṅghika*)
4. "Void are *ātman* and conventional *dharmas*" (*Prajñāptivādins*)
5. "Transcendental *dharmas* are real" (*Lokottaravādins*)
6. "Things only words and names" (*Yahavarika*)

Mahāyāna
7. Emptiness (*Śunatāvāda*)
8. *Tathatā* real but not things (*Lankavatāra Sūtra* and *vādins*) (Awakening of Faith)
9. *Tathatā* beyond description (*Vimalikirti Sūtra*)
10. *Dharmalōka* (Kegon)

The Chinese founder of Kegon systematized the schools as follows:

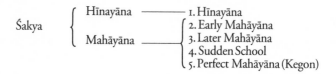

Śakya
Hīnayāna ———— 1. Hīnayāna
Mahāyāna ———— 2. Early Mahāyāna
3. Later Mahāyāna
4. Sudden School
5. Perfect Mahāyāna (Kegon)

Diagram of Hīnayāna and Mahāyāna

Shinran, according to Eidmann, differentiates Hīnayāna and Mahāyāna as follows, in his *Gutoku's Notes:*[126] Mahāyāna teaches the Bodhisattva ideal (the "Great Career") and Hīnayāna the *arhat* (the "Smaller Career"). Eidmann points out, however, that the Theravādins encourage those who are suited to it to follow the Bodhisattva ideal (cf. Bhikkhu Narada Thera's *The Bodhisattva Ideal.*[127]) According to Eidmann, the real difference is that the Hīnayāna is psychological and the Mahāyāna metaphysical:

"Hīnayāna is concerned with states of mind. The *Abhidharma* of the Pali canon[128] is almost entirely occupied with the analysis of the states of mind of man. The whole body of Pāli scriptures is chiefly concerned with the arising and destruction of states of mind, and religious emancipation is attained by realizing [that] these states of mind are without ego. The inner awakening to the emptiness and voidity of states of mind brings the individual saint to the state of *nirvāṇa*. . . .

"Mahāyāna, on the other hand, . . . concerns itself with the ultimate emptiness of the whole universe. Mahāyāna schools seek to destroy the ego by realizing [that] the whole universe is empty and void, and therefore [that] the individual ego also is devoid of any underlying eternal substance. . . .

"Zen, which is sometimes said to be psychological, on closer examination is found to be entirely metaphysical, in that it is not concerned with states of mind, but with the underlying emptiness of the universe.

"Shinshū [on the other hand], is primarily psychological. Its chief concern is with the passions and the states of mind in which *nirvāṇa* can be attained."[129]

These two ways, briefly, are those announced in the *Dṛg-dṛsya-viveka:* the subjective and the objective ways to *nirvāṇa;* and I think that they are quite well summarized in the formula, *way* of the *arhat,* and *way* of the Bodhisattva—as referring not to the activity of the Enlightened, once enlightened, but to the way proposed for the attainment of Enlightenment.

Dorothy arrived at 9:30 P.M., after having managed to get herself somewhat lost on the way from the airfield in Osaka to the Kyoto Hotel. I took her down to the Grill for dinner, then out for a walk through the shopping section southwest of the hotel.

Friday, May 13

Japanese class from nine to noon; then met Dorothy for lunch, and a sightseeing expedition to the Imperial Palace, the Heian Shrine and garden, the Chion-in Temple, the Higashi Honganji Temple, and, finally, Eidmann's dwelling in the Nishi Honganji compound. Eidmann was a very cordial host indeed; had us stay to dinner, and put on a handsome tea ceremony for Dorothy after it was over. She has been in Japan, with the army, for some nine months: had never had a Japanese meal before; had never seen a tea ceremony; had never been inside of a temple or shrine. Back to the hotel, really tired, at about eleven.

Saturday, May 14   *Kyoto—Nara—Kyoto*

The Five-Storied Pagoda at Nara

8:45 A.M. train to Nara. Visits to the Five-Storied Pagoda, Deer Park, Kasuga Shrine, Tōdaiji Temple and belfry; lunch at the Nara Hotel; then back to the station, after another pause at the Five-Storied Pagoda.

In Kyoto by 3:00 P.M. A bit of shopping; performance of the geisha dances at the Kamogawa Theater (my second view of this performance: viewed now from balcony front row—much better than last time: in this balcony, one removes one's shoes and sits on the floor). More shopping after the theater, then dinner at Suehiro's and—dead tired—early to bed.

Sunday, May 15

Breakfast at nine. Then out to take photographs of the Aoi Matsuri procession,* which came right past the hotel. A large tour of Americans had arrived at the hotel to see this procession, and we were such a spectacle

---

* According to a newspaper article, the Aoi-Matsuri Procession (Hollyhock Festival) dates back to Emperor Kimmei (509–71), when crops were seriously damaged by a spell of bad weather. A diviner declared that the deities of the Kamo Shrine had been offended, so the emperor ordered the people to appease them by offering branches of hollyhock. Thereafter the weather improved. In the Heian Period (781–1185) the festival came to be very color-fully observed at the imperial command. Due to a civil war (Ōnin no Ran) it was sus-pended (1467–77, the war), and it was not resumed until 1694. From 1868 to 1885 it was again suspended—then again for some of the mid- and postwar years.

taking photos from a high perch on the hotel fence, that the Japanese were busier photographing us then watching the procession.

The *kebiishi* (mounted) and four *kado-no-osa*

The procession is led by a pair of heralds; next come four police sergeants (*kado-no-osa*) in light brown; next a mounted judicial chief junior (*kebiishi*) in deep blue and a pair of fire masters (*hi-no-osa*) in pink; another *kebiishi*, of higher rank, in vermilion, with another pair of fire masters and some attendants in white bearing spears and bows; next the governor of Kyoto Prefecture in scarlet, mounted and attended; then a big flower canopy (*hanagasa*) and three coffers ornamented with sacred paper strips (*gohei*); a pair of mounted *kuratsukai,* and two racehorses, a mounted official of the Horse Affairs Board, and a lacquered court carriage drawn by an ox come next; another ox follows the cart (the *kae-ushi,* or spare ox); a pair of attendants in pink bear a stringed instrument and six court dancers follow on horseback; the mounted imperial envoy in black and a spare horse come next and seven attendants (*beijū*) on horseback, in purple; a mounted senior chamberlain bears the imperial message that is to be read at the shrine, and at the end come the great hollyhock bouquets.

The procession starts from the Imperial Palace at 9:00 or so and passes the hotel at 10:00. At 11:00 it reaches the Shimogamo Shrine, which is in the Tadasu-no-Mori, "Query Grove." The chief priest greets the procession and leads the imperial envoy into the shrine court. The officials take their seats.

The envoy reads the imperial message; the priest reads a divine message, and hands the envoy a small branch of hollyhock, which he then sticks in his crown. The *meryōtsukai* leads two horses twice around the building, the *beijū* sings a song called "Suruga-no-Uta," "Song of Suruga Province," the court dancers perform a dance called "Suruga-no-Mai," or "Dance of Suruga Province," and out on the racetrack in the grove the two horses gallop.

The procession then proceeds to the Kamigamo Shrine, where the same ceremony is repeated. At about 6:00 P.M., the procession returns to the palace.

After viewing and photographing the procession, I accompanied Dorothy to Osaka and put her on her plane bus, returning to the hotel by about three. The brief view of Osaka was quite impressive—another large and wonderful city, about thirty-five minutes by fast electric train from Kyoto.

In my room, for the rest of the day, I studied Japanese, wrote up my diary, and penned a couple of letters—feeling that I had done something to repay Dan Campbell and Dorothy for the vast introduction they had given me to Tokyo six weeks ago.

The return visits to the palace, etc. and Nara were interesting and pleasant, and from the guide at the palace I learned one new thing, namely, that the three sacred treasures of the realm are: the Jewel (= Benevolence); the Mirror (= Cleanliness); and the Sword (= Courage). One might say that these are actually the dominant virtues and ideals of the Japanese. It is evident, also, that they are symbols known also to Buddhism, with, however, a slightly different reading in that context.

Monday, May 16

Up at six, to study Japanese, and from 9:00 to 12:00 in class; then home, to study until about 3:30 P.M., when I went around to Eidmann's. Found two gents present, an oldish Mr. Mosser, who is living in the Kyoto Hotel and is touring the world with a lot of letters of commendation from American politicians, and a younger, Mr. Gold, who hopes to study in Japan when he leaves the army. After their departure, I remained for supper, which included a breaded whale cutlet that I guessed was either veal or chicken. Liked it very much—and was told that it is the cheapest and least respected meat in Japan.

A couple of points and a plan emerged from our discussion:

What has seemed to me to be a quicker adjustment here than in India to the Western style of male-female relationship is not quite what I thought it to be, yet is closer, even so, than the Indian to the West. The young men and women whom I have seen tête-à-tête in the coffee shops are not young people on the loose or on the search, but either young married people, getting away from the family for a while, or engaged people, whose engagements have been largely arranged by their families. According to Eidmann, when the family intends a marriage, the young people are allowed a first impression of each other (a sort of one-look situation), and then, after they are formally engaged, they may go out together. And the young married people, he tells me, are more numerous than I supposed: some 50 percent or so of the university students are married. Even so, the situation is closer to the Western than the Indian, where heterosexual life, either before or after marriage, hardly exists. The Japanese, retaining their own pattern, could behave in a manner resembling the American, and apparently do so: perhaps this accounts for the less emphatic moralizing resistance and more natural ease of these people in our Western forms.

It occurred to me in the light of all this that in Japan it is largely "the people," and not the aristocracy, that I am seeing in the Western mode. It is probable that the upper classes are holding more strictly to the traditional patterns. But in Europe they hold to a traditional pattern also in their marriages. This "American" pattern is actually a vulgar, popular one. But in India the "people," that is to say, those who are not of the three top castes, have hardly come into their own: they are illiterate and dwell in mud huts. The castes, like the aristocracy here and in Europe, are holding to tradition.

Eidmann pointed out that Buddhism is a religion that has been particularly favored by the merchant classes in the Orient—both in India and in the Far East. I suggested that the universalist—as opposed to vertical-traditional—character of Buddhism might be partly a cause of this circumstance; for the merchants are the ones who travel, whereas the priests and the nobles have their vested interest, so to say, in the local scene. (I think there is a good point here.) Did the universalism of Buddhism inhere in the Buddha's own teaching, or is it something that developed later. (Compare Christ and Pauline Christianity.) Is Aśoka the Universalist?

We discussed the matter of superstition and concretistic anthropomorphism in religion. How many Buddhist priests believe, when they engage, for example, in a spring rite, that their prayers or magic actually affect the weather. Catholic priests certainly think, when they pray for rain or boons, that there is an actual personal God who hears their prayers and might do something about it. Undoubtedly, this level of belief exists in Buddhism too. But when the Kegon priest dips water from a well in order to bring rain: "the all is in the atom," "the ocean is in the drop," etc. "in a single hair is an infinitude of lions"—where are we?

Eidmann feels that of the Buddhist sects, Tendai and Shingon are the most superstitious; that Zen, too, has a lot of magic and hocus-pocus; and that Jōdo's worship is very close to *bhakti*. He was willing to admit also that even in Shinshū there might well be many who, in spite of all the sermons, thought of and prayed to the Buddha as an actual person.

About my studies of Buddhism and Japanese; Eidmann made a number of fine suggestions. First, he felt I should continue at the language school, but commence study of kanji right away.[130]

He also suggested that I begin learning the *sūtras* by heart in Japanese: written in kanji, they are an excellent introduction to the chief characters in the Buddhist tradition

I had another massage for my feet and legs, which are in pretty bad shape after all this walking (Achilles' tendons; sprain still swollen; cramps from Ace bandage; all at once), and I returned home at about eleven to commence my reading with kanji:

Kanji characters = small, river, person

Tuesday, May 17

An item in this morning's paper on a meeting of the International Chamber of Commerce in Tokyo: much talk about the poverty of Asia and the need for civilization to take account of this fact if it is to prosper. The great problem: average per capita income (1949) in the world $230 per annum: in Africa $75, and in Asia $50.

OK. But the forgotten point is this: that Asia has not contributed and cannot contribute a single helpful technological or political thought to the contemporary world. All it has, apparently, are raw materials, which are of value only because they function in the context of an Occidentally invented and -furthered technology. Europe and the U.S.A. are contributing hundreds and thousands of new inventions a year (medical and agricultural included): the Orient, however? Nothing.[131]

At noon, after my Japanese class, I went downtown to have my visa extended to August 31. I had to have three pictures, so I went to a photographer and though the picture isn't great, it at least is human—which is *news* for Joe Campbell. No trouble getting the extension and—(amazement!)—no payment necessary. Then I went for a haircut and since I could not direct my barber in Japanese had to submit to what happened. I found that when a Japanese has a shave the entire face, forehead and all, is shaved. I saved my forehead, but that was all: besides, I didn't ask for the shave; it just followed the haircut before I realized what was up.

Returning home at about 3:30, worked a bit on my Japanese and diary before setting off at 6:15 for a dinner party to which Ellen Psaty invited me last week. The other guest was the new director of the U.S. Cultural Center in Kyoto, the city that is the cultural center of Japan: and he is one who knows nothing about Japanese culture (and confesses it), and very little about American. He doesn't like Japanese food or Japanese tea; he hopes that a simple, natural, American, person-to-person approach will win the hearts of the Japanese; he questions the "sincerity" of Japanese courtesy; he objects to the slowness and lack of initiative of his Japanese staff—and is generally an archetype of the wrong man in the right place.

Wednesday, May 18

Up at six; class until noon; lunch at the hotel; a bit of Japanese study, and then off to meet Ellen Psaty and her interpreter at the Municipal Modern Art Gallery, where there is a huge exhibition of Kyoto paintings. As in India, the gouaches are better than the oils. The first galleries that we visited were exclusively gouaches, and it seemed to me that they showed such similarities to each other that four-fifths of the works might have been by the same artist. Definitely, the artists were skillful and had taste. There was a consistent clarity of design and color, a firmly maintained aesthetic interest, subdued dramatic values, a predominance of nature and city sub-jects—few, but elegant (though un-"psychological") portraits: a number of really lovely realizations. I was told that this style was an intentional "museum" style, for exhibitions of this kind, in the European manner, and that to see what the same artists were *really* doing I should have to go to their studios, where they were painting for *Japanese* homes and environs.

We proceeded to the oils—and here (as in the oils in India) the imita-tion of the West seemed not to have been assimilated so well: the parodies were outright, unashamed, and with no suggestion of a Japanese con-sciousness, system of values, atmosphere, or line of interest. Still worse was the sculptural exhibition, where there were nothing but studio nudes, por-trait heads, a few nonobjective organizations, and a single little piece of original effort and inspiration. I was disappointed also in the ceramics and screens, and, of course, could not understand at all the rooms of cal-ligraphy.

We were joined by one of the museum directors, who conducted us next to a small building in the Reizei-dōri area—the "oldest, smallest, and dirtiest" art studio and academy in Japan: built in the 1890s by an Italian, the site from which Occidental art spread out through Japan. The director showed us the two rooms, in one of which two young women, students, were doing charcoal sketches from plaster casts, in the good old Occidental way: the other room was full of easels bearing the pictures of a standing nude. We sat and talked for a while, then took a trolley to our several des-tinations.

I had dinner at Suehiro's and, arriving in the hotel at about 6:30, sat down in the lobby to read the *Life* article on Indian religion, in which I had had a hand last spring[132]—when along came the gentleman named Mosser, whom I had met at Eidmann's, and we chatted about travel till about eight. Then up to my room to study Japanese.

Thursday, May 19

Up at six—school till noon. Downtown then to fetch from the customs office an air-mailed copy of my final Zimmer opus, *The Art of Indian Asia*. I was distinctly disappointed in the quality of the reproductions: the proofs were better, I thought—or perhaps it was simply that the margins here were too narrow, while the great two-page spreads fell apart in the gutters. Anyhow—the ordeal is far behind me and the book leaves me feeling that I'm glad I'm heading now for something of my own.[133]

I studied Japanese, and after dinner paid a visit to Eidmann. He tells me that in Japanese Buddhist meditation the aim is not trance—*samādhi*—but repose of spirit. Trance is somewhat suspect; but nevertheless in Noh, the actors often go into trance and perform in that state. Tea masters sometimes perform in trance—these trances, apparently, are one or two steps beyond the "inspired trance or state" of the performing and functioning artist or athlete in the West.

On television, these days, the sumō championship now being held in Tokyo is being shown. I've seen two sessions. Eidmann tells me that sumō originally was connected with ritual—and certainly the whole atmosphere suggests a rite. The announcements are made in a manner suggesting Noh. The wrestlers' tossing of salt and sipping of water have ritual moods. And the final swinging of the bow suggests ritual too.

Fillmore is studying calligraphy with the brush, and the effects here resemble those announced in *Zen in the Art of Archery:*[134] it is all one grand continuum.

Eidmann gave me a couple of books to help me commence my study of kanji and a nice little translation that he has made of the *Sutra of the Teachings Left by the Buddha.*[135]

Friday, May 20

Up at six. School. Studied kanji and reviewed my class lessons till about five. Sumō on TV in the hotel lobby (a couple of quite wild falls) and a tempura dinner in the hotel, then back to my Japanese. Mosser dropped into my room for a chat from about 7:00 to 8:30. To bed at 1:00 A.M.

CHAPTER VI

TEA AND FIRE

Saturday, May 21

To Eidmann's at 9:30, just in time to arrive at the start of a tea ceremony, with Yamauchi himself, the leading tea master in Japan, sitting in the place of honor, and a little old lady of eighty-six—Eidmann's teacher—in the place at the door. I was given place two, and made a mistake at the outset by crossing thither directly, instead of going around everybody's back— but no one said anything and I had a nice time watching the master and little old lady, as well as Haru (Eidmann's secretary), who made a couple of mistakes—he told me later—while conducting the affair.

We went next for a little stroll through the temple grounds—greatly crowded in honor of the festival of Shinran's birthday: the neighboring streets, too, were decorated, and many of the store and house windows contained little scenes, depicting episodes from the legend of Shinran's life. Airplanes flew low overhead scattering paper lotus petals, and the crowds were enormous.

We next returned to Eidmann's house for a pleasant lunch and then set off for the Noh theater in the temple compound—where there was a lovely crowd to see the Noh plays. We, however, took our departure after the opening few minutes of the first play, and, pausing briefly, to watch a group of college students practicing sumō, proceeded to a temple of the Shinran sect—westward of the Nishi Honganji—to see a *goma* (from Sanskrit *hōma*) festival conducted by *yamabushi* ("mountain hermits"), which turned out to be one of the really great experiences of the year.

The temple is the Fudō-dō Myō-ō-in and was originally built (it is said) in the ninth century in what then was the palace area. Kōbō Daishi is supposed to have brought to it Buddha statues from China, which, at the time of the civil wars, were buried in the ground beneath the temple, where they are supposed to be to this day. The Buddha image now worshipped in the temple is supposed to have been made by Kōbō Daishi.

The temple is closely associated with a Shintō shrine, and the two, indeed, are so closely mixed that one cannot tell where the Buddhism ends and the Shintō begins. While we were waiting for Haru to make arrangements at the temple for us to attend the ceremony, a large car pulled up and a Shintō priest stepped out in full regalia. Where he went, after entering the precincts, I do not know. Also to be seen were a couple of young Buddhist monks, wearing (which is unusual in Japan) a yellow-robe-like element over the normal black habit: suggesting the worlds of Thailand, Burma, and Ceylon.

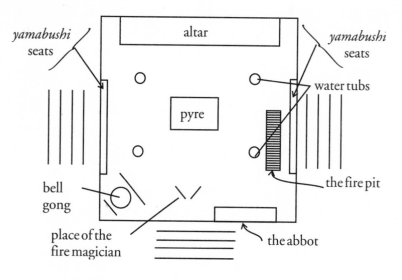

Yamabushi ceremony setup

We arrived good and early for the ceremony and were given seats on the front row benches facing the altar. There was a large, square, roped-off area before us, with a big, square pyre in the middle, covered with evergreen boughs. Beyond that was an altar, the length of one side of the area, set with offerings: cakes, oranges, etc., all neatly stacked. At each corner of the area was a large wooden tub of water with a long-handled scoop—to be used on the fire. And in the corner at our right was a large bell-gong set on a table.

The *yamabushi* arrive

At about 4:30 P.M. the *yamabushi* arrived—in their fantastic costumes. They had been on a procession through certain parts of the town. This curious order of monk-magicians is said to have appeared in the eighth century, as a protest against the governmental control of the Buddhist religion (comparable in a way, I should say, to the hermit movement in Christendom after the rule of Constantine).[136] Refusing the usual ordinations by the government, they retired to the mountains and lived as holy hermits, and, like the friars of later Europe, were responsible for spreading the religion among the common people. Buddhism in Japan before their time had been largely an aristocratic affair. Moreover, they were strongly influenced by the seventh century Tantric lore and principles (compare Zimmer's discussion of Borobudur[137]).

It is most remarkable that in the *goma* fire sacrifice that we were about to witness, elements of the Brahmanical *soma* sacrifice, as well as of the much later Tantric Buddhism of the great medieval period, were synthesized, and colored, moreover, with a tincture of Shintō. Hanging around the sacred area were strings bearing the jagged paper offerings characteristic of Shintō—not white however, but colored.

The arrival of the *yamabushi* was heralded by a blowing of conchs; they entered the area, after passing behind us, from the lower right-hand corner, and then circumambulated the pyre.

Next, they stood in two rows before the altar, and, beating time with the jingles of the staffs and batons in their right hands, chanted, ensemble, the *Prajñāpāramitā Hṛdāya Sūtra*. This finished, they went and settled on the seats prepared for them at the two sides of the area. The abbot in his robe came to our side and sat facing the altar. And another, very nice gentleman, who was a kind of second abbot, came and thanked us for being present.

In a moment, another, smaller group of *yamabushi* arrived and were ceremoniously challenged at the entrance by two *yamabushi* guardians. In a kind of Noh play dialogue they were asked a lot of test questions—imitating the procedure of more ancient days, when strangers coming to

Shooting an arrow into the air

yamabushi sacrifices and rites were actually challenged, to prove that they were not fakers and frauds. In the dialogue, the newcomers, through their leaders, were asked the meaning of the term *yamabushi* and the reason for each of the elements of the costume. The replies were given with great force—as though an actual battle were taking place; and in the end, when they had proven themselves, the new group was admitted and allowed to sit with the rest, after ceremonially circumambulating the pyre, and praying before the altar.

The next great event was performed by a little *yamabushi* who had arrived a good deal earlier than the others and while we were waiting had sat alone inside the area. Haru and another young Japanese with us had conversed with him over the ropes. He now got up, with a long bow and a sheaf of arrows, and at each of the corners pretended to shoot an arrow into the air (in the forest, he would have let it go, but here in the city, he finally released the arrows gently at his feet).

Next, another *yamabushi* got up with a sword, and, after praying before the pyre, waved it at the pyre, and then returned to his seat.

The abbot then stood before the pyre and read a *sūtra* from a piece of paper which then was tucked into the pyre. The nice gentleman who had greeted us did the same. And then the stage was ready for the great event.

It began with two *yamabushi*, bearing long, flaming faggots, one at either side of the pyre, reaching in, low, and setting the pyre aflame. It went up with a great belch of smoke, which billowed heavily to the left (our left) and completely engulfed the *yamabushi*. Since I was taking pictures, I was glad that the breeze leaned in that direction—though the air seemed, actually, quite still. Rather soon, that side of the area cleared and the smoke curved around back of the pyre and over to the right, and then, rapidly, it engulfed our part of the area: remaining, however, only for a moment, it was, presently, back where it had been at the start. It was a terrific mass of smoke, full of sparks and blazing fragments, and when it came around our way again it burned a couple of neat little holes in my blue dacron suit—which has been my chief suit throughout this journey. There was a great chant in progress that reminded me more of the noise of the Navahos than anything I've ever heard, and the general atmosphere was a bit exciting. One of the young men inside the area came over and said something to Haru, who then pointed out to me a *yamabushi* who was sitting about

The *yamabushi* making the smoke go round

eight feet off my starboard bow. "That's the one," he said, "who is making the smoke go round." I looked, and I suddenly realized what I was witnessing. The chant was filling all the air. The smoke, definitely, was circulating in the clockwise direction...

...and this *yamabushi,* with an attendant beside him, sitting on his shins, was moving his hands, pushing, conjuring, and pulling, like a cowboy turning a steer with a rope—only the rope couldn't be seen. I was so surprised I felt a sudden thump inside me, and I began taking photos of this little man, like mad. Four *yamabushi* with water scoops, meanwhile, were dipping water onto the sides of the fire—ostensibly,

Clockwise swastika

to keep the flames under control, but perhaps also to give a bit of mechanical assistance to the magic.

After a while, when the smoke diminished and the flames increased, my *yamabushi* began, ceremonially, tossing little stacks of wooden tablets into the fire, on which the votive prayers of individuals in the congregation had been inscribed. There were hundreds of these little tablets, neatly stacked between the water tubs, in rows, like cords of wood. When the magician had begun this tossing, the other *yamabushi* in the area took it up—conjuring prayers into each packet as they held it in their hands and then giving it a toss into the flames. When all the packets had been thrown in, the pyre was pulled apart and the logs were dragged over to a pit on the right side of the area over which they were placed, as a kind of log lid. Beneath, the flaming coals and smaller wood then was shoveled, so that tongues of flame leapt up between the logs—and many of the people of the congregation, removing their getas and zōri, prepared to walk across. The nice gentleman who had welcomed us would be the first to go. The wizard was at one end of the pit conjuring a power to cure into the fire and cooling the flames; his assistant was at the other end, doing the same. And so, since I had seen, through his work on the smoke, that he was a true master of fire, I caught the fever and began to decide that I might walk across too.

I was wearing on my right ankle—the one that I had sprained at Angkor—an Ace bandage, which it took me a while to undo. This made me the last on the line, but the flames were still leaping up high between the logs—say some eight or ten inches. Two youngsters just in front of me dashed across as fast as they could, but I decided to take my time and see what it really was like to walk on a wizard's fire. My first step, with my right foot, was a bit timid, and a bit off to the side, where there were no leaping flames. But then I thought, "Well now, come on!" and seeing a nice fat flame right in front, I put my left foot down on top of it, squarely. Crackle! The hairs on the lower part of my leg were singed and a pleasant smell of singed hair went up all around me, but to my skin the flame was cool—actually cool. This gave me great courage, and I calmly completed my walk, strolling slowly and calmly right down the center of the road. Three more steps brought me to the end, and the hands of several *yamabushi* helped me off. I went back to our seats, and the two ladies in our party were gasping with amazement at what I had done. I went out to one of the water tubs to wash my feet and get into my socks and shoes—and it was only when I was putting on my right shoe that I noticed that the swelling in my ankle had gone down. All the pain had disappeared too. Around the remains of the fire in the center of the area a lot of the little old women were standing who had gone over the fire, holding their hands out to the burning cinders and then rubbing their poor, aching backs—dear souls. It had certainly been a great and wonderful event. The courteous gentleman was greatly pleased that I had participated and invited us all to come back some day. We gathered our things, and presently strolled away.

We strolled back to the neighborhood of the Nishi Honganji Temple, where we looked again at the shop displays and then bade good-bye to the two ladies who had been with us. I was a bit high from all the excitement, and so, returned to Eidmann's for dinner and an hour's talk, before returning home.

A detail from the history of the American military Occupation of Japan: The Taishō University library was taken over by the U.S. Army (no Christian university in Japan was thus treated) and in the clearing of the rooms the card file of a Sanskrit-Japanese dictionary, on which 1,000 scholars had been working for some twenty years, were simply dumped. The Japanese hysterically sent crews to rescue what they could and many (perhaps most) of the cards were recovered: but a vast task still remains of classifying these thousands of mixed up items again. No funds are available for the work and it remains undone.

Besides dumping the cards the military gentlemen stole a number of rare and very valuable books. (This would seem to indicate, by the way, that not all of them were utterly ignorant of what they were doing.)

Sunday, May 22   *Kyoto—Nara—Hōrinji—Kyoto*

At 8:30 my Japanese student friend, Hisashi Mita, arrived at the hotel and we started off for Nara and Hōrinji. A magnificent day.

Stop one was at Nishinokyō, where we visited the Tōshōdaiji and Yakushiji Temples. The chief images in the first were made of japan and cloth and were large and handsome. The chief of these was of Kanshitsu. At his proper right was a Senju Kannon. The guardian to the right carried a *vajra*. Off to the left side, against another wall, was a large wooden statue of the *Ādi* Buddha with his hands in the *lingam-yoni mudrā*. We left this building (the *kondō*, or main hall) and strolled around the beautiful grounds; then entered the *kōdō*, or lecture hall, where some more fine images are preserved—among them a figure of Fudō Myō-ō—and I suddenly realized the sense of the rites in which I had participated yesterday. Fudō Myō-ō, whose name means "very still, even in fire" (according to Hisashi Mita), is a red figure sitting in a fire, with the red flames up behind him, as a kind of backing; his left eye is closed (as though gone: cf. Wotan) and his right is open.[138]

We remained an hour in this temple area and then walked to the neighboring Yakushiji Temple, where there was a lovely three-storied pagoda, and, within the main hall, three beautiful bronzes—a beautiful Kannon, and two standing Bodhisattvas, Gakkō (Moon) and Nikkō (Sun).

We returned to the station and took the train on to Tsutsui, where we changed for a bus that took us to the neighborhood of Hōrinji, which we reached about 1:00 P.M. We had a bowl of rice in a roadside restaurant and then walked on to the temple—one of the great experiences of the year. Lots of photographing: many beautiful images, including a glorious, very tall and gaunt Kannon (the so-called "Kudara Kannon," a gift from Korea in the Asuka period), and the Buddha trio illustrated in *The Art of Indian Asia*—to my shock, with the Bodhisattvas transposed—and, finally, that celebrated seated image of the world-contemplating Bodhisattva. All were beautifully exhibited, but the room of the last was usurped by a little class of students, listening to a young instructor spout such nonsense as "archaic smile," and "frontality."

Our next event was a little walk across country, to a pretty temple area called Hōryūji, where there was a charming little garden as well as some fine images, featuring Kannon. There were some *vajras* before the chief image. The temple had once been of the Shingon sect, but now is Hossō (according to the nice little lady who showed us around).

Our final walk was to the nearby Hokkiji Temple, prettily set in the country and with a small but handsome pagoda. We walked back to the road, under a slightly showery sky, past the peasants in their fields (one, a very handsome young woman wearing her makeup, but in peasant clothes), and caught the bus back to Tsutsui.

The train had trouble getting home, due to some failures in the electricity, but we arrived, finally, at seven, and, after a nice steak dinner at Suehiro's, voted it a wonderful day.

Special item: the rain was falling as we walked from Hokkiji Temple to the bus, but the sun was shining. "We call this in Japan," said Hisashi, "the marriage of the fox."

Monday, May 23　　　　　　　　　　　　　　　　　　　*Kyoto*

All day, Japanese. A letter from Jean, however, in which she reports on the trials and success of her production of her Saroyan play, as well as the sale of Abu (1938–1955)[139] and purchase of a new car. Had dinner at a pleasant Chinese restaurant, Hamamura, where I fell into conversation with a young American named Stoops, from California, who is working at the university and teaching. Like everyone else, he regarded the Fulbright group in Japan as a very poor lot.

Tuesday, May 24

All day, again, at Japanese. I am trying to get my hand in on kanji. The going is very tough. Went around to Eidmann's after dinner for a pleasant evening's chat. He suggested that, while in Japan, I should study tea, but somehow this didn't appeal to me very much. I think I'm just about jammed, now, as I am.

Wednesday, May 25

Another day of Japanese, and nothing but. Dinner tonight, and last evening, at a very good and reasonable restaurant called Fujiya, on the corner of Sanjō and Kawaramachi, right near the hotel.

Thursday, May 26

Still more Japanese. If this doesn't get me over the bump, I don't know what will! Dinner at another cheap restaurant, The Star, but not so good.

Friday, May 27

After my Japanese class, a long visit with Eidmann, from 2:00 to 10:30 P.M. I brought over my copy of *The Art of Indian Asia*, and we had a good deal of talk about the making of books. I am trying to stir him to write a history of Buddhism in Japan. He loaned me, some days ago, a nine-page paper on the history of Buddhism in Japan.[140]

Eidmann has mentioned also the fact that in Ceylon Buddhism is having to put up a fight to recover ground lost to the Christians during the period of British rule. Only some 2 percent of Ceylon is Christian, yet the Christians hold 50 percent of the radio time—and since most of the civil service group is Christian, they are not yielding.

One more point with respect to Japanese Buddhism—this time, in contrast to the Buddhism of Tibet. The chief period of continental influence in the Japanese tradition is that of fifth to eighth century Tantra—that of Tibet is the tenth to twelfth centuries, with its stress on the Yab-Yum motif.[141]

Going over *The Art of Indian Asia* with Eidmann and Haru, I became somewhat reconciled to the beauty of the book: which is certainly below the level of my expectations; but I had a few shocks as I went through the plates and text: a number of mistakes that I recognize—and a number of overly bold statements challenged by Eidmann and Haru.

Saturday, May 28

Japanese all morning, then with Eidmann and Haru to a delightful lecture on Nagasaki prints by the Dutch consul in Kobe, at the monthly meeting of the Kansai Asiatic Society. The prints and the lecture presented a pleasant and illuminating little view of the Dutch-Japanese interplay in the Nagasaki area from the seventeenth to the nineteenth centuries. The lecture itself was really elegant—urbane and charming; and while the gentleman talked, I had thoughts of my own about my problems when I return to New York. I want to hang on, as far as possible, to certain things that I have commenced here in Japan, and, at the same time, develop my own major work. My basic formula, worked out at the lecture, looks like this:

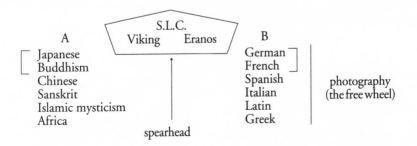

A Campbell plan for life

The approach to side A is to be through Japanese at first: Japanese language records, Vaccari's kanji, the Buddhist *sūtras* in Japanese, and modern Japanese scholarship.

The approach to side B is to be through a thoroughgoing refreshment of my European languages, commencing with German, which I now want to speak like a civilized man. Eidmann has given me some good suggestions for the refreshment of my Spanish and Latin.

My principal task at the outset, undoubtedly, will be my Sarah Lawrence class, where I shall have an opportunity to reexperience my whole experience of the present year in the light of my earlier thoughts and lectures on mythology.

My next task will be that of catching up with the Eranos series.[142] This will bring me back into the context of my *Basic Mythologies* plans.[143]

And my third problem will be, to get started as soon as possible on my first Viking contract—a book on mythology, which has already been slightly planned.[144] As soon as possible, I should begin to alternate my three-month stints on this book with those (to be commenced later) of my *Basic Mythologies*. I begin to feel, now, that I should not go to Europe next summer, but go on working diligently to get my writing and notes into gear.

Extremely important, however, is that times and plans should be arranged immediately on arrival in New York for the continuation of my Japanese, and then, as time permits, for a return to German and French, with a commencement, at some point, of Italian (for Ascona).[145]

And finally, let's see what can be done along the photography line.

Sunday, May 29

All morning writing letters. All afternoon and evening at work on my diary. At 11:15 P.M. I am precisely here. And I feel that I have now pretty well caught up to myself. I have a few more subjects for this journal, but they can wait until I have a bit of time: they have to do with my new thoughts about my own dawning point of view—in contrast to the Zimmer-Coomaraswamy matrix from which I now emerge; and about India and Japan; for I find that in Japan I have become reconciled to India—as Orient. Finally, about anti-U.S. elements in Asia, and why.

Monday, May 30

After a morning and early afternoon of Japanese, sent a letter off to Alan Watts[146] and read Eidmann's paper on the contrast of Shinshū and the *bhakti* of the Gītā. According to this little opus:

1. The Gītā distinguishes two eternal principles, ever distinct—the material body (including its psychic elements) and the immaterial soul, which is without qualities and inactive. (Problem here: Jain formula vs. Vedantic: actually, Vedanta is somewhat ambiguous, since it insists both on non-duality and on the primacy of *ātman:* perhaps another example of two-faced India wanting its "spirituality" both ways. Try to think this out.)

2. Shinshū and Theravāda Buddhism deny that man has any innate Buddha nature (*ānata*): Mahāyāna, however, though still professing *ānata,* has brought the soul in by the backdoor as "Buddha nature."

3. The Gītā teaches that the ignorant confuse body and *ātman,* imagining that it is their souls that suffer, but that the sage, distinguishing, is released.

4. Buddhist release comes in the recognition of the illusionary nature of the so-called soul substance denying both the concept of any innate Buddha nature and that of a permanent, pure, inactive soul. (I think Eidmann is here straining on a gnat. Coomaraswamy has pointed out that the *ātman* of Vedanta is not "soul"—not the soul that is denied by the Buddhist term *ānata.*)

5. The God of the Gītā is a personal God, who assumes incarnations to save the world of men. But the supreme form of God is revealed only as a rare act of grace (e.g. to Arjuna).

6. In Shinshū, the idea that God's (or Buddha's) true form can be seen is regarded as an apparitional concept. Moreover, *whatever good man does or ought to do is of purely social value; it has no bearing on his salvation.*

7. The Gītā teaches three main ways:
   a. That of knowledge (*sānkhya*)
   b. That of action (*yoga*)
   c. That of devotion (*bhakti*)
   It prefers the way of "indifference in action" (unselfish performance of duty), to that of knowledge and inaction.

8. The Shinshū concept of the two divisions of Buddhism is somewhat similar:
   a. The Entrance by the Holy Path (*shōdōmon*) and
   b. The Entrance by the Pure Realm (*jōdōmon*), i.e. by faith. (In Japanese Zen the concept is especially strong that somehow salvation comes by the performance of one's duty perfectly.) Shinshū insists, however, that any Buddha body seen in vision, which can be measured and depicted, is not the True Body of Buddhahood. Moreover, whereas the God of the Gītā is personal, Amida is defined in the *Topics for Discussion of Peace of Mind* (*anjin rondai*) as not a person.

9. *Karma* in the Gītā is due not to action itself, but to the desire underlying the action: acts performed without interest in their outcome have no binding

effect. In fact, it is not only wrong, but even impossible, to refrain from action: man must do his duty—which is not defined, yet accepted as a kind of categorical imperative.

10. *Karma* in Buddhism too is due not to action itself, but to the desire underlying the action. *Shinshū, however, finds no possibility of the ordinary person creating "barren karma"* (Theravāda term). Shinshū insists on the Kegon principle of conditioned arising: because man cannot free himself of his passions he suffers countless reincarnations, and he has within him no power to act unselfishly in life.

11. Devotion (*bhakti*), in the Gītā, brings man to Salvation. God is sometimes spoken of as intervening to bring his devotee to the goal; but in the main, it is through his own power that man advances in devotion.

12. In the Gītā, it is peculiarly important for man to fix his mind on God at the moment of death: indeed, the time of death is so important that the Gītā* declares that man attains salvation only if he dies at a favorable time with his mind fixed on God: waxing moon, and six months when the sun moves northward.

13. Some Buddhists, too, emphasize thinking about Buddha at the instant of death, *rinjū shōnen,* as the true cause of attainment; but Shinran rejects this theory, as well as all emphasis on auspicious times.

14. Faith in Shinshū is not the same as that of the Gītā. *Faith in Shin is an instant of perfect egolessness in which all self-confidence is surrendered.* This egolessness is not acquired by any internal power within the believer, but is *entirely due to the power of the main vow of Buddha.* (I should like to know what is meant by this last line—and whether the effective vow is the Buddha's or the devotee's.)[147]

Without quite realizing it, or knowing why, I seem to have undergone a considerable change of feeling with respect to India in the past few weeks. In the first place, with the immediate annoyances gone and some of the major shocks now taken for granted, I have begun to remember the majesty of the majestic things, the wonder of the wonderful, and the interest of the interesting. Going over *The Art of Indian Asia* the other evening with Eidmann, and seeing there the beautiful photographs of the beautiful things I had seen, I felt that all of my petty little quibbles were really petty.

Furthermore, finding in Japan much of the great Oriental past, which in India has been shattered, has given me an improved position from which

---

* Bhagavad Gītā, viii, 23–27.

to feel my way back into what once was there: what must once have inhabited those ruined shells that lie all around the land.

I don't know whether I've set this down already in my notes, but it seems to me now, that, whereas in India the upper classes have lost their Oriental character and are, for the most part, a lot of conceited fakers and confused jackanapes, in Japan it is the upper classes that have preserved their Oriental tradition; and, vice versa, in India it is the squalid illiterate lower castes that have preserved their Oriental character, whereas in Japan the lower classes—largely literate and decently groomed—are taking on the West in a big, fast, and wonderful way.

I have also new thoughts about my new thoughts, vis-à-vis the old thoughts that were inspired, largely, by Zimmer and Coomaraswamy.

A fresh approach to the Orient by way of Japan and Buddhism, on the one hand, and perhaps Persia and Islam on the other (Corbin's writings),[148] will break me decisively from the old position. My own view of India has discredited entirely, for me, Coomaraswamy's high tone about the caste system; and the mistakes of Zimmer that I had to correct while writing and that I have discovered since, have discredited for me, as a final attitude, the rather slapdash intuitivism of my dear master. I am now for a very careful, meticulous checking after all the lovely intuitions: we have got to have both, if we are going to have a book.

Tuesday, May 31

During my visit with Eidmann last Tuesday a number of interesting points emerged from the pleasantly rambling conversation, which was largely inspired by the marvels of the *yamabushi* magician. Fillmore was present, and was interested in the matter; and when he asked how it could be approached philologically, I suggested that a paper on the *philology of the words of power* would be fun: one should study the relationship of power words and divine languages (e.g. Sanskrit and Hebrew) to psychological principles. We spoke of Tantra, Kabbala, Ang, etc. Then we spoke of Purāṇic-Eddic connections, and of European witchcraft: all of these things should be approached afresh.

Eidmann declared that in Japan there were many definitely secret groups continuing some of the old mysteries: the *yamabushi* were an example. But there was also a kind of self-defense system (not sumō; not jūdō) which is taught only to elaborately and profusely recommended people of the highest character. In Tokyo an old Japanese gentleman sent two GIs who annoyed him into the moat at the Imperial Palace. The army became interested; but the old man would not teach.[149]

Eidmann mentioned also the attested miracles of the spies in ancient times: they could disappear, they could be invisible. Furthermore, on huge kites, they would ascend to look at the enemy camp (a connection here, perhaps, with the chatter in modern India about the "airplanes," etc. of "Vedic" times).[150]

Also discussed were the swordsmen (of whom there are still a few) who could pull a sword longer than their arm from its scabbard, cut off a head, and return the sword to its scabbard, so quickly that nothing of the act could be seen.

And finally, Eidmann declared that one of the reasons that the Christians were feared and suppressed in sixteenth-century Japan, was that their magicians were a particularly powerful lot.

In connection with the Purāṇic-Eddic discussion, Eidmann suggested a connection between Buddhism and the Eddas. I pointed to the Wotan-Śiva, Śiva-Buddha continuity as a possible explanation of an apparent influence; but now I think the connection (fifth to twelfth centuries A.D.!) may have been more direct. Consider the closed and the opened eye of the Fudō Myō-ō figure that I saw last week at the Tōshōdaiji Temple: the Bodhisattva "very still, even in fire."

Out of all this I drew the idea of a little work on *the actual mysteries of the Orient, which might be regarded as validation enough of the exaggerated legend of "the mysterious East."*

As for the contemporary East, some new facts and thoughts, worthy of note. In this morning's paper a letter from a troubled "foreigner," who found himself excluded from a number of eating places in Kyoto: one even exhibited a sign "Japanese Only." (In Patna I saw a sign on a hotel: "Hindus Only.") "As one who has traveled to almost all parts of the world," this letter writer writes, "nowhere before had I been so insulted or embarrassed.... Except in Communist-influenced areas, never before had I witnessed such an intense anti-foreign feeling. Discussing this saddening experience with other foreigners, both tourists and businessmen, I learned that almost all had encountered the same experience in various Japanese cities."

One could speak of the anti-foreign feelings that a Japanese might encounter in Tennessee or certain parts of California: but the point is that such feelings certainly do exist in Japan—as throughout the Orient.

An article in yesterday's paper mentioned and discussed the problem of slave girls in some of the harems of India. The problem has come to light in a number of specific cases: girls bought in childhood, forbidden to leave, tortured when reluctant, etc. Undoubtedly this phenomenon exists in India today—and if there is now an outcry against it, the cause of the outcry is the humanitarian influence from the West.

In general the crimes of the Orient are no less spectacular than those which American journalism spreads as news from the U.S.A. out all over the world. The Oriental journalists are not so efficient: they are content to fill their papers with American boilerplate (even Occidental jokes and cartoons, that can mean nothing at all to the Oriental). Result: America's fine reputation for crime, and a sanctimonious face on your Hindu "holier-than-thou" gentleman of absolute leisure.

In Japanese, we are now just halfway through the book. The term ends July 8—and I think I'll stick it out. My first plan was to spend about six weeks at this, and then push off for more touring; but June, I am told, is a month of sheer rain—and I'm learning much here in Kyoto. Another five weeks of this sort of thing won't do me a bit of harm.

Having caught up pretty well on my letters and diary, and having doubled the track on my classmate at school by learning the kanji as well as *rōmaji*[151] texts of our lessons (the regular plan of the school is to review the whole thing in kanji next term), I am beginning to feel that I may be getting some place in this deep dig, after all.

After class today I had lunch at Fujiya, and then studied and wrote in my diary till about six. Dinner at Fujiya (which is turning out to be my great standby—lunch for ¥150 and dinner for ¥300; total, about $1.35), and then to Eidmann's, where I found a young woman missionary named Mary Jones. The talk was around religion and I learned a few things:

1. Gandhi's introduction to the Gītā was in England, through a visit to a class or lecture of Annie Besant.[152] (We hear nothing of this in India today. The Ramakrishna monks are playing up the Ramakrishna connection.)

2. About 1917 Annie Besant had practically persuaded the Congress Party to accept England's terms for a free India. Gandhi moved in against her. Result: Besant's work occluded by the great Gandhi movement: all kinds of patriotic spirituality—and an India divided.

3. The first Shinshū patriarch is Nāgārjuna[153] and the second Vasubandhu.*[154]

4. Among the Christians of Japan is a very influential group known as the Mukyōkai (no church), who meet together and read the Bible, but belong to no congregation. Among them are such influential personages as Yanaihara, president of Tokyo University;[155] also his predecessor. Eidmann claims that the direction of their thought is toward Shinshū.

5. Eidmann feels that in Zen today there are very few who represent the true Zen teachings. In the old days, in such a temple as that of Kenninji there would have been some three hundred monks, with three or four attaining satori: today there are about twenty monks: and in all of Japan there are not more than five or six *rōshi*.[156]

6. Mary Jones promised to bring me a book, at school tomorrow, about modern Christianity. I told her about the argument I had in Madras with the people who had dropped the myth of the Fall and Redemption from Christianity, and she seemed to think that the book she was going to lend me would show me what it was all about.[157]

When Miss Jones left, at about 10:00, Eidmann told me of Professor Kasugai's reaction to *The Art of Indian Asia:* he was completely knocked out. "I would never have even dreamed of dreaming of such a book appearing in a dream." He is taking it to a meeting of top Japanese scholars in Tokyo today and believes that it will totally upset all their ideas of both American scholarship and the significance of the work that has been done on India in Japan. (Eidmann claims that the Japanese underestimate American scholarship because they mistranslate the English: they read the word *passions,* and their dictionaries give them *bonnō* instead of *netsujō*.)[158]

Professor Kasugai is going to have the Chion-in Temple treasury opened and exhibited to me: The last exhibition was last year, and the next should be some fifty years hence; but this is going to happen for me because of the wonder of my book. He is simply overwhelmed.

And well, so am I—by his wonderful response.

Two letters today from Bollingen. One from Vaun,[159] asking if I would like to accept an offer for a Spanish (Mexican) translation of *The Hero;*[160] the other from Bill McGuire,[161] stating that a paper edition of

---

* See Junjirō Takakusu, *The Essentials of Buddhist Philosophy* (Honolulu: University of Hawai'i Press, 1949), p. 12 for a view of the relationship of these to the older Buddhist sects.

The Hero is about to be launched. Both announce that the publication date of *The Art of Indian Asia* was May 23: the day after my trip to Hōrinji and the day of the arrival of Jean's letter announcing our new car.

Oh yes—last Thursday a cable from Harold Taylor announced that the college yearbook for this year had been dedicated to Horace Gregory, Alistair Reid,[162] and myself (the three absentees), and would I please cable my greetings at once to the graduates? So I guess I can say that the year is over—and the pull of the next job, next year, can already be felt. Apparently, we are going to be about four thousand dollars in the hole, Jean and I: so the main job apparently again, is going to be to rake in a good bit of cash. No doubt just what is needed to pull me out of my dreams.

Wednesday, June 1

A letter from Harold Taylor today, offering me a raise for next year and asking me to give the convocation address on September 30. So the college is now really pushing in. The opening day is September 21, thirteen days after the opening of Bard[163]—which should give me time enough to get a haircut and buy a new pair of shoes.

As soon as I hit New York, I must go to work on *Eranos,* make arrangements to carry on with *Japanese,* get in touch with Volkening,[164] and start work on the Viking presentation. That, I believe, is to be my first flight of tasks.

The second flight is to be connected with the opening of *Sarah Lawrence:* preparing my course and the convocation address.

Next, I must turn to the task of oiling up either *my German or my French* (perhaps, for Jean's sake, it would be well to commence with the French), and finally some way must be found to keep the game of *photography* going. Let us schedule it, tentatively, as follows:

> September 8–20: Japanese/Eranos/Volkening: commence work on the Viking presentation and book
> September 21–30: S.L.C. convocation address and class
> October 1–10: French (or German) and photography
> December 26–March 26: Commence work on *The Basic Mythologies*

At 4:30 today, after my usual morning at the Japanese language school and early afternoon of work in my room, I headed for the Heian Shrine, to meet Hisashi Mita at the entrance and attend a wonderfully interesting presentation of Noh plays on a temporary stage erected in the court. There were about five thousand people present: a wonderful audience. Three plays and one comedy were presented. The first I had already seen in Tokyo: in fact, it was the first Noh I had ever seen, *Arashiyama*—only, this time, a fantastic episode was added of a company of monkeys enacting Noh in monkey language. The audience loved it. A comedy came next; then the lovely Noh called *Izutsu,* "The Well," and finally an astonishing piece, *Shōzon,* in which duels were enacted in a sort of Kabuki style. It was a beautiful night with a lovely moon—just a month since that magnificent evening of the Festival of Ten Thousand Lights at Nara.

Thursday, June 2

All day on Japanese—with a couple of letters, one to Jean (we are running into a money problem), one to Harold Taylor (sending in my signed contract), and one to the Batteys (about Jean's teaching this summer at the Tokyo Cultural Center).

An idea for the opening of my Viking book:

"For then only do we know God truly," wrote the great Christian theologian, Saint Thomas Aquinas, "when we know that he far surpasses anything that man may say or think of God." The great saint and theologian then, in the remainder of his work, proceeded to analyze and characterize God, until that catastrophic morning, when he was saying mass, when... etc. (get a good reference for this anecdote).[165]

"..." (Give next a comparable quote from some Pawnee or Hottentot medicine man.)[166]

(And then:) This is the sense of the whole world of myth, as it blossoms from the mind bent on the knowledge of the transcendent and the manifestation of the ineffable.

Next: Christ's life, as the typical "Life of the Hero." To be followed by Jensen's rendition of the Celebes *dema* mythos.[167] After this, the Greek Alexandrian complex, and therewith the Hebrew formula of the Hero race. Bible and Babel should then be developed.

(An idea for my classes: have a wire recorder in the room and use the lectures then as bases for either a book or a series of short articles.[168])

Two long spans: (1) The Christian theme of God's love and the myth of Hainuwele; and (2) Zen in the Art of Archery and the wall paintings at Lascaux and Pêche Merle.

An important classification: mythology as

1. *Artha* } magic (Frazer)
2. *Kāma* }
3. *Dharma* } "religion" (Durkheim: Coomaraswamy)
4. *Mokṣa* }
5. Entertainment
   a) Folktale
   b) Literary ornament

Classification of mythology

Two poles of interpretation: (1) Literal, concretistic (popular—exoteric—extrovert); (2) Metaphorical, symbolical (elite—esoteric—introvert).

CHAPTER VII

SURPRISES AND TRANSFORMATIONS

Friday, June 3

Two months in Japan! And how full of surprises and transformations. And three more months ahead!

I've been reading the book about Christianity that Mary Jones spoke about and handed me after Japanese class. Title: *The Christian Faith,* by Nels Ferré, abbot professor of Christian theology, Andover Newton Theological School. Going through this work here in Japan, at the close of my year in the Orient, has made very vivid to me a very important point:

1. *The traits peculiar to Christianity are not:*
   Belief in God (*Īsvarā*)
   The doctrine of the Fall (*avidyā*)
   The Incarnation (*avatāra*)
   Redemption (*mokṣa*)
   Love and selflessness as redemptive (*karuṇā*)
   Heaven-Purgatory-Hell
   Judgment (Osiris)
   Progress toward the Kingdom of God (Zarathustra)
2. The traits peculiar to Christianity are:
   a. Finality of the Personality of God (Judaism)
   b. Old Testament plus New Testament as Word of God
   c. Old Testament Fall as severing man from God to such a degree that a

special New Testament revelation was required for redemption. Also, a vocabulary of Fall and Redemption

    d. Jesus of Nazareth as the unique revelation of God's New Testament (incarnation)

    e. B.C.-A.D. division of all time (historical rather than spiritual reading of symbols)

    f. The Church as the unique vehicle of Salvation

    g. Specific Christian inflection of traditional rites

3. Compare this (point-by-point) with the traits peculiar to Judaism analyzed by Steinberg:

    b. Old Testament as the unique Word of God

    c. This point receives less stress in Judaism than in Christianity

    d. The prophets

    e. Jew-Gentile distinction

    f. The ultimate justification of the Jewish race, who give the world its savior. The "Remnant"

    g. Specific Jewish inflection of traditional rites

Note in Ferré's account of the break with the Social Gospel that led to democracy and the Romantic that led to progressive education.[169] This honestly severs the tie-up that the Christians in Japan are trying to make between Christianity and democracy.

I must try, now, to find a good analysis of *Islam*.

At about 5:30 today I called for Ellen Psaty at her dwelling, was delightfully greeted by Obasan—who had liked my Japanese over the phone; and took her to the second evening of Noh up at the Heian Shrine. The crowd was even greater than last time. Two seats (very bad) had been saved for us by a young army couple named Poor, and we remained only through the first two plays: *Yashima* and *Hajitomi*—the latter, particularly fine, with its emergence of the Lady Yūgao from her bower. The long solo speech in *Yashima* (by Zeami) was most remarkable. Ellen tells me that in these Noh companies only the principals are professionals; the others are amateurs.

よし子

Japanese characters = "Yoshiko"

It was about 9:00 P.M. when we left—quite stiff and sore from the craning and sitting—and went for dinner to Suehiro's. Next we proceeded to a Japanese bar in the Pontochō: or Yoshiko. Two guitarists were tinkling away, the proprietress was chic and cordial, a gentleman arrived with three middle-aged geishas (these seem to me to be the most charming women in Japan!) and had a nice time on one glass of beer. In and out came other parties and finally an American couple, the girl looking a bit disgruntled and the pleasant, tall, and amusing gent having a good time testing his Japanese on the hostesses. It was a fine view of Japan's response to the Western manner of enjoying "night life." The man with his geishas went out as gaily as he came in. We had a couple of brandies and at 11:30 left.

Saturday, June 4

A wire this morning from Joe Lillard[170] suggesting that I should wire greetings to our Columbia class on its thirtieth reunion. Too late for a wire—and besides, why?

Spent the morning concluding my notes on Ferré and afternoon on my Japanese. At five I went around to Eidmann's for dinner and an evening's conversation.

Last evening at Suehiro's Ellen and I were asking each other what is so attractive to the Japanese (and Asians in general) about Communism.

My view: Asia resists the problems raised by individualism, the personal equation, etc., yet requires the machine. Communism offers a clue to a kind of Asian machine civilization.

Her view: The caste and social blockages are very strong. The paths open to graduates of Tokyo University are quite fixed; those to Kyoto grads are different; those to Doshyo[?][171] are far inferior, etc. etc. Communism promises a leveling of these barriers.

The other evening at the Gass Lump,[172] Hisashi said, rather cautiously, that the ideas of Communism had a great appeal to him. He was afraid, he said, of the "bad effects of competition." I described what seemed to me the good effects: but it's the same story as the one I encountered in India. Communism has become a kind of Asian dream.

And we agreed that the U.S.A. should not lean or hope to lean on Orientals, whose whole system of concepts and needs is so different from ours that the term "democracy" can hardly be experienced as a requirement.

Ellen spoke of several elegant young Japanese whom she has met who have studied in London, Paris, and America: they think it would be wonderful to visit India or Norway...thinking of the new Socialist style. And why are so many young of the wealthy, who live on pillows, enthusiasts for the Communist cause? Same reason, I guess, as at S.L.C.[173]—anti-Papa, plus slanted teaching.

An additional thought about the Christians: "Jung writes," says Ferré, "that the basic cure of much mental illness is religious in nature. But modern man is in search of something more than his racial, unconscious self. It is true that he must break the circle of his isolation and be reunited to the roots of his deeper self, but that self is what George Herbert Palman called the 'conjunct self.' In Royce's terms he can find it only in the 'beloved community.'"[174]

It is this proud notion that Christianity—the Christian community—is the only door through the absolute wall of "sin," that is the Christian message. Hence, a fundamental antagonism to (a) the psychological-pedagogical romanticism of such movements as that represented by Jung and progressive education, which seek to release the "image of God" that is in man as a competent force, (b) the Social Gospel of democracy, and (c) such true tolerance as that represented by the sentence in the Gītā: "By whatever path a man seek me, even so do I welcome him, for the paths men take from every side are mine."

Clearly, Christianity is opposed fundamentally and intrinsically to everything that I am working and living for: and for the modern world, I believe, with all of its faiths and traditions, Kṛṣṇa is a *much* better teacher and model than Christ.

Amen, then, to that.

The claim of Christianity to consideration as a world religion is refuted by its confining of the concept of redemption to the Christian community, which is but one community in the wide world. Kṛṣṇa's welcome is to all communities, whether of the present or of the past: with no totalitarian, imperialistic implication either; no claim or hope that Hinduism shall ultimately be the one religion of mankind.[175]

It is this universalism that may be said to constitute Hinduism's first claim to our consideration.

The second claim is its proof, through such selfless, released (i.e., redeemed) teachers as Ramakrishna, Ramanan, and Krishna Menon, that Man can be and has been released from his natural selfishness without the mediation of any messenger of Jesus Christ.

The fact that, against these claims, many modern (in fact, perhaps, most modern) Indians are besotted sectarians, superstitious, and careless of the well-being of their neighbors, is secondary. Just as Christianity has been born from the history and societies of the Mediterranean-Atlantic zone, so Hinduism from that of the Himalayas and the Vindhyas.

When I get home, instead of brooding on the inadequacies of the modern Indian transportation system, the hordes of beggars, and the conceited fakirs, I must keep my mind on this central truth; remember also, the beauty of the ancient temples; then think of the millennium of Islamic, Portuguese, French, and British wars, and be surprised that there is as much as there is of the ancient lore: indeed, it comes spouting from the mouth of everyone in the land—no matter what his actual life.

The other side is the political-economic, psychological crisis of the modern period. This I must always discuss with care and understanding—but never without remembering the force and actual threat of the anti-Americanism that I felt in every house.

My primary loyalty, now, is definitely to the West, which as I now see, is prodigiously the hope, as well as transformer, of the modern world. All other cultures are provincial—and they are facing, ten to a hundred or even five hundred years late, the tensions between the new and the old that have been—and are being—faced and resolved first in the West.

In every continent the claims of religion are being reduced: religious geography, astronomy, moral dogmatism, etc., are in full retreat before the scientific revelation; and the fundamentally religious function of "salvation/redemption/*bodhi* ('awakening')," as rendered variously in the various religions, now has to face the claims of the psychological schools, as well as the differing claims of each other. Finally, perhaps, the religion whose "myths" accord most properly with the needs recognized by psychology will be the one to survive—if any survives. And I should say, definitely that in this crisis Christianity (with its mortal sin and its one and only adequate redeemer) is out. The Gītā, as I realized very well in Ahmedabad, can not only support but can also supplement psychoanalysis, without bringing any antipathetic principle into play. Christianity cannot do this.

Christianity and Freud, by the way, have something important in common, inasmuch as for both, man's rational consciousness is absolutely sealed away from the unknown root of his soul. The Christian needs Christ's Minister and the Patient needs the Analyst. Jung, on the other hand, is more distinctly in the optimistic romantic tradition: pagan, one might say, as opposed to Judeo-Christian.

The chat tonight with Eidmann was very pleasant. Before going to see him I glanced at Henry van Straelen's "The Religion of Divine Wisdom, Japan's Most Powerful Religious Movement"[176] and learned of Tenrikyō, founded in 1838 by Miki Nakayama,[177] "in order that the true happy life and the real peace of the world might be realized and we all become brothers and sisters." "If we had mutual love among ourselves, this world of ours would be converted into a brighter and happier world," we read in one of the speeches of the present patriarch, Nakayama Shōzen. "The cause of all our troubles is our shortcomings in the love of humanity. Human beings today are driving themselves into a trap. Today we must love mankind as never before. This is our reason for introducing to the people of the world—the Religion of Heavenly Wisdom."[178]

The sect has "a few million believers, 14,200 churches with 80,000 preachers," and is constantly expanding. And I ask myself: what would Professor Ferré say of *this* religion of love? Might it not be "sufficient unto Salvation"? If not why not?

Eidmann showed me a book by Ferré, *The Sun and the Umbrella,* where it says: "Jesus never was or became God."[179] This is not an easy one to reconcile with the statements of the book by the same author that I have just read: we talked a bit about the confusion in modern Christian thinking. We discussed also the problem of *relationships between Buddhism and the early Christian tradition.* I mentioned the Vulture Peak–Mt. of Olives parallels, Peter and Ānanda, the pattern of the Sage with his followers; Eidmann mentioned the problem of the Essenes as possible Buddhists and the probable Buddhist influence on Ecclesiastes.[180]

To illustrate the difference between the Christian and the Buddhist attitude toward relics, he told the tale of *The Dog-Tooth Relic of the Buddha,* which, he declares, is a well-known and oft-repeated Buddhist tale.[181]

I brought up a query about the passage in the Acts of the Apostles in which the apostles are forbidden to go into Asia. Eidmann did not know the text: we hunted for it and found it in Acts 16:6. An explanation is still to be found.[182]

Some other matters:

Eidmann holds that plural marriage is still practiced among the Mormons; he himself was introduced to the six wives of one of the leaders of the movement. The religious idea involved? A school for altruism and a breeding of bodies for souls.

Eidmann's view of Christianity is that the two logical extremes are Unitarianism and Mormonism, the former absolutely monotheistic—and empty, and the latter polytheistic.

About marriage: *The First Commandment* in the Bible is in Genesis— to beget and multiply. All Jews must marry and have a family. And so what about Jesus? Well, read again, very carefully, the text of *The Marriage of Cana.*[183] And consider—as the Mormons do—Jesus' relationship to the sisters of Lazarus, Martha and Mary, and to all those other young women...

In modern Japan there is taking place a measurable lowering of the general IQ. Forces operating: the Shintō idea that all must think alike; government control of the universities, the exclusion of adventurous thinkers. The control is exercised via Tokyo University. Government to Tokyo University to all other universities. Faculty appointments in all Japanese universities have to be controlled from and approved by Tokyo. He told me also of a form that he has just received asking what he is now *studying*. (Compare the Council of Learned Societies form that I received at the time of the war.)

As a kind of stunt, to illustrate the capacity of the trained Japanese mind, Eidmann called Haru in, read off to him a list of twenty-five objects that we had just written out. He recalled them, perfectly—and then gave us the list again, about two hours later.

The last act of the evening was my introduction to the art of using a Chinese dictionary.

Sunday, June 5

An amusing situation has developed around *The Art of Indian Asia.* Kasugai brought the book to a scholars' dinner in Tokyo, and the waiters held the soup course in their hands for an hour and a half while the group swooned and went crazy. One man, whose son had just returned from a trip to India to make photographs, jokingly declared that he could have saved a lot of money and had good pictures if he had only seen this book first. Eidmann is stressing the fact to them that this work was produced in America through the support of Mellon money—capitalistic money. He asks them all to guess the price, and when they shoot between $150 and $300, he gives them the $19.50 and they are shattered. I think that Jean in India and this book in Japan have been the greatest blurbs for the U.S.A. that have come to the Orient without any government support this lovely year.

My thoughts are beginning to point in very strongly toward the problem of returning to New York with my present set of new feelings, plans, and studies fully functioning. One problem is going to be to assimilate the dance situation when Jean arrives. That must be worked out here. And when we hit New York the new program must be brought into play immediately.

The whole emphasis in reading is to be on Mythology and Comparative Religion. In Japanese, I must try to find simple story-texts of Japanese myths and legends, also Buddhist *sūtras;* in French or German, I must read Corbin, etc. and the Eranos volumes; at Sarah Lawrence, I must rebuild my class notes (and perhaps use a wire recorder to catch my lectures), and with Viking, I must get back into the writing swing.

As a book to follow my Viking myth volume, I am thinking more and more of the story of *Apollonius of Tyana.*[184]

And I am thinking also that, one way or another, I must manage to come back some day to Japan.[185] My visit, I feel (though it is only two-fifths done), is almost over.

All day at work on diary, letters, and Japanese.

CHAPTER VIII

A Vast and Difficult Question

Monday, June 6

Some thoughts on the current U.S.-Japan situation.

The visitor to Japan distinctly has the feeling that a lot of American big wigs and little wigs are getting a lot out of what is going on here—and represent an interested force. I should like to know a lot more than I do, for example, about what goes on in and around the so-called PX.

Japanese public opinion is permeated by pacifism and antimilitarism. Much of the vote of the Socialists during the last election came from women registering a protest against rearmament. The clause renouncing arms that the Occupation wrote into the constitution is used with a telling effect by opponents of a new army. Japan is contributing no more than 2 percent of its national income to defense. Their own armed forces are not popular with the Japanese.

U.S. forces are too much in evidence throughout Japan. Many U.S. officials question whether long-term relations with Japan are not being seriously endangered in order to continue the short-term advantage of using U.S. forces in the Far East. Responsible Japanese unanimously report that the best means of improving relations would be to withdraw all

American ground troops within a year or more. The navy has moved the bulk of its activities south.

The continuous display in the cities of American GIs on leave is a quite bad job, it seems to me. Conceited, complacent, bulky boys in shirt-sleeves, for the most part, on the look for girls or with girls on their arms. Eighty-five percent are said to be "shacking up." On Limits strip joints, photo joints, conspicuously and obviously for GIs; rough and ugly behavior (e.g. pimps thrown into the Ginza's river). Around all this is a vast civilian army of "carpetbaggers" and "dependents," the latter extremely unpliable and intolerant of Japanese customs: pippin housewives from Nebraska, Ohio, Michigan, etc., continually complaining about their hard lot, when they have more servants than any of their counterparts in the States. They raise their comparatively noisy children, and are generally uninterested in anything else.

学生の美術史

Japanese characters = "Art History for Students"

After dinner I visited Eidmann and commenced work with him on the reading of a little Japanese text: *Gakusei no Bijutsu-shi.* Also, spent an hour listening to the Japanese conversation records, of which I finished section one. Felt distinctly that my work on Japanese had entered a new phase. This week my original six-week enrollment in the language school ends; but I'm going to remain till the end of the term, July 8. This will leave me about twenty days in which to reach Tokyo and meet Jean: a time to travel a bit and try to put my Japanese to use.

Tuesday, June 7

All day on Japanese. Met Stoops again at dinner—this time in Fujiya, and he invited me to visit a lively bar with him over in the Gion area: set the date for next Tuesday.

A letter today from Ezekiel in Bombay, inviting me to write for the new magazine *Quest* that he is now editing. Am not going to think of writing anything, however, till I return to New York.

Wednesday, June 8

In the paper this morning: a report on the inquiry on the death of a newspaper man, Gene Symonds, murdered by a mob in Singapore last month. The reports indicate that a police car stood by, at about three hundred to two hundred yards distance, doing nothing. The mob shouted, "We want to beat up Europeans. We want to assault Europeans." The racial affinity of the majority has not been stated, but it must have been Chinese. Articles have been running recently about the prodigious Communist influence among the Chinese in Singapore: it is both ideological and patriotic. They constitute a vast portion of the population and regard China as their home.

Themes that are not sounded in the worldwide Communist-led clamor for "justice": U.N. membership for Japan; Russian imperialism in Eastern Europe (Bulgaria, Romania, Hungary, Czechoslovakia, Poland, Estonia, Lithuania, Latvia, and a chunk of Finland); Chinese imperialism in Tibet;[186] the prodigious size of the Russian army—large long before the U.S.A. reversed its disarmament efforts after the collapse of Czechoslovakia; and the propriety of India's claim to Kashmir.

At 6:00 P.M. today a student called on the phone, to whom Stoops had given my name last night at his lively Gion bar: I shall see the youth tomorrow. All sounds a bit odd to me just now.

After dinner visited Eidmann and read with him another paragraph in the *Gakusei no Bijutsu-shi*.

A nice letter from Jean today about our finances. Joe Lillard has helped her calculate, and it seems that with a loan of $1,500 from her mother, plus the $1,700 loan that I received from S.L.C., we are going to make it—just!

Thursday, June 9

These days, I am just midway in time between my departure from India (March 4) and my arrival in New York (about September 6). My chief experience at present (besides that of the wonders of Japan and the Japanese language) is that of a beautiful refreshment of all the young plans, hopes, and ambitions with which I left Germany for New York in 1929![187] I feel as though I had been given that *second chance* which people dream about—and essentially, though on a larger base, my hopes and plans are about what they were at that time. This I find most remarkable.

My plans for the return are becoming quite firm. The first problem (and the only really delicate one) will be to get going immediately on Japanese— before I lose this perilously perishable load of vocabulary and rules so recently and too rapidly acquired. That attended to, I shall—as scheduled above[188]— get going on my Eranos readings, Volkening-Viking myth book, Sarah Lawrence convocation address and classes, French or German.

For the Japanese four operations seem indicated:

a. A purchase of the record course
b. A systematic continuation of my readings (Vaccari's reader, probably, and whatever small text I may have in hand)
c. The discovery of a good teacher, to help me with free conversation and systematic reading, perhaps once a week
d. The opening of Japanese connections in New York (Honganji-Zen etc.)

And while I am voyaging between Tokyo and New York (one week in Honolulu; a couple of days in San Francisco) I must keep going on the reading: probably with the Vaccari reader.

Just now, I am *beginning* to feel that I may be catching on.

Stoops's young man arrived at 5:00 P.M. and I talked with him, over coffee, in the hotel lobby: talked at first as though his major interest were in getting to the U.S.A. after graduation; then I realized, from a couple of restrained but definite remarks, that this was the old homosexual club. Got rid of him at six, went up to my room to sit down and think a minute; then started for a good steak at Suehiro's.

On the way, a very small boy on a very small bicycle hit my right foot, coming from behind, and though the blow was slight, it was precisely at the point of my sprain. The kid fell off his bike, and I bade him Godspeed; but the ankle is a bit the worse for the shock.

As I approached Suehiro's, Stoops's young man overtook me, and I bade him good-bye again at the door of the restaurant.

After dinner, returned to my Japanese.

Friday, June 10

Time is certainly flying. A letter from Jean: she leaves next Tuesday for New Orleans, where she will give a performance, and her last class in Colorado will be July 22. She will start then for Tokyo and is now due to arrive July 25. She also has had my air ticket to New York sent on to Kyoto: I picked it up today after my morning of Japanese.

And so, the circle has been closed.

A note from Adda,[189] in praise of *The Art of Indian Asia,* which she has just received; also, one from Carl Schuster,[190] who saw a copy on the desk of John Pope[191] in the Freer Gallery in Washington, D.C.

A letter from Bill McGuire,[192] stating that plans are going ahead for paperback editions of *The Hero* and *Philosophies.*[193] New York begins to seem very much alive.

Notes from George Gurow and Martin Wong in Taiwan—inviting me back, with Jean. Unfortunately, that can't be done. Our money and time are too tight.

A good article on India by Kōji Nakamura appeared in the *Mainichi* this morning, with a number of points that help to underline some of my own ideas—which are still pretty confused:

Economically India is undoubtedly at the lowest level in the world. Per capita income, circa $50 per annum. Illiteracy 83 percent. This, certainly, has to be the starting point for any discussion of the country.

"The Four Evils" (Nehru's terms) that must be eliminated if there is to be an improvement:

1. Casteism
2. Linguism
3. Provincialism
4. Communalism

These are still everywhere and very strong.

The government stands for a welfare state based on a "socialistic pattern of society," and a neutral country in the arena of international politics. Indeed, no other formula could solve even a fraction of the gigantic problem.

Saturday, June 11

Friday, after class, Mary Jones came to the school and loaned me Ferré's *The Sun and the Umbrella,* which I glanced through, briefly, at dinner. When she gave me the book, I told her that my chief criticism of what she was giving me was that it wasn't, as she had promised, without mythology, but actually stressed the chief themes of the Christian myth, namely:

1. Sin, as something that cuts man off so radically from the divine that only a special savior can save him; and
2. Jesus of Nazareth as that unique Redeemer.

"But sin," she said; "do you mean to say that sin isn't a fact?"

"Sin isn't a fact," I said, "it's a way of interpreting facts—and implies a belief in God, God's commands, our knowledge and disobedience of God's commands, and everything else." At this point Father Moss entered the room and Mary Jones fled.

In *The Sun* [God] *and the Umbrella* [the Church's teachings, which shut God away from us instead of bringing Him close] Ferré is apparently against Christian mythologizing, and yet he accepts, as facts, 1 and 2, as above. He is in quite a tangle, however, when he tries to interpret the relationship of the human Jesus to the God who was made manifest through and in him—but then, that's a grand old Christian agony and a natural consequence of taking mythology as fact.[194]

"God was thus organically present in Jesus, fulfilling His purpose and our destiny. Here is revelation. Here is Incarnation. Here is power for the forgiveness of sin and the making of the new community in Christ. Christ is God's love come to earth. He is the Logos, the Word...."[195] There is a concession to the operation of God's will through other teachers, but the redeeming fullness, it is maintained, was only in Jesus.

The rains have come. Today is overcast and wet. This will last, I am told, for a month—which is to be the last month of my attempt to grasp my Oriental pearl—a Mikimoto pearl—my hothouse knowledge of Japanese. So, here goes!

To Eidmann's after lunch, and a very pleasant visit till 10:30 P.M. A number of important items:

In one of the U.S. Marine camps near Kyoto, the continuous ratio of venereal disease was circa 70 percent. The army gave women permits signed by commanding officers, if they would stick with one man as his steady—this as an attack on the venereal problem. If the couple was accosted by an MP the girl would have to show her permit. In general the "On Limits" dives constitute the army's solution to the sex problem. The pay of a U.S. private is higher than that of a Japanese general and most of it goes, apparently, on liquor and women. The relationship of the present deterioration of morals in the U.S.A. to the education of U.S. Army draftees abroad is a problem that would bear study.

While sanctioning and cooperating in the relationship of the GI to the prostitute, the army has done everything possible to balk marriage to a decent girl if one should be found. The girl has to be examined for disease; the couple has to be questioned by a long series of officers and during the course of this ordeal the soldier is often transferred to another post; and finally the marriage has to be sanctioned by an army chaplain—who is frequently anti-Buddhist, anti-heathen.

One U.S. Army chaplain in Japan wrote a little booklet of warnings: all Japanese women are immoral heathens; those who meet GIs are inevitably prostitutes to boot. This booklet was translated into Japanese and caused quite a stir.

The Japanese do not understand the American army man, who, on entering the army, expects to return home alive. The Japanese in the army expects to die—and this gives him a character very different from that of the civilian. (Banzai attacks in the World War, for example.) The Japanese, indeed, are afraid of restoring their own army to life and will resist all American efforts to change the constitution, to make an army legal.

The present Japanese army is unconstitutional—and with American connivance. This has created an extremely awkward and ambiguous situation. The Japanese are used, however, to "open secrets," and prefer living with a broken law to reforming a law that seems to them proper and good.

The Japanese army entered World War II expecting to lose—and had it not been for the emperor's revolution, they would have all died fighting.[196] Actually, they were practicing in the streets with bamboo sticks. How to explain such an attitude logically? Perhaps the attitude toward death of the early Christian martyrs, who actually courted death, is the nearest analogy in the West.

Near Sendai there is a mound with an inscription that is now read as identifying it as the tomb of Christ. The legend: that Jesus was not dead when removed from the Cross; healed by the medical arts of Joseph of Arimathea, he sailed to Japan in a boat and now lies here, buried.

The basic teachings of the various Buddhist sects in Japan have been summarily formulated in four-word aphorisms which proliferate from each other in each system in amplification of the lore; e.g.

即身是佛

Zen formula #1

Soku shin ze butsu
This body is Buddha

即身成佛

Shingon formula #1

Soku shin jō butsu
[That] this body [may] become Buddha

總別安心

Jōdo formula #1

Sō Betsu An Jin
General [&] special peace [of] mind

Japanese characters to Zen formula and Shingon formula

Anjin, "peace of mind," in Jōdo is not synonymous with Enlightenment; and the problem implied by the terms *sō betsu,* "general and special," was one that was particularly important in the Heian period; namely: is the attainment one that is known only in a special moment, or is it maintained through the whole life. According to Jōdo, as a result of the achievement and maintenance of this Peace of Mind, one achieves Enlightenment (i.e., is projected into *nirvāṇa*) at the moment of death.

Shinshū was developed by Shinran out of Jōdo and advanced beyond it. Eidmann did not give me the number 1 Shinshū formula, but discussed two of the subordinate formulae and contrasted with them the Christian position; as follows:

> *Shinjin shōin*
> Faith awakening true cause
> [The true cause (of salvation) is the awakening of faith]

The Christian counterpart would be:

Kiristo shōin
Christ true cause
[The true cause (of salvation) is Christ]
Shōki nimbo
Object (of) refuge, person (or) law
[Is the object of refuge (or worship) a person or the law?]
For Shinshū the proper object of refuge is the law
For the Christian the object is the Christ, i.e., a person

This whole principle of formulation and presentation seemed to me extremely interesting: one that could be well employed both in analysis and in pedagogy. An excellent exercise would be that of finding comparable formulae and proliferations of formulae for the traditional (and even some of the modern) thinkers of the West. Indeed, I might ask myself some time: *What is my own basic formula?*[197] Clue One, a little statement made to Eidmann: "A myth is the imaging of a conception, or realization, of truth."

In connection with all this: a little passage then found in Ferré's *The Sun and the Umbrella:* "The Christian faith believes not that God is too holy to behold sin but that He comes to seek and to save the sinner. The Christian faith knows no absolute, either, which like an inverted rainbow dips from the eternal into finite existence only to return again to perfection; G*od Himself, in coming to save us, rather, for our sake 'becomes sin';* he lives with us, among us, in us and for us."[198]

"What is this?" I asked Eidmann; giving it to him to read: "Tantra!" he said. "Exactly!" But, of course, Ferré doesn't follow this inspiration to its conclusion.

In Korea nowadays, according to Eidmann, there are two interesting phenomena: first, riots before the American embassy in Seoul, protesting against America's support of "pro-Communist Japan." Second, Korean married monks beating up the unmarried monks and nuns who have been ordered by the government to supplant the married monks in their temples. The married monks actually were established in Korea by the Japanese to break down Buddhism. Many of them are sheer thugs. For *it was an expressed intention of the Meiji to root out Buddhism.*

Ironically, since the Occupation and the new constitution, it is possible to favor Buddhism without danger to your career. (This, I think, must be balanced against the excessive Christian propaganda.)

Japan in Asia is not trusted. (The situation, probably, is comparable to that of Germany in Europe.) The Japanese actually had the idea that they could be the saviors of Asia—(and they may yet be, as the Germans may yet be the saviors of Europe). After their defeat, however, and in the face of the general anti-Japanese picture in Asia, their attitude became that of "To hell with it; let us cultivate our own garden." One great problem, however, is that they *do* need markets.

I have the feeling that we should never forget Spengler's warning about the anti-mechanical character of the Asiatic mind. They will learn to use the machine to throw off the West—but their yearning is for an Asian style of life, to which the machine is intrinsically alien. In many individual cases—chaps brought up in the Western manner—Asians *seem* to be not less at home with the machine than Occidentals (e.g. Krishnan at Bhubaneshwer). But in the character-shaping tradition itself, which is the force that affects the unconscious, an anti-mechanical principle is at work,* which in the long run and in the great mass, will probably work as Spengler warns.

And in this connection one more idea. If Nehru would come to Tokyo instead of falling in love with his brother Asians of Peking and Moscow, he would find an Asiatic nation really capable of furnishing him with the machines and technical aid that he needs. The co-prosperity sphere would really begin to come into being.

"Yes, but..." I hear, from some imaginary knower of Japan. Well, I want to hear what the but might be.

Worked with Eidmann on kanji and on the reading of a little introduction to Shinrikyō.

Sunday, June 12

I went today with Hisashi Mita to the Takarazuka Revue in Takarazuka. An excellent revue, by one of their three or four troupes; this one "The Snow Troupe," *Yuki Gumi.* First section: *Blue Hawai'i*—an amusing set of hulas, by about eighty girls, with a little plot; then, the main revue, *The*

---

* See Lily Abegg, *Ostasien denkt anders: Versuch einer Analyse des west-östlichen Gegensatzes* (Zurich: Atlantis, 1949).

Tales of the Four Flowers, and I felt again the real charm and excellence of the Japanese theater: scads of good dancers and beautiful girls; kimono and Western styles equally well done; superb stage sets and transformations; an ability to flash out and into depth (opening the stage forward, backward, and to the sides, that yielded really wonderful effects); perfect taste and lovely invention in the curtains, backdrops, scenes, and lights; a great ability to keep things moving, changing, and surprising. One of the leading ladies in a set of geisha dancers nearly knocked me out.

A couple of additional observations:

Remarkable how many of the themes culminated in suicide (compare the Kabuki: suicides and honor killings of one's own children etc.). Think now of the banzai attacks and the Pearl Harbor hara-kiri.[199] Formula: life is lived to the limit, according to a certain principle, concept, sense of the possible, or simply pragmatic plan—and when this leads to an impasse, instead of transformation (changing the lifestyle) one chooses death— which, after all, in a world where reincarnation is taken for granted, is a way of changing the style of one's dress. Contrast with this, however, the equally Japanese formula of "rock with the waves."

The first of the *Tales of the Four Flowers* was about an Ainu[200] romance (Romeo and Juliet theme of feud and suicide), where the Ainu were handled much as American Indians in, say, a revue of the Rose Marie type:[201] the forest idyll.

After the show, we strolled through the zoo and botanical garden, then took the train home: dinner at Suehiro's with Hisashi, and then a good evening of work on my Japanese.

I hope Jean can see this Takarazuka job: it will be an inspiration to her, I am sure: a city of dancers!! Four troupes of about a hundred each! Add this to the picture of the Kabuki and Noh companies! The American theater falls apart in comparison. Steady, perfect "stock" company work: A new show every month: theater, theater, theater, theater. No wonder the performances are good beyond belief. Not a ham in the whole of Japan!— except, of course, what I saw in the so-called modern dance.

A nice letter from Alan Watts, when I returned, suggesting that I look up some people in Kyoto: P. D. Perkins, at a bookstore near my hotel; a Zen priest named Sōhaku Ogata, who speaks English and who spoke to Alan's pupils at Northwestern; and a painter named Sabro Hasegawa. He also expressed amazement at *The Art of Indian Asia* and suggested that Jean and I plan to visit him at Big Sur: the latter an elegant suggestion.[202]

I have about decided to remain in Kyoto until after the Gion event July 17–18; then simply go to the Ise Peninsula for a few days, and proceed from there to Tokyo, to meet Jean.

Monday, June 13

Bad day at Japanese school: one teacher ill, and Father Moss, my classmate, managing to break down the learning tension by cracking jokes. This tendency has increased as we have gone on into the more difficult stages. I am actually beginning to wonder whether I might not do better, for the remaining three or four weeks, approaching the language some other way. We have reached lesson thirty-one—about two weeks late, and I doubt whether we shall complete the full sixty at this rate!

In the paper there has been a discussion of the question of antialien attitudes in certain Kyoto restaurants. Some "dismayed foreigner" complained May 31. The Japan Travel Bureau now replies.

The U.S. Army has classified restaurants hygienically as class A, B, or C; sending MPs around to see that no GIs are in B or C restaurants. Many army men are in civvies when on leave. Such restaurants have learned to avoid incidents by refusing service.

A number of restaurants have suffered damage to furniture from foreigners; also injury to people and the bilking of bills. GIs also may bring in their own liquor and ask for a bottle of soda; then get nasty. It is not ideology or racism that leads restaurants that have had this experience to resist foreigners.

Some restaurants are the haunts of streetwalkers: gentlemen (as distinguished from GIs, I suppose) are not welcome in such places.

Many Kyoto restaurants, especially in Gion, do not serve chance customers, whether foreign or Japanese.

Shyness, on the part of people who do not speak English, may be misinterpreted as brusqueness.

After reading this article, and after seeing what I have seen of Americans in Asia, I think it might be well, if I am to give the S.L.C. convocation address, to deal with the question of the educated American as America's only ambassador. Some further thoughts:

The idea of cultural missions—Russian and Chinese missions to India; Indian to Ceylon; The NBC Symphony in Japan; Jean in India.

In general the American citizen is being very badly served in Asia thanks to:

a. Communist ideologists and the Japanese unions
b. Businessmen and the U.S. agencies
c. Senator junkets
d. Illiteracy of the foreign staffs: two-year stints; cocktail circuit (contrast the English and the clergy)
e. Christian missionizing masquerading as democracy
f. U.S. Army wives and personnel
g. Sheer tourists

For Sarah Lawrence, I should emphasize the aspect of education through which each can serve as a human example: educating, refining, cultivating *yourself:* not learning about current ideologies only, but making yourself into a civilized character.

Moreover: solution of world's coming problems lie right here: right on this campus (S.L.C.); for the U.S.A. is the prow of the world ship right now—the individual can become self-reliant *outside* of the governmental institution.

Hisashi, yesterday, discussed a little series of incidents that have taken place on his campus, that of Kyoto University. The first took place three years ago, the second last year, and the third last week. The first occurred when the emperor arrived: a group surrounded his car and sang "The International."[203] The occasion for last year's event I failed to catch, but the students went on a strike. Last week they locked the president in his office.

There is considerable Communist sympathy among the students; the faculty, on the other hand, is very conservative. Whence the student organization and coordination Hisashi didn't know.

At dinner Hisashi said to me: you are very enthusiastic about Japan, but if you stayed here longer you would find some things you wouldn't like.

In India I had to force myself to seek the things that I could admire; here, for balance, I must recognize the "things I wouldn't like"; for example:

1. The Communist anti-Americanism—which is certainly present, but certainly not as overt (by any means) as it was in India
2. The general rudeness of men to women in the RR trains and cars: young students will sit, sprawled out over the seats, and let a woman stand with a baby on her back

3. The generally Oriental rudeness of everybody to the people with whom they are not directly in contact for the moment: pushing in ahead of the line for tickets, elbowing into and out of crowds, etc.

What else?

An apt image for my visit to India occurred to me today as I was walking to catch my trolley to school. *It was like a visit to a vast, haunted house.* The first impression was of the debris and squalor that had piled up during the centuries. Under this heading, all the bad news about poverty, disease, etc. After a while, however, the lineaments of a magnificent, ancient edifice began to be apparent beneath and behind the appalling clutter. Here, the temples, and the vestiges of ancient societies and doctrines. And, throughout, there were curious sounds and apparitions, purporting to be manifestations of the spiritual realm: but whether any of these were genuine, or all tricks, remains a matter of doubt. It is my belief, however, that one or two were real. But now comes the problem of whether anything or how much of this archaic mansion can be salvaged for contemporary living. That is a vast and difficult question, because the answer depends not only on how the supposed spirituality of the place is evaluated, but also upon our evaluation of the characteristic phenomena of the modern world.

Still another idea about India: it is a land with more people and fewer thoughts than any on earth.

A telegram, tonight, to Jean, who leaves New York tomorrow for New Orleans, Boulder, San Francisco, Honolulu, and Tokyo.

CHAPTER IX

TEMPLE TREASURES

Tuesday, June 14

My day: Japanese: letters to Bollingen and Jean: more Japanese.

Officially the "rainy season"—*tsuyu*—began Sunday, but the days have been sunny and rather warm. The heat is coming, and I'm told it can be great!

Wednesday, June 15

Some ideas for the S.L.C. address. Lay stress on:

1. The privilege and responsibility of a year of American education (compare conditions in Asiatic colleges)
2. The irony of what may be called the "barbarism" of the people that we send abroad:
   a. Experts and specialists
   b. "Halfbrights" (The Fullbright "scholars" who don't really prepare themselves adequately, nor go to the cultural depth required.)
   c. Diplomats who know nothing about either American culture or the culture of the land to which they are sent
   d. The army
   e. The missionaries
   f. The "carpetbaggers"
   g. The tourists (pink pants in Kyoto—ugh)

    h. The movies and news items

        (An idea of slaphappy spontaneous crudity as the measure of demo-
        cratic virtue—that is an international disaster)

3. Our responsibility to the Free Nations—indeed, to freedom: We *do* have
   masters who support it and represent it. Why can they not find their way
   to visibility?

4. The counterbalance to the "barbarism": NBC Orchestra, Jean

5. Responsibility of those being educated—to become civilized: not for the
   forests of Hiawatha, but for modern civilization. For instance, What is
   the matter with our children? (Asian mothers "professional," Asian fathers
   too.) The unsolved inner conflict: what is it?[204]

6. The prow of civilization, the brunt of the beating: individualism vs. the
   past—a psychological problem that *each* has to solve. Individual cultivation vs. traditional cultivation. S.L.C. at the forefront here

A serious task, and not a task of *work,* but of attitude, direction, understanding of culture.

Specialization and technology—yes, but—without culture, humanity,
civilization, it is identical with the menace that all of mankind despises:
Titanism.[205]

Discovered theme, then: *Titan or God?*

Specialization (etc.) as Titanism—known to the myths (that is to say,
the images of human evolution) of the whole world: Leprechauns, etc. who
make men's shoes, but lack mankind's culture: and here is the danger for
the U.S.A. On the other hand, there is no point in trying to play the role
of God: we just haven't what it takes for that. But we *could* be human, if
we tried a little: we have all the facilities: and, in fact, when I look at you
beautiful creatures, I know that we *are* human, and delightfully so, at least
in the feminine portion of our social anatomy. What then is the explanation of what I saw as I looked at America from Asia?

The American in Paris of the 1920s: the American in Tokyo of the
1950s.

The U.S.A. in Asia, supporting the British and the French; result:

1. Loss of prestige among the anti-Imperialists

2. No gain of prestige among the Asiatics, who still admire the British and
   the French (and these, by the way, are often identical with the first sort;
   for their idols—the British and the French—despise us, and make this
   very clear in every word that they utter)

Now add to this the picture of (a) through (g) above. Quite a fine
tableau.

Conclusion as to what is the responsibility of the American student. At home: to become civilized and to assist in the civilizing of the American. Abroad: to behave in a civilized manner.

This evening I went to Eidmann's after dinner and found Miss Margaret (Peg) McDuffy chatting with him. They had not yet had dinner. I listened to Japanese language records till they were through, then returned to the room and remained after Miss McDuffy left. Some news and the beginnings of a schedule.

I have made plans to study Japanese with a young man named Iguchi, who has been helping Fillmore. The problem is, that the work at the school has not enabled me to find a way to make Japanese work outside of the classroom. We are covering a lot of territory there, pretty fast; but I have no core of speech habits for either the actual situations of my stay in Japan, or the subjects that I care to discuss. My hope is to begin work with Iguchi as soon as Eidmann leaves for Hokkaido, and to increase my hours with him when the school closes.

Plans, also, to concentrate on a systematic learning of kanji, based on a frequency listing, as soon as school closes.

I have exactly a month, now, in which to clinch what I can of Japanese. Also, to see what I haven't yet seen of Kyoto.

Thursday, June 16

Real rain: the "rainy season" (*tsuyu*) has come for fair.

This morning at eight, right after my breakfast, Professor Kasugai arrived to invite me to the temple treasure viewing tomorrow. He brought with him a young nun, and we had tea in the lounge of the hotel. He also brought a number of photo-graphs of *Indonesian structures with roof forms suggesting the "dragons" on the Japanese temple roofs.*

I mentioned that I had seen a number of interesting monks begging—one, a chap with *a basket over his head and a flute in his hand.* Professor Kasugai told me

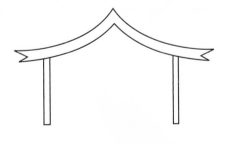

Japanese temple roofs

that this order represented a fusion of Tendai philosophy, Shingon costume (basket), and Zen symbolism (flute: the voice of nature). The leaders are called *komusō: komu (śunyatā) sō* (priest).

Kasugai and the nun left at 8:30 and I took a taxi to school: taxi home again at noon—rain and very heavy clouds.

Found something of interest in *Life,* May 30: Einstein, on a few basic matters of popular interest:

1. The mind can proceed only so far upon what it knows and can prove. There comes a point where the mind takes a leap—call it intuition or what you will—and comes out upon a higher plane of knowledge, but can never prove how it got there. All great discoveries have involved such a leap.
2. The important thing is not to stop questioning. Curiosity has its own reason for existence.
3. Try not to become a man of success but rather try to become a man of value. He is considered successful in our day who gets more out of life than he puts in. But a man of value will give more than he receives.
4. [His] belief is in the brotherhood of man and the uniqueness of the individual.

Last evening Eidmann suggested that *the three major religious developments in America*—that is to say, major native American developments—were:

Mormonism
American Unitarianism
Christian Science

And I believe he is right. Perhaps one should add the Peyote cult of the American Indians, in the light of what is now happening to Aldous Huxley et al.[206]

At five today, went around to Eidmann's, to help him buy a camera and some shirts. We had a very long stroll—to my camera shop and shirt shop; had dinner at his favorite Chinese restaurant: and I returned to my room, rather tired, at ten, and went directly to bed.

Friday, June 17

Up at six, greatly refreshed. A rotten morning, however, at school. "Moss-san," Father Moss, my classmate, is now learning practically nothing and wastes more than two-thirds of our three hours with his fumbling and stalling. After class I asked the principal, Hayashi-san, if I could shift to private lessons in the afternoon. She said it was too late to do so for next week, but that something might be arranged for the week following. I am kicking myself, that I did not ask for this some three weeks back.

After class, I grabbed a chocolate bar for lunch and went up to Chion-in for Professor Kasugai's exhibition of temple treasures. He showed me, first, a huge book with the list of all the treasures, then showed me the eight choice items that he had selected for my viewing:

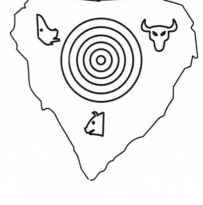

1. A Chinese kakemono map of "India" as *Iambu Dvipa* (copy ca. A.D. 1350 of earlier original) with the names of the main sites in kanji. The area included was Tibet, Afghanistan, Nepal, etc., India, and Ceylon. In the center of the Tibetan zone was a curious, mythological, snake-spiral, emanating, threefold, from three animal heads: one, a sort of hippo; one, a sort of boar; one, a sort of ox. No one knew how to interpret this.

Iambu Dvipa in the form of a heart.

2. A kakemono showing *Amida in meditation;* hands in posture in lap. Picture believed to have been brought to Japan by Kōbō Daishi (ca. A.D. 794). It is a Central Asian piece, thought to date from the second or third century A.D. (If so, probably the oldest artwork—or even object—in Japan.) The figure sits on a double-storied lotus in a white aureole, and is *clothed in a dark red (cf. Red Cap lamas)*. (Kasugai thinks an original yellow robe may have turned red; but I doubt this.) At the four corners of the picture were four Sanskrit syllables on lotuses; added later, apparently, in Japan.

Amida's hands

3. A beautiful kakemono on a broad black square of silk. Descent of the Buddha Amida, on a roadway of cloud, to a meditating personage in a house. In the upper right-hand area is a city or castle in a circle; possibly the Tusita Heaven.[207] The Buddha is accompanied by Bodhisattvas and sages. In the area between the Tusita Heaven and the house (lower right)

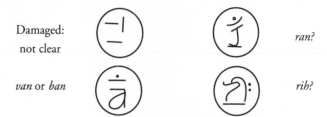

Damaged: not clear

van or *ban*

ran?

rih?

Four Sanskrit syllables (in Sankrit)

are a number of small *arhat* figures—as though precipitated from the atmosphere. In the lower left is a mountain landscape. The natural areas are naturalistically colored, so too the Tusita circle. Amida and his entourage, however, are clothed in gold.

Buddha's descent

The work is thought to have been painted by Eshin (Genshin) (ca. A.D. 950–1000), the patriarch of Hiei, and a patriarch of Shinshū. It is possible, however, that silk of this width was not made in Japan that early—in which case, the ascription would have to be revised: ca. 1280? This panel, according to Professor Kasugai, was the left-hand member of a tryptich.

4. A kakemono showing the Buddha (Śākyamuni perhaps, or Amida) in meditation, with two standing Bodhisattvas: at his proper left,

Avalokiteśvara, with Buddha image in tiara; proper right, Mahāprasthana, with water bottle (looks like a *stūpa*) in his tiara. Date: ca. A.D. 1280? This

work is a Chinese illustration of the *Smaller Sukhāvatī Vyuha* (Nanjo #200[208]), also, the *to-shwo-kwan-wu-lien-sheu-go-kin* (Nanjō #198), the Buddha robe is red.

5. An immense Chinese *kakemono* (too big to hang from the ceiling: lay half on the floor), showing a three-fold epiphany of Amida and attendant Bodhisattvas, with a red sun at the top; and multitudes of attendants and lotus pedestals. At the sides of the sun are soaring musical instruments. Among the attendants are groups playing lutes, flutes, drums, and panpipe reeds (*shō,* such as I heard at Nara?). The probable date of this glorious piece is ca. A.D. 1200–1300.

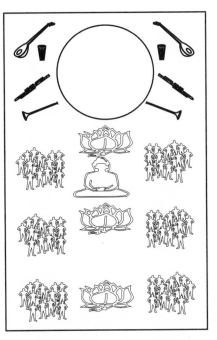

Chinese kakemono. This work is an illustration of the *Amitayur-jñana Sūtra.* The robes of the meditating figure are red.

Professor Kasugai could not explain to me the threefold trinity, but suggested Buddha of the past, the present, and the future. The Bodhisattvas accompanying the three central figures are Mahāprasthana and Avalokiteśvara.

6. A Chinese *kakemono* resembling number 5, but slightly smaller, and with a three-legged bird in the sun. No one could explain to me the three-legged bird. The date of this piece is ca. A.D. 1200–1300. Note: three-legged bird, three-fold Buddha manifestation.

7. A Chinese embroidery of ca. 500 A.D., hung as a kakemono, showing a Buddha figure in meditation with accompanying Bodhisattvas, and with a set of eighteen small scenes down the sides as borders. Again an illustration of the *Amitayur-jñana Sūtra.* The Buddha figure here has a Mongolian moustache (so too have the Buddhas in some of the other works, but I forget precisely which: I think numbers 5 and 6, but possibly also 4.). This Buddha looks very much like a Chinese Confucian sage. Whereas the tone of numbers 2, 3, 4, 5, 6 is dark, that of 7 is yellow and a kind of chartreuse-green.

Screen with conchs and *vajra* bells border

8. A vast screen, mounting as a triptych *an embroidered vestment brought from China* ca. A.D. 1200. The traditional date assigned to this work is fifth or sixth century A.D.; however, some of the elements depicted on the border suggest, rather, post-seventh or eighth century A.D.; namely—*conchs and* vajra *bells.*

Kasugai and a Jōdo nun exhibit screen

The central motif in each panel is an island: from the central one a Buddha emanates; from the other two, nothing emanates. That at the observer's right is a half circle: the half moon? Its opposite is a full circle: the full moon? The central island too is circular: the sun? On the central panel the *three-footed bird* is twice represented. At the lower right-hand corner of the (observer's) right-hand panel is a wonderful four-footed Chinese dragon. Other panels depict *jātaka* scenes[209]; rabbit churning butter with a watching frog, etc.

One suggestion for the three-footed bird is that there is a legend somewhere of three crows (*karasu*) in the sun.

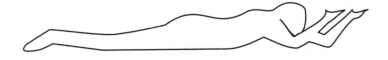

Prostrated figure

In illustration of one of the postures represented among the devotees of kakemono number 5, Professor Kasugai showed me two forms of prostration: the *turīyamaṇḍala*, with knees and hands on the floor, and the *panchamaṇḍala* (the most profound) with the head also on the floor, but, instead of the hand the elbows; *the hands being raised with palms upward to receive the feet of the Buddha.*

According to Professor Kasugai, such pictorial maṇḍalas as were exhibited in the kakemonos of this display are not actually used in modern Japanese worship. Shingon and Tendai use mandalas, but not of these types; and the other sects use none. It is possible that pictures of this type were used in Japan as illustrations and foundations for public readings of the *sūtras:* first, the *sūtra* to be read in Chinese, and next, a translation to be read.

A number of people were present at the viewing: Eidmann, Haru, a Brazilian Nisei, Mr. van Vest (a Dutch gentleman who has been some forty years in Japan), a number of young students (theological), and two Jōdo nuns (one the visitor of yesterday morning). It was a lovely afternoon, with tea, twice, on the floor of the vast room. Then we all went to Eidmann's favorite *amazake* outdoor restaurant for a sip, and finally to a little semi-Shintō shrine to some Indian snake god (*Urūgana*, messenger of

Maheśvara, symbol of women) where there was a stone *stūpa*-lantern show-ing two Buddhas in one frame and, hanging on the temple walls, two or three bunches of hair offerings, made by women for favors received.

At Chion-in Temple. The two figures at the left are Jōdo nuns. To the right is Professor Kasugai and Rev. Phillip Eidmann seated in his wheelchair.

It began to drizzle, about this time, and we strolled down the Chion hill until a taxi arrived, into which the Eidmann party and I climbed. To Eidmann's for dinner and an evening's chat. E. showed me some sixteenth- and seventeenth-century Chinese-Japanese-Sanskrit *sūtras,* with the Sanskrit furnished with kanji translations and hiragana pronunciations.

Saturday, June 18

Morning writing in my diary, to catch up with yesterday's marvels. After lunch went around to Eidmann's again for an afternoon and evening with Eidmann and Kasugai. Lots of talk: quite a number of interesting matters:

In India (Elūrā, Ajaṇṭā, etc.), the figures flanking the Buddha figure are, typically, Maitreya (*stūpa* in tiara) and Avalokiteśvara; in China and Japan, Mahāprasthana (water bottle, which looks like a *stūpa* to *me,* how-ever) and Avalokiteśvara. Is *Prajñāpāramitā* the basis for this change?[210]

We discussed the problem of the origin of the two-Buddha formula (is this what we saw yesterday at the snake-god shrine?). It is based, apparently, on the *Saddharma Pundarīka*. If no examples of the formula occur in India, the problem is: why? When and where was the *Saddharma Pundarīka* composed?[211]

According to Eidmann, *Buddhism is intrinsically a positive, not a negative, way*. His points are as follows:

1. The teaching of the Buddha was originally directed as much to laymen (King Bimbisara and King Sakka, the donor of the gold-paved garden[212]) as to monks. Since, however, the tradition has come to us largely through the monks, for whom those teachings had no immediate relevance, they have disappeared. (I wonder about this.) The stress on the Four Noble Truths is largely Western: one hears little of them in the Orient. (I wonder whether this is really so.)

2. Buddhist monasticism is not negative in the same way that Hindu and Christian are. Westerners are quite happy as Hindu monks, but few have made out well as Buddhist. Their quest for escape is not served by Buddhism, which throws them on their own: they become neurotic. Consider the Buddhist nuns of yesterday afternoon in contrast with the Catholic of yesterday morning. (There is certainly a difference of some kind, but I don't know whether it can be called that of the difference between the positive and the negative approaches: from the outside, at any rate, both look like refusals.)

3. The Mahāyāna—obviously—is positive.

It seems that American (Occidental) movies and plays, when seen in the Orient, are shockingly sexy. Peg McDuffy surprised and puzzled the little Ohtone boy the other day by asking him whether the photo of a certain little girl was of his "girlfriend." He had no idea what she meant—whereas in America even the tots have their boy and girl friends (for instance in Bronxville). This led to my rehearsal of my new theme of the problem of personality-evaluation and free choice in marriage. *In Japan—as in India—at least three-quarters of the marriages are arranged by the families*. In Japan, however, the shift will not present quite as many problems as in India, because the inter-communal love problem does not exist. The culture is comparatively homogeneous.

I had some ideas for a Bollingen investment discussion:

1. The condition of education (student interest, discipline, etc.) is very low in postwar Japan, and the tendency of the Japanese is to blame this on the Occupation. The blame is misplaced (compare India and the English), and yet American influences and investments have been unfortunate enough to give some semblance of justification to the criticism.

a. American aid (Rockefeller, etc.) has gone to the big state universities (Tokyo etc.) and to the Christian universities (Dōshisha, for example), but not to the Buddhist universities. The feeling among Japanese professors (e.g. Kasugai) is that American foundations will not give money to Buddhist universities.

b. The American Culture Center in Kyoto has no books on Buddhism, and yet American scholars have done important and good work in this field—cultural ties would be greatly improved by making this evident. The Japanese themselves lack funds for the purchase of the American books in this field. In contrast to the lack of books on Buddhism, there are many in the library on Christianity: but there are fewer than 400,000 Christians in Japan. *What is the function of the Cultural Center?* To serve as an agency of cultural harmony, or to serve as an agency of the Christian missions?!

2. The Japanese scholars are *not* very good: they favor narrow specialization; they seek fields that will give them prestige among their fellows; they will not dare to argue against a theory presented by a member of their profession who holds a position of prestige—and yet, they think that they can despise American scholarship:

a. Their translations from English are very bad (based on bad dictionaries), so they really don't know what the sensitively chosen technical terms of our American scholars actually say.

Therefore, Project A: Support of careful translations of key works on the Orient into Japanese. No more Bible stuff: there are tons of that; indeed, one would think that the U.S.A. and Christianity were the same thing, to listen to what is being said and published by the Americans in Japan.

b. They are very quick to seize upon minor errors as evidence of worthless work; e.g. Professor Kasugai's glance at the American Encyclopedia donated to his university by the Occupation. He found that the dates of Aśoka given in two articles ("Buddhism" and "Asoka") differed, and concluded that the whole work was worthless. It would certainly work against such quick decisions if more American works (and good ones) were available on Buddhism and the other native subjects in which the native scholars are interested.

Therefore, Project B: Bollingen books, Harvard Oriental Library books, etc.—no more Bibles—to the Oriental universities.

c. The majority of the postwar Japanese who have studied in America are now anti-American. They lecture against, write books against, etc. Why? Compare the problem of Russians who studied in Germany in Turgenev-Tolstoy's time becoming anti-German. Dominant culture inspires negative reaction.[*]

---

[*] See Hans Kohn, *The Twentieth Century: A Mid-Way Account of the Western World* (New York: Macmillan, 1949).

Therefore, Project C: A program of selective fellowships for special ends; as follows:

The present, overly academic, stultified and stultifying condition of Japanese education is largely due to the concentration of power and authority in Tokyo University and the prestige pattern associated with the ranking universities in this system. It does no good to put more money into those universities, as the Rockefellers are doing: these funds only enforce the bad situation and align the U.S.A. with the reactionary team.

The most influential group outside of this structure is precisely the group of universities that the Americans are *not* supporting; namely, the Buddhist universities; and among these the most influential, with the most students, are the Honganji Shinshū and Jōdo. *These universities cannot begin to compete with the state systems largely because they cannot attract and hold good faculty.*

And here is the point:

I asked: "Why don't they offer higher salaries?"

Reply: "They don't have the money!"

I asked: "Why don't they *raise* the money?"

Reply: "They don't know how."

The Japanese universities are run on the fees paid by the students: they have no functioning alumni associations, no big fund-raising campaigns: but there is money in Japan, just as there is in India, and—just as in India, where enough is spent on a wedding to endow two universities—it is never donated to education. What about tapping the big department store universe?

Project C, then:

1. To bring two young men from the Nishi Honganji and two from the Jōdo sect to the U.S.A., to study school administration, fund raising, etc.; these men to be selected by the *hoshus* (patriarchs) of their order. Four young men selected in this fashion will have immense influence when they return— more than a hundred selected in the "democratic" fashion of competitive exams.

2. To set up public speech departments in the universities of these institutions, with which readings in modern problems will be included. There are thousands of students in these temple universities who are going to be the teachers and preachers to the great majority in Japan: they know nothing about the U.S.A.—and yet they are preaching against its influence today from every pulpit in Japan. Why?

We talked further about the anti-American picture, and especially the problem of Okinawa:

A survey team (Japanese) presents the following picture (from the *Mainichi* of June 17):

Many infringements of the basic human rights of islanders have occurred because of their dubious status under the American Occupation. From the legal viewpoint they are Japanese nationals, yet they are governed by the U.S. military administration. They are not protected by American laws, yet they are under American power.

U.S.A. should compensate those whose farmland has been appropriated by American forces for military use in line with land expropriation laws of Japan.

American forces employ 36,800 civilian workers of various nationalities; 80 percent are islanders who lost bond as the result of expropriation. The Japanese earn ¥25 (Okinawan yen) per hour (i.e. circa 2 cents), while Filipinos earn ¥196 and Americans ¥702.

Eidmann adds that Japan is full of Okinawans who are not permitted to return home as permanent residents, and that the Japanese know what is going on there. The disparity between American talk about democracy and illustration of the principles in action is so great that the Japanese do not trust (or respect) America—the Orient, indeed, does not trust the U.S.A.

Some additional projects for foundations:

Project D: Japanese to study the work of American philanthropic foundations.

Project E: $20,000 to two private universities for a study of the proper techniques for the teaching of kanji. (Perhaps the Keystone Co., manufacturer of the tachistoscope, will assist here.[213])

In connection with all of this: I saw the letter from Shantineketan[214] to Professor Kasugai containing a statement of the salary that he is to receive when he goes there this fall for a stint of from three to five years, bringing with him his family:

1. Three hundred rupees per month!
2. Scale 175 - 15 - 400 rupees (Whatever that means)
3. "Dearness allowance" of 30 rupees per month (Whatever that means)

We discussed for a moment a book by Charles Morris, *The Open Self*,[215] in which thirteen "ways of life" are listed and discussed; namely:

1. Apollo
2. Buddha (actually Shōdōmon [Hōnin])

3. Christianity
4. Dionysos
5. Islam
6. Prometheus-Zoroaster
7. Maitreya (actually Jōdomon)
8. Epicurean
9. Taoism
10. Stoicism
11. Meditation
12. Physical activity
13. Self as instrument of forces other than oneself

Apparently, Morris took some kind of straw vote and found that the ways preferred by Americans were numbers 2 and 7.

I had a long discussion with Eidmann (before Kasugai's arrival) of the problem of "revelation" in the religions of America. The discussion commenced with my mention of Tenrikyō (about which I have just begun to read)[216] and Ramakrishna and voodoo. Eidmann then launched into an excellent review of the "Restoration Movement" in America, from Puritan times; as follows:

The Puritans fully expected revelations in America (Zion); the revelations, however, didn't come. Roger Williams, for instance, believed church had failed, and that Christ would have to return.

1740–50: an enthusiastic movement of revelation was put down by church, which was by then a closed corporation of businessmen.

1. The Enlightenment asked: why is there no revelation today?
2. Thousands converted to Unitarianism (Harvard)[217]

1803–4: Movements for restoration of the primitive church (e.g. in Kentucky: this was a small, extreme phase, however): Disciples of Christ (Campbell)[218], Methodists of U.S.A. Then a splash of revelations claiming valid authority:

1. Mormons
2. Pentecostal movements
3. Shakers
4. Utopian movements
5. The Millerites to Mary White to the Seventh Day Adventists (the world was supposed to end in 1844: after 1844, the prophecy was reinterpreted as the beginning of a world renovation: the cleansing of the tabernacle in heaven): Battle Creek: Kelloggs products

1844–45: Spiritualism

After the Civil War: Judge Rutherford, etc., Mary Baker Eddy

1880s: New Thought Movement; Kansas City Unity

1885: Jehovah's Witnesses

World War I: Moral Rearmament Movement

All this got us talking about Restoration Movements now beginning to incorporate the World Religion theme:

The American Indian nineteenth-century "renovation" movements were probably linked to Mormonism. For the Mormons, the American Indians are descendants of several small groups of immigrants belonging to the tribes of Judah and Benjamin (*not* the ten lost tribes). Indians were intitiated into Mormon rites. Were the Mormons' esoteric "garments" the model for Ghost Dance shirts? According to this movement, the Indians were again to reclaim their land. (See Dale Morgan's *Bibliography of Mormonism,* a copy of which is probably in the 42nd St. library.)[219]

Related themes: Swedenborg;[220] and the Bah'ai faith, which is a restoration movement in the Orient; and a World Religion movement in the West.[221]

Consider the World Religion theme of Ramakrishna: the Brahmo Samaj[222] influence and Unitarianism (also, German romanticism, and again Swedenborg): I think, also, that the work of such men as Bastian[223] may have had some influence here.

I have been greatly impressed by what I have read about Tenrikyō—and shall discuss this later: just now—hold the comparison of Miki,[224] Ānanda Mayī,[225] Ramakrishna, voodoo, and Pentecostalism. Nineteenth-century transformations of culture, dissolution of fixed patterns, and individual quest. See Radin on Peyote.[226]

Eidmann stresses the Jōdo Shinshū influence on Tenrikyō: idea of gratitude (Jōdo and Shinshū); idea of *kanro,* "sweet dew" (Jōdo and Shinshū from India's *amrita*).

In Mormonism, revelations now fail to come and the claim now is that inspiration is enough.

Query: Why do revelations no longer come in the traditional Western religions?

A night of pouring rain.

Sunday, June 19

Woke up last night with my first real insomnia since New York—after Eidmann's dinner of tempura. Tried to study a bit of Japanese. Back to sleep, and awake at 8:30—just in time for 9:00 o'clock breakfast and a 9:30 departure with Hisashi Mita for the puppet plays of Osaka in the Bunraku theater. A marvelous experience: 11:00 A.M. till 4:00 P.M. Five plays.

On the way, in the train I could see the Japanese rice fields happily flooded and the peasants everywhere at work in their hats and with grass rain mats on their backs, transplanting rice, blade by blade, from their first beds into fresh, more widely spaced rows; also many ploughing their rain-soaked fields with their oxen. A lovely spectacle.

Hisashi spoke a little more about the "Incident" two weeks ago at the university, and it fits into my Project B picture.[227]

The student organization had asked for a Russian-style party of good fellowship; had been denied; were angry, stormed the president and struck him: he was to leave next day (June 3 or 4) for a law conference in Greece and they were eager to rush their project through. The student who struck was a fourth-year literature student. The student organization has been dissolved, and protest scribblings (Communist-style) are now appearing on the walls: "To strike the president was bad; to dissolve the organization is worse."

Whence the inspiration to the students of the organization? Largely contacts with Japanese union organizations (the same unions as those forced on Japan by our American Occupation economic theorists—our beloved Reds of the forties). Most of the interested students are economics majors.

The big point: U.S.A. is supporting a highly conservative faculty with almost *no* student contacts. Why is Russia, instead of American democratic campus life, the only available model for these students? *Our* fault: our capitalists support the state system; our Reds advertise Russia via the unions. And so where, in all this, is the actual American ideal?

The Bunraku was full of marvels, chief among them the singer-storytellers and their samisen accompanists.

Next, the curious puppet situation, where each single puppet has three men in black to work it, and yet one's concentration goes definitely to the puppet. The leading puppeteer works the body and the right hand; the second works the left hand; and the third works the legs. The plots are Kabuki style, but I read in the program that, actually, in the eighteenth century, it was the Kabuki that borrowed from the puppet play, and not vice versa.

Quite remarkable was the competence of *all* the performers, from old Bungoro Yoshida (eighty-five years old) to the young boy who sang the boy's part in the first play. The expansion and contraction of the stage, transformations of perspective, etc., were in line with what I have come to expect of this absolutely infallible world of the Japanese theater. And the whole thing was a sheer delight.

After returning home, I went to work on my diary and my Japanese.

Monday, June 20

A pleasant, quiet day. Japanese in the morning; letters, diary, and Japanese all the rest of the day.

A slight brain wave this morning for the possible *convocation address* as follows:

"To know that you are a sparrow and not a swan; or, on the contrary, a swan and not a sparrow: to know this and to be sure of it, and to know that there is no possibility of your being otherwise—not even in your dreams—gives a great security, stability, and quality of harmony and peace to the psyche. You are not only reconciled to your place, but permanently at home there, and, since (as Lewis Mumford once wrote) 'values emerge from life at all its levels,' you are rich in life. But, on the other hand, if you are continually thinking one minute that you must be a sparrow, or then, perhaps, with a fresh inspiration, that you are possibly a lion or a whale, you will soon become so profoundly implicated in your own psychological agony that you will have little time or energy for anything else, and certainly no sense whatsoever of the bliss and wonder of being alive.

"The security, strength, majesty, and competence of man living in the rigidly stratified societies of the ancient Orient, is something that one can still see and experience in the East. . . .

"The problems of modern America, on the other hand . . . on our campus, here, they are challenged and invoked . . . *our* problem, when solved, becomes a model for the coming world. There is no question about this:

we are the growing point of humanity—humanity, at least, this side of, and halfway through, the Iron Curtain. But in our failures, conversely, we are a menace to mankind, and a danger to the human species, a really foul and disgusting example of barbarism: unformed 'primal matter.' In fact, the great question that is hanging in the balance today is precisely this: are the values of the unique, unprecedented individual which we are seeking to develop here at Sarah Lawrence, and which, I believe, are the powers that our culture itself is in principle dedicated to develop—actually the boon that we suppose them to be; or is it going to be necessary for mankind to crush them out again, as they have been crushed since the very dawn (apparently) of human society?"

The power of the ancient, nonprogressive ideal to shape men and women who are harmonious and noble, is conspicuous throughout the Orient, where the "value" of archaic man outshines even the degradation of his present cultural shipwreck: in India, in particular, one is aware of this; and this, I believe, is what constitutes the fascination of India. In a different, very vigorous and vital way one feels it also in Japan—shining through the lights and noises of the great modern cities: mingled with—but transforming and assimilating (or so, at least, it seemed to me) the miracles and gadgets of the machine age. In Japan the *cultural* life of the Orient still is unbroken—and one can see in it an elegance of style, a richness of experience, and a competence for life that (to me, at least) seem almost miraculous.

In contrast: the fumbles, amateurism, self-interests, partial systems in conflict with each other of America (e.g. the American Occupation in contrast to America's democratic talk). The result: a universal distrust of America in the Orient—on many levels, joined maddeningly with a will to imitate—for, I can tell you, the lure and promise of the individual's development (which is what we hold in promise for mankind) is a lure to which every young heart in the world spontaneously responds: it is the lure that the archaic societies were designed specifically to crush.

Theme: the danger of our educational system: the production of specialist barbarians (Titanism)—this, perhaps, is what the world most fears and the Russian peril is balanced against this. If we could convince the world that we are civilized, Communism wouldn't have a chance. (And I believe the Communists have known this for some time. One of their formulae, when their influence was strongest in our colleges in the late thirties and early forties, was to deprecate cultural subjects as "ivory tower." The political insanity of that idea is now apparent in every quarter of the civilized world.)

Tuesday, June 21

My last Japanese class with Father Moss. He looked a bit shocked and resentful when he learned that I was leaving him to flounder alone in his own swamp.

At 2:30 I went over to Eidmann's for one of the most charming afternoons of the Kyoto visit. Professor Kasugai and two of his young colleagues conducted us through the beautiful Nanzenji (Zen) Temple, with its garden of gravel and rocks, and in its beautiful hill-and-forest setting. He then took us to a delightful garden nearby, where there were little platforms for "picnic" parties—and we were served a fabulous meal of *yudōfu* by the women who prepare these bean-curd dishes for the temple. In the lovely garden with its pond and shrines and temples, six of us sitting in a circle with our bowls and chopsticks—it was like a trip into a Japanese picture.

Nanzenji Temple and garden

Returned to Eidmann's for a chat about Zen. He maintains that all the great Zen masters (e.g., all of those mentioned by Suzuki) were Chinese, and that in Japan Zen early became an instrument of the government. Its closest associations are with the spirit of Bushidō. And the beautiful gardens, for which the Zen temples are celebrated, actually are vestiges of a garden culture that was originally that of T'ang China, and was subsequently common to all the sects of Japan: plus a kind of Shintō temple-grove idea.

Ironically, Zen (government-supported) has been a Buddhism of garden retreats, whereas Honganji (against governmental control) has its great temples in the midst of the cities and (as in the Tokyo temple that I visited) is rather for modernization than for picturesque retreats. The reason, Eidmann declares, is that the Honganji is in battle for an idea, and so has advanced, so to say, into the field of life.

Eidmann is going to arrange for me, next weekend, to experience a bit of Zen meditation.

Wednesday, June 22

All morning in the hotel, at my Japanese: afternoon, from one to three, at the school. Much better! Then I went to Eidmann's, to commence a series of private conversation lessons with a young Japanese student, Iguchi-san, whom he has found for me. Monday, Eidmann will be leaving for Hokkaido, and I shall continue with Iguchi-san at his house. I begin to feel, at last, that I may crack this thing before I leave Japan.

Thursday, June 23

Morning: study in the hotel lobby and in my room: really very pleasant. About 10:15 the room quivered a little—and I had survived my first Japanese earthquake. Afternoon, one to three, Japanese school. Evening 3:30 to midnight, Japanese study in my room. Dinner at my favorite cheap restaurant, Fujiya. The ideal day!

Friday, June 24

Hotel study in the morning. Class from one to three, then to Eidmann's for my second lesson with Iguchi-san. Observable progress. Professor

ether

air

fire

water

earth

Indian five-element symbols

Kasugai and his colleagues arrived about dinnertime—and we all went out to make "rubbings" of a Mongolian stone carving in the temple compound, brought by the father of the present patriarch from his expedition to inner China. I caught a glimpse of the present patriarch (in shirt and trousers, carrying a briefcase). And heard a hawk, whose cry sounded almost like the music of a Japanese flute. Nature imitating art? After dinner, a long, pleasant, rambling chat developed, during which we viewed a great number of snapshots of a type of Japanese lantern-like *stūpa* in which the Indian five-element symbols are distinctly represented. This, apparently, is rather common in Japan after the fourteenth century—but is not found in China. What is the relation to India? One thinks also of the five buildings built by Milarepa in his initiation.[228]

I was presented with four rubbings of Buddha figures on a stone at the Imamiya Shintō Shrine in Kyoto, as well as with some photos of our earlier parties. Tuesday, at the garden, I had been presented with photos of two Japanese gardens. I promised to write to Carl Schuster[229] to learn the history of the *stūpa* form.

CHAPTER X

AT THE SEVENTH STEP

Saturday, June 25

A curious, badly broken up day. In the morning at ten, Mr. Masao Handa, the father of one of the younger teachers at the Japanese school, arrived to have me criticize his poetry and help him with a textbook on English poetry that he is composing. He remained until noon. Then, at 2:30, I went around to the meeting of the Kansai Asiatic Society to hear Ellen Psaty deliver a lecture on modern Japanese art. But I was one hour too early and so read all the copies of the *New Yorker* on the shelf until the meeting began. Mr. van Vest was presiding. I met Mr. Perkins (whom Alan Watts had written me to look up), and met again the Dutch consul, de Roos, from Kobe, who had lectured last month. After the talk, the consul and his wife drove Ellen and me to the Kyoto Hotel, where we had tea. Another Dutch couple arrived and we had more tea. Then the Dutch people left, and Ellen and I went to a cute little two-by-four bar ("Le Nid") for a drink. Cracked walnuts and drank Johnny Walker on the rocks till she had to meet a 7:45 train. Had my own dinner alone at Fujiya and returned to my room to write letters and bring my diary up to date. Somehow, even with nothing to do but study Japanese, I am managing to fall behind all the time with my mail. A system of *some* kind must be found before I return to New York, or I'm a goner.

One month from today, Jean arrives in Tokyo. Two months from the day after tomorrow we leave for Honolulu, San Francisco, and New York. Amen to a miraculous year.

Some notes on Ellen Psaty's talk, and my conversation, later, with the Dutch consul, who has been in Japan since 1921:

It seems that Europe had already received the impact of Japanese art in the late 1860s: an exhibition took place in Vienna in 1873.

Japanese interest in their own art and architecture as something of national importance began with the visit to Japan of Fenellosa,[230] circa 1878. He lectured in Kyoto in 1882, 1884, and 1886. In 1884, under his influence, an association of painting was founded. He returned to Boston after 1886.

Kakuzō Okakura[231] was Fenellosa's protégé. In 1885, he went with Fenellosa to Europe. In 1885, he and Fenellosa were responsible for the founding of the Tokyo School of Fine Arts. Okakura's interest—like that of the whole Meiji Restoration—was predominantly nationalistic: namely, that Japan should achieve rapidly what the West had achieved through the centuries in the way of skills; and this was to be achieved as a kind of national-racial triumph. Art was to be an instrument of national prestige. The tendency, therefore, was to imitate the big, the recognized, the academic, in all of the arts—instead of that aspect of the Western development that was actually closest to the Japanese sphere of taste and feeling. The whole course of Japanese modern art was thrown off the line by this insincere, unaesthetic emphasis. Moreover, what was imitated was the art of a period in the European development that is one of the lows in the whole Occidental tradition.

The art of the Orient has generally a much stronger literary emphasis than that of the (modern) West. No Western artist would feel that a picture with a poem written across it, and requiring that poem for its proper understanding, was a proper picture. But in China and Japan, the relationship between calligraphy and painting is intimate. The Japanese modern artist seems never to have broken with this feeling, and so, has never really caught the essential problem and intention of modern Western art.

By the close of the Tokugawa period Japanese art had become ossified: fixated to the imitation of a limited range of models. Western art was experienced as a refreshing change. The available teachers, however, were not good: Westerners accidentally present in Japan, who could paint or draw. In 1876 an invitation was issued to European professionals; but those who arrived were only second- or third-raters. In 1887 the Japanese who had studied abroad began to return: but their main emphasis was on the academic.

No tradition for independent individual judgment and expression has ever developed in the modern art movement in Japan. Indeed, this goes so far that the artist tries to suppress information about his life that does not fit into a fixed picture of what the artist life should be. It is almost impossible to find the material for an honest, objective study of the life and work of a modern Japanese artist.

The artist in Japan was, formerly, a craftsman with a fixed social status in a fixed social structure. The breaking of that structure has resulted in a great struggle for success, which would seem to be the primary aim of the modern artist in Japan. This leads him to do the kind of work that he feels ought to be done, to win.

The influence of the dealers (the big department stores, etc.) in creating and maintaining the careers of the artists has an immense impact—as far as the visible picture of modern Japanese art is concerned.

One sees a certain favored, relatively small number of "public" pictures that appear in many exhibitions, and are reproduced in catalogues and books. The relationship of the recognized value of these works, and their artists, to the actual condition of the modern art of Japan is impossible to estimate—for, at the opposite end of the situation we have the fact that in Japan the idea prevails that value depends on how few have seen an object or picture. People buy pictures and they disappear: no one ever sees them; no one knows where they are. The artist himself cannot tell you what has become of his work. It is impossible, therefore, for any critical, comparative estimate of the condition of modern Japanese art to be arrived at. Nor can the public form its own opinion—since the works, other than those being currently exploited by the dealers, are unavailable. And finally, to give an idea of what is behind all this: whereas an excellent traditional Japanese work of art will fetch about ¥2,000,000, the works of the top moderns sell for as much as ¥4,000,000.

Partly as a result of the emphasis of Fenellosa and Okakura on the past of Japan, there has developed no Japanese scholarship devoted to modern Japanese art. Articles on the subject appear only in magazines. And the art dealers, dealing in ancient art, do not handle the moderns. They represent two worlds. And the values of the past have not been able to leap the gap.

There are a number of Japanese words that are applied to pictures and always receive translations that do not quite fit the application. It is probable that these Japanese words, actually, are themselves based on Japanese misunderstandings of the European words by which they are now translated. Examples:

seishin-teki — spiritual

shasei — sketch

shajitsu — realistic (actually: naturalistic)

As for "spirituality" in Japanese art: the Japanese seem to feel that any picture with a lot of space in it is "spiritual." Actually, much of what they would call "spiritual" is what in the West would be termed "sentimental."

My own bright thoughts after all of this:

"History," in the Occidental sense, can be written only in, for, and about the Occident—where at least a considerable proportion of the significant events and people are publicly known: it is a way of writing about life in the world that befits the public character of our Occidental life. No proper history of the Orient, or of anything Oriental, can be written—since the keys to all the movements, facts, and surface appearances are, as far as possible, hidden. The Orient has an intrinsic need and love for the esoteric.

The Japanese listening to Western records (e.g. in those Tokyo coffee shops where record programs are presented) is not doing the same thing as a young Westerner also listening to records. The Japanese wearing Western clothes is not as Western as he looks: the whole context of feelings, requirements, and loyalties of the spirit within the body within the clothes is non-Occidental.

Mr. de Roos supported this, as follows:

You never know an Oriental until you know his family: he has not accepted you as a friend until he has introduced you to his family.

The process of individualization in the Orient is something that is taking place very slowly—or, perhaps, not taking place at all.

Sunday, June 26

Today, what I should call a considerable crack in the glass. First, as I was about to leave the hotel, at 11:00 A.M., a phone call from Tokyo —from guess whom: Ed Solomon,[232] who will arrive for a week's stay in the Kyoto Hotel tomorrow afternoon. Second, when I arrived at Eidmann's I was told that the Zen *rōshi*, Eishū Takeda, whom we were to visit today and at whose monastery I was to get a taste of Zen meditation, would today be attending a funeral—and so the date is off. Eidmann leaves tomorrow for Hokkaido—and that's that.

I was introduced, however, to a young Japanese student who is to go with me, two weekends hence, to the Tenrikyō center for a two-day visit. His name: Kuchiba. The name of the Tenrikyō abbot: Fukaya.

After a nice lunch, I bowed my farewell and thanks and returned to my room to bring my mail, diary, and studies up to date. It is a rainy day, and a good day for work.

Miscellany:

1. *Possible subject for a book: Pope Joan*[233]
2. Name of the deity in the temple in the little Zen *yudōfu*-restaurant garden, before whose entrance two rampant boars serve as guards (one, on observer's right, with mouth open; opposite, with mouth closed): *Maricheta*. In the area near the pond was a little shrine to the "Master of the Pond"—probably a *nāga*.[234]
3. In Zen: Rinzai is a way to Enlightenment; Sōtō is not. (I don't think I understand this!)
4. In Japan, when letters are addressed to important personages, they are addressed to—
   XXXXX, to his basement; or
   XXXXX, into his wastepaper basket; or
   Abbot XXXXX, just outside the circle of his holy radiance.[235]
5. The Buddha figures that Zimmer called "*Dhyāni*" Buddhas might more properly be termed "apparitional" Buddhas. The *Dhyāni* Buddhas are eleventh- through thirteenth-century figures, proper to the Buddhism of Nepal. The figures under the bells at Borobudur would be called in Japanese *keshin* Buddhas; they represent the *Nirmānakāya;* or *hōben hōshin*, representing *Dharmakāya*.[236]

Monday, June 27

Studied Japanese all morning, left a note for Solomon at the hotel, went to Fujiya for lunch and had my classes till three. Taxi (with one of the teachers of the school whom I left at the railroad station, and with whom I found myself actually able to say a few things in Japanese) to Nishi Honganji, for my conversation lesson with Iguchi. Eidmann and Haru had left in the morning for Hokkaido—and I found Obasan learning tea from the little old lady whom I had met here before. I tried to converse a bit with them, and was on the edge of being able to say something. I feel that if I continue a bit longer, this thing will break.

After my lesson, returned at six to the hotel and found Ed in his room (two doors from mine) in his shorts. Took him out to dinner at Suehiro's, then showed him bits of the town and finished in a cute little bar (which I first visited with Ellen Psaty), where, again, I made my Japanese begin to work. We returned to the hotel at about 10:15, and I went back to work on my Japanese.

Tuesday, June 28

Ed at breakfast—and we talked till nine. Then, Japanese till dinnertime, and with Ed to dinner at Alaska (where I dined my first evening in Kyoto). Steered Ed toward the Gion geisha quarter after dinner, and returned to my Japanese.

Some notes on the conversations with Ed. I am assuming that he was sent by God, as everything else has been on this trip, and that I may think of him as standing at the opposite pole from myself, looking at the same objects. By comparing the two views I may calculate for the parallax. Actually—what I have seen white, he has seen black, with few exceptions. We both agree that the Sarabhais are great, that India is a kind of horror, and that it was nice to get to Tokyo.

Ed feels that the U.S.I.S. is doing a good job in the Orient—my feeling is precisely the opposite.

Ed feels that we should go on giving aid to the Orient: I feel that everything we send should be paid for.

Ed excuses the gaucheries of the American grantees and technical people in the Orient: I don't and I think they're a scandal. "But they're farmers!" said Ed. "Well, haven't we got any civilized city people to send out as evidence of some kind of cultural development and sophistication in our country? The Chinese and Russians send artists and we send farmers."

Ed asks why, with all the literacy in Japan, their pattern is authoritarian, not democratic, and why they behaved so militaristically in their conquered provinces. I suggest that democracy may not be the only possible term of literate ideation, and ask why the American authorities in Okinawa are militaristic, not democratic, in their government.

In a subtle way, it has been good for me to have this meeting here with Ed; for it has helped me to realize that I am still on Earth, and it has prepared me to take disparate opinions into account in my preparation for the Sarah Lawrence address.

Wednesday, June 29

News today from Tokyo. Jean's program there is shaping up. A day of Japanese—no view of Ed. I had another lesson with Iguchi from 4:00 to 6:00 P.M., and had dinner alone at the Shijō Fujiya.

Thursday, June 30

Bumped into Ed as I left my room at noon. He has spent the last two evenings at the little bar to which I introduced him and has met the president of the Kyoto Rotary Club. The latter, who was waiting downstairs with his car, announced that Gautam and Gira Sarabhai were due to arrive in Kyoto about July 17th. "All moves to one great end!" I went off to Fujiya for lunch and to my Japanese class; then returned to my room to study. Ed found me and dropped in around 5:30—and I was a little annoyed, but held together: suggested we should go to a Chinese place for dinner, so that I might return early to my work. Phone call, meanwhile, from Ellen Psaty, to ask about our tentative date for tomorrow night. Found, when I returned from dinner, that my watch (Dad's watch: "To Charles W. Campbell, from his friends in the Hosiery Business"—given to him at the farewell party in New York before his departure in 1940 for Hawai'i) had dropped from my wrist and was gone. Felt very badly. The jinx of last Sunday's turn seemed to be continuing to work. Studied Japanese till about midnight and went to bed.

Friday, July 1

Studied Japanese all morning—with a brief conference with a policeman who came to the hotel for information when I reported the loss of my watch. Saw Ed—looking a bit the worse for a hangover—about to go off on a short excursion with a couple of Japanese students. He has found a nice gang of people to help him, and so I probably shan't have to worry about him much more. Lunch at Fujiya; Japanese class; to Nishi Honganji for my conversation session with Iguchi: and there was a letter there from Tenrikyō, declaring that it would be OK for me to visit the place next weekend with my interpreter, Kuchiba. Well, that much, anyhow, is going to work out: and Mrs. Sasaki returns to Kyoto Saturday, so I may yet get a bit of the Zen world.

Fetched Ellen Psaty at 6:45 and we went first for a drink to the little bar (not the one to which I brought Ed) on the canal road. After this, we went to an excellent little restaurant at the edge of the Gion district, called Tsubosaka. Walking down the street, away from it, she showed me another restaurant, Hamasaku, which is also good. We had coffee at a coffee spot called Bel Ami, near Pontochō, then found a bar in Pontochō for a

Japanese characters = the restaurant name, Tsubosaka

brandy—where there was a lively crowd of Japanese, having their fun with the bar girls. We remained for about an hour, then strolled around the town some more and ended in another very nice coffee place, François, where there was a Frenchman sitting at a little table alone, behind a stack of manuscript, as though in a French café. Ellen knew him: Jean-Pierre Hauchecorne, from the Institut Franco-Japonais du Kansai. We invited him over to our table, and he talked, with a continuous, compulsive flow of loosely associated themes, till about 12:30, when we picked up and departed. Meanwhile, three young Japanese homosexuals—two with auburn hair, quite wild—entered and had their coffee at another table.

Hauchecorne's themes: "I am Zen. The great Zen saying: 'If you think you see the Buddha, do not pause; if you do not see the Buddha, pass quickly by.'" I noticed that he patted, occasionally, the handsome cut of his hair, and that his sole interest was his own character as a person who had experienced or seen many interesting things and would presently write three novels and a guide to Kyoto. He knew what the titles and contents of the novels would be and something about the style that they would have. He told of some of the startling effects he had achieved with his Zen bark (like a dog), and strung out a long tale about some interesting chap whose diary he was editing. He was a very pleasant fellow: and I guess he gave me, in the course of all this, my touch of Zen—namely, when he was saying something about the seeing or not seeing of the Buddha I suddenly realized that—well—the banality of Ed Solomon was perhaps my vision of the Buddha in Kyoto. Here, Ed had come all this way to bring me the message, so to speak, of his Buddhahood: his phone call, last Sunday, was, in a way, the cry of the Buddha-child at the seventh step:

"Hello, that Joe Campbell?"

"Yes."

"Well, this is Ed! Ed Solomon!"

"Oh, hello Ed. Where are you?"

"Tokyo!"

"Well, isn't that nice? What are you doing!"

"Coming to Kyoto! Tomorrow."

"Well, isn't that just fine? Where you going to stay?"

"Kyoto Hotel."

"Why, that's where I am."

"Yes, I know."

Actually, as I now can think of it, such a revelation of the Buddha would be the most appropriate possible for myself, whose life is to be at Sarah Lawrence and in New York—not in the Zen temples of Kyoto, which, after all, I could have chosen for my residence during these weeks here, had I been so disposed. I chose the comfort of the Kyoto Hotel. The revelation has come in the form appropriate to the recipient.

During my two hours, this afternoon, with Iguchi, we got onto the theme of the mystery of Buddhahood, and he gave me the Japanese names of some of the fundamental concepts:

Eien no shinri the permanent Truth (= *śunyatā*)

1. *Hōshin: Dharmakāya:* the "body" of *dharma:* Truth, *dharma,* itself
2. *Hōjin:* the "Rewarded" "body" of the Buddha; now in *nirvāṇa*
3. *Ōjin:* the Earthly body of the Buddha

Some theologians believe that the *hōshin* can be seen—which would bring it down (it seems to me) into the realm of ideation.

The term *aru*—existing—cannot be applied to the Buddha: the proper term for the Buddha is *sonzai suru*—(*sonzai* = being).

The *ōjin* appears in the realm of *jikan*—time. I decided that the best term to use in the translation of our word "eternity" would probably be *eien no shinri.*

Iguchi tells me also that, according to what he is being taught, the Mahāyāna is divided into two main schools: the Kūkan Gakuha ("*śunyatā*," or "idea School") of Nāgārjuna; and the Yuishiki Gakuha ("One *Vijña* School") of Vasubandhu,[237] devoted to Maitreya. I hope to hear more about all this next time.

Saturday, July 2

Up at about 7:30 (without my watch) and, after breakfast, to work on my Japanese—with a curious feeling that in concentrating on this Japanese—which I may not learn, after all—I have perhaps missed most of what I might and should have learned and experienced in Kyoto. Ed came to my table in the lounge for a ten-minute chat about his most recent night of joy, and I was pleased that he had found his crowd (actually a very nice crowd) and was not going to be on my hands. After lunch I went around to the Nishi Honganji to meet Iguchi and Fillmore, who were going to make a little tour of temples. Just when Fillmore had given up all hope of being released from the army in Japan, instead of in Minnesota, a wire came from Washington, and he is going to be able to stay.

We took a pleasant sort of picture-taking tour of the Nishi Honganji and Higashi Honganji compounds, and then went to a Zen temple, the Kōfukuji, of the Rinzai sect, supposed to date from ca. A.D. 1300. I took the trolley back to Fujiya after a brief walk through a rather poor section of the city, and studied Japanese till about ten. Sort of tired. Early to bed.

Sunday, July 3

Up at six, for the craziest day of my Japan visit. Professor Kasugai had invited me to accompany him and his students to Nara for a visit to a couple of curious and exceptionally interesting monuments. I was to meet them at 8:00 A.M. at Kyoto Station. Without my watch, I misjudged things and arrived about twenty minutes early, after stopping at Nishi Honganji, to pick up a lunch package from Eidmann's housekeeper. The party—which included Professor Kasugai's wife and kids—began appearing at about 7:55, and we caught, finally, an 8:40 train.

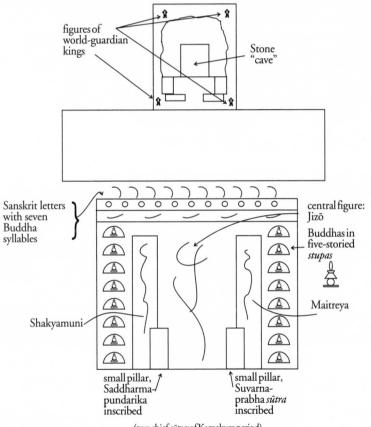

figures of world-guardian kings

Stone "cave"

Sanskrit letters with seven Buddha syllables

central figure: Jizō

Buddhas in five-storied *stupas*

Maitreya

Shakyamuni

small pillar, Saddharma-pundarika inscribed

small pillar, Suvarna-prabha *sutra* inscribed

(two chief *sutras* of Kamakura period)

The temple of Jurin-in

The first of the monuments visited was the Jūrin-in, a neat little building constructed around a stone shrine, which had been built ca. A.D. 1200 in the form of a small cave sanctuary. The founding of the temple is attributed to Kōbō Daishi. (Kōbō Daishi is the "Mayflower" of Japan.[238])

We next went to a large earth mound, like an Indian *stūpa*, with trees and plants growing all over it and occasional stones bearing Buddha figures and inscriptions. The place is known as Zutō, or "Head," Stūpa, and is supposed to have been built on the site where the head fell off a demon slain in the air. The date is ca. A.D. 800 and the Abbot Genbō is supposed to be the founder. The *stūpa* is due south of the great Tōdaiji Temple, which can be seen from the summit.

As one walks around the *stūpa* one sees the following Buddhas. First, on the lowest tier:

> South—*Maitreya*
> West—*Amida*
> North—*Śakya*
> East—*Vaisajaya*(?)

On the next tier, seven Buddha scenes:

> Three unidentified, then
> Birth
> Enlightenment
> Meditation
> Paranirvāṇa of the Buddha

In Japan, eight scenes are common, including Descent of Elephant and three others. In the upper tier: two Buddhas, unidentified. On the summit, a small *stūpa*.

The plan, apparently, was, to have lunch at this spot; but the caretaker seemed to suggest that it would be better for us to eat elsewhere; so, after he had burned some incense for us, in honor of the Buddha, we departed, and walked about a mile and a half in the broiling sun, to the deer park, where we found the shade of a tree and ate—with the deer poking their noses into our meals.

Our next visit was to the Tōdaiji, to see what the cute children called "Daibutsu-san." We went up onto the platform and walked around, where we could see the engravings on the bronze petals of the Buddha's lotus: pictures of astronomical signs, magical continents, thirteen Buddha worlds in layers, etc.

Daibutsu-den Temple, Tōdaiji Temple, Nara

Kasugai told me that the main figures in this temple are: at the observer's left, Akaśakośa; right Avalokiteśvara; and center, Mahāvairocana. After this visit, Mrs. Kasugai and the two children went home, and I should certainly have gone with them; for up to this point it had been a good day. Now, however, we returned to the Zutō mound and spent about three hours, dallying and then suddenly writing down the various inscriptions and taking photos. After this—when I thought we might now go home—we returned to the Jūrin-in and made some rubbings of a couple of stele in the yard.

It should be noted also that in the yard of this temple there was a *small* stūpa-*mound of earth, that looked a bit like the great Irish burial mound,* and if one peered long into the pitch-black interior a small Buddha image could be seen (so, at least, Kasugai told me; for I peered, but could not see).

Stūpa mound

It was after 6:30 when all this was finished, and I was really tired. But, after we had taken a bus to the station, Kasugai-san wanted to visit still another temple; so we boarded another bus and headed out into the country. The visit, this time, was to a small temple in a weedy lot, with a tall thirteen-stage stone pagoda at the side, and around the pagoda was a series of stones bearing the forms of Buddhas and Bodhisattvas, some with many arms. The temple was called Hannyaji, was founded A.D. 654 and rebuilt in the thirteenth century.

From the point in the road where we waited for the bus back to Kyoto, the great Tōdaiji roof and building could be seen towering far above the roofs and trees of Holy Nara.

The bus got us back to Kyoto Station about 8:40 P.M. I went to Fujiya for beer and dinner, and home directly to bed.

Monday, July 4

A very disheartening day. Rather dazed, after yesterday's heat and fatigue, I performed very badly indeed in my Japanese classes.

In my class with Iguchi, from four to six, I talked about Buddhism, and suddenly realized, what I should have known for some time, namely, that *the various sects are founded on the main tenets of the various great* sūtras. The approach to the study of Japanese Buddhism, consequently, should be through the *sūtras* here involved.

Left my class with Iguchi a little early, to rush to Mrs. Sasaki's for dinner—she having just returned to Kyoto from New York. The center of the Zen Institute of America is at 156 Waverly Place, New York City(!!!), so it is obvious what one of my early moves should be on returning home.[239]

We talked of many things, pleasantly, and had a beautiful Japanese dinner, served by her lovely girl servants, in her beautiful house, which is in the grounds of the Daikokuji Temple.

We spoke on several themes, among them the disappointment, not only of her American friends, but also of her Japanese friends, who have visited India. A sense of decline and decay.

Second, the curious generosity of Americans, which seems to be unique in world history and is universally misunderstood. This generosity is *not* a function of Christianity, which, in Europe and Asia, for instance, does not yield this pattern. The explanation may be in our frontier heritage, and in the broad margin of abundance in our rich continent.

I learned that the reason the smoke revolved around the fire at the Shingon ceremony of the *yamabushi* was—that *the fire was laid in a certain secret and complicated way.* This I believe. It suggests, however, a question that I must bring to Mrs. Sasaki when next I see her: what is the real point of the *yamabushi* making believe that a fire, which they know has a mechanical reason for its behavior, is controlled by magic?[240]

In Zen, it seems, the great road and chief exercise is *sitting in meditation; reading and study* are also strenuously practiced—in spite of all the sayings which would seem to suggest precisely the opposite. The meaning of the sayings is not that meditation and study are rejected. (The meaning would seem, rather, to be something like Spengler's rejection of the books.)[241]

All the odd goings-on of the quaint boys of the John Cage type have nothing to do with the real character of Zen.[242] (Likewise, I should think, of the dog barking of friend Hauchecorne.)

It occurred to me that Huxley's interest in the actual visions experienced after mescaline is a kind of materialistic interest in another world of things; whereas, in visionary writings, the images are not in themselves interesting, but are metaphoric of the ineffable. (There is an important point here: don't forget.)

Before I left, Mrs. Sasaki promised to have me meet a *rōshi* before my departure: so it may happen, after all.

Tuesday, July 5

No Japanese classes today (they are having exams for the upper class groups). I had a brief chat with Ed Solomon at breakfast and spent most of the remainder of the day on my Japanese—with time off for naps, however; for I'm still pretty tired after Sunday's event.

During the course of last week, I managed to complete arrangements by letter for Jean's teaching schedule in Tokyo: also, received a nice wire from Jean, stating that her Colorado recital, June 30, was a success. So this concludes, I think, all the agonies of the year.

Today was a real rainy day: a bit depressing, but a good day for work. Solomon went to Nara and Hōrinji with a social scientist from Chicago named Macmillan, whom I spoke with for a moment in the lobby of the hotel. He had spent some weeks lecturing at the University of Hawai'i, where he had been annoyed by the press as a "fellow-traveler": Aunt Louise Dillingham actually tried to have a public lecture that he was to give banned.[243] (I love the Americanism of the Dillinghams! Freedom of speech, Tom Paine, etc., seem to have nothing to do with it. It was amusing to hear this story right after reading all the Fourth of July blather in the *Mainichi* about the Rights of Man, freedom of speech, etc.)

Saw Ed again at about 9:00 P.M. (He and I tonight are the only residents on the seventh floor of the hotel.) His trip to Hōrinji and Nara had been fun, in spite of the rain. It included a couple of American social science women who have been here for some time. They visited a convent in Hōrinji and interviewed a Buddhist nun, who had been placed in the convent by her family when she was about two years old. Her life, according to Ed, was "flat": no study, no social work, just meditation. I should have loved to have heard that dialogue via interpreter, between a cluster of American social scientists of Protestant and Jewish backgrounds and a Buddhist nun.

Ed made a point, during our chat, about the inability of the Oriental students and experts to work with their hands. The Oriental tradition of scholarly study does not include anything like our *field trip* or *do it* ideas. I think that this may account for a lot of the mechanical troubles through-out the Orient. Handwork is left to ignorant laborers or to artisans whose crafts are traditional, while the new technologies are studied by men who cannot soil their hands.

Compare now the two worlds: social scientists judging the life of a Buddhist nun without themselves ever having experienced anything like meditation: Orientals judging Western life without themselves ever having worked with their hands. This might be called the polarity: *Zen meditation vs. Sarah Lawrence field trips* (or, more seriously, the lab. and the techno-logical work).

A couple of further points from the chat with Mrs. Sasaki. The Zen people in Japan tend to contaminate their idea of the message they have to give the world with the accidents of Japanese culture. One gentleman, for instance, who wanted to see Zen spread to America, suggested erecting a Japanese Zen temple in New York, serving Japanese tea, teaching tea cere-mony, etc. When Mrs. Sasaki pointed out the American resistance to bitter tea, sitting on the floor, and so on, he thought the attitude rather crude.[244]

American fellowships for Japan should be for two or three years, not one. The Fulbrights come with their families, take a couple of months to get adjusted and settled, do not know the language, and are practically ignorant of Japanese culture: by the time they begin to learn something, it is time to pack and leave.

Wednesday, July 6

Morning on Japanese; brief conversation with Ed, whose nightlife continues to yield new friends and larger visions. Le Nid (the bar), apparently, is the trapdoor to infinity. My Japanese classes today went better. I am within three lessons of the end of the course, but only one day remains: tomorrow. Friday there is going to be a little graduation ceremony—but next week I'm going to continue, as a special student, and keep at it till I start for Tokyo, on about July 21st.

A nice class this afternoon, also, with Iguchi. We have commenced reading his college text on Buddhism: *Bukkyō Gaiyō,* and I think this is going to be an excellent bridge to Japan.

佛教概要

Japanese characters = *Bukkyō Gaiyō*

At 6:00 P.M. I arrived at Mrs. Sasaki's for dinner (she had phoned this morning to invite me) and we had an excellent dinner again and a fine talk.

We discussed the point that has been on my mind ever since Calcutta and Orissa: the sacrifice of the personal factor in the Orient: archetypalization and the consequent lack of personal initiative. She declared the principle was operative here too, and that it was particularly strong among the better families. Everywhere there is a lack of what we would call personal initiative. Three extreme examples:

1. The young American instructor who assigned a paper to his class of young women and returned after the weekend holiday to find that all the papers were exactly alike. He flunked them all and was summoned before the president, who rebuked him. The girls' families had paid to have them get degrees that were required for their place in society. His notions of scholarship and student performance had nothing whatsoever to do with the reason that those young ladies had come to college. They had worked conscientiously to produce a paper for him, and had succeeded. Now, let him return and give a proper mark.

2. The professor who asked Mrs. Sasaki for a criticism of his paper on Buddhism. She thought she recognized the prose and when she mentioned

this to him, he said quite frankly, that yes, of course, it was all taken from Suzuki, but rearranged. (This is the kind of thing, by the way, that *we* frequently get from journalists, sophomores, and book reviewers—but we do not represent it as an ideal.) Consider in the light of this example, the stability of Oriental art and the pattern of the commentary in Oriental literature and philosophy.

3. The experience of Mrs. Sasaki's maid, when required to bake a cake *alone*—not with the help and advice of everybody in the household. This experience of doing something alone and making something that was *her own* was an entirely new one (and reported as a pleasurable one) for this excellent cook.

Everyone in Japan is implicated in a firmly fixed hierarchy and finds it very difficult (actually impossible) to relax and get on even terms with associates. Even the language (as I now realize) renders the crisis of a change of degree of intimacy quite considerable. The French shift from *vous* to *tu,* or the German from *Sie* to *du,* is as nothing compared to this![245] The result of this fixed external situation is a considerable context of interior tensions—which, in turn, the peculiar social institutions of Japan (geisha world, sake drinking, theater and festivals, and so on) take care of, and pretty well at that. (Mrs. Sasaki's report on the Japanese pattern of getting bingled[246] was that they relax, warm a little, and then become just silly.)

The Japanese attitude toward life, in contrast to the Indian, is definitely affirmative. (Hara-kiri, which is a social phenomenon, has nothing to do with negativism of the Indian type.)

Japanese luxury is optical, says Mrs. Sasaki (how wonderfully true!) They don't go in for great physical comfort, as we do in the West, but insist on beauty—and get it.

Japanese Buddhism is affirmative. The Epicureanism of the Zen *rōshis.* Monastery life, with tea, music, and meditation.

Japanese nuns, like the monks, are devoted primarily to meditation and worship. In some instances convents are in charge of temples. A special phenomenon (that encountered by Ed) is the tradition in the royal family and its branches of placing certain daughters in convents.

The *yamabushi* are noted for the magic of curing. The revolution of the smoke around the fire had a magical effect. One gets two layers here:

1. that of the apparent, but deceptive, influence of the priest's motions upon the fire, and
2. that of the influence of fire upon the cures that were effected.

Shinran's philosophy (Shinshū) was actually extremely profound: the popularization represented in the Amida cult is a misrepresentation—and yet it gives to the many what they want and require. The man who has been working all day in a rice field (or, one might add, broker's office) is hardly fit to follow, or to require, the teachings of the profoundest thinkers of the race.

(Enlarge, and we have the problem of modern India. The corollary, however, is that what the rice-field worker requires is hardly what the philosopher-scholar is thirsting to imbibe.)

Shinran, by the way, according to Mrs. Sasaki, had his own way with women—and this is a point not stressed by the Shinshū teachers of today. Indeed, she declares, the temples of the Heian period were hardly puritanical.

The Buddha himself was an affirmer, not a negator, of life. One has to consider the forty-nine years of his life given to teaching, after Enlightenment, and remember that his last meal but one was in a great courtesan's house. He was a teacher of kings and princes, as well as of monks and nuns.

The problem of Buddhism for the West: what is the essence of the teaching and how can it be carried without the accidental traits of Oriental life adhering to it and rendering it, not only unpalatable, but unsuitable to the Occidental mind?

Thursday, July 7

In this morning's paper, a lovely article about India's intent to enforce, gradually, a state of total prohibition—as though the country weren't already dismal enough! A still more amusing article yesterday pointed to the situation in Nepal—which is just about ripe for a Communist coup. The Indian army is ready to jump in, in that eventuality. What price "peaceful coexistence"!

Ed reported this morning that his bar life had finally hit the geisha jackpot: one of his companions, at 12:30 A.M., had invited him to a geisha session. A lovely time was had by all—"just plain good fun!" said Ed with sparkling, though somewhat baggy, eyes. He introduced me to an American woman of the somewhat dreadful social science type, who spoke of the tensions and frustrations of the Japanese, while trying to make cat's cradles with a rubber band: she spoke of suicides, bed-wetting, psychological advice, therapy, etc., and I was transported, as on the wings of dream, back to Sarah Lawrence.

My Japanese class today was not a great performance on my part, but by 10:00 P.M. this evening I had finished lesson fifty, the last in the book—just in time for my graduation day! Had a session also with Iguchi, who made a couple of good points about the distinctions between Zen, Jōdo, and Shinshū:

1. The emphasis of Zen is on meditation. The individual attains satori through his own force and effort. Moreover, the results are known and experienced in this world. The Indian counterpart is *rājā yoga.* Zen monks tend to retreat from the world.
2. The emphasis of Shinshū is on the recitation of the *nembutsu.* The individual attains the Awakening of the Faith through the power of Amida. The Awakening of Faith is experienced in this world (but is not Enlightenment?).247
3. Jōdo stands between the two: the stress is on *nembutsu,* but the effect is the result, partly of one's own force and effort, partly of the grace of Amida. Enlightenment is not experienced in this world, but in the Pure Land.

In contrast to Zen, in Jōdo and in Shinshū the stress and effort is toward bringing Buddhist teachings to mankind. (In Zen, perhaps, we have a large dose of Taoism: the atmosphere of old-roguism [as Lin Yutang calls it] is much the same.)248

Jōdo nuns taking tea

4. Tendai, according to Iguchi, leans in the direction of Shinshū and Jōdo, while Shingon is closer to Zen. (According to Mrs. Sasaki, Shingon is the main base of the *yamabushi*.)

Friday, July 8

The graduation exercises at 10:00 A.M. were something never to be forgotten. The graduates were, of course, all missionaries of one kind or another, four or five nuns, a couple of priests, and a company of assorted Protestants. Diplomas were distributed to applause (mine, however, postponed until I finish my further course of two weeks), after little talks had been given in English and Japanese by Miss Hibbard (principal of the school), Hayashi Sensei (the dean), and a Scandinavian chap who is the student of longest standing. Following the distribution of diplomas there took place the prize event of the day; namely, the singing of the school song. The school has no song, and so we sang *Aloha* in Hawai'ian, to the accompaniment of Miss Hibbard's zither. I nearly wept: the combination of the ridiculousness of the whole thing and the pathos of the whole missionary effort to reconstruct in alien lands—with zithers, for example, instead of cathedral organs—the accidents of their culture, hit me in a funny way, and the occasion amounted to an experience. We next went into the yard to have our pictures taken, while the Japanese kids in the large school building across the street looked on from the windows. And finally, we returned to the schoolhouse for cookies (Western and Japanese types), iced coffee, and some more singing to Miss Hibbard's zither and word games. The party ended about noon, after one of the graduating ladies sang a solo—again to the zither—with a kindly smile, but the sort of seriousness that indicates artistic effort and achievement.

Good-byes at the door of the little schoolhouse, and, after my beef sandwich, coffee, and "fruit punch" for lunch at Fujiya, I returned to the hotel for a nap. The heat is beginning to build up hard, and I'm beginning to feel the same sort of sudden fatigue that used to hit me in India.

At about 3:30 I went to Eidmann's place for my reading lesson with Iguchi, then returned to Fujiya for dinner and had another amusing experience. The waitress brought me the menu and as I took it I said what I thought was *"Konban wa"* ("Good evening"). *"Hai!"* ("Yes!") she said, and she took away the menu, wrote something on a slip of paper, and disappeared into the kitchen. I looked at the paper. Something was scribbled in katakana, and the price was written ¥170. Well, I thought, I can't go too far wrong for ¥170, so we'll just wait and see. In about ten minutes she brought me a chopped-steak platter, with spaghetti, beans, and a fried egg![249] I felt that the language school had done well to postpone the granting of my diploma. I returned to my room, to study diligently till it was time for bed.

Saturday, July 9   *Kyoto—Tenri—Kyoto*

The day opened with an amusing surprise. I was about to leave to have breakfast with Mrs. Sasaki, when there was a knock on my door: Ed Solomon. "Come," he said; "I've something to show you." He had been packing, to leave for Tokyo, when, in his suitcase, he found my watch. Mystery. How did it get there? Guess: stolen by one of the room boys, inscription on the back rendered it unmarketable (also, I had notified the Kyoto police); returned, not directly (too obvious) but via my friend.

A very nice breakfast chez Mrs. Sasaki, and a couple of interesting points emerged in the conversation:

About the Catholic Church and the Occupation—why there are so many Catholic priests and nuns now in the language school. She made several points:

The first is gossip: that when MacArthur was in the Philippines a number of the Philippine businessmen helped him to handle his money so well that he made a fortune: became a very wealthy man. The gossip goes that he promised to promote the cause of Catholicism in Japan.

The second is fact (from "reliable sources"): The U.S.A. foresaw and looked forward to a second Russo-Japanese war; but a people, to fight, must have something to fight for. People fight for two reasons: (1) their food and livelihood, and (2) their God. The Japanese had already fought one war for their food and livelihood and were not likely to engage in another right away for the same cause. Buddhism and Shintō, on the other hand, supply no real God, in the Biblical sense of the term, for which people would fight. Ergo: the Japanese must be given a God for whom to fight. The Catholic Church, as the staunchest anti-Communist force in the Western world and the best organized church outfit besides, was given the go-ahead and U.S. government aid. Project: to convert one million Japanese a year, so that in ten years there should be ten million Catholics in Japan. Result: fiasco. All the Christian sects together cannot count more than some 400,000, even after ten years of the most ambitious plans. The Catholic share, after the ten years, seems to be about 250,000. Nevertheless, the nuns and priests are continuing to push in: as witness, my cute little school.

Mrs. Sasaki told of hearing an Episcopalian bishop get the brush-off in Washington at precisely the time when the Catholic Church was receiving every possible aid. No double optics in Operation God!

Mrs. Sasaki told of hearing a sermon in St. Patrick's Cathedral, delivered before the cardinal by a very handsome young Irish priest, wherein the story was told of a nun, who would probably soon be beatified, who claimed that the Holy Trinity dwelt within her. The priest asserted that the Holy Trinity dwells within us all.

Problems: What is the function, then, of the Church? Is it that the sacraments alone open the gates to this interior trinity. Is the body of the Virgin Mary, who was assumed into Heaven, likewise in every heart?

Mrs. Sasaki suggested one explanation for the dismal failure of the Christian project in Japan; namely, that the Japanese feel that they can read the Oriental Bible at least as well as Westerners can—and they do not find in it precisely what is found by the Christian churches.

Reviewing in my mind the whole conversation, I felt that it helps me to understand the curious Religion-Business-Politics tie-up that has become so prominent in America since the war.

At about nine, Mrs. Sasaki's Japanese secretary, Takemura, arrived, and at 9:30 we went around to the Daitokuji *sōdō,* to see Oda Roshi and view the temple. The visit to the *rōshi* was great. At the entrance to his residence, Takemura gave a short call, and immediately there was an odd call in reply, shortly after which a young monk appeared and made a deep kowtow. We bowed, and Takemura said that we had an appointment with the *rōshi.* Off went the monk, to return shortly, inviting us in. We were placed on cushions in a moderately large room, facing a kakemono, before which there was a cushion for the *rōshi,* who presently arrived and took his place: a handsome, middle-aged, Buddhist monk. We had tea. Compliments were exchanged; conversation was held, through Takemura, first, with respect to Mrs. Sasaki's New York voyage and return, then with me. On learning of my interests, the *rōshi* first spoke of Shintō and then asked me about the religions of America. I spoke first of the American Indians, then of the interest of the moderns in primitive and non-Christian traditions. He invited me to return some day and tell him more about the Indian religions, in which he was greatly interested. His own discourse on Shintō made the following points:

An earlier branch of Shintō, known as the Yamato, is rather primitive in character and stresses themes of purification. Another branch, Izumo, possibly of Korean provenance, shows similarities with Buddhism.

After the interview the *rōshi* brought us to a shrine in which a tooth—relic of the founder of the monastery—was preserved. Beautiful rooms, beautiful, black lacquer altar and steps, beautiful gardens opening into and out of the rooms at every turn. Mrs. Sasaki told me that it was this wonderful openness of the Zen temples to nature, as though there were no difference between the two worlds, which endeared her to Zen. We visited with another monk to conduct us through the meditation halls, teahouses, and the room where the acolyte faced the master. We returned to Mrs. Sasaki's for another glass of tea, and then I made off, at about noon, for the hotel.

Packed my bag, had lunch, and went to Eidmann's, to meet Kuchiba, who was to be my guide to Tenri. Fillmore was there, with a tall friend, and we had tea; then Kuchiba and I made for Kyoto Station. It turned out to be one of the great events of the year.

Mr. Fukaya, our host, met us at the station with a car and drove us directly to the Tenri main temple—a large and very handsome structure with a great, square excavation at its center, within which there is a wooden pillar—on the very spot that the mythology of Tenri regards as the origin place of mankind. When all of mankind has accepted Tenri, this pillar and the temple itself will be transformed into stone.

While we knelt on the great tatami-covered floor, worshipers came in and out, and while reciting their prayer they clapped their hands occasionally, and moved their hands in a pleasant little hand dance: the idea being that thought, word, and action should be one. Prominent among the decorative elements of the temple were the *shimenawa* and the white paper hangings of the Shintō shrines. Priests, in what seemed to me to be a modified Shintō vesture, sat behind the altar rail in immovable repose, and we saw more priests of this sort when we left the main hall of the temple and began walking through the long and spotless circumambulatories.

Inside the Tenri temple

Before we left the temple hall, a number of men with cleaning cloths arrived and began polishing all the woodwork in the great hall—and as we then walked through the long corridors, we passed a number of groups on their hands and knees, wiping the floors and singing as they moved along. These were worshipers, doing one of the standard services. It was actually an extremely touching thing to see. Mr. Fukaya said that I should point out any one of the worshipers I wished, and he would ask him why he was here. I said, "Well, how about one of the people in this group right here?" He touched a young man on the shoulder, who got up, and after a brief moment of embarrassment, told us that he had been ill about the waist and had lost his joy in life; but had come to Tenri and been cured and now was healthy and happy again. Like most of the many thousands whom I saw at Tenri, moving about in work groups, or with their friends, this was a peasant type; intelligent, however, in contrast to the Indian peasant, and wearing the standard coolie-jacket uniform of Tenri.

Our next visit was to the sanctuary where the foundress, Miki Nakayama, is supposed to be in living presence. Within the great room was another room, and within that still another—her dwelling, where she is clothed and fed and put to bed as though alive (cf. Ramakrishna, Ānanda Mayī).

Mr. Fukaya next brought us to the charming guest house, behind a bamboo fence, and with several rooms and pretty gardens, which was to be our residence for the night. Tea was served by a very nice woman servant, who presently called me to my bath. I had asked for a good hot one, and, by golly, that's what it was. I got in, quarter-inch by quarter-inch, and then soaked for about fifteen minutes, came out, dried off, and got into a nice after-bath kimono. What a luxurious affair—and, after all, so simple!

I didn't realize that Kuchiba was to use the same water, and so, pulled the plug; but we saved the situation at the last possible moment—and he was very generous and forgiving.

Feeling clean, and blithe, and wonderful, we were conducted, shortly after the bath, to the home of the patriarch—great-grandson of the foundress: we had to put on getas for the short walk—and this was quite a feeling. (Somehow, I felt much less ridiculous in this rig than I did when wearing the *dhotī* in Orissa!)²⁵⁰ We entered a room where a Yale professor of sociology, named Lassway, or something like that—a man of about sixty—was asking questions through an interpreter (a splendid young man named Professor Saitō, I think), and receiving answers from a couple of Tenri people. Had Tenri ever been persecuted and how had it met the persecution? What disciplinary measures short of excommunication did it bring to bear for infractions of its rules, doctrinal and moral? At the time, the questions seemed very important, but actually, they were a bit off to the side of Tenri, and the answers, given willingly and carefully, added only one important bit of news to what I already knew about the cult. This was, that, some twenty-seven years ago, there was a man, Aijirō Ōnishi, in Yamaguchi Prefecture, who claimed that the center of the world was not at Tenri but within himself. He was excommunicated and formed a heretical group called Tenri Honmichi, "True Road Tenri."

At about 7:15, one of the men being questioned got up to attend the evening service, and I asked whether I might be present at the morning service. Answer: Yes. The service takes place at 5:00 A.M.

Dinner was at about eight, on the floor of a large and beautiful room, for a company of about twenty gentlemen and one lady—Mrs. Nakayama, the wife of the patriarch. It was a perfectly delightful evening. A troop of little Tenri girls served the sake and innumerable dishes, and while Professor Lassway, at my left hand, sat across from and conversed convivially with the patriarch, I had the good fortune to be face-to-face with the very handsome and charming Mrs. Nakayama; Kuchiba, at my right, helped me to converse.

At about nine, a company of gentlemen arrived who were introduced—curators, professors, and a monk. They remained a while and departed. They had been present—as had the patriarch—at a memorial service, held in Nara, for Professor Warner of Harvard (whom I met, two years ago, with Mrs. Coomaraswamy).[251]

The patriarch (a really cordial and even jolly host) gave us copies of his world-tour book, showed us some photos taken on the trip (one at the bedside of Professor Warner), and then invited us to a European-style room for more tea and conversation—I was a bit surprised to see how bad the decoration was of this room, after the perfect Japanese rooms and gardens everywhere else. And now Professor Lassway began a rather fine series of questions for the patriarch to answer—out of which the following points emerged as (for me, at least) the most interesting:

First, that, in contrast to Christian Science, Tenri believes that not all disease is to be cured or accounted for by mental states: it is therefore not antagonistic to the medical profession and actually has hospitals and infirmaries on its estate.

The gifts of money, made by many, are not required of the devotees, but are voluntary. For some, the "Cheerful Life" (Tenri's ideal) is best attained by renouncing property.

Third, there has as yet been no theological controversy over the point of literal vs. symbolic interpretation of the mythology. There has, however, been contention between the patriotic and non-patriotic readings—with the latter favored by the temple.

The company retired at about 11:30 P.M., and I spent my first night in a truly Japanese bed, on the floor.

CHAPTER XI

BAKSHEESH REVISITED

Sunday, July 10

Woke up every half hour, on the dot, and finally, at 4:30, got up, shaved, and was ready when Fukaya arrived to take us to the service. There were, I should say, about five thousand people in the temple. The patriarch himself—a rather different man, it seemed, in this role—conducted the prayers, which were recited in unison to the beating of a large gonglike drum. The hand movements accompanied the words. Then the company stood, and while praying, went through a quiet little dance. We moved to the hall of the foundress, and deep in the inner chamber a woman could be seen whose function it was, apparently, to serve the foundress.

Our next event was a visit to the mausoleum of the foundress, which is on a lovely height. Then we returned to the guest house for a Western-style breakfast.

Mr. Fukaya very generously answered a long string of my questions at this time, and the following main points emerged:

1. Reincarnation is taken for granted.
2. The body is a loan from God.
3. The borrower of the body was created by God, is not itself God, and yet is not distinctly different from God.

4. The moment of creation was 999,999,999 years before the moment of Miki Nakayama's revelation. This number, however, may be interpreted, simply, as meaning, a very long time ago. This is the beginning, I should say, of allegorical exegesis, to allow for scientific views.

5. Human consciousness has evolved through three great stages: (a) that of minute forms in the muddy waters, (b) that of the gaining of mental power, (c) that of reading and writing.

6. Man's consciousness is free—free to make mistakes, and does so. When man's thinking does not accord with the *michi,* or true way of God, he goes wrong and sickness, as well as other ills, result.

7. There is (or seems to be) no idea of a moment of general catastrophe in the past, like that of the Fall (or, in primitive mythologies, the discovery of fire), when mankind as a whole lost its pristine state. Mankind, as a whole, is progressing. The mistake is made by the individual.

8. The mistake is to forget that the world is one.

9. As the result of bad deeds a man may descend in the scale of progress and take birth as a plant or animal. The word "death" is used in this connection, but in no other. When such a soul returns to human birth, it is said to have "come again."

10. Some of the ills experienced in this life are the effects of earlier lives. Problem: how to break this claim of cause and effect in daily living.

11. The first thing to realize is that the body is borrowed. This realization gives happiness ("the cheerful life"). One's expression of this happiness (so achieved) is one's "daily contribution."

Mr. Fukaya says that Tenri is not opposed to, or in conflict with, other religions: one can be a Buddhist as well as a follower of Tenri. The God of Tenri is the One God—the same as the one who gave to man Buddhism and Christianity. On the other hand, the non-active, meditative lifestyle of Zen is regarded as precisely the opposite of that of Tenri (compare the Zoroastrian opposition to the yogi).

Tenri is not inclined to metaphysical speculation. There is no thought about death in its system: one does not go to any heaven or hell after death. There is little speculation about "the borrower of the body." The orientation is essentially practical, and directed to the actualization of the "cheerful life" (*yōkigurashi*) and the effective use of the "daily contribution" (*hinokishin*).

One example of the practical program is that of the work teams of one hundred young men apiece, who come to work at Tenri for ten-day periods. Their work is a form of prayer through labor—and actually, as we sat talking in the pretty guest house (which had been built, like all the other buildings in this fabulous city, by the voluntary labor of people who came here of their own free will and actually paid their own room and board while doing the work), there were the songs of the passing work teams all the time: the whole city was full of song. And one group of older men, whose voices were no good, went to work with drums and horns, whose music was no good either, but at least it could be heard and was certainly cheerful. 1,982,000 people have worked in this way at Tenri during the past year and a half. (Many, of course, are repeats.)

The great majority in this remarkable city are distinctly of the peasant type, but the clergy, professors, and intellectuals who talked with us for twenty-odd hours, were not peasant simpletons by any means. Their impression, I think on Lassway as well as on myself, was frank, intelligent, practical, and honest.

Mr. Fukaya showed me copies of the newspaper (weekly) and the magazine that he publishes. Fifty thousand copies are sent to Tenri churches; two hundred thousand to Tenri people.

I was told also of the *besseki,* or "basic instruction," and holy blessing that is given in the seminary of Tenri: it gives one the power to help people cure themselves by giving them again their intrinsic sense of proportion—clearing dust.

In Tenri there is the main temple with its immediate precincts, and then many subsidiary churches with their surrounding dormitories—the latter, looking much like fine Bronxville mansions, but à la Japanese. Tenri has about fifteen thousand churches, including some in Honolulu, Los Angeles, Seattle, and Chicago.

At about 9:30, Mr. Fukaya left us, to go to his work, and Miss Lois Uchida, a very nice young Nisei girl whose father was head of the Los Angeles Tenri church, took over. She brought us to the museum (good ethnological collection—of Peruvian textiles, especially); the library (on religion, philosophy, anthropology, and so on), where we had a brief talk with the librarian; and finally to the vast new school structure being built by voluntary labor in an elegant style, and—like all of the other buildings—sturdily and well.

A delightful lunch was served by the nice little lady in charge of our building; we took a final stroll about the grounds, for me to take a few pictures, and finally, at 4:30, a car called to drive us to Kyoto, in the company of Miss Uchida and a nice young, rather silent man.

I invited the lot to Suehiro's for dinner. Kuchiba had some other date, but the rest joined me—and, as a final fillip to a prodigious weekend, as we were about to enter the restaurant we saw the most amusing procession (Kyoto is simply nutty about processions): four groups of tiny boys; one group as samurai; one, like little peanuts on the backs of horses; one, dressed as geese—with their mothers diligently fanning them; and one (very tiny) as little Jizō with the clanking sticks of the Bodhisattva.[252]

Bade my friends good night at about 8:00 P.M. and strolled home to bed.

Monday, July 11

My first morning of special classes at the school. It went very nicely. I was invited to converse for two hours about my family, which I more or less did.

I felt a bit fatigued and feverish after lunch and slept from 12:30 till 2:30. A voyage to Eidmann's to see Iguchi was fruitless—Iguchi was absent, not well: but I got in for another session of tea. Returned home to write up my diary. Dinner at Fujiya and to bed at about 10:30.

An interesting item in the morning paper about Indian journalists interviewing Japan's new ambassador to New Delhi, Seijirō Yoshizawa. Their questions: Would Japan recognize Red China? Does Japan subscribe to the *Pancha Sīla?*

Replies: At present Japan is committed to recognize Nationalist China; but because of Japan's proximity to the Chinese mainland and the need for trade, Japan favors "some adjustment of our relations with China."

Japan is pledged to the United Nations Charter and was a party to the Bandung Declaration—both of which embody the principles of coexistence.[253]

And finally (that soul balm for India): "Japan entertains an age-old sentiment toward India as a great source of cultural heritage which has contributed to the formation of our national characteristic."

Phone call this evening from Mrs. Sasaki, inviting me to meet another *rōshi* tomorrow afternoon.

Tuesday, July 12

After my Japanese class, I went to the Kyoto branch of the Kansai Customs Office to have a blank page added to my "Foreign Exchange Record Book" and had a very amusing hour, while six young men took time off from their game of Go to discuss the problem and finally do the wrong thing. After dinner, I received a phone call, asking me to return tomorrow to have the mistake corrected.

At 1:30, I appeared at Mrs. Sasaki's for our trip to Ryōanji (with the celebrated rock-sand garden) and visit to Gōtō Rōshi at the nearby Daishu-in. Daishu-in means "Great Jewel Temple," and Ryōanji, "Dragon-Peace Temple." Gōtō Rōshi was a lovely old man of seventy-seven, clad in white: more like the Indian monks, I should say, than the comparatively formal and stately Oda Rōshi, whom I met Saturday. He is Mrs. Sasaki's Zen master, and the meeting was delightfully simple and informal. A tall, thin, young monk, who is to be the *rōshi's* successor, served us our whipped tea, and an *obasan* rolled up the shades and pattered here and there. The *roshi* talked to me about Kōbō Daishi and Dengyō Daishi, and their masters in China, and brought out a book showing the spiritual lineages of all the great Buddhist teachers from the time of Gautama to 1909. He spoke, also, briefly, of spiritualism in the religions of Japan, declaring that in Buddhism it was confined to Shingon and Tendai (or, at least, this is what I understood).

Mrs. Sasaki's secretary again acted as our interpreter, and we were accompanied also by a pleasant, rather typical, American literateur-homosexual of about fifty-seven, who prefers Noh to Kabuki and goes to all the Jūdō movies (why are they *always* the same, these guys?). He was sweet and so was everybody else. He is reading *Finnegans Wake* with the *Skeleton Key* and asked the standard question: When are we to have a key to the *Key?*[254]

After visiting the *rōshi*, we visited the rock garden, but the setting was destroyed by a lot of chaps setting up shop in the temple for an exhibition of kimonos. This led me to ask Mrs. Sasaki about the poverty of the monasteries—and there came out some more news about the Occupation.

The great land reform—to break the feudal system and turn land over to the peasants—allowed individuals (which includes the abbots of temples) to hold no more than six acres apiece. Result: the temples were deprived of both their own lands, and the support of landowners who for-merly had had property and wealth from which to make donations.

(Query: Was this land reform supposed to represent the American way of life? If not what was the way, and who were the authors of the reform? Three guesses.[255] Query two: What chance would a bill restricting church properties in this way have of enactment in the U.S.A.?)

The pattern of trade unionism imposed on Japan is some twenty years ahead of that of the U.S.A., and far beyond Japan's means to support it.

The school system was completely knocked apart, and reformed ideal-istically, according to American ideas and again beyond Japan's means to furnish adequate support.

The big trouble: a combination of ultra–New Dealism and American provincialism, according to both of which, local conditions are not to be regarded; nor local ideals, preferences, traditions, or habits.

I returned to my room at about 6:15, for an evening of study.

Wednesday, July 13

Japanese in the morning. Another trip, at 11:00, to the customs office to have the Go players correct their mistake of yesterday, and, at 8:00 P.M., a visit from Professor Kasugai and his disciple, the Buddhist nun, to have me autograph the Zimmer volumes that I'm giving him as a present. Otherwise: a day of pleasant study—in spite of the heat, which, now that the rainy-season clouds have cleared, is hitting the middle nineties.

Thursday, July 14

A phone-call slip, this morning, from Gautam Sarabhai,[256] who is at the Miyako. I left a message that I would phone him at noon, and went off to school. Today, I finished the primer and started into the first reader, at page 125. Studied Japanese all afternoon and at 7:30 P.M., Gautam and Gira Sarabhai arrived and we went off to the Alaska for dinner. Quite a remark-able experience comparing notes on Japan with the Sarabhais. They feel and look more alien here than I do; believe—as I do—that Japan is as dif-ferent from India as it is from the U.S.A. They are trying, I think, to be not too greatly impressed. Of course, as far as eating goes, they are having it a bit hard. Alaska had almost nothing that they could eat.[257] We then took a stroll through some of the cuter streets and at about 10:00 P.M. they taxied back to their hotel.

Gautam says that in the textile market, Japan has lost considerably to Indian competition, but that in the manufacture of machines they can sell to the Indian market. In Japan there are five major and nine minor export firms through which all the exporting is done. One is met and entertained by the members of these firms and does not get through to the manufacturers. The employees in the textile industry are girls, average age 17.9 years, who work for three years, eight hours a day, get room and board, plus from ¥4,000 a month to ¥7,000 (the last year), and, besides, continue their schooling. When they quit, they have a dowry and are ready for marriage. One girl can tend 4,200 spindles, which is the highest record in the world. The top in the U.S.A. is about one man to 4,000 spindles. This whole situation transforms the labor problem: it is very different from that of a country in which the work in the mill is a lifetime job.

While walking with Gautam and Gira through the streets of Kyoto, I was interested in trying to recall the picture of India: what I noted was the comparatively heavy, stoop-shouldered slouch of Gira in contrast to the springy vitality of the Japanese women: the dark languor in contrast to the flash and brilliance of these people—and, of course, all the ritualism and arrogance about food. They found seaweed difficult to like; it has, unfortunately, been the most common of the Japanese-style vegetable elements. They prefer the Western-style restaurant to the Japanese. And by a curious misfortune, I had the luck of ordering, by accident, a veal curry: my first since India.

Gautam said that Japan didn't seem anything like the rest of the Orient to him, because it is industrialized, and the rest of the Orient is agricultural. He also wondered whether the Japanese are warm friends: they seemed to him cold and formal. He was impressed by the politeness and cleanliness. (Those were the only good things he said voluntarily about Japan.) When I said I had been to Formosa, Gautam asked what I had found there: "Like being in America, I should think," he said. When I told him I was learning Japanese, he wondered what good there could be for me in learning this language. In speaking of Rangoon, he told of the dangers of brigands, only a few miles out of the city. I could feel no enthusiasm at all for any of the places in the world, outside of the borders of India. Hong

Kong is a kind of resort city. He has not yet visited Bangkok. I had a curious feeling of dullness and tediousness about Gautam and Gira this
evening, whereas in Ahmedabad they had twinkled with life. Maybe it's
my contrast of India with Japan that makes the difference, or maybe
it's just that their pattern is that of provincials in a really alien world: self-
protective and slightly piqued. The pattern is *very* strong, I feel, in Gira.

Gautam's words about *agriculture* and *industry* can be carried a long
way. The agricultural, peasant ideal, for example, is expressed in the great,
heavy hips of the Indian women, whereas the trim, reedy, willowy figures
of the . . . but no! China's women are willowy too, and China is definitely
agricultural; and the women of Japan were this way before the Meiji era.
This idea isn't so good. Perhaps one should say, rather, that the willowy
ideal of the Far East prepared its world to accept the machine age without
too much psychological tension, whereas in India, where the *anima* image
cannot be jammed into a bathing-beauty's bikini, there is a fundamental
spiritual antagonism to the new age. Ha! A nice cocktail party thesis. Very
nice indeed.

Friday, July 15

Called for Mrs. Sasaki at her home at 8:30 A.M. and then, joined by a fine
young man named Walter Noak, went up Mt. Hiei, to spend a marvelously interesting day. To begin with, we spoke on several points in the
taxi and on the trolley on the way to the Mt. Hiei finicula.

A nice counterpart to the Sarabhai reaction to Japan: the reaction to
India of a Japanese, Mr. Tsunoda, formerly at Columbia University, as
reported to me by Mrs. Sasaki. He spent ten days in the New Delhi area,
and brought the following report:

On a trip to a holy mountain some two hundred miles north of New
Delhi: upon arrival at the hotel he had a bath drawn and found the water
very muddy. Tsunoda-san decided to let the water out of the bath and fill
the tub again: he pulled the plug; the bath boy maintained that his pre-
rogatives had been usurped, that his status had been endangered, and that
the whole social structure of India had been insulted. He would supply no
more water—and Tsunoda-san was openly despised by all the servants of
the hotel for the period of his stay. His impression was that although in

India people talk of doing away with the caste system, they are actually doing little to change the present situation.

His car, returning, was held up at a railroad crossing for about forty-five minutes: ten or fifteen minutes before the train arrived, twenty or so while the freight train shunted and shuttled back and forth within sight, and about ten minutes after the train had moved on. Meanwhile, multitudes urinated, defecated, and did other "dirty things," all over the place, while waiting.

In his conference with Radhakrishnan,[258] he had the impression of a vain, loquacious dilettante, spouting airy platitudes and regarding these as evidence of high spirituality, while disregarding completely the actualities of the world scene.

Mrs. Sasaki spoke about the kōans of Zen. They are not odd (as the writings of Suzuki and Alan Watts would seem to suggest). Each, on the level of consciousness from which it comes, makes good sense, and receives its only possible answer in the traditional response. You have to stand on the level from which the kōan comes to appreciate its logic, however. The main road of Zen is not the kōan, but meditation; the kōan is public evidence of the level of consciousness attained.

Mr. Noak is the young man who had the experience of the students who handed in identical papers.[259] His students are studying to get the certificates of accomplishment that are prerequisite to a good marriage. In Japan (also, I think one can say, in India) a certain supersenitiveness to Western criticism leads to the maintenance of a surface (e.g. exams in college); but the true function of the elements of that surface are not what they would seem to the Western eye.

Our first visit when we reached the top of Mt. Hiei was to Jōdo-in, a small but important temple, within which is the tomb of Dengyō Daishi. The young monk in charge of this temple, and living there practically alone—with only a couple of men and boy servants to assist—is named Sōmon Horizawa. His function in the temple is to conduct all the services, utterly alone. He has been two years in the temple and is to remain there ten more—without coming down from Mt. Hiei. He is now twenty-six years old; he joined the Tendai order at the age of twenty-one, after quitting Kyoto University before receiving his degree. His day commences at

2:00 A.M., with the recitation of *sūtras* before the two shrines, which we visited—that of Dengyō Daishi and that of Amida. By 7:00 A.M. this phase of the day's work is done and he is free for breakfast, cleaning house, and a bit of reading. At 10:00 A.M., another spell of services, till about noon; and then there is another two-hour spell at about 4:00 P.M. The rest of his time is free, and the time that he spent with us today was that between 10:00 A.M. and 4:00 P.M. (I don't understand what happened to the 10:00–12:00 worship.)

Our first visit in his temple was to the main chapel. When one faces the altar one is facing also the tomb of Dengyō Daishi, which is just outside the back wall. Sōmon slid the door open and let us look at the tomb building—with the great tall California-like trees all around it. (Dope! I had left my camera in the front hall!) Two trees from India flanked the tomb; the one at our right was a sal tree, that at our left was supposed to be (but wasn't) a banyan.

We next visited in this temple the smaller Amida chapel. Here the paraphernalia of worship were of the Shingon type. The monk had to read here the *Dai Hannya Sūtra,* which is stowed in a case just outside the chapel and consists of six hundred volumes. The main image in this chapel is a lovely standing image of Amida: it stands before a tabernacle, within which there is another image, black, supposed to have been carved by Dengyō Daishi himself. This image is almost never exposed. Sōmon himself has seen it only once. (Another example of Ellen Psaty's law: in Japan, the value of a thing is estimated by the fewness of people who have seen it.)

This chapel was small and dark and silent. The wind could be heard outside in the tall trees—and Mrs. Sasaki told me to try to imagine this place in the winter with the young priest performing his offices in the solitude and darkness. The whole spirit of Tendon was right here: the whole thing: the sense of solitude, darkness, and therein the Buddha's apparition—a very different world from that of Zen, with its openness to the fair garden of the world. Even the incense, said Mrs. Sasaki, has a different smell.

After visiting the two chapels we sat in the young monk's main room and drank orange juice. Nearby was a long calligraphic kakemono. I asked its meaning. The young monk smiled: he couldn't read it—nobody could: it was in a very difficult calligraphic style known as the "grass style" (a "grass-style scroll"). Again—the sense for mystery of this curious world. I had to think of Joyce and Mallarmé. On Sōmon's desk, among many books, was one by Hakuju Ui, who, Mrs. Sasaki said, was the leading Buddhist scholar.

Sōmon got into his walking clothes and, wearing getas,[260] accompanied us on the day's excursion, as our guide. We visited first a moderately small temple with vivid red decor, called Amida-dō, then passed on to one of the most important spots in Japan, the so-called "Command Platform." This was established by Dengyō Daishi as the place for the valid ordination of monks—in rivalry with the "Command Platform" at the Kegon center in Nara, which, up to that time, had been the sole legitimate site for ordinations. After the establishment of this platform on Mt. Hiei, the capital could move from Nara to Kyoto.

Sōmon Horizawa atop Mt. Hiei

At this platform the Tendai monks are ordained to this day. Sōmon was ordained here. The ordination takes place after a long period of ritual bowing, days and nights on end with only minimal pauses for naps and nibbles, has culminated in a vision of the Buddha. Sometimes three years are required before the vision is seen: in Sōmon's case, the ordeal lasted two-and-a-half months. At the ordination itself, the candidate makes his bow before the high monks of the order, at the altar in this temple. The central Buddha of this altar is Shaka, with Miroku at his right and Monju[261] at his left. The candidate then is shaved here and takes the commandments. Sōmon said that during the course of the bowing ordeal, the neophyte sees many other visions besides that of the Buddha, music is heard, flowers fall, and the radiant Bodhisattvas of the *sūtras* appear.[262]

As Mrs. Sasaki pointed out, Zen is opposed to such visions as traps in the spheres of illusion. Zen's orientation is non-, trans-, or anti-mythological, in contrast to that of Tendai.

We moved on to a vast and impressive, red-painted temple (all of these Tendai temples, in fact, have red decor), known as, and dedicated to, Dai Nichi Nyorai, "Great Sun *Tathāgata*." This Buddha is the Absolute Buddha of the Kegon sect. We entered by a side door, and Sōmon told of a ritual in this temple where the worshiper has to get through this door quickly, just as it is being banged (slid) shut (*Symplegades* motif[263]). Within, right at the door, was a little shrine of the seven kings (Shintō motif[264]).

Our next visit was to the largest and most impressive temple of all these on Mt. Hiei, the Konpon Chō-dō,[265] "Hall of the Origin of the Teaching." The decor of this large and beautiful building was freshly painted: we went into the main building and found, behind the main room, a darker, older, equally large chamber with some images in a large tabernacle; one, the so-called Yakushi Nyorai, supposed to be by Dengyō Daishi.

Time for lunch was now approaching, so we hiked off into the lovely hills and finally settled on a little height with a number of tombstones, overlooking the beautiful hills and the prodigious reach of Lake Biwa. The air was full of insect calls and of bird notes ("the Japanese nightingale") that sounded more like the bird songs of our northeastern American forests than any I've heard in Asia. It was a lovely, refreshing rest, and when it was over, we started downhill to visit Hagami Shōchō Acarya in the Mudōji Temple. This temple is dedicated to Fudō ("not moving"), the god of the *goma,* or fire ceremony;[266] and the name of the temple has almost the same meaning as the name of the god: Mudō: "immovable"; as "without" (*mu*) "moving" (*dō*); Fudō: "not" (*fu*) "moving" (*dō*). "Temple of the Immovable, Mysterious God."

The path that we followed to this temple was an extremely precipitous and tortuous one, and has an interesting function. It is part of a long route of some eight *ri* (about seventeen miles[267]) that Dengyō Daishi is supposed to have walked every night for one hundred nights. It is known as Kaihōgyō, and today is used in connection with a specific Tendai discipline. Through a period of seven years, for one hundred nights each year, the trainee walks this path, wearing the long "coiled-lotus" hat of the Tendai monks. Mrs. Sasaki walked the way one night and declares that the monks go at a fast, steady clip, without pause or alteration of speed, almost as though on air, moving like feathers in the breeze—and this in the dark. I asked whether she thought the discipline might have a value somewhat like that of *Zen in the Art of Archery,* and she answered yes. If that is so, the discipline would be that of a sort of transcendence of the ego-centralized, rational control of the body.

At the Mudōji Temple, Hagami Shōchō Acarya, who was a very pleasant and friendly man of about fifty, showed me, among other things, the "lotus-curled" hat and I took a couple of color photos. The temple is in a wonderfully romantic spot, with precipitous paths and a glorious view out over the lake.

One more bit of news about Mt. Hiei. In the sixteenth century Nobunaga destroyed the whole mountain community, to crush the power of the monks, and this was the end of the predominance of Tendai (ca. A.D. 850–1550). Hideyoshi gave permission to rebuild, and the present community dates from his time.

According to Mrs. Sasaki, the rise of the power of Zen took place in the Kamakura period, in the twelfth–fourteenth centuries. The history of Buddhism in Japan, she declares, is intimately tied up with the history of politics: the flourishing of the different sects is tied up with that of the various political teams.

An interesting point: our young monk Sōmon, apparently, feels that he is approaching an impasse in his Tendai-style of discipline and is interested in learning more about Zen. I asked, when we had said good-bye to our mountain friends and returned to the Kyoto Hotel bar for a drink, whether such a shift in discipline would amount to a radical trauma for such a monk. Walter Noak seemed to think it might. Mrs. Sasaki, however, said that in the great period the Tendai and Shingon monks had all practiced Zen: in fact, Zen had been the meditation aspect of their discipline.

We talked a bit, finally, about the Orient-Occident problem in general, and a few good points arose.

According to Mrs. Sasaki, today it is the West that is idealistic ("spiritual"), and the Orient that is grossly materialistic.

I pointed to the laughable character of much of the "democracy" and "human rights" talk of the Oriental journalists and politicians. They keep saying that the economic inequalities of the world must be corrected and love the sound of the phrase 400 million people: and yet, from those great 400 millions not a single profitable, generally useful idea has come into the modern world. The Orientals may be able to copy the machines that are supposed to, and are perhaps going to, save them, but they have not contributed one useful thought to the whole tradition. In compensation for this failure, they try to make a great thing, in India, of their "spirituality."

In Japan, according to Mrs. Sasaki, the compensation is that of the impenetrability, for Westerners, of the Oriental mind. If you say you like their food, houses, art, etc., they are delighted—but if you say you yourself actually sleep, sit, and eat on the floor, in your own home, by preference, the screen goes up and you are frozen out—because, it is *impossible* for a Westerner to do and enjoy these things. (I was amused, by the way, to find that for Gautam and Gira the Japanese style of sitting is as difficult as it is for us.)

It is a general Oriental notion that Oriental philosophy and art are impenetrable for the Westerner, and I am not inclined to contest the point. It is also true, however, that very few modern Orientals have been able to write as well on these subjects as the Occidentals. Indeed, in English, at any rate, the Indians, at least, quote from Occidentals without using quotation marks and often abuse the Occidental mind while doing so—as I learned for myself in Calcutta.[268] My own inclination, right now, is to leave the Orient, therefore, to the Orientals and point my own work toward that particular work which is perhaps the *great* work of the Occidental scholar in the field of Culture Studies, namely, the Comparative approach. This is almost completely alien to the Oriental mind, as far as I can see, and belongs to what I shall henceforth think of as the *Cartesian approach* to culture and religion.

A striking fact about the Orient is what may be termed its provincialism. Each country tries to date things by short kingly eras. It took the West to conceive of a general dating system—coordinated from the "birth of Christ," or the Augustan age of Rome. It took the West also (namely, the British) to regard the whole globe as one field, measured from Greenwich. And so, it is not remarkable that our culture has become the unique world culture of all time, and our science, philosophy, etc., the unique world science, and comparative culture field.

(Compare Nietzsche—the present age, the age of comparative competition and survival. Our age, actually, is of the formation of what is to be the common-field culture of the whole world. We have the luck to be alive and working at this wonderful moment, in this wonderful coming-into-being of the common field: and the great question for each living—as opposed to dying—culture is this: what can it contribute, what has it to contribute, to the common pool; not, what can it get by one strategem or another, from its creative neighbors. As far as I can see at present, the Orient's contribution will be in the psychological field, via the work of Western-style scholars on materials dating primarily from the fifth century B.C. to the eighth century A.D.)

Resolution: *Comparative mythology* (philology, in the German sense) is indeed my field—and the method is to be first of all *philological* (*The Basic Mythologies of Mankind*) and secondly, that of the Jungian *amplification* (example: *The King and the Corpse*[269]).

Saturday, July 16

Today and tomorrow, the great Gion Festival of Kyoto. The floats have been standing along Shijō for about a week now. Kasugai phoned to say that he would call for me at 5:00 P.M., to visit some of the floats; and when I phoned Gautam, I suggested that he and Gira join us at that time.

Worked all day until 4:45, then went to the lobby to meet my friends. Gautam and Gira were the first to appear—with a Japanese gentleman who is trying to compete with another Japanese businessman in entertaining them. The Kasugais arrived with his wife, two youngsters, Buddhist nun, and five students. We sent Gira and most of the Kasugai team off first, and while we were waiting for the car (Sarabhai's friend's car!) to return, Saitō arrived with *his* wife and child. On Shijō, at the Moon Spear float, we were met by the second Buddhist nun-friend of the Kasugais, and entered the temple building associated with the Moon Spear float. We visited the float, sat around a bit, and then went out strolling about the crowded, prettily decorated streets, saw many more floats and visited a couple of little places where children, cutely dressed, were singing hymns and lighting candles.

Japanese children beneath paper *gohei* offerings

At about seven the Sarabhais, their friend, and I bade good-bye to the rest of the company and were taken, by the friend, to Prunier's for dinner—after which we visited the beautifully lighted Yasaka Shrine, strolled around, bought a few toys, and then commenced a long quite wonderful walk (till about 11:15 P.M.) through the crowded, beautifully lighted streets of Kyoto.

Gautam and Gira now seemed to have caught on to Japan, and were liking it a lot. Our conversation covered a number of points worth recording:

Ed Solomon's visit to Ahmedabad: Lois Murphy, in her letter to the Sarabhais, had built Ed up as a rather important member of our faculty: *Director of Field Work, Sarah Lawrence College.* Gautam figured that this sounded like someone in the social science field and made appropriate plans. Ed arrived. He wasn't really interested in anything; just wanted to sit around among nice people. He said he liked adolescents, played the guitar for them, and had a nice time. Perfectly wonderful advertisement for Sarah Lawrence! Gautam thought he was a kind of joke.

I asked Gautam about India: was he pessimistic or optimistic about India's possibility of pulling out of the ditch? "What ditch?" said Gautam. "Well," I said, "according to the standards of other countries that I've visited, India's economic and health conditions would be regarded, if they were ours or theirs, as catastrophic. One of the things that one learns when one visits India is that people can go on living under these conditions. But I understand that the Indian government is trying to improve them. Do you think they are going to succeed?" And then came one of the revelations of my year's visit to the Orient. *Gautam spoke as though the conditions were actually not so bad and were pretty well under control.* The antibiotic drugs, he said, were conquering disease. Russia was going to give a steel mill: England, in competition with Russia, was going to give another steel mill, and there was even a third somewhere in the offing. Cotton quality has been improved, so there will be no need, now, to import African or American cotton. And the rice supply has been brought up to a surplus level: a great economic plan for Burma, devised by a team of Americans and based on the assumption that the export price for Burmese rice would be at a certain level, had been wrecked by India's success in growing rice (which itself had been somewhat assisted, Gautam *didn't* add, by American technical aid).

Talking with Gautam I gained (or perhaps refreshed) the impression that *the Indians do not regard their condition as being as desperate as visitors tend to:* the only point of course, though, is that other side, which one must always look for in the Indian; namely, that the baksheesh pattern was even present in Gautam's delight at the Anglo-Russian steel-mill competition— and that in India itself it is the predominant motif. Every young or old man you meet in India complains about the money he's getting; and so the conditions are *not* actually satisfactory. And one more detail: when I talked with Gautam about disease in India, I said that when I was in Calcutta they had smallpox, bubonic plague, and everything else. "All you need to protect yourself against smallpox," Gautam said, "is vaccination." "I know," I said; "but I wasn't talking about myself; I was talking about disease in India...." When tuberculosis was mentioned, Gautam said that they also had a lot of tuberculosis in Japan. *His whole pattern was defensive of the actual Indian situation.*

Gira made a good remark about Japan; namely, that whereas in most places there is a kind of hierarchy of the arts, in Japan everything—sculpture, pottery, woodwork, temples—seems to be regarded with equal seriousness and attentive respect.

While wandering about the streets, Gautam wondered why the Japanese did not keep their pretty kimono tradition instead of going over to the Western clothes. I suggested that *in Japan there is not the same patriotic antagonism to the Western style that one finds in India.* These people have accepted the machine age and made it their own. Besides, the girls are excellent seamstresses and many of them make their own clothes—they do not feel them as alien.

I do not know how to summarize the system of feelings about India that has begun to crystallize from my hours with Gautam. Perhaps if the Indians don't regard their condition as horrible, let us not regard it as horrible either—and let's withhold our baksheesh. The anti-Western feeling is definitely present, though, even in Gautam. The benefits that India is deriving automatically as a consequence of Occidental advances (antibiotics, etc.) are simply accepted as a matter of course. In this sense, India's anti-Westernism is something very much deeper than the Japanese. Gautam, viewing the pleasant character of the Japanese crowds, had to remark that in the West, where people get drunk, there were always unpleasant episodes at festivals.

With respect to India and Pakistan, according to Gautam, no one in India regards the tension as serious any more. Nothing really serious will break between the two countries. And with respect to China: when I said that India had fallen in love with China, Gautam said that actually there was a feeling of rivalry between the two: India does not want China to get ahead of her, and yet is afraid that she is doing so.

This flashed a thought in my mind: India, China, and Russia regard themselves as the big three of Asia, fighting, perhaps, for place. Actually, the great nations of the world, today, are five: U.S.A., Britain, Russia, Germany, and Japan—in that order. The rest are beggars, or else auxiliary to one or another of the big five. Switzerland is the exception.

Sunday, July 17

Off at 8:15 to see the parade of the great floats. A field day for shutterbugs. Special license for anybody with a camera. I was at it from 8:30 till about 11:30. Iguchi found me in the multitude (minor miracle) and accompanied me to Fujiya for lunch, then to the hotel for a chat. When he left, I retired to my room for a long nap—nearly dead with heat of the sun on my head and the weight of the pavements on my feet. A wonderful day.

Gion festival procession in Kyoto

At 7:00 P.M. I went out for another stroll and at 8:15 P.M. Hisashi Mita called for me with a friend of his from the swimming team of some university and we went around the town again. The city was still very gay and there was a shrine-bearing procession that we kept bumping into: a large team of chaps in modified sumō costumes bearing the shrine (Dionysian element) and a procession of stately gentlemen coming along behind them. I thought of Lafcadio Hearne's descriptions of such processions.[270]

As we walked, Hisashi mentioned the connection of all this with the advertising campaign of the Daimaru Department Store—and, in fact, there is an important (though to me obscure) connection between the department stores and the religions (as well as secular-cultural) life of Japan. The lanterns hanging so handsomely on all the shrines generally bear advertisements for the department stores—as do the curtains in the theaters.

And something else occurred to me as we walked through the lively, pretty streets—namely, that in Japan there is a wonderful feeling for the brilliant surface of things: *the surface flash;* and this, without much thought of what in the West would be an important consideration, namely, the form-world of the sentiments. Snatches of Western tunes are thrown together in their advertising broadcasts, television shows, etc., without consideration of what we would regard as their formal relationships. Perhaps one can say that in Japan *the surface flash rides directly over* śunyatā: the in-between world (which has been the main concern of the West), *the world of the feelings and sentiments remains unexpressed*—a secret, as it were, except, of course, in the formalized plot and catastrophe patterns of the Kabuki plays, at which everybody has a good cry.

Following our walk, we returned to the hotel to view, for a minute, on television, a Western-style wrestling bout between some American and Japanese champions. How vulgar, fake, brutal, and even ridiculous they looked, in contrast to the sumō, viewed some weeks ago on the same television set. The bouts looked choreographed to me—not convincing at all—with their punching of the umpire and everything else.

Bade good-bye to Mita and returned to my room at about 10:15 for a bit of study before bedtime.

CHAPTER XII

PENELOPE RETURNS

KYOTO, YAMADA, TOKYO, AND HOKKAIDO

Monday, July 18

My last week in Kyoto. After my Japanese classes, went to the Japan Tourist Bureau to arrange for my trip from Kyoto to Tokyo via the Ise Peninsula.

Something suggestive in this morning's paper: an article on T. E. Hulme,[271] by Yoshizō Miyazaki, which caught me just at the right angle and gave me what I think is an important suggestion for the linking of my work on mythology into the field of contemporary American literary acrobatics.

According to Miyazaki, Hulme's *Speculations: Essays on Humanism and the Philosophy of Art* laid down a philosophical basis for the nature of modern poetry:

1. The central idea of the Renaissance is that Man, not God, is the measure of all things. This notion produced humanism and the sciences, then degenerated into humanism in Rousseau and the French Revolution.
2. This notion is not true in itself, because it leads us to assumptions that are false and invalid; e.g.—that man is intrinsically good; that man is a well of

possibilities. "The humanist canons are, I think, demonstrably false," declares Hulme.

3. Hulme's antihumanist thesis:
   a. We must not "introduce into human things the Perfection that properly belongs only to the divine, and confuse both human and divine things by not clearly separating them."
   b. "We are painfully aware that nothing actual can be perfect."
   c. It is therefore necessary to take up a kind of "religious attitude" and to be aware of the "futility of existence."
   d. "This realization of the tragic significance of life makes it legitimate to call all other attitudes shallow."
4. Hulme's utter pessimism: "Man is endowed with Original Sin. He is essentially bad, he can only accomplish anything of value by discipline..."
5. Hulme's anti-Romantic argument: "What are Romanticism and Classicism?" The Classical poet never forgets the limit of man; he may jump but he always returns: he never flies away into the circumambient gas. The Romantic, on the contrary, is always flying up into the eternal gasses. The Romantic poets are sloppy, furthermore; always moaning or whining about something, always craving for the infinite.
6. Hulme's ideal for poetry: It should be dry, sophisticated, and exceedingly exact in its choice of words, since poetry "is no more nor less than a mosaic of words." This is Classicism in poetry. "I want to maintain," he said, "that we are in for a classical revival."
7. Hulme's *Humanism-Romanticism, Classicism-Religion Formula:* Romanticism fails to recognize the division between the religious attitude, which postulates absolute values by which man is judged as limited and imperfect, and the humanist attitude, which regards man as fundamentally good and perfectible by his own efforts. Hulme identified humanism with romanticism and the religious attitude with classicism.

Miyazaki goes on about T. S. Eliot and the heritage of Hulme.

1. He says that Hulme's identification of humanism with romanticism and classicism with the religious attitude was taken over, refined, and elaborated by Eliot in a more orthodoxly Christian fashion.
2. Romantics, according to Eliot, are in fatal error, because they never see the hopeless imperfectibility of man and are so naive as to believe in the spontaneous secretion of human emotions. [*sic*—?!]. Emotion is not the sole subject of poetry. "There is no method except to be very intelligent."

Finally, we are told about Hulme and the American poet-critics:

1. According to these last, Hulme defined the mood and perspective of our age: Tate, Ransom, et. al. "Ours is an age of intellectual chaos and spiritual disunity." The decline of organized religion is at the bottom of the trouble, according to Tate. A system of religion is necessary because it provides standards by which man can measure his own imperfections. Man is essentially imperfect, hence humanism and romanticism are heresies.

The whole discussion seems to me sophomoric, archaic, and ridiculous—based on an identification of religion with Christian pessimism (Original Sin context) and a very sloppy use of the terms divine and absolute (see Nietzsche); furthermore, the argument that because standards are needed in poetry, organized religion is a necessity, one can hardly credit to such touted names; and finally, the tendency to regard the quandaries of our literateurs as the typical agony of our time ("intellectual chaos and spiritual disunity") is a major mistake.

Yet the connection of all this with the blather of the current book boys is obvious, and I think I should at least make a try at indicating the relationship of my studies in mythology and comparative religion to the refutation of this position. *Perhaps something of this could be touched upon in my S.L.C. address. Perhaps, also, this problem could give the touch-off to my Viking book on Mythology.* In other words, my task now is twofold:

1. Basic Mythologies: a historical study
2. Viking Mythology Volume: an amplification of the contemporary literary and aesthetic horizon

Yes, I think so!

A new thought that has come to me about the significance of Japan—in contrast to India—for the modern world:

Gautam's first remark about Japan was that it differed from the rest of the Orient in that its economic pattern is industrial whereas that of the rest of the Orient is agricultural. Paradoxically, however, it is my feeling that the elite aspect of the Oriental spiritual heritage survives here better, certainly, than in India, and possibly better than anywhere else in the world. Here then, as nowhere else, one can study *the functioning of traditional principles in a modern, industrial society.*

Not only is India not industrialized, but her traditions survive largely on the folk level: among the upper classes largely in the dilettante style. When Gautam asked me if I was going to continue to study Sanskrit as well as Japanese, I answered yes, since the main language of India seemed to me to be Sanskrit (i.e. the main importance of India is archaic, not modern); Hindi, I said, seemed to me not very important. "It is important for *bhakti,*" said Gira. "I'm not interested in *bhakti,*" I said—and that's it! *Hindi—Bhakti—Folk—Agriculture* (by exploited peasants): second-growth India, one might say, the great elite tradition having been cracked by the Mohammedans.

In a sense comparable to India's *bhakti* are the vastly popular Japanese Buddhist Shinshū and Jōdo sects, yet, according to Eidmann, there is a difference (I have yet to discover just what it is). Zen, which is certainly an elite tradition, with a strongly secular as well as a monastic side, was developed in Japan precisely during the period of the collapse of India under Islam. Shingon and Tendai seem to me to represent a Japanese inflection of the fundamental magical and religious principles of the classical Orient. Kegon, I believe, is the gift of the Asiatic mainland.

A new thought, today, in connection with Gira's remark about the hierarchy of the arts. The idea of such a hierarchy, I believe, is Western. What she has found here is the fundamental Oriental view (artist-craftsmen) which in her own India has been lost. A nice example for my contention that what India has lost is alive in Japan.

And so now I think I am beginning to find a basis for my future discussions of my visit to India:

1. Traditional Hindu culture shattered by Islam
2. Second-growth civilization: communalism and folk-level survivals (e.g., *purdah, bhakti*); local princelings, etc.
3. England's restoration and modernization of India:
   a. Modern cities, govt., etc.
   b. Publication of Indian texts
   c. Development of a literate class capable of reading about India's past
4. *Svarāj:* Westminster-Peking polarity: U.S.A. as scapegoat and focus for baksheesh-resentment structure
5. Dead center: the quest for the past and for the future
6. In Japan: the past and the present simultaneously present (Tradition plus Industrial Society)
7. In Japan: Tradition in the patterns of the elite—Occident in the play of the folk (honky-tonk with a pretty surface flash)
8. The Orient in general concerned to maintain its self-esteem in the face of an obvious Occidental triumph:
   a. *Japan's formula: to match the West at its own game* (this is a progressive, vitalizing, refreshing motif). Symptom: Japan's easy adoption of Occidental clothing
   b. India's formula: *to fall back on an unwarranted notion of Indian "spirituality"* (a world-alienating, reactionary, and sentimental attitude). Symptom: India's sentimentalism about the sari (costume—Orient à la Occidental tourist ideology)
9. The future of the world in general is in our young people of college age— who, though in various lands and with various minor inflections and local stresses, are being taught one great system of thought: the secular thought

(scientific, cultural-historical) of the Western world. For them, as for us, the problem exists of coordinating this New World teaching with inherited ideas—and the inherited ideas (fundamentally) are those of the mythological archetypes, in their various local inflections

Some thoughts about the early lectures of my course, this fall:

Ovid: mythology in a *literary* application
Frazer: *artha-kāma:* myth as magic
Durkheim: *dharma* aspect
Freud and Jung: *"mokṣa"* aspect

What is left for religion? Does religion serve any of the above ends better than science?

Answer: Religion teaches us to view the whole range from a transcendental position (there is a contradiction in the adjective). The whole field viewed from the requirements of *mokṣa: mokṣa—dharma—kāma—artha.*

But, actually, have the religions done this? Totemism and Sectarianism bring Tension. Is Buddhism the exception?

Tuesday, July 19

After my Japanese class, went to Japan Tourist Bureau and concluded arrangements for my trip to Tokyo via Ise. At 3:00 P.M. Kasugai and the Buddhist nun came for a little good-bye exchange of presents, and at 5:00, Gautam and Gira arrived for a final chat and a promise to meet in Tokyo. At 6:30 I went for dinner to Ellen Psaty's and at 10:30 I returned to the hotel and hit the hay. The heat, these days, is a bit on the debilitating side. Some items from the day's conversations.

Gautam notices that in Japan, small industries—even "cottage" industries—are able to compete on fairly good terms with big business. Also, modern inventions are being utilized on the cottage level. A comparable situation exists in Europe (e.g. in Switzerland) but not in the U.S.A.

Why is it that the U.S. Occupation of Japan smashed the Japanese big-business trusts, while in the U.S.A. itself the comparable trusts are in a fair way to engulf the whole business situation?

Ellen spoke of the "screen exhibitions" at the time of the Gion Festival. Last Saturday, homes possessing fine screens were thrown open to public view—in half the city. Next Saturday, those in the other half of the city will be thrown open. This is an old custom of Kyoto—and many of the screens exhibited are priceless. She had quite a day, hopping around with a camera. She had received news this morning of a Rockefeller grant that will permit her to remain in Japan another year. We talked a bit of the weird matter of American grants and grantees.

Wednesday, July 20

Japanese classes in the morning. In the afternoon, visit with Iguchi and Augusto Yamazato to the Shūgakuin Detached Palace: a hot but pleasant afternoon. Dinner with Iguchi and Yamazato at Fujiya, and farewell. Home for an evening of Japanese.

Another fragment of thought for the S.L.C. convocation:

The Culture Problem is not that of Orient against Occident, but instead:

1. Frozen vs. Fluid Culture (Spengler: Civilization vs. Culture)
   a. Traditional patterns vs. experiment
   b. Religious ambience vs. free thought
   c. Acceptance of ideas vs. testing of ideas
   d. Borrowing & adaptation vs. invention
   e. Archetypology vs. individual
   f. Formality vs. informality
2. Provincial vs. Global thinking
3. Imprecision vs. Precision (cf. language contrast)
4. Periods of Creativity in Ancient "Orient," e.g.:
   a. Old Kingdom Egypt
   b. Upanishadic India
   c. Alexandrian Near East
   d. Confucian China: T'ang China
   e. Haroun's Baghdad
   f. Fujiwara Japan
5. Some dangers of the free path
   a. Titanism (ego stress, barbarity, specialization)
   b. Amateurism
   c. Group disintegration ("ivory towerism")
   d. Romanticism of "The Great Fool"

Thursday, July 21

As I walked to my trolley this morning—the next to last morning of my Japanese session—I noticed that the tiny tots of the big school on the way were not on the sidewalks this morning, coming prettily on their way to class. Apparently yesterday, July 20, was the last day of the term. The weather, moreover, is really hot: we are well into summer. Took a nap after lunch, and during the rest of the day attended to my packing and study problems.

It is a happy period of my trip that is ending, and a happier one is about to open. My large, general plan worked out rather well, I feel. It now seems to me that I got everything out of this year that I had hoped to get, and a lot more that I had not foreseen. My apprenticeship to Zimmer, Coomaraswamy, and India, certainly, is ended, and a generally fresh orientation has come of my visit to Japan. I think I've really learned enough Japanese to continue profitably with the study, and the glimpse of Japanese Buddhism has been immensely important. My program for my opening days in New York should carry me well into the work of the year—and, furthermore, I can now see no reason for accepting any outside pressure as obligatory, from now on. "Joe's Friendly Service" is closed.

A formula can be worked out for discouraging the people who ask me to do their work for them. Establish three periods a year when the "Friendly Service" is available:

One week at Christmas

One week at Easter

One week in mid-August

Accept work only with the understanding that it will be handled in the next available "service period"; and accept only as much work for each period as can be finished in five workdays of five to eight hours each. At my basic rate of $100 per day for professional side work, this amounts to a donation of about $1,500 per year to sheer friendship—and I think that's just about enough.[272]

At about 9:30 Kasugai phoned, wanting to come with Saitō, who had a gift to present—a plate of brass, laquered, with an inlayed scene in mother-of-pearl. They came at 9:45; chat, and farewell.

Friday, July 22   *Ise Peninsula*

Japanese classes till eleven. Farewell greetings. Lunch at Fujiya. Vacate room at noon, and catch 1:40 train for Yamada, Ise Peninsula. Before entering upon this phase of my story, let me conclude the account of Kyoto with one more motif from the morning paper, namely, an article in the *Mainichi*, by Marquis Childs, on Nehru and Tito,[273] "Two Apostles of Coexistence."

The point that reached me was this: that what Nehru and Tito have done has been "to bring into being...a third sphere of influence made up of those who are determined to prevent a clash of the two giants. This today is a very powerful influence which has made itself felt on both sides of the Iron Curtain. By their personal diplomacy and by their stress on the necessity for independence of action, Nehru and Tito have helped to focus the hopes of many different peoples, who formerly felt themselves helplessly drawn along in the wake of one or the other of the two giants. Whether this is the way to true peace or the road to appeasement and disaster, as the critics of both leaders have often said, future events alone will tell."

Somehow this dissolved my India problem into what may be its final elements. From India's point of view: the success of the "Coexistence" position. (As noted already in my India notes.) But from America's point of view, the danger of this position, if our experience of Russia since 1945 means anything. However, with American strength and success and Russia's economic difficulties turning the tide (apparently) in favor of the West, Nehru's position may actually be functioning in everybody's favor— helping to ease the tensions, and urging Russia, as well as the West, to relent. This leaves only one big complaint against Nehru, and that is his consistently anti-American, pro–Chinese-Russian propaganda, where he is actually taking the Red side in such questions as Formosa and in accusing the West of all the aggressive moves. This, I think, plants him far enough on the pro-Red side to make American aid to India a bit paradoxical.

And so now back to Japan.

An amusing train ride, third class, among peasants and schoolkids. The former, in contrast to those of India, neat and literate: showing to each other the cellophane-wrapped bolts of cloth bought in Kyoto, and calculating their expenses in little notebooks. The ride, a bit sooty (why didn't the Japan Travel Bureau book me by the fast and cleaner electric railroad?), but the country, with its rice fields, beautiful mountains, and lovely towns, was delightful. Arrived in Yamada, 6:00 P.M. Took taxi to the nearby Seiki Ryokan Inn, Japanese style—and I was immediately and at last in Japan, thanking God for my three months of Japanese.[274]

At the door of the inn, six or eight women in kimonos: welcome, in the grand style. I was conducted to my room, passing a cute snatch of garden. Tea was served, and a young man was sent to help me make plans (in Japanese) for the big day tomorrow. Next, the hot bath—in a little bathroom: not quite as hot as that in Tenri, but hot enough—and I came out, cleaned of the dirt of the journey. More tea—and I, now, in kimono. More planning for tomorrow (the problem: how to get my luggage to Toba). Then my dinner, with a special young woman at my side (the one who had taken me to the bath), to pour my beer, cut up my meat, etc. A lovely dinner—and, connecting this in my mind with my other Japanese tatami experiences, I suddenly got the formula. During my planning of the day, I mentioned the Ise Peninsula dances, of which I had read in the guidebook. After dinner my waitress brought me a little booklet, in Japanese, about the Ise dance (*Ise ondo*), and told me to wait a minute, left the room, and presently summoned me to the cutest exhibition of the year. A chair had been placed for me in a large, gaily decorated room, and seven young ladies of the inn's staff danced the *ondo* for me, in three parts. It was a nice little folk dance, quiet, and gentle, and charming. So, here we are on the brink of the geisha world in a simple little provincial inn. It is one, very consistent Japanese pattern of pleasant living—and it certainly is pleasant. Look what I've been missing, just because I can't speak Japanese. (Without the bit that I have, this whole thing would be simply impossible!)

My hostess, after preparing the floor bed and truly beautiful mosquito net of green with red trimmings—which filled the center of the room, turning the bed into a special sort of sleeping area—sat down and chatted with me till I dismissed her at about ten.

Saturday, July 23

Woke up and got up at about 6:30. At seven, the sliding doors made their sound and my friend's voice: "*Sumimasen.*"[275] She came in with tea, and then led me off to the hot water for my shave. Ham and eggs for breakfast and at 8:40 my other friend, the young man, arrived, to help me on my sightseeing for the day. The bags would be transferred to my inn in Toba and we departed from the inn, with bows and good wishes, at about nine.

Unfortunately it was pouring rain, so the whole day had to be enacted under umbrellas. Somehow, however, it didn't much matter. The magnificent scenery was only the more romantic in the rain—and the schoolkids, of course (but now on vacation and prettily dressed—all with umbrellas), were everywhere.

The first visit was to the *gekū* ("outer shrine"), in a glorious grove of gigantic evergreens, much like the forests around San Francisco. The architecture is pre-Buddhist—and simply stunning. The shrine dates from 478 A.D., and is dedicated to the goddess Toyouke, who came down to earth by the order of Amaterasu.[276]

We took a trolley to the second shrine, the *naikū* ("inner shrine"), which is in a grove even more glorious than that of the *gekū*, and is supposed to date from 5 B.C. Besides the torii and the great shrine itself, there is a "Horse Stable" (*umaya*), with a white horse used in ceremonials—and a great dance sanctuary, where, for a contribution of ¥1,000, I saw six damsels and five musicians (big drum, small drum, reed-musette, flute, and reeds/koto),[277] perform a ritual dance before the empty shrine of Amaterasu: a priest recited a prayer to the goddess, sending my name up to her as the donor, and again, my year touched one of its climaxes.

Another trolley brought us to Futamigaura, where the two rocks, commemorating Izanagi and Izanami,[278] stand just offshore, joined by a great straw rope that is renewed every January 5.

Then a bus to Toba: a boat ride around the lovely bay (suggesting to me very strongly that of Sitka),[279] and finally a visit to the Mikimoto Pearl Island: view of the process of growing pearls, and at about 3:30 four of the girl pearl divers put on a little performance for a gallery of schoolkids and American tourists: still in the pouring rain.

My guide left me at the Toba railroad station, where he put me into a taxi and sent me to my next hotel, where I have a second floor with a balcony, overlooking the beautiful bay.

Bath and dinner—less glamourous than last night's conditions, but still rather great. I seemed to be quite alone in the inn till about 7:30, when a party of (apparently) three males arrived in the next room—and it was they, I then realized, for whom all the glamour of the establishment had been reserved. Clapping of hands initiated the singing of a series of geisha songs—and then at the other side, three young lady guests began clapping hands for a song of their own, and now (at 10:00 P.M.) the two parties seem to be beginning to get somewhat together. At any rate, the inn is in a very, very, very, lively condition. The only problem is, that I'm going to have to get up at about six, to catch a 7:15 train.

Sunday, July 24   *Tokyo*

Things quieted suddenly at about 10:45 P.M. Good sleep. Breakfast in my room, Japanese breakfast!—seaweed soup, rice, little dishes of things, and—two fried eggs, to be handled with chopsticks. Train at 7:15. At Nagoya the 10:00 o'clock express arrived one hour late and there was no place to sit. Stood for six-and-a-half hours in the crowded aisle. Arrival in Tokyo 5:30. Settled in Yashima Hotel again. Good steak dinner at Suehiro's, and to bed.

Monday, July 25

Cab to Haneda to meet Jean, whose plane arrived on the dot of 8:40: Jean looking fine. Cab to hotel. Lunch at Imperial, after visit to U.S. Culture Center, where Jean is to teach. 1:00 P.M. four dances by Tōhō Kabuki Company, at Takarazuka Theater: last dance used symphony orchestra in combination with samisen—rather interesting amplification of volume all of a sudden, without breaking effect. Home for a rest, then dinner at Suehiro's and stroll through Ginza with stop at a coffee shop.

Tuesday, July 26

Jean off to teach in the morning, and I have Japanese lesson at the hotel with Miss Somekawa—nice lady; good lesson. Lunch with Jean and culture center people (Irene Pines and Mr. Kobayashi) at American Club. Good conversation.

1. Buddhism-Existentialism link
2. Japanese sense of "all's well with the world": sin idea missing: sense of harmony and accord

Rest, after lunch, then to Shimbashi Enbujō to see Osaka's Bunraku theater group. Wonderful show, including an amazing exit by the Benkei puppet,[280] and a curious fox scene at the end of the last piece. Jean was pretty tired and kept falling asleep. We had dinner at the theater, and, before retiring, stopped for a cool glass of orange juice at Mon's, the coffee shop across from the hotel.

Wednesday, July 27

In the morning, to the Japan Air Lines office to meet Mr. Akira Wakasugi, who had helped Jean with her tickets when she passed through Tokyo in January. He brought us around to the Japan Travel Bureau, where Mr. Takeichi planned for us our trip next week to Hokkaido. Japan Air Lines is making a free gift to us of the air passage, round trip. Wakasugi took us to lunch—and carefully admitted, when I made the point, that it would be a good thing for international accord if the U.S. Army pulled out of Japan: their behavior has not been exactly good.

Jean and I went to the Kabuki this afternoon, where we saw two traditional and two modern plays. Some important facts became apparent:

1. Loss of musical factor in the modern plays
2. Loss of dance (movement) in the modern plays
3. Stress on dialogue (people sitting and talking)
4. Stress on problems—psychological and social
5. Realistic, rather than styled, action in the modern pieces
6. Inferior utilization of stage space in modern pieces. In general, we thought the earlier style far superior to the modern

The second piece was an amazing dance: one male and eight female (old hag) characters, in a restrained dance of senile lechery.

The last piece dealt with the problem of a doctor in the nineteenth century, trying to introduce Western methods. Very interesting sociologically, but inferior to the early Kabuki, as "theater."

Dinner at the Kabuki theater, and a coffee at Star Fire before bed.

Thursday, July 28

Jean's teaching and my Japanese lesson in the morning. Lunch at Ginza Fujiya, Japan's Schrafft's. Department store visits in the afternoon, and then a rest. Sukiyaki dinner at Suehiro's fourth floor restaurant and a visit, after dinner, to Asakusa. Coffee at Mon's, and to bed.

Friday, July 29

Shopping and purchases in the morning at Takashimaya Department Store. Rest in the afternoon (the heat is terrifically wet and sticky). Visit, at 5:00, to Shinjuku Gyōen, to get seats for the outdoor Noh plays, which commenced at 6:00 and ended at 8:30. Saw *Aoi no Ue, Yo-uchi Sōga,* and a Noh comedy. Vast crowd. Good evening. Dinner at Irene's Hungaria. Coffee at Mon's, and to bed.

Saturday, July 30

Jean's teaching and my Japanese in the morning. Lunch at Fujiya—and an early afternoon of shopping. Bumped into Gautam and Gira in one of the shops and made a date for tomorrow night. Home for a rest, and then, to the Sumida River Fireworks Festival, which was certainly the most amazing and beautiful fireworks display either of us had ever seen. Dinner, late, at Suehiro's, and home to bed.

Sunday, July 31

Lots of plans and resolutions are shaping up for the period of our return to New York. For Jean—stress on her solo programs and teaching at Bard; for me:

1. Japanese (teacher to come to apartment)
2. Henry Volkening—Viking Press Conference
3. S.L.C. convocation address
4. S.L.C. course plans
5. Eranos work
   a. finish reading
   b. work on outline
6. Commence work on Viking book
7. French—for Jean and myself (teacher to come to apartment)
8. Commence party schedule
9. Photography

My big problem, we agree, is going to be that of warding off the Joe's Friendly Service projects. Nikhilananda and Mrs. Coomaraswamy are already the major entries. Our second problem is going to be the telephone. We think that we should arrange for a telephone answering service and a secretary of some kind.

I shall take a vow not to reply to the phone, except on certain specified days at certain hours. And the answering of letters should be handled through a secretary.

The giving of parties should be a regular task, so that we capture and hold the lead in this game. Our acquaintances seem to fall into four groups:

1. Friends
2. Work connections
    a. Dance
    b. Bard
    c. Publishing
    d. S.L.C.
3. People profitable to cultivate
4. Miscellaneous (fill-ins, old shoes, etc.)

The idea is to begin as soon as feasible with some parties for the first group, and to go on then at the rate of about one event a fortnight. We must also commence an exploration of the fun possibilities of New York— to try to make it come up to Tokyo and Kyoto in interest!

Through our conversations a couple of points seem to have come out with a fresh clarity.

1. Three levels of interest:
    a. Aesthetic organization
    b. Mythological organization
    c. Zen realization (trans-mythological)
2. My leading projects
    a. Bollingen book: stress on the magical charm of the myth world: narrative emphasis
    b. Viking book: stress on the intellectual interest and problematic of the myth world: philosophical emphasis
3. Intrusive commitments, to be assimilated:
    a. Lectures—my fee $250 (this will stop them!)
    b. Book reviews—accept only from Salmony & Block
    c. Articles—do only those that grow naturally from work in hand, or that clearly further careers of Jean or myself
    d. College tasks—be careful of their number

At 11:00 A.M. to the Bunraku again—for a wonderful performance. Finished at 4:15—at about 5:30, to the Japan International House to see Gautam and Gira and to meet Mr. and Mrs. Yoshimura (he, the architect of this new building and of the Japanese house at the New York Museum of Modern Art); also present, a music critic, Yoshida (interested only in Western-style music) and an American gentleman named Greeley who works with the NHK (Japanese Broadcasting Company). Pleasant chat. Good-bye to Gautam and Gira, who leave tomorrow for home. Dinner at the International House with the Yoshimuras and the Messrs. Yoshida and Greeley. To bed at eleven, after a sip of coffee and cocoa at Mon's.

Monday, August 1   *Chitose, Hokkaido*

All morning packing; lunch at the hotel. Departure at 1:45 for Japan Airlines and the 3:30 plane to Hokkaido. Arrival at Chitose Airport: bus to Sapporo Grand Hotel, where we arrived about 8:00 P.M.

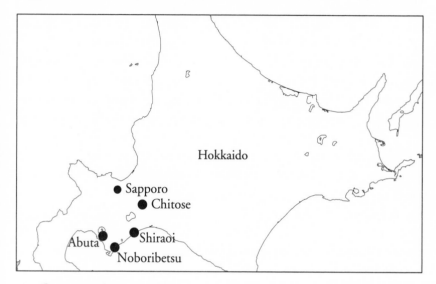

Great surprises:

1. Vast airfield and American military base at Chitose. (Our airplane landing, by the way, was the best of the year: only the squeak of the tires hitting the pavement: not even a slight jounce.)
2. Countryside not Japanese: somewhat sandy soil and scrappy vegetation, then well-forested and cultivated areas: more work horses than in Japan proper; peasants in less-pretty clothes; houses with American-style roofs or a thatch rather different from the Japanese; two or three farms with barns and silos that could have been in Indiana: grazing cattle here and there.
3. Sapporo, a large city—sort of frontier atmosphere: I thought of a combination of Alaska (Juneau) and the West: bright lights: one charming, carnival street along which we strolled after dinner.
4. Hotel, brand-new, American style, excellent food, nice little room and bath: quite a surprise.
5. Boomtown atmosphere everywhere.

Tuesday, August 2   *Shiraoi—Noboribetsu*

Up early: breakfast, and off to catch a 7:44 train. Arrived at Shiraoi at 10:30. Followed Japanese tourists to an Ainu village, where an old Ainu couple put on a lecture-demonstration in the almost utter darkness of a large Ainu house. A crowd of Japanese students and I tried to get good photos, meanwhile. After the talk of couple no. 1, Jean and I strolled to another Ainu-style house (quite new) where a second old man donned ceremonial robes and allowed me to take his picture—again, however, in semidarkness. They put a robe on Jean, who became suddenly shy about having her picture taken. We strolled, next, to the beach, where a lot of kids were playing, and then back to the main road. On the way, I found old lady no. 1 pushing a baby carriage: took her picture, and when I handed her a sixty-yen tip, she pointed to the hair on my arm and to that on hers: I put my arm against hers and the skins were the same. We laughed, and the mystery of the Ainu race's presence in Japan remained as deep as ever![281] Photographed another old man, carving bears, and then Jean and I walked to a sawmill, sat on one of the logs, and commenced eating our picnic lunch—which had been put up in very pretty little carrying boxes by the hotel.

A motorcycle pulled up, and a very pleasant, big Texan, here with the air force, got off and asked if I could change his army currency into yen. I couldn't but we invited him to join us with our sandwiches, and had a pleasant talk for about an hour. Learned about radar checks on the Russians, etc. When he left, we returned to the station and sat for two hours, waiting for our 4:05 P.M. train. Funny little railroad station, with nice people.

At 4:33, arrived at Noboribetsu and took a taxi to the Noboribetsu Grand Hotel at Noboribetsu Spa. An interesting synthesis of Occidental and Oriental elements. Japanese-style rooms: European dining room: Japanese big bath, with a pleasant mixed bathing situation, which reminded us of the Penning pool.[282] One lady took her child systematically to every pool in the big room—varieties of sulfur bath, supposed to be good for the health. After the bath, cooled off in our room, and then had dinner. Tried to locate the temple at which Eidmann is to be tomorrow, strolled a bit—but rain fell and we returned to the hotel, pretty tired after the day, and went early to bed.

Wednesday, August 3

Some good thoughts emerged at breakfast:

1. The Japanese road of approach to the divine is the aesthetic way.
2. The Japanese do not refer their morality back to the dictates of "God," but

regard the rules as social rules—extremely important social rules, for the serious breach of which hara-kiri may be the only answer. *Dharma,* that is to say, is here relative to society, which, of course, is correct.

3. It occurred to me that the Western concept of Order is now that of efficiency—mechanical—and that perhaps the Japanese concept of aesthetic order, joined to this, or playing against it, may be the main motif of the contemporary search for form: for instance in modern art.

4. The Japanese *dharma*-as-social idea seems to be related to the Chinese Confucian orientation.

After breakfast, wrote letters, then went for a walk with Jean to see if we could find Eidmann. Went up a hill road to a school at the top and came down again—paused at a temple where a young man told us that Eidmann was at the Grand Hotel. Visited a large area of sulfurous springs and boiling pits, where we took a few pictures, then returned to the hotel, only to learn that Eidmann was not there. Lunch, more letters, and at about 3:30 the phone rang: Eidmann, downstairs. Professor Fujiwara and Haru were with him. We had tea and a pleasant chat and arranged to have Eidmann and Haru with us for dinner.

At the sulphur pools near Noboribetsu

Jean and I went to the bath while Eidmann and Haru took a stroll through the town. Then they returned for dinner in our room, Japanese style, and we had an excellent talk. A few major points:

In the village of Shiraoi, which we visited yesterday, one block, or section, is wholly Ainu. In all of Hokkaido, there are probably no more than one hundred full-blooded Ainus, but twenty thousand or so who participate in the Ainu culture. All but a dozen or so speak Japanese as well as Ainu. There are a number of Ainu dialects. No thorough study has been made of the language.

The *bear sacrifice* is the principal Ainu rite. The idea is, that the gods come to the Ainu as bears, but then cannot get out of their bear incarnations, unless killed. The rite returns the god to his proper form, and the meat and skin are left behind, to the Ainu, as a gift. The Ainu keep bears as pets; the women nurse the cubs. The pets then are sacrificed. Eidmann thought the ideas absurd—but I find here the *dema* complex,[283] associated with the Animal Master (Moon Bear? Sun Bear? Totem Bear?). Is there possibly an old Stone Age connection here, comparable to that of the Eskimo-Magdalenian continuity? *I think I should use this bear myth in my Basic Mythologies.*[284]

1. In northern Hokkaido some stone circles have been discovered; also, some Paleolithic-type caves. They are regarded as late (circa A.D. 1000) and not associated with the Ainus. (Perhaps some Malekula connections?)[285]
2. According to Buddhist belief, every grain of rice in your rice bowl is a Bodhisattva; hence the Buddhist monk or priest (Haru, for instance) eats every speck of rice in his bowl. (Compare the bear sacrifice of the Ainus. I indicated the connection, and Eidmann was a bit embarrassed!)

Actually, *all religions are absolutely absurd if their symbolism is read concretely*—and the trouble with the majority of religious people is that they always read it that way.

Eidmann and Haru left at about 9:45 after preparing whipped tea for Jean; the girl prepared our room, and we hit the floor.

Thursday, August 4   *Abuta*

Off in a bus, after breakfast, to the station. Eidmann and Haru left at the same time for a visit to Shiraoi. We reached Abuta at 11:05 and went by bus for a beautiful ride to Lake Tōya and our next domicile, the Manseikaku Inn. Bath: lunch in room: walk through town: lovely boat ride on the beautiful lake with a young lady at the microphone announcing all the news, and twice giving us Japanese songs.

Eidmann, at the railroad station of Noboribetsu, told us the three main surprises that the Japanese experienced from his speeches:

1. That Christianity and democracy are not synonymous
2. That the money for the Christian missions is not supplied by the U.S. government
3. That missionaries are not political agents

Following our boat ride, we returned to our room for a bit of a nap, then had dinner in the room and went early to bed. Jean beginning to feel a bit queasy in her gut, after our recent Japanese meals.

One little matter of today that is worth a note; namely, the Japanese-American gentleman from Los Angeles who spoke to us in the train and then was with us for the boat ride: Mr. Mori. Twelve years a member of L.A. Rotary Club, he served as a delegate for them to conventions, including Paris, 1938. Then, when the war came, they asked him to resign. They are now asking him to rejoin: but the stab struck too deeply. Now sixty-seven and retired, he is devoting himself to the work of the Congregational Church.

Friday, August 5

Jean still a bit heavy. Spent the morning writing letters; then, at 1:30 P.M., commenced on magnificent mountain bus ride to Jōzankei: the Shikanoyū Club. Another Japanese spa—this time in a wildly mountainous area, in contrast to the beautiful lake area of yesterday.

Some things I've noted about Hokkaido: Ainus are regarded about as the Indians in the U.S.A.; farms larger than those of Japan proper, with crops like those of America—wheat, corn, beans; fields worked by horses: blacksmith shops in villages; forested areas resemble Oregon mountains: beautiful vistas, wild and rugged, with many big trees; lumbering; difficult mountain roads. Apparently, having been developed first in the Meiji period, Hokkaido, in contrast to the rest of Japan, followed Occidental models.

Saturday, August 6   *Tokyo*

Tenth anniversary of the Hiroshima bomb.

Went for a pleasant stroll, this morning, through the town and at 1:15 boarded an electric train for Sapporo and the conclusion of our trip. Delightful ride, and a magnificent plane back to Tokyo—5:30 to 7:40: one hour faster than the journey north. Back in our room at the Yashima Hotel by 9:15—cocoa and cake at Mon's, and early to bed.

Sunday, August 7

At 11:00 went to the Meijiza to see the Ichikawa Girls Kabuki. The girls were less strong than the men, of course,[286] but in their second piece, *Sennin Katawa,* which was a charming and amusing dance piece, they were really wonderful. I thought, also, that in the women's roles of the regular Kabuki pieces they were really better than the men. In any case, they have done a bold thing here, invading the male actors' domain, and have actually succeeded in presenting a magnificent show. The pieces: *Yoshitsune Senbon-zakura* (which I have seen already in male Kabuki), *Sennin Katawa, Keisei Awa no Naruto,* and *Kanjincho* (which I have seen in the Bunraku, and in a film of Kabuki that was shown in New York in 1953).

After the show, we went to Takashimaya Department Store, to shop a bit, and then saw, at the Nippon Seinenkan Hall, what turned out to be a children's ballet school, performing *Swan Lake.* Left after the first curtain and went to Irene's Hungaria for dinner—then to Mon's for an iced coffee, and to bed.

Monday, August 8

Dance and Japanese classes in the morning. A bit of shopping in the afternoon. Arranged air passage to and from Kyoto. At four-thirty, return to the Ichikawa Girls Kabuki (joined by Irene Pines, of the U.S.I.S.), for another wonderful show: again, the dance pieces were the best. Iced coffee at Mon's, afterwards, and to bed.

Tuesday, August 9

Dance and Japanese classes again in the morning. The weather is again pretty hot, and so, after a bit of shopping, we took it easy in our room till about five. Dinner at Suehiro's, and then to the Kabukiza, to see *The Teahouse of the August Moon.* The play is good, but the production (Itō's brother[287]) slowed the action considerably and did not do justice to the stagecraft of the Kabukiza. A wonderful satire on the stupidities of the Occupation. For me, after my four months in Japan, the charm of the Japanese phase of the play was quite delightful—excellently performed by a Japanese cast (American parts by Americans). Unfortunately at the concluding moment (reconstruction of the teahouse), the maladroit stage crew broke an important element of the set, and the curtain had to be rung down and the audience dismissed.

CHAPTER XIII

CLOSING THE CIRCLE

TOKYO, HAWAI'I, CALIFORNIA, NEW YORK

Wednesday, August 10

Began calculating the job ahead in the purchasing of presents for Honolulu, San Francisco, and New York: eighty-five persons!

At one I had lunch at the hotel with the artist Sabro Hasegawa.[288] We had an excellent chat, from which the following main points emerged:

There has been in Japan a ten-year pendulation rhythm between Occidental and native movements. The defeat took place just ten years ago this month and was followed by a strong Occidentalization tendency. The reaction is due to begin (and, I dare say, will have something of a Communist tinge).

My notion that the dual life of the Japanese businessman (business suit and chairs during the day, *yukata*[289] and tatami at home) brings the Unconscious and Conscious of Japan into conscious dialogue has to be modified by the realization that for the majority this dialogue is not intentionally fostered. Hasegawa cited one friend who stated that he *had* to return to the simple life at home "because he is poor." (This, of course, would not reduce value of the dialogue.)

Hasegawa himself has felt the tension of the East-West struggle in his painting career—in the beginning he worked in oil (Western manner) but now has turned to ink and paper. Hasegawa, in his own quest for form, has found his best base and support in Tea. Tea, for Hasegawa, is intimately linked with Zen. (Contrast Eidmann, who stresses disconnection.)

Zen, according to Hasegawa, has two sides, monastic and secular. The great stress on meditation (see Mrs. Sasaki) belongs to the monastic aspect. The secular aspect operates through Tea, flower arrangement, Noh, and so on, to render life itself the field of contemplation. Hasegawa's chief masters are the founder of Sōtō, the founder of Tea, Zeami,[290] and Bashō.[291]

According to Hasegawa, the businessmen of Japan have begun to take a genuine interest in the support and development of Japanese art and culture. Hence the *department store art programs.* To be worthy of civilized patronage, the businessman must himself be civilized. This idea was derived from China, Hasegawa believes, during the thirties.

During the afternoon we shopped—heavily; and for dinner, we went to Suehiro's with Eidmann and Haru. We sparked Eidmann on the Zen-Tea theme and got the following reactions:

The founder of Tea had eight disciples: seven were Christians, one may have been a Christian, and the tea equipment went to the Yamauchi family. Moreover, the founder, compelled to commit hara-kiri, was not "calm" but greatly disturbed by the prospect. There is nothing here of Zen.

Zen temples today sell *amulets and charms:* Eidmann and Haru bought several in Hokkaido.

After dinner we took a little stroll about the Ginza, and stopped in the Shirobasha for iced coffee. Haru's amazement at the decor of the Shirobasha was a delight to see.

Thursday, August 11

Jean not feeling very well this morning. Took it easy all day. I had my Japanese lesson till noon. We had lunch at Mon's. Took a nap and did a bit of shopping in the afternoon, and for dinner joined Eidmann and Haru, first at the Shirobasha and then at an Indian restaurant. The proprietor (from Trivandrum) had learned from his Japanese wife how to be tidy. For me it was rather fun to have to enthuse again about dhal and curry. When I mentioned Indian music to the proprietor, he said that the long time that one had to wait for the singer to warm up taught patience. (Always, Jean said afterward, they have some moral handy: anything but the pleasure of experiencing art.)

We bade good-bye to Eidmann and Haru, whom we shall visit, next week, in Kyoto—and went to a "Hawai'ian Coffee House" for iced coffee, then home to bed.

Friday, August 12

Jean went off to teach her (postponed from yesterday) dance class and I wrote letters and diary all morning. A bit of shopping and resting, then cocktails at Imperial at 4:00 with a Mr. Sperry, whom Jean had met on her first visit to Tokyo. We had seen him yesterday in the Indian restaurant with an Indian couple and had made this engagement at that time. He told us now that the Indian couple were not liking Japan: the woman thought Tokyo a "man's" city—I thought, what gall: an Indian woman calling the Japanese society a man's world! Jean and I went to see the Takarazuka show at Takarazuka Theater (same show as the one I saw in Takarazuka). Then had a late supper at Peter's Restaurant and home to bed.

Saturday, August 13

Japanese and dance lessons in the morning. At about 3:00, Irene Pines called for us in her car and drove us to a curious and amusing session of *gengaku* and *bugaku* music and dance at the garden, arranged by the Asahi News and the Japanese camera business as a photo competition. Six hundred photographers—mostly Americans—politely competed for space from which to photograph the small stage. It was sort of crazy, but Jean had a chance to hear the music and to see a bit of the sort of dancing that was presented, May 1, at Tōdaiji in Nara. After the show we went for a "Mongolian-style" dinner at the delightful Genghis Khan Restaurant.

Sunday, August 14

Started our packing job in the morning. Afternoon with Sabro Hasegawa at his home. He knows Cage, Isamu, Watts,[292] and his talk about Zen and Tea had a bit of the sound of our Eighth Street friends' chitchat on the subject.[293] He served us tea, showed us his work (success just dawning in America: practically unknown in Japan), and, after a light supper with the family, we went to the station—watched the Bon dance for a while, and took the train back to Tokyo. Packing. To bed.

Monday, August 15   *Kyoto*

Went with Jean in the morning to her dance class at the American Culture Center and took photos of the class. After lunch, we headed for Haneda Airport. We had a lovely flight to Osaka, then by *densha*[294] to Kyoto. A taxi to Nishi Honganji—and the beginning of a large and wonderful visit.

The gate was swung open for our taxi by Eidmann's manservant and we drove directly to the door of the house. The visit commenced with a special kind of tea (*sencha*) prepared by Haru, then a viewing of some pictures (kakemono) that Eidmann had bought in Hokkaido and a general discussion of plans for the week. In the room with Eidmann when we arrived was Professor Kasugai, who would take care of our "sightseeing" till his departure Friday night.

We were put into kimonos and after dinner went out to see the Bon dance in front of the Nishi Honganji Temple. Jean, Haru, and I joined the dance for one round. We returned to the house, had a cup of some curious little sweet infusion, a bit of fruit, and at about midnight retired, after Haru conducted a little prayer service.

Tuesday, August 16

Temple gongs and roosters woke us at 5:30 A.M., and after breakfast we proceeded to one of the Nishi Honganji teahouses for a morning tea ceremony, conducted by Haru, and attended by the little tea-ceremony old lady who has taught tea to the whole Eidmann household. Next, we visited the other beautiful Nishi Honganji teahouses, the tea garden, and the temple. We saw the last part of a ceremony in the main hall, with a concluding bit of *shō* music, and then went through the palace rooms.

After lunch we paid a visit with Haru to the seventeenth-century house of Ieyasu—full of escape passages and trapdoors—and after dinner went up to the roof of the Ryūkoku University library building, to view the five fires built for the Bon ceremony on the hills surrounding Kyoto. Before retiring, we visited the Bon dance in front of the Higashi Honganji.

Wednesday, August 17

Met the Kasugai family, 9:30 A.M., at the Imperial Palace. After visiting the palace, we proceeded to an extremely interesting Tendai temple (Manshū-in), with a glorious garden representing Lake Biwa. Many important paintings were here, and the abbot told me that the founding abbot, back in the sixteenth century, (ca. A.D. 1600) had been very much interested in Christian-Buddhist parallels, liturgical and otherwise; Tantric parallels, etc. We had our *obentō* in this temple and then went on to view the glorious Shūgaku-in garden—three levels, representing the three worlds.

At four we went to Mrs. Sasaki's, to attend a beautiful tea, served by a young Zen monk, Sōhaku Kobori, in the Daikō ("Great Light") monastery, near the Daikokuji. This young man is a direct descendant of Enshū Kobori, one of the earliest tea masters, and his ceremony was conducted with considerably more ease than Haru's. After the ceremony, I had a brief discussion with the young monk on mythology.

He declared that in Zen Buddhism there was no mythology, and when I referred him to the mythological motifs associated with the birth of the Buddha, he declared that these were given spiritual interpretations by the Zen teachers. I had cited the incident of the newborn Buddha's seven steps: he paralleled it with the kōan:

"What is the origin of all the Buddhas?"

"The Eastern Mountain crosses the river."

It was a little hard for him to realize that no matter what the mode of interpretation the motif itself was still a mythological theme.

This led me to the following idea; namely, that *four levels of mythological interpretation are to be distinguished:*

1. The magical—where the symbols are employed to achieve magically-caused effects; e.g. Navaho rain rites; the Mass.
2. The concretistic—where the symbols are interpreted historically; e.g. Fall and Redemption, Christian style.
3. The mythological-psychological, where the deities, etc. are interpreted as spiritual principles; e.g. Shinshū interpretation of the Buddha (according to Eidmann).
4. The "allegorical," where the reference goes past the whole context of the symbolical to a transcendent, ineffable realization; e.g. the elite Zen interpretations of the Buddha motifs (according to Kobori).

After the tea ceremony, we had dinner with Mrs. Sasaki, and a beautiful conversation followed, which lasted till about 11:15. The main points:

A fundamental contrast between Occidental and Oriental thinking rests in the precision and intellectual consistency of the Occidental as contrasted with the multifold (or vague) and tolerant style of the East. When I (a Westerner) was through with the Church, I was through with it. In the Orient, on the other hand, Buddhists will pray to the fox-god . . . etc., and *rōshis* will participate in popular worship.

Such an interpretation of the Buddha as I had heard from Kobori this afternoon is hardly shared by the multitude of Japanese Buddhists. We, in reading of and studying the Orient, come in touch only with the *crème de la crème:* the multitude hold to comparatively primitive, concretistic interpretations. Mrs. Sasaki is convinced that the vast majority of the Buddhists in Japan have quite simple ideas about the Buddhas whom they worship: they literally believe that the Bodhisattvas are going to come for them when they die, to conduct them to the Paradise of Amida. (Eidmann, however, contests this view for Shinshū.) Even the actual behavior of *rōshis* is disappointing. For example, the two Zen *rōshis* whom I met on my earlier visit to Kyoto had a little affair between them in which one managed to buy a large number of laquer boxes from the other at cost, forty each, instead of for the four thousand each, which the other expected.

"The idealists in the world today are the Americans; the Japanese, as well as the Indians, being materialists, through and through."

"Life" is not Zen but Tao: Zen is a way, a method. Zen has influenced Tea, gardens, Noh, archery practice, etc., but these are not Zen. (Contrast, here, the view of Hasegawa—see page 254.)

The Buddhist scriptures are so numerous that in the temple compounds an entire building is generally assigned to them. "*Various* sūtras *have been stressed at various times and by various teachers and these have furnished the bases of the various sects.*" (Eidmann's remark, while showing us the Nishi Honganji compound, July 16.)

The basic text of Kegon (Chinese: Hua-yen) is the *Avataṃsaka,* or Flower Wreath, Sūtra. During the Nara period, under the emperor Shōmu, this sect was the leading sect in Japan (Tōdaiji Temple). Its influence has been carried on in a number of the later Buddhist sects, and notably in Zen. Of the various themes stressed in the *Avataṃsaka Sūtra,* Zen makes a special point of that of the *Dharmadhātu* (*hokkai*), "the Universe," i.e., the Fourfold Universe as the Field of *Dharma* and Realm of Absolute Truth. This theme is developed as follows:

1. *Ji-hokkai:* the World of Things
2. *Ri-hokkai:* the Noumenal World. Śunyatā: the World of the Absolute Principle: the World of Zen: Egolessness: Unity with the Great Self
3. *Ri-ji-muge-hokkai:* the Harmonization and Unification of the *ji-hokkai* and *ri-hokkai:* the Principle of Things Without Obstruction: Phenomenal and Noumenal Worlds as identical
4. *Ji-ji-muge-hokkai:* the Realm of the Harmonious Interpenetration of All Things with Each Other, Indra's Net. The Universe as One Whole: The Eternal, Self-Recreating Play of the Absolute[295]

This is what was signified by the episode of Gautama's holding up of the flower: each existence is the totality of life.[296] (Scholium: This is the goal-thought: Consider in connection with this the conversation with Sri Krishna Menon.)

5. A fifth step or sphere is to be added, namely that of the Return to the Natural: the manifestation of our realization in our everyday life: each work, each act, is a holy world-supporting act. It is no longer necessary to think of the religious aspect. This is the state known as *mushin* (No Mind), "Having Nothing in the Mind"

One is filled with:

1. gratitude to all beings in the past, for having brought about the conditions of our enlightenment;
2. gratitude to all beings in the present, for the same reason; and
3. a sense of responsibility to all beings in the future.

(Query: How to reconcile this with the "No Mind" idea?)

After our evening with Mrs. Sasaki in her house in the Daitokuji compound, we returned to the Nishi Honganji, to find Eidmann still sitting up. We had tea, and retired at about 1:00 A.M., after discussing a bit with Eidmann some of the themes of our Sasaki evening. Result, a few more ideas:

Eidmann contested Mrs. Sasaki's statement that popular Buddhism is unilluminated. It is his belief that the followers of Shinshū really understand the Shinshū doctrine of the Buddha. An exception must perhaps be made for the cities, especially Tokyo, Kyoto, and Osaka, where the purity of the belief is contaminated by contact with the followers of other sects. Shinshū is concerned with Preaching and Lay Practice, not only with worship for the layman while the monks practice meditation. Hence, the lay community in Shinshū is well informed. The crux of Shinshū is the mystery of *the Awakening of Faith*. The object of worship in Shinshū is *myōgō*. (The term *kigō* = symbolic logic.)

As for the ontology of the Buddha: to say that the Buddha *is* or is *not* is to miss the point. The corollary: to say that the Buddha is a myth or is not a myth is equally beside the point.

Kegon is the key to Japan. It is strongest today in Shinshū. It is talked about in Zen (e.g. Suzuki).

Hōnan, the founder of Jōdo, is an object of worship in the Sōtō Zen temple in Ōjōji, Sendai.

Just as Christianity in Japan is a vehicle for the introduction of Occidental elements, so was Zen for that of Chinese. The Japanese-Chinese vocabulary from the Zen era carries a Zen tone. Zen Buddhism reenforces the Chinese influence in Japan. The term Zen in the West is associated immediately with Zen Buddhism; but in the Orient it has a broader reference—Zen = Egolessness = *muga* = *mushin* (see above , no. 5). As for *Zen in the Art of Archery:* Zen was introduced into the context of archery by Honda, a Tokugawa archer who had practiced Zen. In archery, Zen = egolessness. (Here Zen reenforces a principle that may have entered into archery already in the Paleolithic.)

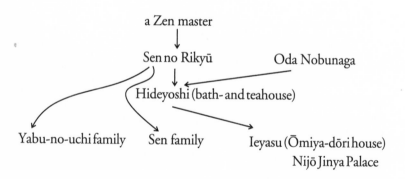

The genealogy of Tea

The idea of *mushin* in Tea: it is a kind of spontaneity (Spengler's "in Form seen") that comes *beyond* the sphere of the complicated learning of what is correct. *Note:* it is not the abandonment or loss of form (an idea that I got from my conversation with Hasegawa.) The idea of form, as it appears in Tea, permeates *all* the spheres of Japanese life (e.g. the formalities of polite conversation). Mastery (and even trance-action) consists in going *beyond.* Jean points out that in modern India, where there is no sense of this form principle, trance-ecstasy is associated with the *rejection* of society—this is a very important point. The essence of Tea (as of archery, athletics, dance, all effective action, yoga, Zen, and whatnot) is *activity and calm together:* form and ecstasis.

With Mrs. Sasaki I discussed the matter of the Zen kōans. Apparently kōans were used in China but not graded and employed in a series. The grading took place in Japan, ca. 1680, and has since become a standard and typical Zen principle. During the course of our discussion I tried to figure out the probable sort of reply to be given to the kōan announced by Kobori (see page 257), but Mrs. Sasaki laughed and said that that kind of rational cogitation was precisely the opposite to the kind of understanding that was required.

In the course of some conversations with Jean, it occurred to me that in Japan I had found examples of both:

rājā yoga—Zen meditation; and

bhakti yoga

1. Shinshū "Awakening of Faith." (Minor meditation, to calm the spirit, but with no goal of enlightenment through meditation, or symbolical understanding of the Buddha)
2. Jōdo: *Namu Amida-butsu:* Illumination at death

but that I had seen nothing of:

karma yoga, or

jñāna yoga

In conversation with Eidmann, I asked what he thought of this and he suggested as a possible example of *karma yoga* in Japan Ippen Shōnin's Jishū (thirteenth century), which, he claims, exerted a great influence on the development of Japanese culture. It now has only three or four hundred temples, and is definitely a minor sect. He pointed out, also, that in certain early Buddhist *sūtras three Bodhisattvas* are mentioned: Virgadika Bodhisattva, Śraddhadika Bodhisattva, and Panadika Bodhisattva; the path or method represented by the last, he suggested, might be likened to that of *jñāna.*

These three Bodhisattvas are sometimes represented as independent of each other, but sometimes, also, as standing in a graded series. This reminds me of the Gītā's lack of clarity about the primacy or interrelationship of the yogas. Perhaps the great answer here is that the Oriental mind (see page 258) does not, or cannot, make strict or final decisions or distinctions in matters of this kind.

Bushidō, according to Eidmann, represents not Buddhist *karma yoga,* but Shintō.

The Fujiwara term *aware* is very difficult to translate. It means "pity," but is not the word for *karuṇā,* which in Japanese is *jihi.*

According to Professor Kasugai, the Noh play was an expression of Zen. The voice of the Noh play is the voice of the Void. The word *Noh* means "everything."

Tendai, according to Professor Kasugai, is based on the *Saddharma Pundarīka Sūtra.* The worship of the *stūpa* is a Tendai trait, as is also the worship of Two Buddhas.

The whole question of the relationship of Zen to Tea, Noh, archery, etc., is one that I have been trying to work out, these past few days. Eidmann is most emphatic in minimizing the influence of Zen in these matters. Hasegawa, on the other hand, saw Zen everywhere in Japanese life. Professor Kasugai asserts the influence of Zen in the shaping of Noh, Tea, and gardens; Mrs. Sasaki gave what seems to me to be a quite good formulation of the relationship (see page 258). Returning now, however, to the viewpoint of Hasegawa, perhaps it would be correct to distinguish with him the points of view of the layman and the monk. Kasugai, Eidmann, and Sasaki are definitely on the monk's side of the question. If we stand on the lay side, perhaps we can say that Zen has helped us to see how the arts of Tea, archery, theater, etc., *are* ways to enlightenment—i.e., have helped *us* (if not the monks) to regard them in the manner of the *karma yogin.* Whether the Zen of the monasteries is capable of teaching intentionally what we laymen have, perhaps accidentally, been able to learn from Zen, is then beside the point.

Eidmann holds that the school of modern Zen enthusiasts, who see Zen as Life, stems from the romanticism of Kakuzō Okakura.[297] And as for the relationship of traditional Japan to the works of Japanese modern art: when Japan's true aristocrats buy modern art at all, they buy only the best (who, however, is to judge?). Modern Critics of the Yoshida type, on the other hand, spurn the traditional arts entirely. There is a full split here. They pretend to be Western (Paris, Vienna: "Tokyo is a large village," etc.), but are really not Western. *Western art is a function of Western Life*—not of the attempt of an Oriental to associate himself with the West.

In my talks with Jean I have managed to formulate some of my notions about the primary traits of the West, and their relationship to the problems of the modern Orient:

The first contribution is *the development of the interest in the uniqueness of the individual,* perhaps via the troubadour, erotic tradition and its later manifestation in marriage for love. This leads on to "Progressive Education" and Sarah Lawrence College.

The second contribution is that which I now call *the Cartesian concept of Space and Time* (B.C.–A.D., instead of dates by reigns; latitude and longitude for the whole planet). This led to:

1. The actual expansion of Occidental civilization
2. The universal application of the Scientific Method (other peoples had invented occasional engines, etc.)

And then, on the bad side

3. A totalitarian pathos and urge (Christianity, Democracy)

Then, finally, the West's third contribution: the machine.

One of the charms of Japan is the nontotalitarian character of its life: the various arts (Noh, Kabuki, etc.) survive without contaminating each other, etc.; whereas in the West we tend to have Modern vs. traditional, etc. The Indian counterpart is what Nehru calls the curse of Communalism.

The Asian penchant for Communism is perhaps to be explained as a desire to gain the material advantages offered by the machine (Contribution 3) without facing up to the spiritual-psychological problem of individualism (Contribution 1).

As an example of the nonpersonal character of Japanese life: the standard formalities of speech, which are in Japan accepted as adequate expressions of personal feeling, and to me were embarrassing to utter, as sounding insincere and merely mechanical.

Thursday, August 18   *Nara*

At 8:00 A.M. we met Mr. and Mrs. Kasugai at Kyoto Station for the trip to Nara. At Nara we were joined by the monk Jōkai Hiraoka (son of the archbishop of the Kegon sect, Abbot Myōkai Hiraoka, whom we also met) of the

Tōdaiji Temple. We visited the Nigatsu Temple, where a ceremony was taking place, with two monks sitting in facing chairs, at either side of the altar, exchanging words in a mock philosophical discussion (sometimes in the Honganji Temples, Eidmann later told us, such discussions are held in earnest); other monks chanted *sūtras;* we were shown the blackened ceiling—blackened by *goma* fires which, miraculously, do not ignite the building.

The Campbells and the Kasugais at Nara

We then looked at the great bell (ca. A.D. 752; forty-eight tons), and a chapel wherein the portrait image (twelfth century) of a disciple of Hōnin, and an image of Jizō into which a nail was driven, to keep it from leaving its place and walking about to shelter children.

Then we went on to the Tōdaiji Temple and the Great Buddha. Mrs. Roosevelt[298] was there with a small party of guides and journalists. We went up to the high platform and walked around the image. On to the temple with the many-armed Kannon, and finally the temple with the Four Kings and twofold Buddha shrine (see above, May 1, page 72).

After viewing the temples, we entered the reception building with the Reverend Hiraoka and had tea: he invited me to write to him for books and information and presented me with a picture book of Tōdaiji. He gave Jean and me fans, bearing rubbings from the former reception hall, which had been destroyed by the U.S. Army.

We proceeded, having said good-bye to our guide, to a hotel, for lunch, then went to the Kasuga Shrine and ran into a large practice session of the performers (dancers and musicians) who were to participate in a great festival the following day. Koto players in one room, *shō* in another, flute in a third, and musette in a fourth—each with instructor. We heard them all severally, then were treated to a brief ensemble. Also viewed the dancers (same style as that of my Ise visit).

Jean Erdman and the Kasugais at the deer park in Nara

We slowly strolled back to the station through the deer park and past the five-storied pagoda, and arrived in Kyoto about 5:00 P.M.

Jean and I went to the Kyoto Hotel, just to get to a decent Western-style toilet, and then I showed her Theater Street and the Pontochō. We returned to Eidmann at 6:20.

Eidmann bid us sit down and talk—but when 9:00 P.M. arrived and no dinner, I asked whether he knew that we had not eaten. He pretended surprise. I told him not to worry: we could go out to Fujiya. He insisted on joining us, and we all taxied to the Shijō Fujiya—where Haru and I had an amusing battle for the check.

Friday, August 19   *Kyoto*

In the morning, an amusing visit from "Cook-san" and "Mini-san"—Jean's family's old servants, who after a lifetime of service in Hawai'i, have now returned to Japan. They landed in Yokohama August 16, where they were joined by their family—two grown sons and a daughter and their children. This morning they arrived in Kyoto, after having wired us they would visit us at 9:00 A.M. Eidmann had planned to have us see Chion-in with Professor Kasugai at 10:00; but we postponed our meeting and waited around for Cook-san and Mini-san till about 9:45, when I decided to go look for them at the Nishi Honganji front office. I walked twice around the temple compound and was beginning to wonder whether they were going to show up at all, when, in my second round, I spied Cook-san standing quietly at the threshold of the front office, neatly dressed and patiently holding his hat in front of his stomach. Mini-san was standing inside, chatting with a number of people—her sons and some strangers, as well as some of the people of the office. Cook-san finally caught her attention and she greeted me very sweetly and charmingly. They both looked well and happy, and, apparently, were being very well taken care of by their families. I went back to our cottage and fetched Jean: then we brought Cook-san and Mini-san back to our rooms, while the family waited in the office.

It was a nice little visit. Cook-san had been sixty years in Hawai'i, and had a little trouble making himself comfortable on the tatami. Eidmann's boy servant, Hayashi-kun, brought us tea, and we chatted for about three-quarters of an hour about Jean's mother, Hawai'i and Japan, Mini-san's plans for living in Japan, and our own trip. At about 11:30, Eidmann appeared in the door and conversed hospitably in Japanese with the guests; and then we took our departure, returning Cook-san and Mini-san to the front office. I noticed that Cook-san had forgotten his hat and started back for it. He followed: we found it in the room. I took a few pictures of our visitors with their family and we bade them all good-bye.

When we came back to the house, Eidmann was about ready to start off with us on the day's adventure, but then Haru returned from a trip that he had made to Osaka. We all started off in a taxi for Chion-in, where we found Professor Kasugai waiting for us in the garden. The day that he had planned for us was one of the loveliest of the year. It began with a beautiful Japanese luncheon on the tatamis of the Hermitage. This was followed by a visit to Chion-in, which concluded with the presentation to me of a great book on the life and works of Hōnin. Next, at 1:30 P.M., we attended a beautiful tea ceremony at a Jōdoshū convent, where five or six nuns did the honors. At the opening and close of the ceremony the notes of a *shakuhachi* solo came from somewhere out in the garden that was faced by our big tearoom, and Jean nearly went crazy with excitement. At the close of the ceremony we viewed some kakemonos painted by an old monk, where the lines of the figures (Kannon, Amida) were composed of verses from the *sūtras*—a tour de force that in one case, at least, was quite successful. The nuns—young and old—were darling, and the whole experience was a sheer delight.

Our next event, at 3:00 P.M., was a magnificent visit to the beautiful Hōnen-in Temple, where we sipped tea and took clear, cool water from the mountain spring in the lovely garden—then attended a "*Namu Amida-butsu*" ceremony, beating "fish mouths" and chanting.[299]

At four we went to the *yudōfu* garden of the Nanzenji Temple for another of those wonderful *yudōfu* feasts. Tall, beautiful lotuses were growing in the pond. They opened the shōjis of the little garden temple for us, so that we could get out of the drizzle that had begun to fall. And when the party was over, at about 6:30, we bade Professor Kasugai farewell—and the Buddhist nun who is his disciple—and drove to town—for an evening of shopping and strolling in the streets.

Saturday, August 20

A day of shopping. In the morning, pottery and dishes; lunch in Alaska, on the top floor of the Asahi building; afternoon at Oridono's, buying silk. Jean had a wonderful time.

After a light dinner at Eidmann's, we set off with Peg McDuffy, in the car that Eidmann has just bought for her, first to see the temple of which Eidmann is to become the master, and then to join the members of the Kansai Oriental Society at a fine dance-play and drumming festival in the neighborhood of a small, Tendai-Shintō sort of temple on the outskirts of Kyoto. The performers were the members of a peasant club of actors. They began by beating in complicated rhythms small but very heavy drums, held aloft by sturdy handles; and then moved on to two to four large drums set up on the platform. Afterwards we had a little series of plays: a comic masked dance of a farmer and his wife; an episode of a samurai defeating, first a ghost, then an ape; and an episode of an acrobatic dragon, confronted and defeated by a second acrobatic dragon, who then was driven off by a samurai warrior. The audience consisted of the peasant people of the neighborhood and the members of the Kansai Oriental Society, who were given special seats and attention. I was struck by the relationship of all this to the pantomime that I had seen during my first week in Kyoto, as well as by the skill and pleasant ease of the performance.

One of the leading figures of the Kansai Society, Mr. Perkins, invited Jean and me to join him tomorrow for a visit to the geishas of the Pontochō.

Back at Eidmann's, we had *sencha,* and went to bed on our mats on the floor.

Sunday, August 21

Miscellaneous shopping in the morning, lunch at Daimaru's top-floor restaurant, and the afternoon with Mr. Perkins. We met him, a Japanese gentleman, and an army-post librarian at the Kyoto Hotel and proceeded to the Pontochō Theater building where beer was being served on the riverside veranda. Three of the geishas joined us—a young one in a full geisha wig who sat like a big cat, in complete silence, at her corner of the table, and two of the older geishas, who turned out to be two of the leading personalities of the Pontochō. Perkins talked about the traditions etc. of the Pontochō. The geishas here constitute a kind of caste, apparently, inheriting their tradition from their families. Those at our table were married to Kabuki actors (I think that this is what I was told). We drank beer and chatted, and at about 5:30 said good-bye.

Jean and I shopped, on the way home, for presents to give to Eidmann, Haru, Hayashi, Obasan and her husband, and, after dinner, made our presentations. The first was a projector, for Eidmann and Haru, the second a print-drier for Haru, and the third a fountain pen for Hayashi. All seemed perfectly delighted with the surprises—and I myself liked the Birdie projector so much that I would have bought one to bring to New York if I had been sure that the light would have worked on the New York circuit.

Monday, August 22

After breakfast, we finished our packing and then took a little final tour with Eidmann and Haru—first to the little *amazake* restaurant up near

Chion-in, then for a farewell visit with Mr. Perkins. We just caught the 12:30 train to Osaka, and took the plane, then, back to Tokyo.

Return to the Yashima Hotel: Suehiro's for dinner: and early to bed.

Tuesday, August 23   *Tokyo*

Jean's dance class and my Japanese lesson in the morning. Shopping for presents during the afternoon. In the evening, a nice dinner party for Jean at Irene Pines's, with lots of dancers and nice people to meet her. Chatted for a while with one Japanese who spoke German and then with another who spoke French. A pleasant, sort of international affair. Jean, I think, met some people who may be able to help her if she ever plans to dance in Japan.

Wednesday, August 24

More shopping for presents for our friends: this went on most of the day, and I began to tire of the whole project. At about 3:00 P.M. I suddenly learned that we had no reservations home on Japan Airlines—we had been on the waiting list only. This sent me scurrying to PAA,[300] and distracted me entirely from the melancholy of having to quit Japan.

Our evening was spent with a Mr. Shibato, editor of the *Mainichi* newspapers, who was entertaining also an American magician named Furst. He took us first for a "Mongolian" dinner to the restaurant in the garden, and then to the nightclub Ginbasha, where I had gone with my friend Campbell, my first day in Tokyo.

Furst declared that both in Europe and in Asia, *the magicians of the world hope only that they can become as good as the American magicians.* Reason: the other magicians of the world have for generations been performing only the tricks handed down to them from their fathers; whereas the American magicians, who regard it as *infra dig.* (below their dignity) to go on repeating the same old tricks, are forever thinking up and performing fresh surprises. This seemed to me symbolic of the whole miracle of America's present prestige and power in the world. It requires neither wealth nor machinery to invent a new trick, but only *an attitude of mind—* and this attitude, it now seems to me, is the real key to our achievement.

Shibato, as soon as we reached the Ginbasha, called for three hostesses to take care of himself, Furst, and me, leaving Jean completely out of the picture. When the music started, however, I asked Jean to dance, and this left him with two to deal with. All the ladies were pleasant and cordial, but my girl for the evening was Jean—and this was not quite in the customary pattern of the nightlife of Japan.

Thursday, August 25

Anniversary of my departure from New York. Dance and Japanese classes in the morning. Shopping all afternoon, and at 4:30 a phone call from the manager of PAA to say (in an American businessman's comforting voice) that he had received a wire in our favor from Honolulu (we had wired for aid) and could assure us that everything possible would be done to assure our departure this weekend, either the 26th, the 27th, or the 28th.

Cocktails at the Imperial, with Jean's friend Sperry, who took us, together with two other American couples, to the Tokyo Plaza for an excellent steak dinner and then, just about at closing time, to a vast nightclub, the Nimatsu. And so we are coasting rapidly out of the atmosphere of Japanese into that of American life.

At dinner I was placed between the two young American wives, who began asking questions about Buddhism, and about whether I was a Christian. Their queries threw me back, immediately, into the worried atmosphere of young America.

"Well then, so what are you living for?"

I said I was living because my parents had begotten me and I had not yet died. As for any great single aim or hope, I had none. I might (and should) have gone on to say that I had not yet committed suicide, because I found life immensely interesting and, in the main, greatly enjoyable. (Ecstasy in the contemplation of God's tenth aspect, i.e. the world: mankind, the tenth angelic choir. Or Zen: "Have you washed the dishes.") Not one great end, but many interrelated ends constitute the rationale of my metaphysically-impelled existence.

"And so, how do you evaluate things."

I replied (here, I think, too ponderously) that "an amplification of consciousness" seemed to me to be the main sign of "evolution" and that perhaps one could evaluate his experiences and deeds in terms of their contribution to such an amplification in himself and others. (Try to bring this into relationship to my first point.)

"What happens to you when you die?"

My body decays and disappears. Eternity, however, is not to be interpreted in terms of time ("long time," "time after death," etc. etc.). It is a dimension of the present, to be known now.

Friday, August 26

Jean's last dance class and my last Japanese class in the morning. At 12:30 Jean returned to say that *passage had been booked for us today* on the six o'clock plane PAA to Honolulu. Irene Pines joined us and helped in the packing, the shipping of packages via Takashimaya's shipping service, farewells to teachers and students, and driving to Haneda Airport.

My dear teacher, Miss Yoshiko Somekawa, returned to the hotel to see us off, and my wonderful visit to Japan was ended.

Haneda, 6:00 P.M., Flight 2, to Honolulu. In Tokyo, a drenching downpour; no visibility; up, and then up into the clear skies above.

Saturday, August 27   *Wake Island*

3:30 A.M. Wake Island: the pause of an hour. A bus ride to restaurant and a stroll back: big army planes and machines, machines, and machines.

Sunday, August 28   *Honolulu*

Recovered (dateline crossing at about 6:30 A.M.). Arrival in Honolulu, after a lovely flight, at 5:15 P.M. Mother, Alice, and Anne, Marion, Da, and Louie at the airport. Long session at the Customs. We drove to Marion's, where Jean and I are to stay, for dinner. Pleasant evening. After dinner, we went with Mother, Alice, and Anne, to spend a couple of hours with them in their cottage in Mānoa.[301]

Saturday, August 27

Up at about 9:15. After breakfast, to the Outrigger Club for a swim with Alice and Anne. Lunch at the club. More sunshine and water. The beaches full of the typical fauna. At about four, up to visit Mother in Mānoa again, and so on.

August 28 to September 3

There has been a vast increase in the population since our visit in 1949. The new dwellings and shops are, in the main, quite handsome; the new hotels, on the other hand, are vivid eyesores—suggesting Nassau, Miami, and the Riviera. Around Waikiki, a large, completely tourist population; all wearing Aloha shirts.

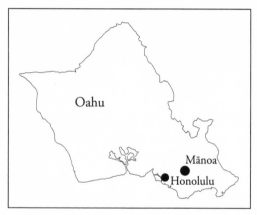

The Outrigger Club has only eight more years on its lease. The land was sold from under it to a "mainland outfit," which wants to raise its rent from $5,000 to $50,000 a year. (Not too much, actually, for the value of this site, but, apparently, too much for the Outrigger Club to pay.) They are going to try to move in with the Elks, into the wonderfully situated Elks Club, near the King's Surf—but this may not work, and all concerned are in sorrow. "This ends Waikiki," is the general word. "And the joke is, the tourists come for just what the beach boys and the surfboards mean."

On Da's birthday (August 31), Jean and I held a dinner party at Don the Beachcombers. Great disappointment. Food mediocre: music third-rate: hula, Tahitian dance, and general atmosphere, quite vapid. Alas, no more beach-boy music or first-rate dancers.

The pity of it is that Vikram Sarabhai arrived (August 31) for a one-night stay (with the Watamuls) and wanted to see a bit of Hawai'ian dance. We invited him to join us at Don the Beachcombers, and then again, the next afternoon, at the Outrigger Beach. During my brief conversation with him on the way up Tantalus, to return him to the Watamuls' place after the party, I got again a strong whiff of India's anti-American, anti-Western, pro-Chinese sentiments. The argument (not too violent) was about America's nonrecognition of China and China's continuous mistreatment of kidnapped American airmen. Just as in India, it appeared that the Chinese were doing nothing wrong and the Americans nothing right.

Wednesday August 31

At 2:30 P.M., a visit to the Bishop Museum with Jean, Alice, and Anne, under the guidance of Anne Harding and her husband, the curator of the museum, Dr. Spoer. We were shown the magnificent collection of feather cloaks (about one hundred fifty in the world; twelve in Russia, some in British Museum, Scotland, etc.; about twenty-seven here: one cloak 66 inches across—for a man over seven feet tall: Kamehameha's beautiful golden-feathered cloak: a long sort of sari-cloak for a four- or five-hundred-pound princess). Kenneth Emory joined us for a while, now grey, but otherwise looking fine. And I met again one of my old students from S.L.C., Pat Cook Peacock, whose husband is now a rancher.

The museum is in much better form than it was before the arrival of the Spoers. René d'Harnoncourt's style of exhibiting has made a great difference.[302] Outstanding were the tapa-cloth and feather-cloak exhibits. Some ideas:

1. The crucial questions for Southeast Asian culture are
   a. Date and place of the first sea-going canoes
   b. Date and varieties of the first cultivated crops (banana, taro,—rice)
2. The Polynesian racial (blood-type) affinities, still an enigma
3. Problem of extent of America-to-Polynesia influences (Heyerdahl's new book, I saw yesterday in a bookstore)[303]

Following the museum visit, we went up to the Spoers' new and wonderful house on Makiki Heights for a drink. Then began the birthday party for Da, announced above.

Thursday, September 1

Breakfast at 8:00 with Walter Dillingham[304] and Louise, Ben and Frances present. Very pleasant and prosperous atmosphere. Louise about to set off for a day of golf, tennis, bridge, and bowling. Walter, at about eighty-one, just recovered from a major intestinal operation, looking fit, though a little older than in 1949. Ben, bulky and *sympatisch*. Walter showed us his beautiful orchids and told a few yarns of the grand old days. "Wish I could give you a piece of the old Dole property," he said to Jean, as he left for his office at about 9:30, "but I don't have any of it to give."

At noon we had lunch with Marion and Louie, and at about four we went to the beach for a chat with Vikram, who had had quite a day of sightseeing and was ready for a swim with the young Watamul. At five we went to visit Dr. and Mrs. Paul Larson and had a lively and very interesting talk. Themes:

The Alexander method of physical culture:[305] the crouched posture suggests fear to the Unconscious and actually stimulates an excessive secretion of adrenaline. Result: excessive energy expenditures and aging. Erect posture, when correct, suggests fearlessness and inspires life. Parallel: yoga and the lion roar.

India's anti-Americanism and the irony of our aid to Asia, which is being turned, by propaganda, against us.

The actual prodigious power of America—and yet our fears: fear of Russia, fear of China, etc. etc. Of the first eighteen airports in the world, all are American except London (which comes in at about nine or ten) and Paris (down around fifteen).

Dinner with Mother, Alice, and Anne, and the beginning of a new idea for Alice, namely, the writing of a book about interior decoration in Hawai'i.

Got our PAA reservations today for September 3 to San Francisco.

Friday, September 2

The chief visits today were two to Jacob Feuerring,[306] who is now staying with his new wife in a cottage not far from Noela Drive and will leave with her on the *Lurline* tomorrow for New York. His themes:

1. Buddhism in Japan is due for a very strong nationalistic trend, which has already commenced.
2. India, in the next twenty years, will recover its spiritual leadership of Asia, with a powerful universalist tendency. (This I very much doubt.)

And my themes:

1. Whenever an Indian thinks of becoming "spiritual" his first impulse is to "throw off" the world; whereas in China and Japan the elite tradition is that of the knowledge of eternity *in* time: is that not the lesson of Tea? Indeed, is that not the lesson of Civilization?
2. For the teaching of men a pedagogical schema is necessary. These schemas become the structures of the various civilizations. When the structure instead of the teaching is taken as final, however, the lesson is lost. And this is the problem of India. The Indians have become so infatuated with the schema of their civilization (e.g. that of the four *asramas* and waiting for the time of the third) that they have lost the message of their own teaching.

We visited Feuerring again after lunch and met his wife and a Chinese artist from Hong Kong named Chang, who says that there is no cultural or artistic life in Hong Kong: it is a port, a good place for shopping.

At five we drove back to pick up Marion and go to Da's for cocktails. Little Jeffie[307] was wheeled into the porch area where we were sitting; Bargie and Tad have been hoping for some kind of miracle to save him. At their church—or rather, in their community they have a very active *"praying group,"* to which they credit a number of miracles: one, the recovery of Mary Lou Erdman from a lethal infection, some two months ago; another, the healing, or rather, disappearance of a brain tumor on the operating table, when the head had been opened and diagnosed as fatal... Bargie is trying, in her mind, to connect this kind of *magic, or miracle,* with the philosophical ideas that she encountered when a student—perhaps the *parapsychological* field is the one that all this leads to. I think of my *yamabushi* experience,[308] the Pueblo rain dances, and these Praying Cures, as belonging in one category.

After the cocktails, we came back to Marion's for dinner and then went to see Tad, Josephine Taylor, et al., in the Community Theater's new play, *Oh, Men! Oh, Women!* by Edward Chodorov.[309] A couple of very good points about psychoanalysis:

There are two schools: one holds the theory that the patient should be "cured" of his habits and impulses; and the other maintains that such curing is impossible and not even desirable, but rather that the patient should be helped to accept his character without fear, melancholy, and neurotic resistances. Compare Fromm's[310] distinction between returning a patient to the patterns of society, and enabling a patient to develop courageously in his own direction.

The real aims of one type of woman in marriage: a trip to Europe, a husband, a baby, and a good figure throughout her life. If husband and wife could realize that this, and not deep love, was all she wanted, things would be relatively OK.

The real aims of another type are to feel needed, loved, and not to be crushed under the spiritual or mental dominance of her husband.

In all this, there was a quite good criticism of Ibsen's *Doll's House,* as proto-psychoanalysis, and as not solving the problem of Nora's unhappiness. What is she *really* looking for "out there"? Is physical departure from the house her answer? And there is a good dig at Nora's husband, who thinks that economic security and protection is all she requires and does not realize the needs of a woman who wants to be loved, as described above. It is this insensitivity on his part that has turned the home into a Doll's House—and sent Nora outdoors to seek what she requires.

This play was handled in pretty good style, as was also a little children's production of *Jack and the Beanstalk* that we saw the day after we arrived here and in which Bargie played the part of Jack's mother. In *Jack,* I was struck (after my year in the Orient) by the character of the domestic image that emerges: the terrible father image and the rescue by magic. I thought of Samuel Butler's novels and, in contrast, of the comparable Oriental motifs. There is a problem here, to be studied. In the modern Orient, I think it is, rather, the terrible mother image that prevails: the mother-in-law vs. the young wife. Also, if one compares this contrast of Economic Titanism and "Magic" with that represented in the Chodorov play, one has a pretty clear line. Problem: Selfishness = materialism vs. Selflessness (Sympathy, Compassion) = "spiritual magic."

I was hoping to be able to chat with Alice today about her economic situation, but no opportunity came, and I shall have to try again tomorrow.[311] Actually, all seems to me to be in pretty good case up there. Alice's circle of friends, whom we met at a party in her cottage our second or third night here, is pleasant and sympathetic. (Her boss and his pretty Filipino wife; Doyle Alexander and his wife;[312] and a couple, whose daughter is Anne's best friend.) The main problem is, to get Alice's income into a higher bracket. She is trapped, as it were, by American Factor.[313]

And finally, about my *own work, as viewed from here:*

In Japan, I was in my dream boat; here, in America, I have stepped ashore. Problem: to keep lines ashore from the dream boat for unloading. How? My schedule in New York, as noted above, three hours writing; three hours outlining.[314] The rest of the day or week will be free for the land-world interests and necessities.

My writing can commence as a continuation and spontaneous expansion of these journal notes. What I now think of as *the "raindrop" approach:* a drop here, a drop there, until the whole ground is wet: a paragraph here, a paragraph there, until the whole book is drafted—after which, the material can be handled as I handled Zimmer's notes.

This journal can be continued, with increased emphasis, however, on the notation aspect and diminished attention to the daily diary.

Saturday, September 3

Last day in Hawai'i. Up to see Mother and Alice in the morning; a brief expedition to the beach at Waikiki; luncheon at Marion's with all the families (about twenty-five people!) and a pleasant run of brooding all the while. A few points to be noted before leaving:

Feuerring spoke of *two kinds of tea ceremony* in Japan—the social and the religious. In the latter no talk about the bowls etc.; more stress on the silently contemplative side.

Both Alice and Da have spoken of *the particular character of the Chinese community in Hawai'i*. Loyalty to family groups (*hui*). No participation in the Community Chest, etc., of the general community. Somewhat arrogant miserliness. Comparatively large accumulations of wealth.

In contrast, *the Japanese are eager to Americanize themselves*. Generosity, community interests, etc.

The luncheon party cleared up at about 3:00 P.M. Jean and I then went into our room to pack. At about five we were ready to push off. Da came for us, and, with Marion, Pini, and Pono,[315] we set off for the airport. Mother, Bargie, and Alice arrived in the lively, crowded airport about 6:15 and the call came for us to board the plane at 6:35. Leis and Aloha.

A jammed plane, filled with a gay company of aloha-shirted and mumu-ed vacationists. Lots of noise. And we were amazed, after the rather lean and perfunctory service that PAA had accorded its "tourist" passengers on the way from Tokyo to Honolulu (where most of the "tourists" had been Filipinos), by the cordial and lavish hospitality of our steward and stewardesses. We figure that the heavy competition of the airlines had something to do with it, and that the fact that a large number of our cabin mates were obviously the members of a large tour of some kind may have helped. In any case—it was cocktails before dinner, a good meal decently served, wine, and then a large cake with ALOHA. Sleep supervened around 10:30 or 11:00.

Sunday, September 4   *San Francisco*

Alan Watts met us at the San Francisco Airport when we arrived, about 7:15 A.M. He looked a bit sleepy-eyed—and why not?—he had had to leave his place at Point Sur at about 3:30 A.M.! The airport was the biggest and busiest I had seen since my departure from New York: planes leaving every minute for everywhere. And the cars in the prodigious parking lot, out in front, were as amazing as anything else. The whole power of America, in contrast to Asia's world, was immediately visible.

And on the long, very beautiful drive down to Point Sur, we were easily and pleasantly returned to the feel of life in the U.S.A. First, the great machine world in and around the airport; then the great farmlands of the Santa Clara Valley; next, the holiday world of the Monterey Peninsula—the fisheries and the canneries, and all the memories I held of my year there in the early thirties;[316] then, finally, the miraculous coast—Point Lobos, Point Sur, and the golden hills. On the broad highways—six to ten lanes wide—the vast American cars seemed not too large. And the various odd rigs of the vacationers seemed not too bizarre, in the broad, traditionless land. It was most remarkable and pleasant that the countryside should have been the closest in America to that of the Ise Peninsula in Japan: and in contrast to the way I felt in Japan—here I felt that I did not really mind the lack of toriis and shrines. Shrineless America was all right too!

On the way down, we discussed Japan, Buddhism, and the U.S.A. Dorothy[317] and the three cute children greeted us when we arrived. We had a pleasant lunch on the veranda, overlooking the Pacific and then retired to our rooms for a nap. More talk at dinnertime and into the night until about 10:00, when, rather sleepy again, we all retired for a quiet, absolutely solid sleep, in the beautiful fresh air. Some of our themes:

As to whether it is proper to call the sort of *Buddhism-in-life* that Alan, Hasegawa, et al. represent, "Japanese Zen"? In Japan, Zen definitely is "sitting." Alan stated that he was sure that the Zen of Hui-neng and the fundamental Chinese texts was not "sitting," but "sitting, standing, walking, and lying." Why not use, then, I suggested, the Chinese word *ch'an?* Might be a good idea. At least, it would rub out the Japanese Zen objection that the Zen being described by Alan and his tribe is not really "Zen."

Alan made light of the kōan system. One is supposed to answer the kōans intuitively, but the field of associations that would inspire the answers must differ according to one's cultural experience. For a Westerner, the Japanese system is hardly appropriate.

Zen, properly, is undeliberated action.

Alan told of the sexual life of a Zen master: coition without movement, until, after hours, the orgasm comes for the woman of itself. *Wuwei. Sahaja.*[318]

Alan wondered whether the emphasis on personality in the Christian tradition might not be a deterioration of the all-in-each idea of Kegon-Zen.

Alan likened the Christian promise of happiness in heaven to the happy-ending formula in the fairy tale. Life itself is validated only by an uncertain future—in which one must have *faith.* Pessimism with respect to life itself: optimism only on the basis of the figment of faith.

In the plane, by the way, I found in *Time* an interesting article on the new Palestine find of *manuscripts of the Essenes.*[319] Perhaps a good point from which to start my Viking book.

Monday, September 5   *Big Sur*

A drive, in the morning, up to see Maud Oakes in her beautiful place eleven hundred feet above the coast.[320] Magnificent views. Nice chat. She is coming tonight to dinner. Also coming is a Jewish chap of the old Woodstock type, named Morgenrath, whose wife once studied at the New Dance Group. We had a picnic lunch in the woods, went for a stroll over the golden hills, paid a visit to another Woodstock-type household (chap who sells Henry Miller's books and runs a little art gallery by the road), then returned to prepare for dinner. Maud, the Morgenraths, and a fine old lady named Porter arrived, who, thinking that I was going to be Joseph Campbell the poet, brought a volume of that good gentleman's poems for me to read aloud.[321]

Lovely dinner and conversation till about 2:00 A.M. Maud left at 10:00 and Mrs. Porter at midnight—after I had read the desired poems.

The conversation was lively, but brought forth no new ideas. During the afternoon, however, Alan had told me something about *the Zen method of training for fencing*—which, after all, may be rather Bushidō than Zen. The main idea is *unfocused alertness*—a readiness to flash quickly in any direction with absolute effect.

Tuesday, September 6 (Labor Day)

Lunch at Maud's, and then good-bye. Alan drove us back to the airport, where we had a beautiful dinner. Departure at nine, United Airlines, on the last leg of my trip around the world.

The drive with Alan was magnificent. It was a beautiful day, and the coast was even more impressive than it had been two days ago, when half lost in mist. Our conversation rattled along and yielded one very good idea—namely, that the kōan test is a Japanese variant of the riddle-test motif—cf. *Eddas*, ca. A.D. ninth century.[322] Perhaps we've hit something here.

Wednesday, September 7   *Idlewild Airport, New York*

At 6:30—Chicago, for a brief stand-up breakfast snack in the airport. Jean, not feeling well, did not leave the plane. Arrival at Idlewild Airport, about 11:45. Bus to air terminal, New York City. Taxi home—and the round is complete.

An Overview of the History of Buddhism in Japan

[This outline is taken from notes that Joseph Campbell took from an article by Phillip Karl Eidmann. See page 128—DKK]

A.D. 552

- Korean king at Paekche sends Buddhist scriptures and images
- Buddhist materials destroyed by Mononobe and Nakatomi clans (Japanese military)
- Soga clan (civilian leaders) favors Buddhism

ca. 585–650

- Korean king again sends scriptures, images, clergy
- Soga-Mononobe feud reopened, but Buddhism remains
- Buddhism adopted first by nobility: within a decade Emperor Yōmei himself was a Buddhist
- Prince Shōtoku (regent of Empress Suiko), a great influence: built temples; instituted a system of diocese; wrote commentaries on three scriptures
- Early monks encouraged to teach arts of road making and bridge building; monastic students included in embassies to China to study in the great monasteries

ca. 650–794 (Taika and Nara periods)

- Major period of influences from China
  - o Six schools introduced
    - **Jōjitsu** (introduced in 625—minor)
    - **Sanron** (introduced in 625—Japanese branch of the *Mādhyamika* school; introduces Nagārjuna's concept of *śunyatā*)
    - **Hossō** (introduced in 653—Japanese branch of the *Yogācāra* school)
    - **Kusha** (introduced in 658—Japanese branch of the Theravādin *Sarvastavādin* school)
    - **Kegon** (introduced in 735—Japanese branch of the Chinese Hua-yen school, based at the Tōdaiji temple in Nara)
    - **Ritsu** (introduced in 754—focused on monastic discipline [*vinaya*]; revived as part of Shingon)

ca. 794–1185 (Heian period)

- Kyoto as the permanent capital
  - o New stability and continuity in Buddhist teaching (formerly, teachers were chiefly Chinese or Korean)
- Great period of translations in China: many systems for ascribing each *sūtra* to a period of the Buddha's life, culminating in some supreme revelation just before his death
  - o **Tendai**
    - Japanese branch of Chinese *Chih-k'ai* School, at Mount T'ien-T'ai in the province of Chekiang: The Lotus *Sūtra* as the culminating doctrine.
    - Dengyō Daishi brings this teaching to Japan and continues the eclectic work by harmonizing Buddhism with Shintō; instituted a new ordination platform, and, on the grounds that the Japanese were already so pure that they did not need the monastic *vinaya* discipline, instituted a new "Bodhisattva Discipline," completely abandoning the Theravādin *Vinaya,* which had been translated earlier.
  - o **Shingon**
    - Kōbō Daishi, while in China, was initiated into the Esoteric, or *Vajrayāna,* school then fashionable there. The school virtually died in China—but continued in Tibet, and in Japan as the Shingon. Mt. Kōya became the center from which he taught his mystical rituals and doctrines.

ca. 700–1000

- Three hundred years of scholastic study and the gradual sifting of Buddhist doctrine down to the people
- Lady Murasaki Shikibu writes *The Tale of Genji* ca. 973

ca. 1000–1200

- Civil wars: weakening of six earlier Buddhist sects
- Idea of the period of the Latter Law: Emergence of new and independent Japanese Schools

1174

- Genku Hōnen establishes **Jōdo**
  - o Since the people live in the period of the Latter Law, they are incapable of rigid discipline; their only hope, therefore, is to be born into the Pure Land of the Amida Buddha and there to attain Enlightenment. The act of praising Amida is itself sufficient for rebirth into this realm.

1192

- Eisai returns from China with *Ch'an*—**Rinzai Zen**
  - o A transmission "outside of the scriptures"
  - o A transmission "from heart to heart, without words"

1223

- Dōgen founds **Sōtō Zen:**
  - o Emphasis on scholarship and research, as well as meditation
  - o Ch'an, a development of Buddhism that grew out of the effort to teach Buddhism to the untutored Chinese farmers, became, in Japanese Zen, the religion of professional militarists—it is the chief component of Bushidō

1224

- Shinran, a disciple of Hōnen, founds **Shinshū**—the most influential form of Buddhism in modern Japan: "In the egolessness of the moment of faith, the efficient cause is created for the attainment of complete enlightenment at the instant of death."

1253

- Nichiren—founder of the **Hokke** (Lotus, or Nichiren) School:
  - o An attempt to reform Tendai, based on the Lotus *Sūtra*
  - o Opposition to Tendai eclecticism, which made the mythical Buddhas and the historical Buddha equal
  - o Lotus *Sūtra* regarded as the teaching of Śākyamuni
    - Nichiren identified himself as Viśiśtacaritra Bodhisattva, who, in the Lotus *Sūtra,* is said to be the one who, in the days of the Latter Law, would proclaim the true essence of the Buddha's teachings.

ca. 1300–1500 (Kamakura, Ashikaga, and Civil War periods)

- Very unsettled in Japan—period of the samurai movies
- Many monasteries became military camps
- Military monks fought in secular causes

1600–1867 (Tokugawa shōgunate)

- Tokugawa peace, feudalistic style
- Exacting governmental regulations affecting even Buddhist regulations: no new doctrines or sects; the focus shifts to scholarship and meditation
- Shintō revival (starting ca. 1650)
  - o A group of scholars and politicians, led by Mabuchi, Motoori, and Hirata created a neo-orthodox doctrine, in opposition to Buddhism

1867 (Meiji Restoration)

- Admiral Perry arrives; downfall of the Tokugawa shōguns
- The principles of the neo-orthodox Shintō revival became the basis of the Meiji Restoration
- Buddhism is virtually outlawed and dissent abolished

1931–1945

- Invasion of Manchuria and Second World War
- Japanese government again outlawed Buddhism

1945–1952

- At end of war, U.S. Occupation policies unfavorable to Buddhism
  - o "Freedom of religion" guaranteed, but nearly all temple lands were confiscated and a number of sects were thus completely impoverished
  - o The religious corporate-body law upset twenty-five centuries of Buddhist tradition by requiring temples to be reorganized upon the congregationalist pattern of United States Protestantism.

THE NATURE WAY: SHINTŌ AND BUDDHISM IN JAPAN[1]

There is a legend telling that when the Buddha once was to give a sermon, he sat for some time in silence and then simply elevated a flower in his hand. Only one of those present understood, but he thereby was illumined. The Buddha caught his eye and smiled and a verbal sermon—the Flower Wreath *Sūtra*—then was given to the rest.[2]

The art of letting flowers deliver the message beyond words entered Japan with Buddhism itself from China, where the Indian Mahāyāna doctrine had become fused with the native Chinese doctrine of the Tao. Then in Japan, the art and Buddhism as well became fused with the native Shintō.

In Japanese art, nature is the model and unsymmetrical balance, the secret of its flight. The composition must also suggest some idea, sentiment, or wish appropriate to the occasion. For in Japanese thought, each moment of time is a total manifestation of Buddhahood and each flower itself a Buddha-thing. This principle that art can fuse nature and thought and carry us beyond both is perhaps the outstanding characteristic of Japanese civilization.

It is already evidenced in the great Shintō shrines on the beautiful peninsula of Ise. Today, every tourist learns on his first sightseeing ride that in Japan there are two types of religious sanctuaries: one is called *o-miya*, the word is translated shrine; the other *o-tera*, temple. Shrines belong to Shintō and are marked by graceful wooden gates like this, called torii. We see in the photograph on p. 291 the entrance to the majestic cedar grove surrounding the grand shrine of Ise, which is devoted to the ancestral line of the imperial house. And this dynastic line, in turn, according to legend, traces itself back to the sun goddess Amaterasu. The architecture of the many buildings dates from earliest Japanese times. The structures themselves are demolished every twenty years to be rebuilt on exactly the same plan so that the wood is fresh and young, but the form more than fifteen centuries old. An important principle here is illustrated, namely that life is an expression not so much of matter as of its informing spirit.

The earliest archaeological remains in Japan date from a long, rather obscure period called *Jōmon*. The word means "cord-marked" and refers to a crude pottery that seems to have begun arising around 2500 B.C. The people of Japan at that time were probably Caucasoid, like the Ainu of today. And they certainly were hunters and fishers at that time. During the next twenty centuries, the arts of agriculture and village life arrive and the population, through a series of incursions, became gradually Mongoloid. Then, about 300 B.C., the so-called Yayoi period opened with arrivals by way of Korea, bearing a high Neolithic style of pottery like that of China 1,500 years before.

The next and final great stage of prehistoric Japan opens circa 300 A.D. with the arrival of the Kōfun or Yamato peoples, who became the nuclear force for what was to become Japanese civilization. They seem to have been of north Asiatic origin and their mythology exhibits many astounding parallels to those of the peoples of northern Europe. Moreover, they brought with them a type of mound burial that is likewise familiar to the West. The royal burials of the Yamato, however, were often of prodigious size. The level of this civilization was roughly comparable to that of pagan Europe of the same period, and as the creative spirit of modern Europe is already announced in Celtic and Germanic myth, so that of Japan becomes evident in the Shintō of this age.

Shintō is a very difficult religion to discuss, however. It rests not on theology but on a certain type of experience, as I learned in a rather amusing way at the International Congress for the History of Religions held in

Tokyo in 1958. Delegates had arrived from every nation in the world, and the Japanese committee had arranged that we should visit, under their auspices, every temple and shrine within reach. Shintō shrines are without images. To a very strange type of music, stately, very slowly moving dances are performed both by choral groups and by solo figures, the latter frequently masked. The music is of an ancient style derived from China of the T'ang period (around A.D. 618–970), when Buddhism from China was entering Japan. In the West, this was the period of Charlemagne. This music has disappeared from China, but in Japan it is used for both temple and shrine rites to summon the spirits, which indeed one can actually feel and even almost see arriving at these ceremonies.

There was a very intelligent social scientist from New York among the delegates at this conference, and after we had visited a number of the shrines and seen a number of the rites, he approached one afternoon a Shintō priest who was also a member of the conference. And my friend said to the priest, "I've been to a number of these shrines now and I've seen a number of the rites, but I don't get it. I don't get the ideology; I don't get the theology."

The priest seemed very disturbed that Shintō had disappointed his guest and he shook his head and he said, "I'm afraid we don't have ideology; we don't have theology. We dance."

It is the function of art to carry us beyond speech to experience, and that is the function also of Shintō. In a welcoming address to the members of that Congress, Prince Mikasa, the younger brother of Emperor Hirohito,[3] made the point that the evocation of a sense of awe before the wonder of being itself is the essence and the inspiration of Shintō. In illustration of this, he read to us a poem of two lines composed many centuries before by a visitor to the grand shrines of Ise, as follows:

> *Unknown to me what resided here,*
> *Tears flow from a sense of unworthiness and gratitude.*

It is this sense of gratitude for the wonder of the world that is the most characteristic feature of the religious mood of Japan and particularly of Shintō. This stands in direct contrast to the modern existentialist mood of shock, *nausea,* and disgust. On the popular level, this feeling of awe in nature is expressed in relation to trees, stones, water, the rising of the moon, flowers, villages, and the play of children. As we read in the Shintō text, spirits reside in all kinds of things. The basic sense of Shintō, then, is that the processes of nature cannot be evil, and since man participates in nature, his own nature partakes of this virtue.

A Shintō ceremony

To participate in the virtue, purity of heart is required. And this quality of heart is symbolized by certain tokens in the great Shintō shrines that are supposed to have been carried down from heaven by the ancestors of the royal house. The first of these is a mirror, which represents the pure heart reflecting nature and heaven without fault. The second is a keen sword symbolizing the courage to manifest virtue and the last is a jewel necklace, the ornament of benevolence.

It was into this optimistic, world-affirming context that Buddhism entered Japan, having originated in India in a period of world disillusionment and having taken root in China in one of political disaster. In Japan, the teachings of Buddha came to a young unbroken people who gave to the positive aspects of the Mahāyāna doctrine of the Jewel of *nirvāṇa* in the Lotus of the World,[4] an extremely powerful interpretation, to a brief history of which we shall now proceed.

Buddhism entered Japan in A.D. 552 and brought with it a continental architecture with stress on the tile roof, which has become the dominant form not only of Buddhist temples but also of secular buildings and now even of Shintō shrines. The art and thought of the great continental Chinese civilization came with Buddhism to Japan and the date of this arrival, sixth to eighth centuries A.D., was exactly that of the arrival of Christianity in Germanic northern Europe. Japan is thus the young country of Asia, related to the civilization of China much as modern Europe is related to the culture of Greece and Rome.

The first phase was marked by the flowering in the eighth century A.D. of the beautiful temple city of Nara, where many of the early buildings still stand. And of these, the most important is Tōdaiji with its Hall of the Great Buddha. Within is an immense bronze Buddha, fifty-three-and-a-half feet high on a lotus ten feet high and sixty-three in circumference. The image was cast in the year 749 and weighs 452 tons. This Buddha is not the historical Buddha, Gautama Śākyamuni, but the great sun Buddha from whom historical Buddhas proceed. The Sanskrit name is Mahāvairocana, and the doctrine represented is called in Japanese *Kegon,* or "the flowering."

Let me explain. Usually, the progression of causality is reckoned as coming from past to present, in our direction, as it were. But since, according to the doctrine of the Yonder Shore, the nondualistic *Prajñāpāramitā* doctrine,[5] "past" and "present" are not to be regarded as two separate things. The chain of causality must be reckoned also as proceeding from the future to present. Furthermore, since "here" and "there" are not to be regarded as two completely separate things, the influence of causality moves from there to here as much as it does the other way, so that all things contribute to the causality of any given situation at any moment—all things past, future, and to the sides.

Another name for this doctrine is the Doctrine of the Net of Gems, in which the world is regarded as a net of gems, each gem reflecting perfectly all the others. It is also called the Doctrine of Mutual Arising, and represents a notion of universal karma, not individually separated karmas. This is the meaning of the term the flower wreath—*Kegon*. Everything causes everything else. The doctrine works, furthermore, on all levels. In groups, for example, the leader and the group are *mutually arising*.

Now let us go on to the second stage of the history of Buddhism in Japan. In A.D. 804, two young Japanese Buddhist monks sailed to China, and when they returned, brought back some new ideas.

The younger of the two, Kōbō Daishi, returned with the doctrine known as Shingon, the True Word. The idea here is perhaps best explained by analogy with the Roman Catholic doctrine of the word "Consecration." When the priest pronounces the words *"Hoc est enim Corpus meum,"*[6] the wafer of the Mass becomes literally, according to Catholic doctrine, the body of Christ. Comparably, when the Shingon monk duly prepared pronounces certain words, a miracle of transubstantiation occurs, not in bread but within the monk himself.

The other young boy, Dengyō Daishi, then returned with the doctrine known as Tendai, the leading teaching of which is that a certain text, the Lotus *Sūtra,* is itself substantially the Buddha. There is a temple of this sect on Mt. Hiei near Kyoto where the text is revered in perpetual meditation.

Yet the heroic, effort-making deed of both of these young voyaging monks was to return with the idea that the native Shintō spirits, or *kami,* were to be regarded as manifestations on a lower life plane of the compassion of Buddhahood, so that the two traditions were now united. And today in Japan people pray in one breath to the Buddha and to the *kami.* In Japan, the main point, as I have said, is not theology, not ideology, but the sense of religious awe.

And now we come to the climax, the period of the ladies and their gallants in the fabulous court of Kyoto, the perfume of whose elegance lingers still in that town. Toward the close of the ninth century, a mad emperor in China had been responsible for a completely ghastly massacre of Buddhist monks and nuns, matched in Buddhist history only by the work of Islam in India and by what is going on right now under the Chinese in Tibet. Buddhist Japan at that time cut off connection with the mainland and from that moment onward, Japanese Buddhism developed on its own.

The first development was in the palace, in the atmosphere of Lady Murasaki's novel *The Tale of Genji.* For the art of courtly love as a knightly spiritual discipline was cultivated in Japan in the tenth century, just as it was to be celebrated in the Europe of the twelfth century. Moreover, in keeping with the Buddhist doctrine of the unity of all things in the flower wreath of mutual arising, the ladies of this love game were known as flower maidens, and their lovers cloud-gallants. In Europe the lover was to be a man endowed with a gentle heart. In Kyoto, he was one who heard the sigh of things. The technical term was *aware:* "to know the sorrow or sigh of things." Thus we hear a flower-wreath palace echo of the Prince Buddha's first noble truth: all life is sorrowful.

Torii gate at Ise

A far more serious development occurred, however, around the thirteenth century, when a series of three great reformers founded the leading Japanese Buddhist sects of the present day. The first was Hōnen, who founded the Jōdo, or Pure Land, sect, the guardian Buddha of which is the figure known as Amida in Japan, from the Sanskrit Amitābha, meaning "immeasurable light." The legend tells that Amitābha refused *nirvāṇa* for himself unless through his achievement he might bring everyone by the simplest means to *nirvāṇa.* And so indeed, anyone who so much as pronounces the name of Amitābha will find himself when he dies sitting like the Buddha on a lotus in the lotus pond of that Buddha. If he has lived and died in virtue, his lotus bud will be open. If not, it will be closed. However, the waters of the lotus pond continually murmur as they ripple, all is impermanent, all is without a self, and the radiance of the Buddha, Amida, penetrates the bud so that eventually the being inside is illumined, the bud opens, and like the rest he achieves *nirvāṇa*.

Zen garden

The second reformer, Shinran, was Hōnen's student, and he also was a devotee of Amida. Whereas Hōnen had gone so far in the affirmation of life that he had rejected celibacy for his clergy—the Jōdo priests are married, which in Buddhist practice is amazing—Shinran went even further, rejecting the specifically religious life altogether, maintaining that the ordinary tasks of life in the world when well done are adequate means to that awakening of faith which is the ultimate gift of religion. This sect is known as Shinshū, and is today the most important in Japan.

Reformer number three, then, was Eisai, the founder of Japanese Zen, which is addressed mainly to the samurai, the military caste, and so required the character of a strictly disciplined exercise, as the attitude of these monks in their meditation hall well shows.

A religion like Jōdo, which depends for salvation on the merits of the savior, is called *tariki* in Japan, which means other's strength, salvation from without. Zen, on the contrary, is of the type known as *jiriki,* one's own strength and self-reliance.

After the middle of the thirteenth century, the Japanese feudal order went pretty much to pieces. A period of baronial warfare followed in which loyalties to the overlord was a high virtue, and the ideals of Bushidō developed, the way of the warrior-caste. This really terrible period in Japanese history, which corresponds both in time and character to the fourteenth or sixteenth in the history of Europe, and is of such importance to the modern Japanese movie screen, was not brought to conclusion until 1600 when the Tokugawa shōgunate was established. All contacts with the outside world were severed at this time and cut off from the rest of the world until Admiral Perry's fleet arrived in 1854. The Japanese culture body became, so to say, completely homogenized. The aristocratic, warrior principle of honor and loyalty to one's vocation soaked down to the very simplest, humblest strata of the society. The Net of Gems, Shintō—all became fused, so to say, coming to focus in the arts that developed at this time, particularly the Zen arts of the warrior way, of painting, of arranging flowers, and of tea.

Indeed, these arts epitomize the whole heritage of the Japanese civilization—whether expressed in the language of Shintō, Bushidō, or Mahāyāna Buddhism. And so, let us now in conclusion consider some details of the method of the *chadō,* the Way of Tea.

The basic principles of the Way of Tea are expressed in the very character of the teahouse. It is a simple house in a garden. "Even a woodpecker," as the poem says, "will not harm this hermitage among summer trees. I went there and I came back. It was nothing special."

Near it you will find a little spring for the libations in the garden. All around, what meets the eye is cool and fresh, the mossy stone basin stands beside the budding branch. The entrance to the teahouse is at about the level of one's knees. It requires skill and delicacy to enter properly. Humility is taught here, the need to get rid of the mind that thinks, This is good, that is bad. Simply live without such thoughts and it is good to live. Inside, a few significant art objects are presented which one is to admire and finally, with the host as guide, comes the sipping of tea.

They spoke no word,
The visitor, the host,
*And the white chrysanthemum.*7

Finally, one regards the bowl, and the whisk that has been used for bringing the tea into the water. In form, the beauty, the simplicity. The beauty here is comparable to that of the joints of wood at the great shrine of Ise in the cedar grove, unknown to us what resideth here. For as in India, the dominant thought of Buddhism is of this world as *māyā*, illusion, a mask over the non-dual reality of *Brahman*. In Japan all things are Buddha things. All things themselves are the real. The fluid aspect of impermanence is itself the absolute state.

In the words of the great Zen master Dōgen, founder of the Sōtō sect of Zen, "Impermanence is Buddhahood.... These mountains, rivers, and earth are all the See of Buddhahood."

> The Buddha Way lies in accepting and appreciating the form as it is, the state as it is. The bloom of flowers and the fall of leaves are the state as it is and yet unwise people think that in the world of essence there should be no blossoming of flowers and no falling of leaves. Buddhahood is not something to be sought in the future, but to be realized where and as we are. The colors of the mountains, the echoes of the valleys, all, all are the form and voice of the Buddha.8

CHAPTER NOTES

EDITOR'S FOREWORD

1. Joseph Campbell, *Baksheesh & Brahman* (Novato, California: New World Library, 2002), p. 164.
2. *Op. cit.,* pp. 290–291.
3. See p. 47.
4. See p. 105.
5. See p. 16.
6. In these journals, this series was conceived of as a single book, tentatively titled *Basic Mythologies of Mankind.*
7. This is the way in which he became most widely known, first for his series of lectures on religion that aired on New York's public television station (the transcripts of one of which provided us with the appendix for this volume, "The Nature Way"), and finally through his interviews with Bill Moyers, aired after his death as *The Power of Myth.*
8. See p. 227.
9. See p. 103.

CHAPTER I

1. Ceylon was to change its name to Sri Lanka in 1972.
2. Though officially known as Thailand since 1949, the country was still referred to by its older name by many Americans.
3. Professor Senerat Paranavitana was the first Singhalese Commissioner of Archeology for Ceylon, from 1940 to 1956.
4. Carl Hagenbeck was a renowned designer of zoos in the early twentieth century. He is credited with originating the modern, barless zoo.

5. A *stūpa* is a Buddhist temple mound, memorializing Buddha. "In its earliest known examples, at Bhārhut and Sāñcī, the form was that of a moundlike central structure surrounded by a railing with sumptuously carved gates. In the course of the subsequent centuries the *stūpa* developed variously, particularly following the spread of Buddhism throughout Asia." —Heinrich Zimmer, *The Art of Indian Asia,* completed and edited by Joseph Campbell (Princeton: Princeton University Press, 1983.)

6. Parakrama Bahu I "the Great" was the Singhalese king of Lanka, or Ceylon, ca. A.D. 1153–86. He ruled from Polonnaruva, reuniting his factionalized kingdom and reunifying the various Buddhist sects. The monument that Campbell is referring to is a statue reputed to be of Parakrama.

7. The Gold Coast achieved independence in 1957 as the Republic of Ghana.

8. Dr. Syngman Rhee (1875–1965) served as the president of the Republic of South Korea from 1948, through the Korean War, until his downfall in 1960.

9. Chiang Kai-shek (1887–1975) was the Chinese general and head of the anti-Communist Nationalist government, first in mainland China, then in Formosa (later known as Taiwan).

10. Campbell is referring to the University of Peradeniya.

11. Campbell meets up with Solomon in Japan, who was the director of field work at Sarah Lawrence College. See pp. 189–201.

12. D. T. Devendra, G. P. Malalasekara, et al., editors, *Encyclopedia of Buddhism* (Colombo: Government of Ceylon), volumes 1 (1963)–5.3 (1992).

13. Ziggurats were the pyramid-like temple mounds of the Sumerians and other Mesopotamian civilizations. They were built with a spiral path around the outside, and a flat top. See Joseph Campbell, *The Masks of God: Primitive Mythology* (New York: Penguin/Arkana, 1991), pp. 145–48.

14. Campbell is quoting Jason Grossman (See *Baksheesh & Brahman*).

15. The South-East Asia Treaty Organization had been established in 1954 (a few months before Campbell's voyage) for countries of Southeast Asia and part of the southwest Pacific, as a defensive alliance on the model of NATO to further a U.S. policy of containment of Communism. Its members were Australia, Britain, France, New Zealand, Pakistan, the Philippines, Thailand, and the United States. The organization was dissolved in 1977.

16. Winged female figures in classical Indian and Southeast Asian art, *apsarases* are "heavenly damsels [that] constitute a kind of celestial corps de ballet are the mistresses of those who in reward for pious and meretorious deeds during their earthly lives have been reborn among the gods." —Heinrich Zimmer, *The Art of Indian Asia.*

17. This is the "curious American" whom Campbell met after a dance performance by his wife, Jean Erdman, in Baroda, India. See *Baksheesh & Brahman,* p. 250.

18. British Overseas Airways Corporation.

19. The daughter of Indian author Dhanvanthi Rama Rau, Santha is a noted author in her own right, best known for her travel writing and for her stage and screen adaptations of E. M. Forster's *Passage to India.* Her husband, Faubian Bowers, produced volumes on Japanese theatre and poetry, and Indian dance. He also served as General MacArthur's aide-de-camp.

20. "In some people—possibly because of infant relationships—the stress goes towards power, in which case the sexual life takes a secondary position. [. . .] Jung calls this person the introvert. His meaning is somewhat different from the common sense of the

word. Jung defines the introvert as a power-oriented person who wants to put through his ego achievement.

"The sex-oriented person, on the other hand, turns outward. Falling in love means losing yourself in another object. This person Jung calls the extrovert. Now, he says, every individual is both, with an accent on one or the other. If you have your accent sixty percent over in the power arena, it's only going to be forty percent over in the eros area.

"Now when you run into a situation where your normal orientation doesn't function, where it isn't carrying you through, you are thrown back on the other. Then this inferior personality emerges. [...]

"Jung uses a fine word for this reversal: he calls it an *enantiodromia*. As you know (of course) from your Greek, *dromia* is 'to run': hippodrome is where the hippos (or horses) run; a dromedary is a racing camel. *Enantio* means 'in the other direction.' So, taken together, enantiodromia means running in the opposite direction, turning turtle."—Joseph Campbell, "Personal Myths," *The Joseph Campbell Audio Collection, Volume IV: Man and Myth.*

20a. Immediately following his enlightenment, the Buddha is said to have meditated at the foot of an enormous banyan tree, in the roots of which lived a serpent king, Mucalinda. The Buddha passed into a state of bliss, unaware or unconcerned with his surroundings. However, an unseasonal storm blew up. Mucalinda issued forth and, with his cobra hood, protected the Buddha from the tempest for seven days and seven nights.

21. Frances Webb Roosevelt (?–1986) was the widow of Quentin Roosevelt II. Quentin, grandson to President Theodore Roosevelt, served with his father, Theodore Jr., in the D-Day invasion of World War II. The father died of a heart attack in Normandy, a month after the landing in 1944, and the son died in an airliner crash in Hong Kong in 1948. The visit to which Campbell is referring must have taken place some time before the war.

22. Professor Veditantirige Ediriwira Sarachchandra (1915–96) was a professor of theatre and religious studies at the Ceylon University in Colombo, as well as an adapter of folk drama. V. E. Sarachchandra, *The Sinhalese Folk Play* (Colombo: Ceylon University, 1953).

23. Dr. Alfred Salmony (1890–1958) was a Hungarian-born professor of Asian art, particularly the carved stone art of China and Japan. Campbell met up with Salmony and his traveling companion, Jason Grossman, and traveled throughout India with them. He seems to have been creating a periodical for the Institure of Fine Art in New York, where he was a fellow. See *Baksheesh & Brahman, passim.*

24. Joseph Campbell, editor, R. F. C. Hull and Ralph Manheim, translators, *The Mysteries: Papers of the Eranos Yearbook,* volume 2 (New York: Pantheon Books/Bollingen Foundation, 1955).

25. Heinrich Zimmer (1890–1943) was one of the scholars who most influenced Campbell's life and work. A friend of Thomas Mann, of Carl Gustav Jung, married to Hugo von Hofmannsthal's daughter Christiane, a great raconteur and a man of immense erudition, Campbell found in Zimmer a challenging fellow spirit. Although they knew each other for only two years, from Zimmer's arrival in New York until his untimely death from pneumonia in 1943, Campbell became a friend, and after his death, at the request of Zimmer's widow, spent twelve years editing and completing Zimmer's work. These works included *Myths and Symbols in Indian Art and Civilization* (1946), *The King and the Corpse* (1948), *The Philosophies of India* (1951),

and *The Art of Indian Asia* (1955), which Campbell had completed while he was on the trip through India (see *Baksheesh & Brahman,* pp. 176, 217, 220, 311, 313–14, 317–18). The arrival of *The Art of Indian Asia* in Japan would serve Campbell as an excellent *carte-d'entrée* during his visit there (see pp. 147–48).

26. Burma officially changed its name to Myanmar in 1989.

27. Formosa is now known by its Chinese name, Taiwan.

28. The nineteenth century Hindu saint Sri Ramakrishna spoke of two attitudes towards God: the way of the monkey (which clings to its mother by its own strength), and the way of the kitten (which mews for its mother to carry it). See *Baksheesh & Brahman,* n. 86.

29. The story may be apocryphal. It is true, however, that the formal entrance of the Taj Mahal Hotel of Bombay, India, faces away from the bay on what might have been the "back" of the hotel.

30. Thakin Kodaw Hmaing (1876–1964) was an eminent Burmese author and peace activist.

31. Ho Chi Minh and his Viet Minh Army had defeated the French at Dien Bien Phu, just north of Hanoi, in May 1954. This defeat led the French to abandon Indochina. In October 1954, the Geneva Peace Accords, which spelled out the terms of the French withdrawal, created the states of Cambodia and Laos, and split Vietnam into two states—supposedly for just two years. An election in 1956 was supposed to create a unified, democratic Vietnamese state. However, in October 1955—just five months after Campbell's fly-over—Ngo Dinh Diem, the head of the South Vietnamese government, renounced the accords, fearing that their implementation favored Ho and the Communist North. The states weren't unified again until the end of the Vietnam War, in 1975.

32. Carl Thomas Rowan (1925–2000) was a widely syndicated newspaper columnist, author, biographer, television and radio commentator, and founder of the Project Excellence scholarship program. The U. S. Ambassador to Finland in 1963–64, Thomas was one of the first African-American ambassadors to a European nation.

33. Dr. C. Martin Wilbur was a professor of East Asian Studies at Columbia University.

34. The United States Information Service is a branch of the U.S. State Department concerned with public relations in foreign nations.

35. The Japanese occupied Formosa from 1895 to 1945. Not all observers agree that the Japanese rule was beneficial.

36. The Kuomintang, or KMT, are the Chinese Nationalist Party, led by Chiang Kai-shek.

CHAPTER II

37. Campbell's family had an apartment on Riverside Drive in New York for several years while he was a child.

38. In fact, the Japanese wear what Westerners think of as surgical masks when they have a cold, so as not to impose on others by spreading their germs. The Jains, in practicing *ahiṃsa,* "harmlessness," mask their mouths to avoid killing airborne microorganisms and insects by inhaling them.

39. Popular in the Paris of the 1920s that Campbell had visited as a young man, Apache (pronounced "ah-PAHSH") dancing involved, at the least, a man and a woman in a sort of cross between ballroom dance and pantomime. The woman was often literally dragged and thrown as part of the dance in a semi-sadomasochistic tango, which was supposed to be an artistic depiction of domestic passion in the demimonde.

40. This would seem to be a specifically Jungian observation, though it actually comes via Campbell's work on Heinrich Zimmer's *Philosophies of India,* Bollingen Series XXVI (New York: Pantheon, 1951): "The pleasure of love... is the bliss... of Shiva and his Shakti in their eternal realization of identity; only as known in the inferior mode of egoconsciousness. The creature of passion has only to wash away his sense of ego, and then the same act that formerly was an obstruction becomes the tide that bears him to the realization of the absolute as bliss (*ānanda*)." —*Philosophies*, pp. 576–77.

41. This is what is known as Kobe beef.

42. This famous hotel was designed by Frank Lloyd Wright, built in 1922 and demolished in 1966.

43. "Gāru" is simply a Japanized version of the English word "girl."

44. A samisen is a three-stringed instrument with a long neck, played by plucking, somewhat like a banjo.

45. This is Campbell's brother, Charles Campbell Jr., one year younger than Joseph Campbell himself.

46. Georges Balanchine (1904–83) was one of the most influential choreographers of the twentieth century. A Russian émigré, he served as the ballet master at the New York City Ballet from 1946 until his death in 1983.

47. The Bollingen Foundation had been founded by Mary Mellon in the early 1940s to advance and preserve learning in the humanities. One of its major projects was the Bollingen Series, a collection of published works on psychology, mythology, and religion. As of 1955, Campbell had written several Bollingen books, including *The Hero with a Thousand Faces,* and had edited and contributed to many more, including the Heinrich Zimmer posthuma, *Where the Two Came to Their Father,* and the Eranos Yearbook series.

48. Katakana is a syllable-based Japanese script used especially for terms adopted from other languages.

CHAPTER III

49. In the seventeenth century, a tsunami, or tidal wave, destroyed a temple building around this bronze Buddha; only the great statue remained. It has sat under the open sky ever since.

50. A Nisei is an overseas-born person of Japanese descent (usually second generation).

51. This is the third or fourth time in this journal that Campbell has undertaken to dampen his polemical tendencies, a self-acknowledged shortcoming with which he struggled throughout his life. His resolve was usually short-lived, as his true feelings continued to surface. See Robin and Steven Larsen, *A Fire in the Mind* (New York: Doubleday, 1991), pp. 507–12.

52. Hiragana is another syllable-based, Japanese cursive script form.

53. Amitābha Buddha, "The Buddha of Infinite Light" (or Amida, as he is known in Japan) is the savior-Buddha invoked in "Pure Land" sects of Buddhism such as Jōdo and Shinshū. Simply put, if one calls upon Amida, he has promised that one will gain *Sukhāvatī,* "The Place of Bliss," or "The Western Paradise." Inspired by Indian masters such as Nāgārjuna (ca. A.D. 150–200), the Pure Land sects place the Lotus Sūtra, or *Saddharma Pundarīka,* at the center of their teaching.

54. The Shinshū sect of Buddhism was founded by Shinran in 1224 and was more aimed at the common person than the then-dominant Tendai. The I.B.A. is the International Buddhist Association.

55. A *Dhyāna* Buddha is literally a "contemplation" or abstract Buddha, as opposed to a historical figure such as Gautama Śākyamuni. The Sanskrit *dhyāna* became transliterated in Chinese as *ch'an,* thence into Japanese as Zen. This form of meditative Buddhism is reputed to have been brought into China by Bodhidharma ca. A.D. 520, and developed by Hui-neng. See pp. 98–101.

56. This is a constant refrain in Campbell's writing, an example he often used of the tendency in Western religions to take a literal rather than a metaphoric reading of myths and symbols. See Joseph Campbell, *Thou Art That: Transforming Religious Metaphor* (Novato, Calif.: New World Library, 2001), p. 20, or *The Inner Reaches of Outer Space: Metaphor as Myth and as Religion* (Novato, Calif.: New World Library, 2002), p. 5.

57. Phillip Karl Eidmann was to serve as a sort of Virgil during Campbell's stay in Japan, a guide and cultural interpreter. A Shinshū Buddhist priest, Rev. Eidmann published many articles and books on Buddhism, both in Japan and in the United States. He was paralyzed from the waist down, apparently by injuries suffered during World War II.

58. Jacob Feuerring. See pp. 274–75.

59. Ruth Fuller Sasaki (1893–1967) was a translator and author of books on Zen Buddhism, as well as a Rinzai Zen priest. Along with her husband, S. S. Sasaki, she founded the First Zen Institute of America. Her daughter, Eleanor Everett, was Alan Watts's first wife.

60. Ellen Psaty Conant was to become a leading authority on Japanese art in general and Kakuzo Okakura (see n. 231) in particular.

61. *Namu Amida-butsu* is a prayer to Amida (Amitabha). The Pure Land sects (Jōdo and Shinshū) practice a doctrine known as *nembutsu,* which holds that contemplation of the Buddha's name leads one to the Pure Land, or *nirvāṇa.* See n. 53.

62. Emperor Hirohito (1901–89) reigned from 1926, through the crises of World War II and the reemergence of Japan as an international power, until his death in 1989. This was his fifty-third birthday; he was almost exactly three years older than Campbell.

63. Statues of the Bodhisattva Jizō (Kṣitigarbha) are found everywhere in Japan. He is said to protect children, especially the dead, whose souls nestle in the sleeves of his great robe. The Mibu-Kyōgen is attended by droves of children, tended by mothers and grandparents. Jōchō (?–1057) was the most renowned sculptor of Buddhist images during the Heian period.

64. It seems almost certain that Campbell left out a sentence before this one.

65. Kannon (Chinese = Kuan-yin) is a female avatar of Avalokiteśvara, the Bodhisattva of compassion or mercy.

66. The origin of this quote is uncertain.

67. See n. 112 for more information on the Three-Body system. *Kegon* means "flower wreath" and refers to the Buddhist *sūtra* of the same name; the sect places that *sūtra* at the center of its teaching, and the Doctrine of Mutual Arising. See Appendix B, n. 2.

68. A *mudrā* is a ritual attitude or posture.

69. This the wish-fullfilling avatar of Avalokiteśvara.

70. Ākāśagarbha, or Kokūzō, is a Bodhisattva who embodies wisdom.

71. The Mantō-e Festival is conducted only once every hundred years. Campbell, by serendipity, was in Nara at just the right time.

72. The *shō* is an extremely sophisticated woodwind instrument that looks something like a large, upturned set of panpipes with a lacquered mouthpiece at the bottom.

73. The Yamato emperor Temmu began to create the warrior class that became the samurai ("those who serve") during the seventh century.

CHAPTER IV

74. "It" is Campbell's ongoing lament, developing ever more strongly, that Americans—especially the diplomats and scholars—were lazy and presented a poor image of their country. He would seek to remedy this upon his return through his own years of service to the Foreign Service Institute and the U.S.I.S. See foreword, pp. XIII–XIV, and Larsen, *A Fire in the Mind*, pp. 426–29, 437, 455, 472.

75. The Noh stage includes a wide platform that serves as the main playing area, with two narrower platforms that extend to either side of the audience and serve as both exit and entrance areas and secondary playing areas. The outdoor theater at the temple follow this design.

76. This floor was made of sprung wood that squeaked or "sang" as it was walked on, thus protecting the shōgun from a surprise attack.

77. There seems to have been some sentiment at this time to remove all U.S. service personnel and arm Japan with its own nuclear arsenal—hence the "J-bomb."

78. *Amazake* is sweetened sake, an alcoholic drink made from fermented rice.

79. *Arhat* is a Sanskrit word, often translated as "saint." Most often, it is used in connection with the Theravādin (or Hīnayāna) forms of Buddhism, rather than the Mahāyāna Buddhism practiced in Japan. In this context it seems to mean an advanced spiritual being who has gained enlightenment. Theravādins find the "Hīnayāna" appellation derogatory; therefore, though Campbell consistently referred to this form of Buddhism as Hīnayāna (having been introduced to Buddhism from a Mahāyāna point of view), we have tried to use the more accepted nomenclature in these notes.

80. Though there is some controversy over Śaṅkara's dates, the most accepted (circa A.D. 700–50) do indeed jibe with Campbell's suggestion; if true, this would render moot the theory that Bodhidharma, the great Indian figure of the *dhyāna* school of Buddhism that was to become Chinese *ch'an* and Japanese Zen, could have been a student of the Hindu Śaṅkara, who is the most famous exponent of the *advaita vedānta* philosophy of non-dualism, which is influential in modern Indian thought. See n. 114.

81. Daisetz Teitarō Suzuki (1870–1966) was one of the most influential early proponents of Japanese Buddhism in the West. His books and lectures had a profound impact on Alan Watts (see pp. 278–80) and Campbell himself. Among his many books were *An Introduction to Zen Buddhism*, with a foreword by C. G. Jung (New York: Philosophical Library, 1949).

82. All of the preceding is Campbell noting Eidmann's opinions. During his stay in Japan, and in the years that followed, Campbell would develop his own thoughts on these subjects, some in line with Eidmann's, and some at odds.

83. See p. 80.

84. Bushidō is the code of behavior pertaining to all traditional martial arts in Japan; it is strongly associated with the samurai.

85. For information on Chiang, see n. 9. For information on Diem, see n. 31. For information on Dr. Rhee, see n. 8; Syngman Rhee was indeed a professed Christian. The Romulo to whom Campbell is referring appears to be Carlos Peña Romulo (1899–1986), journalist and diplomat, who served as the president of the United Nations General Assembly in 1949 and ran for the presidency of the Philippines in 1953. However, it seems likely that Campbell was actually thinking of Ramon Magsaysay (1907–57), who served from 1953 until his death as president of the Philippines. He was a Christian, a strong anti-Communist, and a supporter of U.S.

policy, and came to power with Romulo's support, so Campbell may have fused them in his mind.

86. Professor Shin'ya Kasugai (1917–).

87. Maitreya is the Bodhisattva of the Buddha-yet-to-come.

88. Nāgārjuna (ca. A.D. third century) was one of the great early Buddhist thinkers; none of his own writings have come down to us. Mahāyāna ("Greater Vehicle") and Hīnayāna ("Lesser Vehicle," also known as Theravāda) are the two largest branches of Buddhism. They vary in concepts of monkhood, and in the pantheon of divinely attained humans: *arhats* (Hīnayāna) and Boddhisattvas (Mahāyāna). Campbell compares these two traditions extensively throughout these journals.

89. In Indian religious art, a *vajra* is a lightning bolt representing enlightenment. This motif has corollaries in traditional art around the world.

90. In general terms, it isn't quite accurate to say the Japanese write "in a Chinese sequence"; written Japanese makes use of Chinese ideographs and two groups of simple syllabaries (hiragana and katakana), and the order of the Chinese ideographs in Japanese writing would usually differ from that in a purely Chinese sentence. Campbell seems to be referring to the reading in Japanese of pure Chinese texts. Purely Chinese writings are read by Japanese by actually translating the Chinese into Japanese while reading, with the aid of little symbols inserted into the Chinese text to clue the reader as to the order in which to read and translate the Chinese ideographs. "Writing them on the page in a Chinese sequence" seems to be Campbell's way of expressing what is simply a Japanese person writing in Chinese. The complication perhaps arises from the fact that Japanese uses Chinese ideographs to write Japanese. To give a simplistic example: writing "I am a student of Buddhism" in Japanese would contain some of the same ideographs that would be used to write the phrase in pure Chinese, but with different pronunciations in Japanese. An educated Japanese who knew no Chinese could still guess, through his knowledge of the Chinese ideographs, at the meaning of the purely Chinese sentence but likely not guess at the Chinese pronunciation, whereas a Japanese scholar trained in Chinese could do so. That same educated Japanese person could not write the purely Chinese version of "I am a student of Buddhism." Thus, the written Japanese equivalent of "I am a student of Buddhism" would resemble but not match the Chinese written version.

91. Again, this is the posthumous volume that Campbell edited from the notes of Heinrich Zimmer. See n. 25.

92. This was the seventeenth anniversary of Joseph Campbell and Jean Erdman's wedding.

93. The white *inari,* or Shintō fox-god, is related to sexuality and fertility.

94. Seiiti Miduno and Tosio Nagahiro, *A Study of the Buddhist Cave-Temples at Lung-men, Ho-nan* Tokyo: Zauho Press, 1941.

95. Actually, Seishi (also known as Daiseishi and Mahāsthamaprapta) is most commonly said to symbolize Amida's wisdom. Thus the trinity of Amitābha, Avalokiteśvara, and Mahāsthamaprapta (Amida, Kannon, and Seishi) exemplifies the idea that Amida Buddha's compassion and wisdom together bring the adherent to the Western Paradise of enlightenment.

96. The Suryaprabha Bodhisattva (known as Nikkō in Japan) is connected to light and health. Like Avalokiteśvara, Suryaprabha is often pictured holding a lotus blossom.

97. Tibetan Buddhist *vajrayāna* ceremonies combine the use of a ritual bronze *vajra* in combination with bells to symbolize spiritual awakening.

98. The Tendai Buddhist sect retains a connection to Tibetan Buddhist traditions, hence the *vajras* and the bells.

CHAPTER V

99. Ryosho Takamine (1898–?), scholar on Japanese Buddhism, and Kegon in particular.
100. A kakemono is a hanging scroll.
101. In his later work, Campbell often used the dichotomy between *ri-ji-muge* and *ji-ji-muge* to illustrate the world-affirming and -renouncing strains of various religions. "The Japanese call these alternatives, respectively, the *Ji Hokkai* and the *Ri Hokkai. Ji Hokkai* is the individual realm, *Ri Hokkai* the general. Then they say *ji-ri-muge:* individual, general, no obstruction, no difference. They are, in fact, the same.

  "Now," I continued, "when one of those light bulbs breaks, the superintendent of building doesn't come in and say, 'Well, that was my particularly favorite bulb.' He takes it out, throws it away, and puts in another one. What is important is not the vehicle, but the light.

  "And looking down at all your heads I ask myself, of what are these the vehicles? They certainly are the vehicles of consciousness; how much consciousness are they radiating? Then, I might ask any one of you, 'Which are you? Are you the vehicle—the light bulb—or are you consciousness—the light itself?'"

  "When you identify with the consciousness, with gratitude to the vehicle, you can let it go—'Death, where is thy sting?' You have identified yourself with the consciousness that is really everlasting. It is consciousness that throws up forms and takes them back again, throws up forms and takes them back again. When you realize that you are one with consciousness, you are one with all the forms that contain it. Then you can say *ji-ji-muge:* individual, individual, no obstruction, no difference. This is the ultimate mystic experience on earth." "Episode 1.2: The Spirit Land." *Mythos, Part 1: The Shaping of Our Mythic Tradition* (Los Angeles: Inner Dimension Video, 2000).
102. See *Baksheesh & Brahman*, pp. 201–2.
103. Sanskrit for "not this, not this!" and "it is here, it is here!" these terms express Ramakrishna's teaching that one must meditate on cleansing oneself of connection to the ego before transcending to connection with *brahman*. See *Flight of the Wild Gander*, p. 169, or *Thou Art That*, p. 26.
104. *Śunyatā* is the famous Buddhist doctrine of the emptiness or illusory nature of the world, first propounded in the *Prajñāpāramitā* scriptures, including the *Prajñāpāramitā Hṛdāya*, or Heart *Sūtra*.
105. D. T. Suzuki, *Essays in Zen Buddhism* (London: Rider and Co., 1927).
106. Satori is the Japanese word meaning "sudden enlightenment." It is sometimes equated with *kenshō* ("waking up") and the Sanskrit *nirvāṇa* (which, ironically, means "blown out" like a candle; that is, emptied of self).
107. *Prajñāpāramitā* is translated variously as "the ultimate virtue that comes from wisdom" or "the wisdom of the yonder shore." In Buddhist art, *Prajñāpāramitā* is often portrayed as a female Bodhisattva: "the most spiritual feminine symbol in all the iconographies of the East...."—Zimmer, *Myths and Symbols of Indian Art and Civilization,* ed. Joseph Campbell (New York: Pantheon/Bollingen Foundation, 1946), p. 99.
108. The Hossō sect of Buddhism was one of the earliest to come to Japan, brought by the Japanese monk Dōshō ca. A.D. 664. It is related to the Chinese Fa-hsiang and Indian Yogācāra schools; it is a relatively minor sect in Japan.

109. Campbell makes note of the translation by Eugène Obermiller (1900–35) of this Tibetan Buddhist text, entitled *Uttara Tantra of Maitreya*. There are numerous editions of this translation; there is no record as to which Campbell was referring.

110. The Mahāsāṅghika were a very early Buddhist sect that pushed for the inclusion of not only members of the priestly castes, but also all classes in the practice of Buddhism. Their schism was a precursor to the establishment of what is now Mahāyāna Buddhism.

111. The Sarvastivādins were another proto-Mahāyāna Buddhist sect. The religious text to which Campbell is referring is probably the *Sarvastivādin-vinaya*, the monastic rules for the Sarvastivādin order.

112. The various sects of Buddhism view the Buddha as having various aspects. *Prajñāpāramitā*–inflected sects, such as Tibetan Vajrayāna and Zen Buddhists give the Buddha three aspects, or "bodies": the transformation or emanation body, the reward or enjoyment body, and the *dharma* or truth body. Other sects have different systems. Similarly, a typical Westerner might hold a "two-body" system of the human (mind/body) or a "three-body" system (mind/body/spirit).

113. Georg Cantor was a German mathematician of the nineteenth century who revolutionized the modern thinking about the mathematics of infinity as an acceptable but unresovable abstraction.

114. Śaṅkara, the great Hindu philosopher, taught that all the things of this world were merely *māyā*, or illusion. One day, he told a prince, "You are not actually real nor is your kingdom. It is only an illusion." The next time Śaṅkara came to teach the prince, the prince had one of his bull elephants chase Śaṅkara up a tree. "If this wild elephant is not real, why did you run from it?" Śaṅkara said, "That which you think was me was the one you thought ran up the tree. But that was not actually me."

115. See above, pp. 99–100.

116. There is no record of any major scriptural changes recommended by the Sixth Buddhist Congress of 1954–56.

117. B. L. Suzuki, *Noh Gaku*, Wisdom of the East Series (1932).

118. Apparently, Campbell here means to state his own views, rather than reporting those of Eidmann and Kasugai.

119. Clive Staples Lewis (1898–1963) was a highly regarded scholar of medieval and Renaissance literature and Christian theorist. He is best known today as the author of the Narnia series of children's books and the subject of the play and film *Shadowlands*, which dramatizes his marriage to Joy Davidman.

120. See pp. 58–59.

121. A work that was never published but did serve as the groundwork for the multi-volume *Masks of God*, which was published over the next decade.

122. Wisconsin senator Joseph McCarthy's investigations into the purported infiltration of Communists into the U.S. government—particularly into the Army and State Department—had concluded just weeks before Campbell began his journey to Asia. Though the investigations (or "witch-hunts," as they became known) ended without a single conviction, the image of career diplomats and army officers pleading their Fifth Amendment right against self-incrimination had imbedded itself into the mind of many Americans, Campbell included. He is implying that Communist-leaning U.S. administrators of the Occupation had exercised the same kind of political chicanery at Japanese universities that they complained was being practiced against their brethren in America.

123. Harold Taylor, president of Sarah Lawrence College and a personal friend of Campbell's. See *Fire in the Mind*, pp. 233, 331–32, 357, 414, 504, 545.

124. This is in fact the Indian elephant-god Ganeśa, known as Kangiten in Japan. In Tantric practice, the cakes that Ganeśa holds are said to represent the sweetness of *ātman* (the universal self) within the sordid, personal self.

125. See p. 42.

126. *Gutoku's Notes* is Shinran's brief treatise on the differences between Theravāda and Mahāyāna Buddhism.

127. This is most likely the Venerable Narada Thera's *The Life of the Buddha in His Own Words* (Colombo: Y.M.B.A, no date).

128. A major difference between Theravādin and Mahāyāna teaching that goes unstated (though implied) here is that Theravādin Buddhists concentrate on the so-called Pāli canon of *sūtras*, which they hold to be the true teachings of the Buddha, while Mahāyāna teachings include the broader "Chinese" canon, which includes many of the same writings, but also *sūtras* that are not part of the Pāli canon.

129. This seems to have been a direct quotation from Eidmann rather than from *Gutoku's Notes*.

130. Kanji are Chinese-derived ideograms that form, in addition to katakana and hiragana, the third part of Japanese script.

131. It seems evident that Campbell may have come to change this opinion.

132. This would appear to be "Hinduism," the cover article of the February 7, 1955, issue of *Life*.

133. Campbell was usually disappointed with the published form of his books, especially at first. Later he would become more reconciled to them. With the exception of *Hero with a Thousand Faces*, Campbell had devoted the previous thirteen years to Zimmer's books, rather than writing his own.

134. Eugene Herrigel, *Zen in the Art of Archery*, translated by R.F.C. Hull (New York: Pantheon, 1953, and New York: Vintage, 1971), an autobiographical and now-classic introduction to the subject of *Kyūdō*, also known as "Zen archery." *Kyūdō*, like kendō or jūdō (*-dō* means "Way," from the Chinese *Tao*), is considered a Zen art, a form of meditation through action. It is governed in a general way, like the other martial arts, by Bushidō.

135. Phillip Karl Eidmann, trans., *Sutra of the Teachings Left by the Buddha: Translated into Chinese by Kumarajtva in the Latter Part of the Tsin Dynasty (948–971 B.C.).* (Osaka Koyata Yamamoto, 1954).

CHAPTER VI

136. In the decades following the conversion of the Roman emperor Constantine (A.D. 312), the Christian church became institutionalized. Many nonconformist Christians withdrew from society, either out of protest or out of a need for ascetic retreat.

137. See Zimmer, *Art of Indian Asia*, pp. 298–312.

138. Wotan (or Odin) was the king of the Norse/Germanic pantheon. He had given up the sight in his left eye to gain the ability to see into the future with his right. See *Flight of the Wild Gander*, "Secularization of the Sacred," p. 165.

139. "Abu" was the Campbell's car from 1938 until 1955.

140. Campbell's notes from this paper form the basis for appendix A (see p. 281).

141. The Yab-Yum motif is the symbolic coitus of male and female deities in Tibetan iconography.

142. Throughout the mid-1950s and early 1960s, Campbell was editing the yearbooks of the Eranos conferences on psychology and religion for the Bollingen Foundation.

143. See p. 103.

144. This book, which was much in Campbell's mind during his stay in Japan, was never completed; it seems to have reappeared as the final volume of the *Masks of God* series (which was published by Viking), *Creative Mythology*.

145. Ascona, Italy, on the Lago Maggiore, was the site of the Eranos conferences. See n. 141.

146. Alan Watts (1915–73), author and Western interpreter of Asian culture and (in particular) Zen Buddhism, had been responsible for a few of Campbell's contacts in Japan, and the Campbells would visit Watts in Big Sur, California, upon their return to the U.S. See pp. 278–79.

147. Here the editors have omitted a rather lengthy enumeration of social and political circumstances in Asia that recapitulates earlier material.

148. Henry Corbin, Eranos participant, specialist in the Ismaili gnosis of Islam.

149. The likelihood is that the recondite martial art was aikidō, developed in the twentieth century by Morihei Ueshiba, and still not well-known to Westerners by the 1950s.

150. The "spies" are probably ninja, followers of the skill of *ninjutsu*, the Bushidō-related art invoking stealth, deception, disguise, and martial arts of unusual kinds. The ninja were feared and deadly assassins as well as spies.

151. This is Japanese transliterated into the Roman alphabet—just as the Japanese words in this work are presented.

152. Annie Besant is regarded, along with Alice Bailey, as one of the founders of the Theosophy movement, one of the first Asian-accented philosophical movements in the West.

153. See n. 88.

154. Vasubandhu (ca. fourth century A.D.) was the author of the *Discourse on the Pure Land,* a commentary on the Pure Land *Sūtra* that Shinran claimed was one of the primary texts of Pure Land Buddhism. Thus, he, along with Nāgārjuna, was a spiritual father to the movement.

155. Dr. Tadao Yanaihara (1893–1961) was president of Tokyo University from 1951 to 1957 and was, as Campbell mentions, a prominent member of the Mukyōkai (No-Church) Christian movement.

156. *Rōshi* is a term of respect for a Zen master.

157. See pp. 141–42.

158. *Netsujō* means passion in the sense of fervor or ardor; *bonnō* refers to carnal desire.

159. Vaun Gilmore was an editorial assistant at Bollingen.

160. *The Hero with a Thousand Faces* (originally published by the Bollingen Foundation in 1949) remains Campbell's most influential (and most widely translated) academic work. In it, he examines what he calls the monomyth of the hero's journey: the universal story of the hero's departure from home, the defeat of the shadow enemy, and the return home with a boon, whether that boon is treasure or enlightenment. The Mexican edition to which Campbell refers was indeed published by Fondo de Cultura Económica in 1959 as *El héroe de las mil caras: Psicoanálisis del mito,* and remains in print at this writing.

161. See *Baksheesh & Brahman,* pp. 8, 176, 327, n. 100.

162. Alistair Reid and Horace Gregory were fellow members with Campbell of the English Department at Sarah Lawrence.

163. Jean Erdman taught dance at Bard College in Annandale, New York, during 1955–56.

164. Henry Volkening of the firm Russell-Volkening was Campbell's literary agent.
165. Toward the end of his life, on December 6, 1274, St. Thomas Aquinas was visited with an "ecstasy" during the Mass. When he revived, the priest asked if Thomas was well. When the saint answered that he would not continue his writing, the priest urged him to reconsider, and St. Thomas is said to have replied, "I can do no more. Such secrets as has have been revealed to me that all I have written now appears to be of little value."
166. Campbell may have been thinking of the story of Black Elk, a Sioux medecine man who suffered a similar "shamanic crisis." See *Flight of the Wild Gander,* "Mythogenesis." This style would characterize Campbell's later comparativism— uncomfortable for many traditional theologians—that the insights of a shaman, such as the Inuit Najagneq or Black Elk, might be compared to Aquinas or St. John of the Cross. See *The Historical Atlas of World Mythology, Volume 1—The Way of the Animal Powers* (San Francisco: Harber & Row, 1983), p. 169.
167. A. E. Jensen studied the mythology of the Celebese islanders, who were primitive planters. The myth of Hainuwele described how the *dema*-divinity Hainuwele (whose name means coconut branch) was murdered. Her body was planted, and out of this grew the plants that feed the people. But a door was fashioned, so that the people no longer walk among the *dema*. This story has elements of the rebirth myths that Campbell seems to be considering for his projected book.
168. Indeed, Campbell began to record his lectures from this time on, and many of his later books (including *Myths to Live By* (New York: Viking Penguin, 1993), and *The Inner Reaches of Outer Space*) were created using this system. The Joseph Campbell Foundation has continued to create "new" volumes of Campbell's work such as *Thou Art That* and *Mythic Worlds, Modern Words* by following the same method.

CHAPTER VII

169. Nels F. S. Ferré, *The Christian Faith* (New York: Harper & Brothers, 1942), p. 211.
170. Joe Lillard was a college friend of Campbell's, and served as the Campbells' accountant.
171. The question mark is Campbell's. This is perhaps a reference to Dōshisha University, the Christian university in Kyoto.
172. It is uncertain whether this was a misspelling on the part of the Japanese proprietors of a lounge evidently known as the "Gas Lamp," Campbell's transcription of a Japanese mispronunciation, or a joke on Campbell's part on the comfort of the establishment.
173. Sarah Lawrence College, not Salt Lake City.
174. *The Christian Faith,* p. 192.
175. This realization represents a clear formulation for an attitude that was to become increasingly dominant in Campbell's later years: the Judeo-Christian complex, with its emphasis on exclusivity, was to be resisted in favor of a democracy of myths. See *The Inner Reaches of Outer Space,* or *Myths to Live By.*
176. Henry van Straelen, *The Religion of Divine Wisdom, Japan's Most Powerful Religious Movement,* Folklore Studies, vol. 13 (Tokyo: Journal of Far Eastern Folklore, 1954).
177. Miki Nakayama (1798–1887) founded the Tenrikyō sect, a monotheistic Shintō movement that believes in creation by the *Oyagami,* the "father *kami.*"
178. "Religion of Divine Wisdom," pp. 1-2.
179. Nels F. S. Ferré, *The Sun and the Umbrella* (New York: Harper & Row, 1953), p. 112.
180. The Buddhist Indian king Aśoka sent missionaries throughout Asia and the Mediterrenean. Eidmann is exploring theories that these missionaries had an influence on Judeo-Christian mystic thought.

181. This tale tells of an old woman who promises her bedridden friend that she will bring back a souvenir from a pilgramage. The woman forgets. On her way back to her village, she remembers, and, knowing her friend is too blind to know the difference, she finds a dog's tooth and presents it to her friend as a relic of the Buddha. The old woman is shocked when her friend's "relic" actually affects cures.

182. "Now when they had gone throughout Phrygia and the region of Galatia, and were forbidden of the Holy Ghost to preach the word in Asia...."

183. John 2:1–10. This famous passage recounts the miracle of Jesus turning water into wine at a wedding. At the end of the wedding "the governor of the feast called the bridegroom,/And saith unto him, Every man at the beginning doth set forth good wine; and when men have well drunk, then that which is worse: but thou hast kept the good wine until now." Campbell interprets the bridegroom—whom the governor addresses as the bringer of the wine—as being Jesus himself.

184. Appolonius of Tyana was a neo-Pythagorian mystic who was a contemporary of Jesus. Campbell never was to write on this subject.

185. This plan would be realized in the company of Mircea Eliade and other friends and colleagues at the 1958 World Congress of Religions, which took place in and around Kyoto.

CHAPTER VIII

186. The Chinese had invaded Tibet in 1949 and annexed it in 1951.

187. In 1929, at the end of a two-year Proudfit Fellowship that allowed him to study in France and Germany, Campbell was contemplating "a trip around the world." Because of the onset of the Great Depression, he chose to return to the United States. See *A Fire in the Mind*, pp. 111–15.

188. See p. 148.

189. Adda Bozeman was a friend and colleague of Campbell's who taught political science at Sarah Lawrence College.

190. Carl Schuster (1904–69) was an authority on primitive art.

191. John A. Pope was an expert in Asian art and served as the director of the Freer Gallery at the Smithsonian Institution.

192. See n. 161.

193. Heinrich Zimmer, *Philosophies of India*, ed. Joseph Campbell (Princeton, N.J.: Princeton University Press/Bollingen Foundation, 1989).

194. This problem was to emerge as a central concern for Campbell, and is addressed throughout his work. It is the central issue addressed in both *The Inner Reaches of Outer Space* and *Thou Art That*.

195. *The Sun and the Umbrella*, p. 113.

196. In the days following the American bombing of Nagasaki, Emperor Hirohito broke a centuries-old tradition of the emperor remaining silent and aloof from matters of state. He spoke on radio to his people—it was the first time most of them had heard the demi-divine ruler's voice—and told them to prepare for surrender: "the unendurable must be endured." This is the "revolution" to which Campbell is referring.

197. Compare Jung asking "What is my myth?" (*Symbols of Transformation*, foreword, p. xxiv).

198. *The Sun and the Umbrella*, pp. 27–28

199. Hara-kiri is the ritual form of self-evisceration by which a samurai would commit suicide. Campbell seems to mean that the Japanese chose to attack Pearl Harbor, knowing they would lose the war (see p. 155).

200. The Ainu are a Caucasoid aboriginal tribe native to Hokkaido (the northern island of Japan) and Sakhalin Island. See pp. 247–51.
201. Rose Marie was a child radio star in the 1930s, and then a nightclub and Broadway revue performer of the 1940s and 1950s. The style of her shows was bright, broad, and brash, if occasionally sentimental. Rose Marie herself is probably best remembered as Sally Rogers, the wise-cracking writer on television's *The Dick Van Dyke Show.*
202. Campbell indeed accepted this invitation. See pp. 278–80.
203. "The International" is the Communist anthem.

CHAPTER IX

204. Campbell seems to be struggling to reconcile the constraints of traditional cultures and the naiveté of Americans abroad. Campbell admired the "professional" efficiency of the Japanese style of parenting.
205. In Greek and Roman myth, the Titans were pre-Olympian nature gods of brute force. Campbell seems to be using the term to exemplify unintelligent or one-sided fanaticism. Titanism is also defined as unreasoned rebelliousness, the knee-jerk revolt against authority.
206. The Native American Church movement grew out of the Navaho reservations of the American Southwest during the 1940s. It is a quasi-Christian cult that seeks to bring its followers visions of salvation through the ritual use of peyote, a hallucinogenic fungus. Always interested in comparing indigenous traditions, Campbell is thinking of the peyote cult in relation to Aldous Huxley's discovery of spiritual visions from the peyote-derived hallucinogen mescaline. See Aldous Huxley, *The Doors of Perception* (New York: Harper & Row, 1954).
207. In Buddhist thought, the Tusita Heaven is where the Buddhas-to-be wait to be incarnated in this world.
208. These references are to the so-called "Nanjō Catalogue" of Chinese Buddhist texts, compiled by Bunyū Nanjō (1849–1927).
209. Presumably, scenes from the *Jātaka Tales,* a story cycle that follows the Buddha through his various animal and (finally) human incarnations.
210. It is unclear whether Campbell is referring here to the quality of *Prajñāpāramitā* itself or to the *Prajñāpāramitā Hṛdāya Sūtra,* a Mahāyāna text.
211. *Saddharma Pundarīka* is "The Lotus of the Good Law." Also known as the Lotus *Sūtra,* this Buddhist scripture is believed to have been first written down in India during the first century A.D., although it may have been composed earlier.
212. Bimbisara and Sakka were kings whom the Buddha taught.
213. A tachistoscope is a device used to flash images on a screen for a fraction of a second. It was largely used as a speed-learning tool.
214. Shantineketan is a university near Calcutta. It was founded by the Indian author Rabindranath Tagore.
215. Charles Morris, *The Open Self* (New York: Prentice Hall, 1948).
216. See n. 177.
217. The syncretic Unitarian church developed in America beginning in the Boston area throughout the eighteenth century. By the early nineteenth century, Harvard College was a hotbed of Unitarian thought.
218. Alexander Campbell (1788–1866) founded the Disciples of Christ as an attempt "to unite all Christians as one communion on a purely scriptural basis."

219. Dale L. Morgan, "A Bibliography of the Church of Jesus Christ Organized at Green Oak, Pennsylvania, July, 1862," *Western Humanities Review* 4 (Winter 1949/50): 1–28. Reprinted separately with same title (s.l.: s.n., 1950).
220. Emmanuel Swedenborg (1688–1772) was a noted Swedish scientist and spiritual philosopher. In his later writings, he spoke of the need to found a "new church" in order to create the "New Jerusalem."
221. The Bah'ai faith developed as a reform movement of Islam in the mid-nineteenth century, and has, as Campbell points out, developed as a syncretic World Religion movement in Europe and the Americas in the years since.
222. Brahmo Samaj developed as a monotheistic reform movement in India in 1828. Though it shares some philosophies with Hinduism, it supports neither the worship of idols nor the caste system.
223. Adolph Bastian (1826–1905), a German anthropologist, recognized in the cultures of the world certain recurring motifs. He termed these *Elementargedanken;* the local expressions of these motifs he termed *Völkergedanken*. Like C. G. Jung, Campbell was enormously influenced by Bastian's ideas, and referred to him frequently throughout his work.
224. Miki Nakayama, the founder of the Tenrikyō sect. See pp. 208–11.
225. See *Baksheesh & Brahman*, pp. xx, 200–3, 208–09, 257, 349, n. 207.
226. Paul Radin, anthropoligist, associate of Jung, and Eranos attendee, had presented papers on the Native American Church. After his death in 1959, Campbell wrote the article, "Primitive Man as Metaphysician" in his honor; this essay appears in *Flight of the Wild Gander*. See Paul Radin, *Primitive Man as Philosopher* (New York and London: D. Appleton and Company, 1927).
227. See p. 174.
228. Jetsun Milarepa (ca. A.D. 1052–1135) was a great Tibetan Buddhist saint. His master, Marpa (Naropa), commanded him to build a house for his (Marpa's) son, if Milarepa was to receive Marpa's teaching. Whenever Milarepa had half completed the house, Marpa would say, "Who told you to build the house there?" and then had Milarepa start over again in another location. Milarepa started houses to the north, south, east, and west of the village, before Marpa finally allowed him to build in the center of the village. Then Marpa began teaching him.
229. See n. 190.

CHAPTER X

230. Ernest Fenellosa was a Harvard-educated professor of philosophy at Tokyo University before becoming the curator of the Imperial Museum of Japan. He returned to Massachussets, and promoted East Asian art and literature in the United States. His notes on Chinese poetry and Noh drama inspired Ezra Pound and William Butler Yeats.
231. Kakuzō Okakura (1862–1913), in addition to studying with Fenellosa, was the author of several influential books about Japan and East Asian culture. The most famous is *The Book of Tea* (New York: Duffield and Green, 1906).
232. Ed Solomon was the Director of Field Work for Sarah Lawrence College. Off-campus study (the field trips of which Campbell speaks elsewhere) were central to the curriculum at Sarah Lawrence, and Mr. Solomon's job seems to have been to coordinate this aspect of academic life.
233. This book was never written. Pope Joan is supposed to have served as pontiff from A.D. 853 to 855. She disguised her gender and served, first as a priest, then as a prelate, Pope John. Her deception is supposed to have been discovered when she gave birth to a child.

234. A *nāga* is a serpent-demon in the Buddhist and Hindu traditions.

235. These seem to be Japanese formulae of self-effacement.

236. *Nirmānakāya* is the transformation body of the Buddha, while *dharmakāya* is the *dharma*, or truth body. See n. 112.

237. See n. 154.

238. Kōbō Daishi, a.k.a. Kūkai, was born in the eighth century A.D.; a scholar-priest, he studied in China before founding the Shingon sect of Buddhism in Japan. Campbell seems to be saying that, just as many Americans claim to trace their ancestry back to the Mayflower, many shrines and temples have been attributed to Kōbō Daishi, whether legitimately or not.

239. One hundred fifty-six Waverly Place was less than a block away from Campbell's residence in New York City.

240. See pp. 123–25.

241. Oswald Spengler's view of history, laid out in his multivolume *Decline of the West,* suggests that history is made by the doers, rather than the thinkers.

242. John Cage, a friend of the Campbells' and noted avant-garde composer, used Zen to justify various musical techniques such as surprise and silence in his compositions.

243. The Dillinghams are Jean Erdman Campbell's maternal family. Longtime residents of Hawai'i, they were landed, wealthy, and politically conservative.

244. Subsequent observation shows that Zen has spread to America since Campbell's visit, in part through the traditional disciplines of *cha-no-yu* (Tea), the martial arts, and calligraphy.

245. Japanese includes not only different forms of address for those of higher and lower status, but also what amounts to almost different languages for men and women, including, for example, prescribed ways of communicating between a husband and wife.

246. Clearly Campbell means drunk.

247. In Pure Land sects such as Shinshū, true enlightenment is only attained in *Sukhavātī.*

248. Lin Yu-tang (1898–1977) was a Chinese author and man of letters who lived in the United States from 1936 to 1966. He described the growth of wisdom with age thus: "First the sadness and sense of defeat, then the awakening and the laughter of the old rogue-philosopher." *The Importance of Living* (New York: Reynal & Hitchcock/John Day, 1937).

249. The waitress apparently understood Campbell to say *"hambagā,"* which would be a usual way of ordering the hamburger-steak full meal! *Konban wa* is Japanese for "Good evening"; at lunchtime, *konnichi wa* ("good day") would have been more appropriate, which may have exacerbated the misunderstanding.

250. See *Baksheesh & Brahman,* pp. 85–86.

251. Doña Luisa Coomaraswamy was the widow of the Indian scholar Ananda K. Coomaraswamy. Professor Warner's identity is uncertain.

CHAPTER XI

252. Jizō is the Boddhisattva who protects children. See p. 67 and n. 63.

253. The Bandung Declaration of 1955 asserted five principles (*pancha sīla*) that included peaceful coexistence among nations and respect for human rights. The *pancha sīla* are also the five basic precepts of a good Buddhist life: to refrain from killing, stealing, lying, wrongful sexual practice (i.e. rape), and alcohol.

254. Campbell's first major published work (coauthored with Henry Morton Robinson)

was a gloss of James Joyce's notoriously opaque novel, *Finnegans Wake. The Skeleton Key to Finnegans Wake*, published in 1944, just four years after the publication of Joyce's great work, was a major boon to students, professors, and lay readers alike. Joseph Campbell and Henry Morton Robinson, *A Skeleton Key to Finnegans Wake* (New York: Harcourt Brace, 1944, and Novato, Calif.: New World Library, 2004).

255. Campbell is referring to the Keynsean social theorists who instituted the"New Deal" economics of the welfare state in the U.S. and were attempting to reproduce (or improve) that model in Japan.

256. See *Baksheesh & Brahman,* pp. 187–209, 240–248.

257. The Sarabhais were vegetarians.

258. Sarvepalli Radhakrishnan (1888–1975) was the vice president of India at the time of Campbell's visit. He later served as president. He was also a well-known Hindu philosopher. See *Baksheesh & Brahman.*

259. See p. 201.

260. Getas are thonged sandals, usually with wooden blocks to raise the wearer above the mud.

261. These three Bodhisattvas are Gautama Śākyamuni (the historical Buddha), Maitreya (the Buddha-to-come), and Mañjuśrī (a *Prajñāpāramitā* Buddha).

262. In Zen, these visitations are called *makyō,* and precede the experience of *kenshō,* or enlightenment.

263. In Greek mythology, the *Symplegades* were two floating cliffs that swung together and crushed anything going between them, until Jason's ship, the *Argo,* passed safely through them. They remained still forever after, forming the entrance to the Black Sea. Campbell often used them (and Scylla and Charybdis) as mythological illustrations of the idea of the dualistic world-of-opposites.

264. Campbell is likely referring to the Seven Gods of Luck (*Shichifukujin*) of Japanese folk mythology. (One of the seven gods—Benten—is actually a goddess, a folk variation on Kuan-yin.)

265. Konpon Chū-dō actually means simply "central hall."

266. See pp. 120–25.

267. One Japanese *ri* = 2.44 miles.

268. Campbell discovered that his edition of Heinrich Zimmer's *Philosophies of India* had been plagiarized in an Indian newspaper. See *Baksheesh & Brahman,* p. 63.

269. Heinrich Zimmer, *The King and the Corpse,* ed. Joseph Campbell (Princeton, N.J.: Bollingen Foundation/Princeton University Press, 1993).

270. Lafcadio Hearne, an American writer, arrived in Japan in 1890, and stayed for the rest of his life. He was the author of *Japan: An Attempt at Interpretation* (New York: Grosset & Dunlap, 1904)—Campbell's copy was heavily annotated— and *Tokyo and Kokoro: Hints and Echoes of Japanese Inner Life* (Boston and New York: Houghton Mifflin Co., 1896).

CHAPTER XII

271. T. E. Hulme (1883–1917) was a British aesthetician, and cofounder (with Herbert Read) of the Imagist movement. Read edited Hulme's *Speculations* in 1924.

272. Campbell was unable to carry out either of these vigorous resolves. He did not renew the study of Japanese, though he retained into his later years a great deal of what he had learned in Kyoto, continuing to read and write Japanese. "Joe's Friendly Service" went on for decades as he continued to help friends and younger scholars with their projects.

273. Josip Broz Tito (1898–1980) was the president of Communist (but nonaligned) Yugoslavia from 1945 to his death.

274. To this day the Ise Peninsula remains off the tourist route, though it is a frequent destination for Japanese pilgrimages. Few signs are in *rōmaji* and fewer people speak English than in Tokyo or the Kyoto-Nara region.

275. "I am sorry (to have disturbed you)."

276. Amaterasu, the Sun Goddess, is the most important deity in the Shintō religion. It is her emblem that gives Japan its flag.

277. The koto is a long stringed instrument that lies flat on the ground.

278. In the Shintō tradition, the first wedded couple in the age of the gods (the seventh generation of deities). They gave birth to the terrestrial regions (Ōyashimaguni), mountains, rivers, seas, plants, animals, and men, and became the gods of the earth and of all things on earth. The three most important deities born to Izanagi and Izanami are Amaterasu Ōmikami (the Sun Goddess), Susanoo no Mikoto, and Tsukiyomi no Mikoto.

279. Campbell is here referring to his 1932 trip up the inland waterway to Juneau, Alaska with the biologist Ed Ricketts. (See *A Fire in the Mind*, pp. 200–9.)

280. Benkei was a warrior-priest of the twelfth century who figures in Noh, Kabuki, and Bunraku plays; this particular play is called *Kanjinchō*, and it involves the warrior Yoshitsune's attempt to escape capture by his half-brother, Yoritomo. Yoshitsune flees disguised as a porter of Benkei, his loyal retainer. At a checkpoint, Benkei's resourcefulness and profound loyalty to Yoshitsune make it possible for the company to pass through, and at the end of the play Benkei expresses his joy in a famous exit scene.

281. The Ainu—the early inhabitants of the islands of Hokkaido and Sakhalin—are a Caucasoid race with abundant body hair, not found on most other Asian ethnic groups. This has led to much speculation about their origins. Their culture is characterized by archaic rituals of bear worship that seem to date back to the Paleolithic era.

282. Tom and Elizabeth Penning had a large quarry pool behind their Woodstock, New York, home. During the 1930s and 1940s there were nude swimming parties in the pool.

283. See n. 167 and *Atlas,* vol. 2, part 1, pp. 68–69.

284. Campbell was to follow through with this resolve in both *The Masks of God* and *The Historical Atlas of World Mythology: The Way of the Animal Powers,* as well as in numerous lectures.

285. Malekula is an island in the South Pacific nation of Vanuatu. The primitive islanders created elaborate stone labyrinths, representing ritual descent into the underworld. See *Primitive Mythology,* pp. 444–551.

286. Women performing in Kabuki was an innovation. The women in this troupe were relative newcomers to the art, so Campbell was not surprised that they lacked the technical skills of their male peers, who had trained since boyhood.

287. Teiji Itō, a Japanese-born musician and friend of the Campbells, often performed in Ms. Erdman's dance and theatre productions. His brother evidently directed this production.

CHAPTER XIII

288. Sabro Hasegawa (1906–57) was a Japanese modern artist who studied extensively in the West during the 1920s and 1930s and attempted to combine Western abstraction with

Japanese traditional forms. He returned to his country to paint in 1937, but was detained during World War II for refusing to paint patriotic themes. He moved to San Francisco in 1956, became acquainted with Alan Watts, and died in 1957, just two years after meeting Campbell.

289. A *yukata* is an unlined cotton kimono used as bath/summer wear.

290. Motokiyo Zeami (1364–1443) was a playwright and one of the originators of the Noh form of theater.

291. Matsuo Bashō (1644–94) is generally considered to be the pioneer (and master) of the modern haiku. Haiku is a seventeen-syllable, three-line poem strongly associated with Zen.

292. Isamu Noguchi, a sculptor, was a contemporary and friend of Campbell's. Alan Watts, author/philosopher, and John Cage, composer, we have met before; we will meet Watts again soon.

293. The 8th Street Artists' Club was started by painter Robert Motherwell in 1948. The Campbells would become increasingly involved with the club through the next few years.

294. *Densha* is Japanese for "train."

295. See pp. 96–97.

296. See p. 285.

297. See n. 231.

298. This would appear to be Eleanor Roosevelt, President Franklin Roosevelt's widow and U.N. delegate, rather than Mrs. Quentin Roosevelt (a distant cousin) with whom Campbell had traveled in Thailand.

299. These are percussion instruments with "fish mouths" that make a gonglike sound when struck.

300. Pan-American Airways.

301. Campbell's parents had moved to Honolulu in the early 1940s. Jean was native to Hawai'i. Alice is Campbell's sister and Anne her daughter. Marion Dillingham Erdman was Jean's mother, and Da (Dorothy) and Louie (Louise) were Jean's sisters. In 1955, Mānoa was a village above Honolulu; it is now part of the city proper, and the site of the flagship campus of the University of Hawai'i.

302. René d'Harnoncourt was a former colleague of Campbell's at Sarah Lawrence. He later left Hawai'i to take a curatorial job at the Museum of Modern Art in New York City.

303. Thor Heyedahl's *Kon-Tiki: Across the Pacific by Raft* (New York: Washington Square Press, 1995) explored the idea that trans-Pacific travel could have been achieved by early sailors. Campbell was to expound on some of these ideas in his essay "Mythogenisis," which can be found in *Flight of the Wild Gander*.

304. Jean's maternal uncle and his family.

305. F. Matthias Alexander (1869–1955), an Australian actor who wished to use his body more efficiently, developed the so-called Alexander Technique in the late nineteenth century. It is very popular among actors, dancers, musicians, and athletes. One of the trademarks of the technique is a lengthening of the neck and spine; this creates optimal relaxation and flexibility of the practitioner, but also increases their apparent stature and status.

306. Feuerring had given Campbell references to several contacts in Kyoto, most notably Phillip Eidmann. See pp. 66, 76.

307. Jeffie Fairbanks was the son of Marjory "Bargie" Erdman Fairbanks, Jean's sister. He

was stricken at the age of two and a half (not long before this visit) with a form of paralysis. He lived to the age of twenty-six.

308. See pp. 120–25.

309. A Broadway hit of the previous year, and little theater staple for some years to come, *Oh, Men! Oh, Women!* was described in its publicity as "an hilarious lampoon of sex and psychiatry." The discussion of psychoanalysis that follows was clearly sparked by the play.

310. Erich Fromm (1900–80) was a psychiatrist, lecturer, and author of scholarly and popular books on psychology.

311. Alice Campbell Lenning was Campbell's younger sister, and was probably the sibling to whom he had been the closest as a young man. A sculptor, she and Campbell had shared a cottage in Woodstock, New York, in the early years of the Depression. She had moved to Hawai'i before the beginning of World War II.

312. The Alexanders were old friends of the Campbells'. Doyle Alexander worked with Campbell's father in the hosiery business.

313. The meaning of this last sentence is obscure; we assume that Campbell's sister was working for a company called American Factor.

314. See p. 245.

315. Jean's sister Dorothy's children.

316. Campbell worked as an assistant to famed marine biologist Ed Ricketts (the real-life inspiration for the hero in John Steinbeck's novel *Cannery Row*) in 1932. See n. 279 above.

317. Alan Watts's second wife. At this writing, one of the "cute children," Mark Watts, serves as the Joseph Campbell Foundation's Media Director.

319. *Wuwei* is a Chinese Taoist term meaning "non-action" or "letting be." *Sahaja* is a Sanskrit word meaning "easy" or "spontaneous," used to describe a Tantric ritual of sexual union. See *Baksheesh & Brahman*, pp. 116, 317.

319. These are the *Dead Sea Scrolls*. Though the first of these scrolls had been famously discovered by a Bedouin goatherd in 1947, new excavations at Qumran had uncovered more scrolls in 1955. For Campbell's views on these manuscripts, see *Thou Art That*, pp. 47, 69–70.

320. Maud Oakes was the author and researcher of *Where the Two Came to Their Father: A Navaho War Ceremonial Given by Jeff King*, originally published in 1943, for which Campbell had written the introduction and running commentary (Princeton, N.J.: Princeton University Press/Bollingen Foundation, 1991).

321. Joseph Campbell (1879–1944) was a Northern Irish poet. His best-known work is *The Mountainy Singer* (1909; New York: AMS Press, 1981).

322. A kōan is a paradox for Zen meditation (i.e., "What is the sound of one hand clapping?"). Both the *Poetic* and *Prose Eddas* contain riddle contests—battles of wits. In one famous contest, Wotan, the Norse king of the gods, defeats a giant by asking him, "What did Wotan whisper in the ear of his son on the funeral pyre?"

APPENDIX B

1. This article is drawin from an audio recording of a lecture given by Campbell in 1963 on New York's public television station, WNET, as part of a series entitled *Mask, Myth & Dream*. Originally entitled "The Way of Tea," it is listed as L80 in The Joseph Campbell Foundation audio archive.

2. This is the *Avatamsaka Sūtra,* which is central to the Kegon and Shingon sects.
3. See n. 62.
4. This is a translation of the Tantric mantra *"Om mani padme hum."*
5. See n. 107.
6. "For this is my body." This transformative phrase from the Mass itself transformed into the stage religion's "hocus pocus."
7. This haiku is by the poet Ōshima Ryōta (1718–87).
8. This is Campbell's free translation from Dōgen's "Busshō" (Buddha Nature), a fascicle of his *Shōbōgenzō.*

GLOSSARY

Amaterasu Ōmikami: Sun Goddess, most important deity in Shintō pantheon; born of Izanagi and Izanami

amazake: sweetened alcoholic beverage made from fermented rice

Asakusa: bustling entertainment and mercantile section of central Tokyo

Azuma Odori: begun in the early twentieth century as a vehicle for showcasing the artistry of geisha, annual dance performance presented at Shimbashi Enbujō, Tokyo, in spring

Benkei: twelfth-century warrior-priest, loyal retainer to Minamoto Yoshitsune; heroism dramatized in Japanese theatre arts

Bon: Buddhist summer festival for the dead marked by special dances and a lantern-floating ceremony

bugaku: highly stylized courtly dance form introduced from China during the T'ang dynasty

Bunraku: puppet theatre with origins in the sixteenth century, characterized by stylized recitation, samisen music, and large puppets worked by three operators dressed in black

Bushidō: "Way of the Warrior," feudal-military code of chivalry

Daibutsu-den: seventeenth-century wood structure housing world's largest Buddha at Tōdaiji Temple in Nara

Dengyō Daishi (767–822): founder of Tendai sect (q.v.) of Buddhism in Japan with seat at Enryakuji Temple on Mt. Hiei near Kyoto

Enō (638–713): Hui-neng in Chinese, sixth patriarch of Zen Buddhism whose teachings emphasized "sudden enlightenment," or satori; author of the Platform *Sūtra*

Fudō Myō-ō: God of Fire, usually portrayed with a sword in his right hand and a coiled rope in his left and surrounded by flames

Gakkō: "sunlight" Bodhisattva of Yakushi Nyorai triad housed in Yakushiji Temple (q.v.) in Nara

geisha: "person of the arts," professional female entertainers trained in the traditional arts who entertain guests at teahouses, restaurants, inns, etc.; once widespread but now concentrated mainly in the Gion district of Kyoto and in Tokyo

gekū: "outer shrine," particularly of Ise Shrine near Nara

gengaku: music of traditional stringed instruments

geta: thonged wood clogs for outdoor wear

Go: board game originating in China, using round, black and white pieces and a wooden, grid-pattern playing board

gohei: white paper or cloth strips attached to a stick and offered to a deity at a Shintō shrine

goma: Buddhist fire ritual of purification with origins in ancient India

Hannyaji Temple: dating from the Asuka period (593–710), temple in Nara known for its thirteen-story stone pagoda, the tallest in Japan

hara-kiri: ritual suicide practiced by samurai involving self-disembowelment

Hiei: mountain near Kyoto, site of Enryakuji Temple, head temple of the Tendai sect (q.v.), founded by Dengyō Daishi in 788, and important spiritual and cultural center for nearly a thousand years

Higashi Honganji Temple: branch temple of Nishi Honganji Temple (q.v.) in Kyoto, built in 1602

hinokishin: selfless acts of gratitude performed daily by Tenrikyō (q.v.) followers as an expression of their joy at being alive

hiragana: set of cursive syllabic script containing forty-six symbols that comprises, with kanji (q.v.) and katakana (q.v.), the Japanese writing system

hondō: main building or hall of a Buddhist temple

Hōryūji: seventh-century temple near Nara, whose main hall, built in 680, is said to be the oldest wooden structure in the world

Inari: fox deity

Ippen Shōnin (1239–89): established in 1273 the Jishū sect of Pure Land Buddhism

Ise ondo: folk dance of Ise in which dancers beat rhythm with wooden sticks

Jishū: sect of Pure Land Buddhism established by Ippen Shōnin in 1273

Jizō-bosatsu: guardian deity of children

Jōchō (d. 1057): considered to be one of the greatest sculptors of the late Heian period, who devised a multi-block system of sculpting that allowed for larger, more varied images

Jōdo-in: temple on Mt. Hiei housing the tomb of Dengyō Daishi, founder of Enryakuji Temple, who died in 822

Jōdo Shinshū: Pure Land sect founded in 1224 by Shinran (1173–1262)

Jūrin-in Temple: temple in Nara whose main hall houses an unusual stone image of Jizō-bosatsu

Kabuki: popular theatrical art form that developed in the sixteenth and seventeenth centuries; marked by spectacular stage action, highly stylized dancing, singing, and costumes

kakemono: ornamental pictorial or calligraphic hanging scroll

Kamigamo Shrine: established in 678, one of Kyoto's oldest Shintō shrines and famous for the Aoi Festival held annually in May

kanji: Chinese ideographs used in Japanese writing

Kannon: Goddess of Mercy; Chinese Kuan-yin, Sanskrit Avalokiteśvara

Kasuga Shrine: located in Nara, the main structure was built in 768; features famous Noh stage constructed in the nineteenth century

katakana: set of angular syllabic script containing forty-six symbols that comprises, with kanji (q.v.) and hiragana (q.v.), Japanese writing system

Kenshin Daishi: *see* Shinran Shōnin

kōan: paradox for meditation used in Zen Buddhist training to discourage dependence on reason and encourage intuitive enlightenment

Kōbō Daishi (774–835): also known as Kūkai, founder of Shingon sect of Buddhism, established a monastery on Mt. Kōya in 816

Kobori Enshū (1579–1647): grand tea master and official instructor to Tokugawa shōguns

kōdō: assembly or lecture hall in a Buddhist temple

Kōfukuji Temple: established in 710, famous for its fifteenth-century five-storied pagoda, symbol of Nara

kondō: main hall of a Buddhist temple

koto: thirteen-stringed zither-like instrument with an elongated wood body; placed horizontally on the floor and plucked

Kudara Kannon: carved of camphor wood, statue of Kannon housed in a hall on the grounds of Hōryūji (q.v.), near Nara; said to be of seventh century and perhaps from the ancient Korean kingdom of Kudara

Mantō-e: Festival of Ten Thousand Lights, part of summer Bon (q.v.) ceremonies

Mibu-dera Temple: established in Kyoto in 991, setting for famous spring Mibu-Ky_gen (q.v.)

Mibu-Kyōgen: comic Buddhist pantomime originating at Mibu-dera Temple (q.v.) in Kyoto sometime in the twelfth century, portrays teachings of the Buddha; presented annually in the spring

Miroku: Japanese name for Maitreya

Monju: Japanese name for Mañjusri, Bodhisattva of wisdom and knowledge

myōkōnin: "wondrous good people," a devotee of the Shin Buddhist tradition who has reached and lives in a state of awakened faith

naikū: "inner shrine," particularly that of Ise Shrine near Nara

Namu Amida-butsu: "I take refuge in Amida Buddha," Jōdo Shinshū (q.v.) invocation expressing total faith in and reliance on Amida Buddha

Nanzenji Temple: Rinzai-sect (q.v.) Zen temple established in Kyoto in 1291

nembutsu: repeated invocation to Amitābha

Nikkō: "moonlight" Bodhisattva of Yakushi Nyorai triad housed in Yakushiji Temple (q.v.) in Nara

Nisei: "second generation," usually U.S.-born son or daughter of Japanese immigrants

Nishi Honganji Temple: Kyoto headquarters of Jōdo Shinshū (q.v.) sect, founded in late-thirteenth century by daughter of Shinran, sect's founder; noted for its ancient Noh stage and characteristic Momoyama-style architecture.

Noh: theatrical art form that arose in the fourteenth century and features chorus, drums, flute, and highly stylized dance

o-bentō: box lunch

obi: broad silk sash worn with kimono

Oda Nobunaga (1534–82): military commander who united most of Japan under his rule

Omote-senke: leading school of tea ceremony founded in sixteenth century by tea master Sen no Rikyū (q.v.)

oyako-donburi: chicken and egg dish served in bowl over rice

Rinzai sect: Chinese Zen sect transmitted to Japan in the fourteenth century; emphasizes use of the kōan (q.v.) and the attainment of sudden enlightenment

rōmaji: Roman letters used in transliteration of Japanese

rōshi: "venerable master," title of respect in reference to a Zen cleric

Ryōanji: Kyoto temple founded in 1450, well-known for its rock garden

sake: alcoholic beverage made from fermented rice

samisen: three-stringed banjolike instrument played by plucking

sammon: two-storied Buddhist temple gate

-san: suffix used with personal name as a form of address

satori: experience of spiritual awakening

seishin-teki: mental, spiritual

sencha: green tea

Senju Kannon: thousand-armed Kannon

Sen no Rikyū (1522–91): tea master whose style of tea ceremony gave rise to the three great traditions of tea: Omote-senke, Ura-senke, and Mushanokōji-senke

sensei: teacher or master

shajitsu: objective, realistic

Shaka Nyorai: represents the historical Buddha, Siddhartha Gautama

shakuhachi: five-hole vertically held bamboo flutelike instrument

shasei: sketch

shimenawa: rope of twisted straw hung with strips of white paper used to mark off a sacred area

Shimogamo Shrine: built in the eighth century, one of Kyoto's oldest shrines and well-known in association with the Aoi Festival held annually in May

Shingon sect: esoteric "True Word" form of Buddhism established in Japan on Mt. Kōya by Kōbō Daishi (Kūkai) (774–835)

Shinran Shōnin (Kenshin Daishi) (1173–1263): founder in 1224 of Jōdo Shinshū

Shinshū: *see* Jōdo Shinshū

Shinyakushiji Temple: eighth-century temple in Nara whose main hall houses a statue of Yakushi Nyorai, the Buddha of Healing

shō: mouth instrument made of generally seventeen bamboo pipes and fifteen reeds set circularly in a wooden wind chamber

shōgun: feudal military ruler during twelfth to nineteenth centuries

Shōsōin Treasure House: of Tōdaiji Temple (q.v.), in Nara, constructed in the mid-eighth century, it holds thousands of precious objects dating to the seventh and eighth centuries

Shūgakuin Detached Palace: built in 1659 as imperial villa by Tokugawa shōgun, north of Kyoto

sōdō: meditation hall at a Zen temple

Sōtō sect: brought by Dōgen (1200–53) from China, Sōtō emphasizes sitting in meditation without expectation, with faith in one's intrinsic state of enlightenment

sumō: ritualized, ancient form of wrestling in which object is to force opponent out of a ring or to touch the floor of the ring with any part of the body except the bottom of the feet

Tahō Nyorai: Buddha of Abundant Treasures

Takarazuka: all-women revue troupe based in Takarazuka, near Osaka; first performance was in 1914 *takuan:* salt-pickled white radish eaten as a garnish

tatami: mats made of tightly woven rice straw and used as flooring in traditional Japanese-style rooms

Tendai sect: Chinese school of Buddhism centered on study of the Lotus *Sūtra;* teaching taken to Japan by Dengyō Daishi (767–822)

Tenrikyō: Shintō cult founded by Nakayama Miki (1789–1887) in 1838; based in Tenri, near Nara

Tōdaiji Temple: temple complex in Nara, built in the year 743; its best-known relic, the Daibutsu, is the world's largest gilded-bronze Buddha, housed in a wood building, the Daibutsu-den, which is the largest wooden building in the world

Tokugawa Ieyasu (1542–1616): warrior and national leader, he was founder of the Tokugawa shōgunate

torii: gateway consisting generally of two vertical pillars topped by two horizontal beams, usually painted vermilion, marking the entrance to a Shintō shrine

Tōshōdaiji Temple: built in Nara in 759 by Ganjin, Buddhist priest from T'ang-dynasty China

Toyotomi Hideyoshi (1536–98): warrior and leader who, by 1590, had become ruler of a unified Japan

Toyouke Ōmikami: Shintō goddess of agriculture

tsuyu: season of summer rains

Ura-senke: leading school of tea ceremony founded in sixteenth century by tea master Sen no Rikyū

Yabu-no-uchi: style of tea ceremony established by Yabunouchi Kenchū Jōchi (1536–1627), who advocated a return to the original principles of tea, emphasizing simplicity and aesthetics

Yakushiji Temple: built in Nara in 680; the east pagoda, dating from 730, has remained sound through the centuries

yamabushi: "mountain hermit," wandering ascetics who practiced austerities and cultivated magical powers

Yasaka Shrine: located in the Gion area of Kyoto and famous for its central part in the annual mid-July Gion Festival, its main building dates to 1654

yōkigurashi: "joyous life," basic tenet of Tenrikyō that teaches helping others leads to an actualization of a cheerful life

yudōfu: tōfu simmered in a rich seaweed-based stock and eaten with a soy dipping sauce

yukata: unlined cotton bath/summer kimono

ACKNOWLEDGMENTS

None of the work on *Sake & Satori* would have been possible without the generous and unswerving aid of Jean Erdman Campbell, who as muse to Joseph Campbell begot these diaries, and as president of the Joseph Campbell Foundation at the time of this edition's conception in 1993, was midwife to their production. Jean was also available to help our search for detail, by reminiscing about a time, now almost fifty years ago, when these events unfolded.

Antony Van Couvering was the publishing director for the Joseph Campbell Foundation and managing editor of the Collected Works of Joseph Campbell at the time that the Asian Journals project was conceived and was centrally involved in the tasks of transcribing and editing both volumes of this series. His work is evident on every page of this work.

Robin and Stephen Larsen participated in editing these journals when it was still intended that they be published as a single volume. Their insight into these journals and into Campbell's life makes itself felt everywhere in this volume, particularly in the biographical footnotes.

John David Ebert lent his voluminous knowledge of Campbell's oeuvre to providing many of the endnotes.

Mike Ashby supervised and rationalized the transliteration of Japanese words and names and lent his knowledge of Japanese culture and customs. He also marked, edited, and checked the manuscript for errors and assembled the glossary.

Carol Pentleton drew the illustrations from Campbell's original doodles.

This book would have been impossible without the following good samaritans: Kazuaki Tanahashi (Sōtō information); Maureen Vaughn (Internet access); and James F. Vaughn, Jr. (photographic equipment).

And the associates of the Joseph Campbell Foundation shared their astonishing, eclectic breadth and depth of knowledge, answering questions of quotation attribution, Buddhist metaphysics, and Indian history through the Conversations of a Higher Order on the JCF Web site (www.jcf.org/forum/).

INDEX

ABOUT THE AUTHOR

JOSEPH CAMPBELL was an American author and teacher best known for his work in the field of comparative mythology. He was born in New York City in 1904, and from early childhood he became interested in mythology. He loved to read books about American Indian cultures, and frequently visited the American Museum of Natural History in New York, where he was fascinated by the museum's collection of totem poles. Campbell was educated at Columbia University, where he specialized in medieval literature and, after earning a Master's degree, continued his studies at universities in Paris and Munich. While abroad he was influenced by the art of Pablo Picasso and Henri Matisse, the novels of James Joyce and Thomas Mann, and the psychological studies of Sigmund Freud and Carl Jung. These encounters led to Campbell's theory that all myths and epics are linked in the human psyche, and that they are cultural manifestations of the universal need to explain social, cosmological, and spiritual realities.

After a period in California, where he encountered John Steinbeck and the biologist Ed Ricketts, he taught at the Canterbury School, and then, in 1934, joined the literature department at Sarah Lawrence College, a post he retained for many years. During the 1940s and '50s, he helped Swami

Nikhilananda to translate the *Upaniṣads* and *The Gospel of Sri Ramakrishna*. He also edited works by the German scholar Heinrich Zimmer on Indian art, myths, and philosophy. In 1944, with Henry Morton Robinson, Campbell published *A Skeleton Key to Finnegans Wake*. His first original work, *The Hero with a Thousand Faces*, came out in 1949 and was immediately well received; in time, it became acclaimed as a classic. In this study of the "myth of the hero," Campbell asserted that there is a single pattern of heroic journey and that all cultures share this essential pattern in their various heroic myths. In his book he also outlined the basic conditions, stages, and results of the archetypal hero's journey.

Joseph Campbell died in 1987. In 1988, a series of television interviews with Bill Moyers, *The Power of Myth*, introduced Campbell's views to millions of people.

ABOUT THE
JOSEPH CAMPBELL FOUNDATION

THE JOSEPH CAMPBELL FOUNDATION (JCF) is a nonprofit corporation that continues the work of Joseph Campbell, exploring the fields of mythology and comparative religion. The Foundation is guided by three principal goals:

First, the Foundation preserves, protects, and perpetuates Campbell's pioneering work. This includes cataloging and archiving his works, developing new publications based on his works, directing the sale and distribution of his published works, protecting copyrights to his works, and increasing awareness of his works by making them available in digital formats on JCF's Web site.

Second, the Foundation promotes the study of mythology and comparative religion. This involves implementing and/or supporting diverse mythological education programs, supporting and/or sponsoring events designed to increase public awareness, donating Campbell's archived works (principally to the Joseph Campbell and Marija Gimbutas Archive and Library), and utilizing JCF's Web site as a forum for relevant cross-cultural dialogue.

Third, the Foundation helps individuals enrich their lives by participating in a series of programs, including our global, Internet-based

Associates program, our local international network of Mythological Roundtables, and our periodic Joseph Campbell–related events and activities.

For more information on Joseph Campbell
and the Joseph Campbell Foundation, contact:

JOSEPH CAMPBELL FOUNDATION
www.jcf.org
Post Office Box 36
San Anselmo, CA 94979-0036
Toll free: (800) 330-MYTH
E-mail: info@jcf.org

New World Library is dedicated to
publishing books and audios that inspire
and challenge us to improve the quality
of our lives and our world.
Our books and cassettes are available
at bookstores everywhere.
For a complete catalog, contact:

NEW WORLD LIBRARY
14 Pamaron Way
Novato, California 94949
Phone: (415) 884-2100
Fax: (415) 884-2199
Or call toll free: (800) 972-6657
Catalog requests: Ext. 50
Ordering: Ext. 52
E-mail: escort@nwlib.com
newworldlibrary.com